Animal Passions and Beastly Virtues

In the series

Animals, Culture, and Society
edited by Clinton R. Sanders and Arnold Arluke

Animal Passions and Beastly Virtues

Reflections on Redecorating Nature

MARC BEKOFF

Foreword by JANE GOODALL

TEMPLE UNIVERSITY PRESS
Philadelphia

Temple University Press
1601 North Broad Street
Philadelphia PA 19122
www.temple.edu/tempress

⊗ The paper used in this publication meets the requirements of the American
National Standard for Information Sciences—Permanence of Paper for Printed
Library Materials, ANSI Z39.48-1992

Library of Congress Cataloging-in-Publication Data
Bekoff, Marc.
Animal passions and beastly virtues : reflections on redecorating nature / Marc
Bekoff.
p. cm. – (Animals, culture, and society)
Includes bibliographical references and index.
ISBN 1-59213-347-9 (cloth : alk. paper) – ISBN 1-59213-348-7 (pbk. : alk. paper)
1. Cognition in animals. 2. Social behavior in animals. 3. Animal rights.
4. Animal welfare. I. Title. II. Series.

QL785.B36 2006
591.56–dc22

2005041833

2 4 6 8 9 7 5 3 1

We need another and a wiser and perhaps a more mystical concept of animals. Remote from universal nature, and living by complicated artifice, man in civilization surveys the creature through the glass of his knowledge and sees thereby a feather magnified and the whole image in distortion. We patronize them for their incompleteness, for their tragic fate of having taken form so far below ourselves. And therein we err, and greatly err. For the animal shall not be measured by man. In a world older and wiser and more complete than ours they move finished and complete, gifted with extentions of the senses we have lost or never attained, living by voices we shall never hear. They are not brethren, they are not underlings; they are other nations, caught with ourselves in the net of life and time, fellow prisoners of the splendour and travail of earth.

—Henry Beston, *The Outermost House*

Contents

Foreword

ANIMAL PASSIONS AND BEASTLY VIRTUES is a collection of essays by Marc Bekoff. It is a book for scientists and nonscientists alike. Academic readers will be intellectually stimulated by many of the discussions, and lay people will be fascinated and often inspired. The writing is clear, so even complex subjects can be readily understood by the general public.

The essays in this book cover many topics, and we are able to trace the gradual development of Marc's research and ideas over a thirty-year period. There are those detailing his work in the field of social play and the behavioral ecology of carnivores. Then his interest in the complex issues of animal cognition, emotions, and self-awareness grows stronger. Gradually more and more of his essays focus on moral issues as he discusses the ethics of animal experimentation and the social responsibility of scientists and science.

Marc's research has led, in some instances, to essays that discuss topics well outside the initial framework of the studies. Thus, his study of social play led him to speculate about the evolution of human behaviors that we describe as fairness, trust, and morality—he describes what seem to be precursors of these behaviors, describing them as "wild justice." And his research into animal minds and emotions, to which he has dedicated much of his professional career, has provided him with a growing understanding of animals' capacity for suffering, so that he is able to write with authority against cruel and abusive exploitation of wild and captive animals.

Marc's concern for the destruction of the environment at human hands also is clearly outlined in some of these essays. He writes of the tightly woven tapestry of life on earth, of the close connections between all beings and wild ecosystems. He criticizes those who "redecorate" nature, altering the pattern of the wilderness, destroying habitats, moving or killing wildlife, for their own purposes.

Marc is an extraordinarily prolific writer. He has published books for scientists and for the lay public, and many of his articles have been written both for scientific journals and popular magazines. He has also worked to bring an understanding of animal behavior to children—recently through the Jane Goodall Institute's Roots & Shoots program, which encourages youth around the world to take compassionate and informed action to make the world a better place for animals, as well as for people and the environment. Marc has also worked with senior citizens and prisoners in the Roots & Shoots program.

Perhaps the most powerful essays are those which illustrate Marc's determination to be a voice for the voiceless. He is highly critical of the way animals are so often treated as though they were mere "things" rather than the sentient beings that he—and I—know them to be. His concern, like mine, is for animals both in the wild and in captivity. Marc is not afraid of plunging into controversial topics, such as hunting, the abuse of animals in zoos and circuses, the ethics of animal medical experimentation, and the use of animals for education in schools and universities. These articles, which have been translated into many different languages, as have many of his books, provide information which has been used by others who are also fighting for animal welfare and animal rights around the world.

Marc has the courage of his convictions and is not afraid to speak out—even when his opinion runs directly contrary to that of most of his peers, even when his career could be at stake. When he criticized the reintroduction of Canadian lynx to poor habitat in Colorado (during which many died), the University of Colorado was asked to censure him—fortunately the university supported his right to freedom of speech. And he wrote passionate essays about the infamous dog lab that subjected hundreds of dogs to needless suffering at the university's medical school, pointing out that similar labs had been discontinued in numerous prestigious medical schools with no ill effects on education. The dog lab was terminated in the spring of 2002.

Finally, Marc is an excellent spokesman for animals because he is not ashamed to admit his admiration and love for them. This shines through his writing, as does the sheer delight he finds in simply being with animals, and this will move and inspire many of his readers.

Marc has learned so much from watching animals and empathizing with them, and by publishing this collection of essays he hopes to share this knowledge with as many people as possible.

I will share *Animal Passions and Beastly Virtues* with colleagues and friends around the world.

Jane Goodall
Bournemouth, UK

Animal Passions and Beastly Virtues

Introduction

What Does It Feel Like to Be a Fox?

MY WONDERFUL PARENTS love to recall many stories about my lifelong interest in animals. My father remembers, with a wide smile, that on a ski trip when I was six years old I asked him what a red fox was feeling as he merrily crossed our path as we traversed a frozen lake. When I recently visited my parents in Florida, my father reminded me that I was in awe of the magnificence of the fox's red coat and white-tipped tail and lost track of where I was skiing. And he well remembers that when I was four years old, I yelled at a man for yelling at his dog—and the man chased my father! These two events etched an indelible impression in my heart and in my head. I wanted to study animals when I grew up.

I've long been a recreational ethologist, and I've been fortunate enough to combine my long-time interest in animal behavior with my professional pursuits. My parents have told me that I always "minded animals," that I always wanted to know what they were thinking and feeling—"What is it like to be a dog or a cat or a mouse or an ant?" and "What do they feel?" And to this day, learning about the behavior of animals—all animals—has been my passion. When I study coyotes, I am coyote, and when I study Steller's jays, I am jay. When I study dogs, I am dog. Although I choose not to experience first-hand the odors, the olfactory symphonies, that make up what Paul Auster refers to as a dog's "nasal paradise" in his book *Timbuktu*, I have moved "yellow snow" from place to place, much to the astonishment of other hikers.

GOOD FORTUNE

For more than three decades I have lived in the mountains outside Boulder, Colorado. I willingly share the surrounding land with many animal friends—coyotes, mountain lions, red foxes, porcupines, raccoons, black bears, chipmunks, squirrels, and a wide variety of birds, lizards, and insects, along with many dogs and cats. They have been my teachers and healers, and they keep me humble. They have made it clear to me that they were here first and that I am a transient on their turf. I have almost stumbled into mountain lions and have watched red foxes playing right in front of my office door. Adult bears

Parts of this essay are excerpted from Bekoff, M. 2002. *Minding Animals: Awareness, Emotions, and Heart.* Copyright 2002 by Oxford University Press, Inc., New York. Used by permission of Oxford University Press, Inc.

and their young have played outside my kitchen window. I feel very fortunate to have had these and other experiences, and if I need to make changes in how I live to accommodate my friends, it is just fine with me. I love to see them, smell them, listen to the cacophony of sounds they produce, and take them into my heart. The loss of any of these symbols of their presence would be a marked absence in my daily life.

Although I have always been interested in animal behavior, I have been formally studying animal behavior and behavioral ecology for the past thirty-odd years and love what I do. What an exciting and adventurous journey it has been! I work in beautiful environs, ponder fascinating questions about mysterious lives of magnificent animals, and gather data to answer them—and, of course, the answers generate many more questions. I have always been curious about a wide variety of questions, such as why dogs play the way they do and whether we can learn about fairness, forgiveness, trust, and morality— wild justice—by studying the details of how individuals "converse" during play and negotiate cooperative playful interactions; why dogs and other animals spend a good deal of time sniffing various parts of others' bodies and odors that make me cringe; how or if animals know who they are; how animals communicate using sounds that I cannot hear; what the relative contributions of genes (nature) and the environment (nurture) are to various behavioral phenomena. I have also wondered if animals empathize with one another and how animals make complex and rapid choices on the run or on the fly in the amazingly diverse situations in which they find themselves.

This curiosity brought me to cognitive ethology, the comparative and evolutionary study of animal minds. My colleagues and I investigate questions such as "What is it like to be a dog?" "What do dogs know?" and "What do dogs feel?" I have also studied the nature of human-animal interactions with an eye toward understanding how our goodwill influences their well-being and how animals, in turn, influence our well-being. This collection of some of my essays, *Animal Passions and Beastly Virtues,* covers these and other areas of research. I believe that animals are our consummate companions, because they complete us. And as we learn more about the lives of other animals, we can increasingly appreciate their gifts and abilities and enjoy their presence, even when we think they are a nuisance.

During the past four decades, the study of animal behavior has burgeoned. People everywhere are interested in the behavior of animals, because knowledge about animals enriches their lives. There are many more professional journals in animal behavior and behavioral ecology now than thirty to forty years ago, and many universities offer undergraduate and advanced degrees in the behavioral sciences. The award-winning three-volume *Encyclopedia of Animal Behavior* that I edited contains more than three hundred essays written by colleagues throughout the world, and videos and movies about animals abound. Many people want to remain connected to or reconnect with animals. There is such widespread interest in the field of animal behavior because our brains are not much different from those of our ancestors, who were more connected to the animals with whom they shared their habitats. Our "old brains" seem to drive us to keep in touch with animals and with nature in general. It is not natural for humans to be alienated from other beings, and it feels good to interact with them and to know that they are out there doing what comes naturally, even if one is isolated in a city or spends a lot of time in a windowless cubicle.

THE COMPARATIVE STUDY OF ANIMAL BEHAVIOR: ECOLOGICAL AND EVOLUTIONARY PERSPECTIVES

The field of animal behavior was given a big boost when, in 1973, a most exciting and thoroughly unexpected event occurred—Konrad Lorenz, Niko Tinbergen, and Karl von Frisch won the Nobel Prize for Physiology or Medicine for their pioneering work in animal behavior. Lorenz and others stressed that behavior is something that an animal "has," as well as what he or she "does," and is similar to an anatomical structure or organ on which natural selection can act. Winning the Nobel Prize was an amazing feat for researchers who studied such phenomena as imprinting in geese, homing in wasps, hunting by foxes, and dancing in bees, and some scientists who conducted biomedical research were miffed that such frivolous pursuits merited the most prestigious award, "the prize," for scientific research. And these three men were having fun doing their groundbreaking research, and in many scientific circles this was not acceptable. Lorenz has been filmed donning a fox coat and hopping along the ground to see how geese would respond to him! I remember meeting Lorenz at an ethological conference held in Parma, Italy, and his passion and enthusiasm were incredibly contagious. For hours, he told stories of the animals with whom he had shared his life and never once repeated himself. He clearly loved what he did and loved his animal friends.

Another major figure in the study of animal behavior, Charles Darwin, emphasized that there is evolutionary *continuity* among different species, so it was unlikely, for example, that only humans used tools or had culture. Darwin's ideas about evolutionary continuity—that behavioral, cognitive, emotional, and moral variations among different species are differences in *degree* rather than differences in *kind*—are often invoked in trying to answer questions about the evolution of various behavioral characteristics. On this view, there are shades of gray among different animals and between nonhumans and humans; the differences are not black and white, with no transitional stages or inexplicable jumps. Current work in evolutionary biology and anthropology suggests that linear scales of evolution in which there are large gaps between humans and at least some animals are simplistic views of the evolutionary process. We now know that individuals of many species use tools, have culture, are conscious and have a sense of self, can reason, can draw, can self-medicate, and show very complex patterns of communication that rival what we call "language." So Darwin was correct. We can learn much about humans by studying the roots of human behavior in nonhumans, and often the differences are not as stark as we think they are. This is not to say that humans are not unique, but rather to say that all animals are unique and that we can learn a lot by using what is called the *comparative method*, in which different species are studied with an eye (or nose or ear) toward learning about why they do the things they do in their own particular ways.

While a number of people contributed to the foundations of animal behavior, Charles Darwin's ideas were the most important contributions during the third quarter of the nineteenth century. He appears to be the first person to apply seriously the comparative evolutionary method to the study of behavior in his attempt to answer questions concerning the origin of emotional expression in people and animals.

My major research has focused on canids—members of the dog family—and birds. Some of these beings, especially social carnivores such as wolves, can tell us much about the evolution of human behavior. Most primatologists pay little attention to the comparative literature on behavior, cognition, and consciousness, but I recommend that they expand their horizons, for a primatocentric view does not account for the rich diversity of animal behavior that is played out throughout the animal kingdom. As the primatologist Benjamin Beck once correctly warned his colleagues, there are dangers in being narrowly "chimpocentric."

In my own research on social behavior and behavioral ecology, I stress evolutionary, ecological, and developmental (ontogenetic) perspectives. I follow the lead of such classical ethologists as Lorenz and Tinbergen. I also try to understand individual differences within species and variations among species. Individual differences in behavior are exciting to study because variation provides information that highlights just how different from one another individuals, even closely related individuals, can be. Variation is not noise to be dispensed with.

My approach is called the *comparative approach* to the study of behavior. I have done much interdisciplinary work with geneticists, anatomists, theologians, and philosophers. Scholars from different disciplines need to talk to one another and most importantly listen to one another. My work with Dale Jamieson, Colin Allen, Bernard Rollin, Gay Bradshaw, Lori Gruen, and Jane Goodall, with each of whom I have published papers and books, has been incredibly rewarding and prevented burnout. Each of these people, along with Laura Sewall, the ecopsychologist who wrote *Sight and Sensibility,* stimulated me in many ways and made my science better—I ask more questions and want more in return from my own efforts. Colin Allen, with whom I have done much collaborative work and cycled thousands of miles in the United States and abroad, is always there to pull in my reins and ask, "Do you *really* mean that?" or "What in the world are you trying to say?" Dale Jamieson patiently walked with me through oftentimes tortuous philosophical literature and remains a true friend, although I'd often ask him, "Do you all really spend time pondering this obvious fact?" Benjamin Beck always grounded me and made me appreciate just how dedicated are many people who work with captive animals. These were all very valuable lessons.

While we understand much about the lives of other animals, we need to fill enormous gaps in our knowledge before we can make any stubborn general claims about the evolution and development of most behavior patterns. Caution surely is the best road to take when offering generalizations, especially about complex behavior patterns, animal thinking, and animal emotions. Not only are there differences in behavior between species (called *interspecific variation*), but also there are marked individual differences within species (called *intraspecific variation*). These differences make for exciting and informative research concerning, for example, why wolves and dogs differ and why even littermates and siblings may differ from one another. Many of the coyotes I studied in the Grand Teton National Park in Wyoming lived in packs, but just down the road, coyotes lived either alone or as mated pairs. Thus, making general statements that the coyote behaves this way or that is very misleading, because "the" coyote does not really exist. The same is true for tool use in chimpanzees and orangutans. Not every great ape uses tools, and it is challenging to discover why this is so. Intraspecific variation in behavior has been observed in many animals, including insects. Lumping all members of a species into one category can be very misleading. A bee is not a bee is not a bee, just as a person is not a person is not a person. Humans and other animals are individuals.

I also work at many different levels of analysis. While much of my research is done at the microlevel (for example, analyzing, frame by frame, films of animals at play or animals looking out for potential predators), I am an interdisciplinary holist at heart. I prefer to tackle "big" questions. I also do not shy away from conducting detailed statistical analyses, but never do the animals I am studying get pushed aside as numbers, unnamed variables in an equation, or points on a graph. It is important that the "protective membrane of statistics," as Mary Lou Randour calls it, not shield us from the worlds of other animals, their joys and pains, their wisdom, their uniqueness.

Another consistent thread in my research is that I have always been interested in individuals. Much of my research has been focused on understanding how individual differences in behavior arise during early development, and what they mean as youngsters get older and become independent. I am also interested in the evolution of behavioral variation—why there has been selection for behavioral variation and flexibility.

In addition to writing about science, animal behavior, evolution, and behavioral ecology, I trespass into other arenas. I have always been interested in matters of spirit and have had the good fortune to be involved in two exciting, challenging interdisciplinary programs—Science and the Spiritual Quest II (www.ssq.net), sponsored by the Center for Theology and the Natural Sciences in Berkeley, California; and the Dialogue on Science, Ethics, and Religion organized by the American Association for the Advancement of Science (AAAS), which also publishes *Science* magazine. At meetings of both these programs, participants speak freely about science (evolutionary biology, anthropology, psychology), spirituality, theology, religion, and God, and much progress is made in addressing how science and religion can be reconciled.

AH, IT'S ONLY SCIENCE…

Although my training was strongly scientific, I never felt that science was the only valid approach to coming to terms with the world around me. My early scientific training as an undergraduate and a beginning graduate student was grounded in what the philosopher Bernard Rollin calls the "common sense of science," in which science is viewed as a fact-gathering value-free activity. Assumptions that science is value free never sat well with me, for scientists are humans first and have individual agendas about everything. Furthermore, cut-and-dried normative science is just too confining. I did not worship science and always thought there was room for pluralism and holism.

I believe that the contributions of spiritual and religious perspectives to science are important in our coming to a fuller understanding of animal behavior, in particular the evolution of social morality. I also believe that if science and scientists choose to change their ways, the change will have to come from within the halls of science rather than from, for example, theology, although it will be obvious in many of the essays in this book that I believe interdisciplinary discussions and cooperation are essential for producing change. Indeed, the new field of neurotheology is growing among scholars interested in the biological bases of spirituality, meditation, and mystical and religious experiences. Nonetheless, the philosopher Holmes Rolston claims that "science cannot tell humans what they most need to know: the meaning of life and how to value it." I agree. Science does not usually allow for expressions of sentimentality or spirituality. Unchecked, science could easily produce a soulless society and a loss of human dignity and free will. Questioning science and recognizing the limitations of scientism will make for better science by situating science in relation to fields of inquiry in which it is more acceptable to ponder questions about spirituality, soul, life, death, love, and God.

Having said all this, I want to stress that I am *not* a science basher and that I love what I do. "Ah, it's only science" is not a pejorative phrase. Questioning science is not to be antiscience or a Luddite. I also believe that doing science should be fun and that enjoying science will make for better science. I hope that my enthusiasm for, and my love of, the study of animal behavior will be contagious, and this is among many of the reasons that I wrote this book. I am a biophiliac who loves learning about other animals and nature.

ANIMAL BEHAVIOR AND ANIMAL WELL-BEING

My trek to the study of animal behavior—whole animals in the field—was not a direct one. When I reflect on my academic career, I realize that my parents were correct—I have always been interested in what animals know and what they feel. I have always felt their joys, pains, and sorrows—I have always empathized with them and tried to place myself in their paws and hearts. I have always been suspicious of people who try to denature animal pain and suffering. Pain and suffering have evolved because they are adaptive responses to situations that are dangerous or life threatening. They are part of an animal's nature, and they influence how individuals interact in nature. To take the nature out of pain and suffering is bad biology.

It was during a physiology class, when one of my professors proudly strolled into the laboratory and killed a rabbit using a rabbit punch (laughing as he did so), that my longtime interest in animal protection came to the fore. So it was not really surprising that I chose to leave this program, and then another at a prestigious graduate program in neurobiology and behavior at a major medical school, because I did not want to sacrifice dogs or cats as part of my education. I did some deep thinking and I discovered—really rediscovered—what I wanted to do. I wanted to study social behavior in animals and not, when I was done, have to dispose of ("sacrifice") the animals, individuals with whom I had closely bonded and whom I had named. After moving to Washington University in St. Louis to work on my Ph.D. with the best mentor one could ever have, Michael W. Fox, I conducted research on captive animals, and I allowed mice and infant chickens to be killed by coyotes in staged encounters. I am deeply sorry and haunted by the knowledge that I did this sort of research and would never do it again. I cannot give back life to these mice and chickens, but I have anguished over their death at my hands.

MINDING ANIMALS AND DEEP ETHOLOGY

The phrase "minding animals" came to me on a hike with my companion dog, Jethro, and it means two things. "Minding animals" refers, first, to caring for other animal beings, respecting them for who they are, appreciating their worldviews, and wondering what and how they are feeling and why. The second meaning refers to our acknowledging that many animals have very active minds.

Minding animals led me to develop the term "deep ethology" to convey some of the same general ideas that underlie the deep ecology movement, in which it is stressed that people need to recognize not only that they are an integral part of nature, but also that they have unique responsibilities to nature. As a deep ethologist, following the tradition of ecopsychology, I, as the see-er, try to become the seen. I become coyote. I become penguin. I try to step into animals' sensory and locomotor worlds to discover what it might be like to be a given individual, how they sense their surroundings, and how they behave and move about in certain situations.

As big-brained and omnipresent mammals, we have enormous social responsibilities to conduct our studies in the most ethical manner, to share our information with nonscientists, and also to seek and to use nonscientists' input in trying to determine which questions are the most pressing in our pursuit of knowledge. We also need to seek out the advice of those who hold other world-views, for example, that of indigenous people who have lived for eons in close association with wild animals and nature. All the many different ways of knowing should be considered. In the past, many Western scientists have marched into other countries, studied their exotic wildlife, and departed without consulting with the local people or giving much attention to local problems, such as the influence of grazing on agricultural fields in India or the effects of global warming on animal populations. This practice has changed greatly as Western scientists have incorporated local people into their work and have applied their findings to help solve local problems. Information on many aspects of animal behavior—movement patterns, social organization, and reproductive habits—is useful to people who are studying conservation biology and wildlife management, as well as to those who live alongside the animals under study. There is a very practical side to the heady study of animal behavior.

ANIMAL WELFARE AND ANIMAL RIGHTS

In some essays, I write about animal well-being using terms such as "animal welfare" and "animal rights," terms that are not interchangeable. (Summaries of different philosophies about the general field of animal protection can be found in books by Michael W. Fox, Peter Singer, Tom Regan, and Gary Francione, among others.)

Many animals feel pain and suffer. Although some people believe that it is all right to cause animals pain if the research helps humans, others believe that human benefit does not excuse causing pain in animals. Some people think that animals do not deserve any consideration—at least, their actions strongly suggest that this is their stance.

People who believe that we are allowed to cause animals pain, but that we must be careful not to cause them excessive or unnecessary pain, argue that if we consider the animals' welfare or well-being, we are doing all we need to do. These people are called *welfarists*. People who believe that it is wrong to cause animals any pain or suffering and that animals should not be eaten, held captive in zoos, or used in painful research, or in most or any research, are called *rightists*. They believe that animals have certain moral and legal rights that include the right not to be harmed.

Many people support a position called the *rights view*. According to the lawyer and animal-rights advocate Gary Francione, to say that an animal has a right to have an interest protected means that the animal has a claim, or entitlement, to have that interest protected even if it would benefit us to do otherwise. Humans have an obligation to honor that claim for voiceless animals, just as they do for young children and the mentally disabled. So if a dog has a right to be fed, you have an obligation to make sure she is fed. If a dog has a right to be fed, you are obligated not to do anything to interfere with feeding her. Likewise, if a dog has a right not to be subjected to unnecessary suffering, you have an obligation not to do anything, such as research, that would cause her pain and suffering, even if the research would benefit humans.

Tom Regan, a professor of philosophy at North Carolina State University, is often called the "modern father of animal rights." His book *The Case for Animal Rights,* published in 1983, attracted much attention to this concept. Advocates who believe that animals have rights stress that animals' lives are valuable in and of themselves, not because of what animals can do for humans or because they look or behave like us. Animals are not property or things but, rather, living organisms, subjects of a life, who are worthy of our compassion, respect, friendship, and support. Rightists expand the range of animals to whom we grant certain rights. Thus, animals are not lesser or less valuable than humans. They are not property that can be abused or dominated.

In contrast, welfarists do not think that animals have rights. (Some welfarists do not think that humans have rights either.) Rather, they believe that while humans should not abuse or exploit animals, as long as we make the animals' lives comfortable physically and psychologically, then we are taking care of them and respecting their welfare. Welfarists are concerned with the quality of animals' lives. But welfarists do not believe that animals' lives are valuable in and of themselves, that just because animals are alive, their lives are important.

Welfarists believe that if animals experience comfort, appear happy, experience some of life's pleasures, and are free from prolonged or intense pain, fear, hunger, and other unpleasant states, then we are fulfilling our obligations to them. If individual animals show normal growth and reproduction and are free from disease, injury, malnutrition, and other types of suffering, they are doing well.

This welfarist position also assumes that it is all right to use animals to meet human ends as long as certain safeguards are in place. They believe that the use of animals in experiments and the slaughtering of animals for human consumption are all right as long as these activities are conducted in a humane way. Welfarists do not want animals to suffer unnecessary pain, but they sometimes disagree among themselves about what pain is necessary and what humane care really amounts to. But welfarists agree that the pain and death animals experience is sometimes justified because of the benefits that humans derive. The ends, human benefits, justify the means, the use of animals even if they suffer, because their use is considered necessary for human benefit.

WHY CARE ABOUT OTHER ANIMALS AND BRING THEM INTO OUR HEARTS?

Why do people even care about other animals? As I argue in many of the essays in this volume, it is because they truly are consummate companions, even if we never meet them up close and personal. I argue that it makes us feel good to think about animals and to feel their presence, or to know that they are out there in nature even if we do not sense—see, hear, or smell—them, because our old brains still keep us in touch with other animals and nature as a whole. Many of the books in this series published by Temple University Press show over and over again just how important animals are for our own well-being and how important our goodwill is for their well-being. And there are always lessons to be learned.

It is well known that dogs can help reduce stress in children and adults. Dreamworkers, an Atlanta-based therapy-animal group, cannot keep up with the demand for its animals by humans who need them. In fact, there is a reciprocal relationship. Touching and petting a dog can be calming, both for the human and for the dog. Marty Becker has written a wonderful book titled *The Healing Power of Pets* in which he shows how pets can keep people healthy and happy—they can help heal lonely people in nursing homes, hospitals, and schools. Many heartwarming stories about the importance of dogs to our own well-being are shared by Michelle Rivera in her book *Hospice Hounds.* And, in his book *Kindred Spirits: How the Remarkable Bond between Humans and Animals Can Change the Way We Live,* the holistic veterinarian Allen Schoen lists fourteen ways in which relationships between animal companions and humans can reduce stress. These include reducing blood pressure, increasing self-esteem in children and adolescents, increasing the survival rate of victims of heart attacks, improving the life of senior citizens, aiding in the development of humane attitudes in children, providing a sense of emotional stability for foster children, reducing the demand for physician's services for nonserious problems among Medicare enrollees, and reducing loneliness in preadolescents. Bringing pets to the workplace can reduce stress, improve job satisfaction, foster social interactions, and increase productivity.

Once, while I was visiting my parents in Florida, my father called his friend Ginger, whose husband had recently died, so that she could show me her new treasure, a teacup poodle, not surprisingly named Tiny, whom she carried inside her shirt. Ginger pampered and deeply loved Tiny, who pampered and deeply loved Ginger in return. She brought Ginger much joy in the absence of her husband. But the silly rules of the condominium complex imposed by the homeowners' association did not allow dogs on the premises. I can guarantee you that this wonderful small dog was much less a nuisance than most of Ginger's human neighbors. Yet Ginger had to move, because dogs were banned. What was very interesting to me was that my mother, who had been bitten by a dog when she was young and feared dogs throughout her life, and who at the time was unable to move on her own, also found Tiny to be a welcome and comforting friend. We were all afraid that my mother would become very upset as Tiny landed on her lap. But, to our pleasant surprise, she actually allowed Tiny to lie on her lap and smiled from ear to ear as Tiny burrowed into her blanket and her heart.

On another trip to visit my parents, I read about a homeless man named Jackie Tresize who had been mugged and beaten and whose best friend, a shih tzu named Champion, had disappeared while Jackie was recuperating. Of his canine friend, Jackie said: "He was my little family unit; he kept me from feeling lonely. If I had my dog, I wouldn't want nothing else in life." In my home state, inmates at the Colorado Women's Correctional Facility get to care for and live with dogs who would have been "put to sleep" at the local animal shelter. The experience of walking the dogs, grooming them, and cleaning up after them is incredibly rewarding and beneficial to the dogs, the caretakers, and the prison staff. Prison warden Jim Abbott notes: "They have a terrific calming effect that is very therapeutic for both inmates and staff—in a tense situation they divert it." Says Stephanie Timothy, a caretaker of the rescued dog Charlie: "It helps you feel important that they give you the responsibility.... Just knowing [Charlie] is going to make somebody else as happy as he made me is worthwhile." For another caretaker, Mary Johnson, training Max taught her a trade she can pursue when she is released. And as I was writing this essay, I learned that a dog in Toronto, Canada, was responsible for stopping a man on a killing spree. The dog approached the man and started playing with him, and the man turned himself in to the local police!

The importance of companion animals also made its way into the U.S. Senate. In a landmark speech to the Senate about slaughterhouses, Senator Robert Byrd of West Virginia spoke about the importance of companion animals— our "unselfish friends"—for our well-being.

It's often claimed that because of dogs' long and close association with humans and the strong reciprocal bonds that readily form between these four-legged and us two-legged mammals, they are able to read our facial expressions, body language, gestures, and voices. We share a common language when it comes to many aspects of social communication, and dogs' ability to understand us seems to be a hard-wired instinct. I recently met Hogan, a malamute–German shepherd mutt, in Fort Lauderdale, Florida, and after his human companion told me Hogan was friendly, I did a quick play bow and wagged my head from side to side. Instantly, Hogan was all over me trying to play. He understood what the bow meant and shared my desire to play. I'm sure many of you have experienced similar instantaneous connections on innumerable occasions.

Why are dogs such good healers? Dogs—as well as cats, llamas, and dolphins—help treat humans suffering from terminal illnesses, interminable pain, and severe dementia by providing creature comfort. Caregivers and patients report that animals are "safe" and provide relaxation, friendship, and bundles of love to people in need. If we allow dogs into our lives, they readily ignite and awaken our senses, spirits, and souls. They, and many other animal beings, offer us raw, naked, unfiltered, and unconditional respect, humility, compassion, trust, and love. They are not social parasites who prey deceitfully and selfishly on our goodwill, as some popular writers want you to believe. Rather, as Michelle Rivera points out, dogs are true friends with whom we are tightly bonded and involved in a sort of mutual admiration society. Dogs are intuitive therapists. They truly *want* to make us feel better, to heal us, and we are remiss for not allowing them to do so, to be our best friends. We are depriving them of following their natural instincts. I imagine it is likely that as we allow dogs to do what they do best, comforting us in difficult times, we will discover even more mutual benefits from their unconditional giving. I feel certain that the give-and-take that characterizes dog-human interactions will blossom into even more meaningful and deep interrelationships. Dogs and many other animals truly are consummate companions.

Of course, some people want to learn more about animals to make the case for human uniqueness, usually claiming that humans are "above" and "better than" other animals. But the more we study animals and the more we learn about "them" and "us," the more often we discover there is no real dichotomy or nonnegotiable gap between animals and humans, because humans are, of course, animals. Rather, there is evolutionary *continuity*. Art, culture, language, and tool use and manufacture can no longer be used to separate "them" from "us." Drawing lines between species in terms of cognitive skills or emotional capacities can be very misleading, especially when people take the view that nonhuman animals are "lower" or "less valuable" than "higher" animals, where "higher" usually means primates, nonhuman and human. In many ways, we are them and they are us.

It is essential to learn more and more about the lives of other animals because learning and knowledge lead to an understanding of animals as individuals and members of a given species, and understanding leads in turn to appreciation and respect for the awesome and mysterious animal beings with whom we share Earth. Comparative approaches to the study of other animals allow us to see how different species and individuals solve the myriad problems they face.

There is no doubt that we can learn much about humans by carefully studying our animal kin and also by listening to their stories. One reason for my fascination with the study of animal behavior (in particular, questions centering on animal cognition, animal emotions, animal morality, and human intrusion into the lives of other animals) is that I want to learn more about why both the similarities and differences between humans and other animals have evolved. The more we come to understand other animals, the more we will appreciate them as the amazing beings they are and the more we will also understand ourselves.

MINDING THE BLURRED BORDERS BETWEEN "ANIMALS" AND "HUMANS"

It is very clear that learning about other animal beings—how they spend their time, who they interact with, where they do what they do and how they do it, what their intellectual and cognitive abilities (cognitive ethology) are, and what their emotional lives are like—is essential for gaining a full appreciation of human spirituality and just what it is that is uniquely human. Researchers have now discovered that tool use, language use, self-consciousness, culture, art, and rationality no longer can reliably be used to draw species boundaries that separate humans from other animals. That is, claims that only humans use tools and language, are conscious, are artists, have culture, or can reason are no longer defensible, given the enormous growth in our knowledge of our animal kin. But reflecting on one's own mortality seems to be uniquely human, as might be cooking food. (I sometimes wonder if, and worry that, sadism is a uniquely human characteristic.)

Primatologists have identified about forty different behavior patterns that show cultural variation in chimpanzees (tool use, grooming, patterns of courtship). Female killer whales are known to spend years showing their youngsters how to hunt elephant seals according to local custom. Researchers have compiled a list of almost twenty behavior patterns in whales and dolphins that are influenced by local tradition and show cultural variation. Frans de Waal, a primatologist at Emory University, tells a story of how enamored some art critics were of a painting, only to change their minds when they discovered that the artist was a chimpanzee. In the prestigious journal *Science*, researchers in Germany report that a dog named Rico has a vocabulary of about two hundred words and is able to figure out that an unfamiliar sound referred to an unfamiliar toy. Rico inferred the name of unfamiliar toys by exclusion learning and showed patterns of learning similar to those of young humans. The study of Rico reminded me of a paper published in the *Quarterly Review of Biology* in 1928 about the sensory capacities of dogs, especially a male called Fellow. What I love about this paper is the authors' claim that "much of what the average man 'knows' about his own dog, and about dogs in general is, of course, quite unknown to the animal psychologist." Best to keep an open mind. Just because other animals don't do something when we ask them to do it in certain experimental conditions, or just because we don't see other animals do something we would expect them to do based on our own expectations, doesn't mean that they can't do amazing things in other contexts.

ANIMALS AS "PERSONS": MY MOTHER, BEATRICE, AND MY DOG, JETHRO

Here is a personal story about my mother that raises many questions that I will consider throughout this book. Personhood is a topic that has been increasingly pursued by philosophers, legal scholars, and a handful of biologists. There are practical as well as theoretical—ivory-tower—issues at stake, for how we view animals, their moral and legal standing (Are they objects or property or beings?), often translates into how we treat them. Discussing the status of animals—whether nonhuman animals can be considered persons—compels us to consider what makes us human. The study of animal cognition and emotions is central to questions about personhood.

Once when I was visiting my parents, my father asked, "Marc, can you please wheel Mom into the kitchen and get her ready for dinner?" I answered, "Sure, Dad," and began the short trek. But the journey went well beyond the confines of my parents' home. It remains a difficult and multidimensional pilgrimage for which there are not any road maps or dress rehearsals. I watched myself watching Mom. The role reversal was riveting; I had become my keeper's keeper. I kept wondering, "Where (and who) is the person I called 'Mom'?"

My mother, Beatrice Rose, whom I loved dearly, suffered major losses of locomotor, cognitive, and physiological functions. She did not know who I am and likely had lost some self-awareness and body awareness. She became, as the legal scholar Rebecca Dresser calls such humans, a "missing person." In a nutshell, my mother had lost her autonomy. She had little self-determination. Nevertheless, there is no doubt that others would still think of her as a person whose spirit and soul were very much alive and who was entitled to certain moral and legal standing. And in my view they should.

Generally, the following criteria are used to designate a being as a person: being conscious of one's surroundings, being able to reason, experiencing emotions, having a sense of self, adjusting to changing situations, and performing cognitive and intellectual tasks. While many humans fulfill most if not all these criteria, there are humans who do not, notably young infants and seriously mentally challenged adults. But they are also rightfully considered persons.

Now what about my late companion dog Jethro? He was active, could feed and groom himself, and was very emotional. Jethro was as autonomous as a dog can be. Yet many people would not feel comfortable calling Jethro a person. This irreverence would be a prime example of just what is wrong with academic musings! Dolphins, elephants, and great apes, among other animals, might also warrant being called persons.

Why are there different attitudes toward my mother and Jethro? Why are some people, especially in Western cultures, hesitant to call chimpanzees, gorillas, dolphins, elephants, wolves, and dogs, for example, persons, even when they meet the criteria for personhood better than do some humans? Perhaps it is fear. Many people fear that elevating animal beings to persons would tarnish the notion of personhood. Some also fear that animals as persons would have the same legal and moral standing as humans and would be our equals.

While some may believe this whole exercise is shamefully crass, there are some very important issues at stake. Loving Jethro (and other animals) as much as I do does not mean I love my mother (or other humans) less. Granting Jethro and other animals personhood and attendant moral and legal standing does not lessen or take moral and legal standing away from humans.

Surely, Jethro went through life differently from most human (and other dog) beings, but this did not mean he didn't have any life at all. People vary greatly. There are countless different personalities, but the term *person* is broad enough to encompass and to celebrate this marvelous diversity.

Extending the definition of personhood to nonhumans would not degrade the notion of personhood but would require that animals be treated with the respect and compassion due them, that their interests in not suffering be given equal consideration with those of humans. I hope to convince you that little is lost by calling some animals persons and allowing all human beings to be called persons as well.

UNDERSTANDING AND APPRECIATING THE WORLDS OF OTHER ANIMALS: THE IMPORTANCE OF CURIOSITY, OPEN-MINDEDNESS, PATIENCE, AND PERSEVERANCE

What we learn about other animals can improve their well-being and also ours. The information we gather about their cognitive skills, their levels of intelligence, and their emotional lives—their passionate nature—informs us that individuals of many species are not robots or automatons but, rather, thinking and feeling beings. If animals were merely robots, why would their behavior fascinate us, and why would we bond with them the way we do?

New studies are producing information that shows just how fascinating and complex animal behavior can be. Animals who seemed incapable of much thought have been shown to have remarkable cognitive skills. Who would have imagined that rats might dream about the mazes in which they ran the previous day; that bonobos can tell other bonobos where they have gone by leaving signs for their friends to follow; that chimpanzees are aware of what other chimpanzees know; that elephants can communicate with one another over distances of a hundred or more kilometers, as can whales; that honeybees can learn complex same-difference tasks and generalize learned responses to novel stimuli; or that a parrot can learn to differentiate among objects based on their shape, color, or texture? It's also been discovered that lonely sheep are happier and more comfortable when they are shown pictures of sheep family and friends. And Sissy, a female elephant, left her favorite tire as a tribute to her friend Tina after Tina suddenly died; Carol Buckley, the director of the Elephant Sanctuary in Tennessee, reported that Sissy stood for two days at Tina's grave and left behind her at the grave the tire that she had been carrying around as her security blanket.

Fish also show complex patterns of culture and social cognition, and recent research has shown that fish respond to the pain-reliever morphine and that pain-related behaviors are not simple reflexes. Domestic fowl can control how much sperm they produce depending on the promiscuity of a female. Chickens can recognize and remember more than a hundred other chickens in their social pecking order. Many individual nonhuman animals show distinct personalities and idiosyncratic quirks, just as humans do. There are extroverts, introverts, agreeable individuals, and neurotic animals. Shy laboratory rats might not live as long as more adventurous rats. And it is thought that the stress of living in a lab situation causes premature aging in rats. And there's more. Three years after chimpanzees performed a task that required them to count, they could remember how to count, and a seal showed that he could remember the concept of "sameness" after twelve years. Two elephants, Shirley and Jenni, remembered one another when they were inadvertently reunited after being apart for twenty years. Some animals might also be moral beings (see this book's Part III). Given the linguistic abilities of Rico the dog, I don't think we're barking up the wrong tree when we ponder whether nonhuman animals can have a sense of right and wrong. And why do we think humans should be the measure of what is right and wrong, given what we're doing to other animals, other humans, and the environment?

On the lighter side, fish and snakes appear to communicate by flatulating. What a good and economical use of a natural bodily function! And animals are not immune from rare natural events. Captive hamadryas baboons have been observed to reduce their rates of locomotion and threat behavior during a solar eclipse. And howler monkeys showed a 42 percent decrease in population size, as well as major social disorganization, after Hurricane Iris destroyed the forest in which they lived in southern Belize in October 2001. The list of new and fascinating discoveries is endless.

I like to think of myself as a pluralist—remaining open to alternative views and accepting that there are many different ways to study animal behavior and to explain the behavior of our kin. Solid scientific data, stories, anecdotes, and myths and lore are all needed as we attempt to learn as much as we can about animal behavior. I like to think of the *s*'s that can drive research and explanations of behavior—science, social responsibility, statistics ("hard science"), stories, and skeptics. Hard data do not tell the only story, and in my view it is perfectly okay to be carefully anthropomorphic. In Part I, I discuss the charge of anthropomorphism that so often is used to derail the study of animal minds. And, of course, detailed descriptions of behavior patterns, careful observations, and ethically justified experiments that do not harm the animals in whom we are interested are all important components of a comprehensive approach to animal behavior. A number of my essays show that when we perform research that is invasive, we often are unable to answer the very questions in which we are interested. Often animals are stressed by our mere presence, so we cannot truly study their more natural patterns of behavior. I and my colleagues believe that this is a major problem that needs to be studied and understood so that the data we collect are as reliable as possible and the questions in which we are interested are answered with as little ambiguity as possible.

Animals can do amazing things and accomplish incredible feats, but sometimes they do not do what we ask them to do. They have their own points of view, and on occasion they express them freely. An individual might not be motivated to do something because she is tired, not hungry or thirsty, or just wants to be left alone. It is also possible that we are not tuned in to the sensory worlds of the animals and that we are asking them to respond to a stimulus to which they are not sensitive—a sound that is outside their range of hearing, a color that they cannot see, or an odor that they cannot perceive. The sensory world of many animals is quite different among different species and also varies from our own.

Humans—researchers and nonresearchers alike—often try to package nature and to sanitize and to simplify, or denature, the behavior of other animals. Sometimes simple answers to complex questions suffice, and other times they do not. Experts can disagree, and this is good for science in general and for the study of animal behavior in particular. Disagreements fuel future research by curious minds. Just when we think we know all there is to know, we learn that this is not so. "I don't know" is one of the best phrases a researcher can utter, because admitting that there are mysteries still to be uncovered and acknowledging disagreements can also fuel future inquiries. The Pulitzer Prize–winning poet Mary Oliver captured it best in her lines from "The Grave": "A dog can never tell you what she knows from the smells of the world, but you know, watching her, that you know almost nothing."

While there are many behavioral phenomena about which we know quite a lot—we can make very accurate and reliable predictions about what an individual is likely to do in a given situation—there are some areas in which we know next to nothing. The minds of other animals are private (as are human minds), and their sensory capacities often are very different from our own and each other's. So even though we might know much, academically speaking, about the physiology and anatomy of a dog's nose or of a bat's ears, we still do not know with certainty, experientially, what it is like to be a dog or a bat. Wouldn't it be nice to be a dog or a bat or a termite for a while? And, when, using mirrors, we study the concept of self-knowledge in animals, it is possible that even if we collect data that suggest that dogs do not have as high a degree of self-awareness as do chimpanzees because dogs, unlike chimpanzees, do not respond with self-directed movements when they look at their reflection in a mirror, it remains possible that dogs do have a high degree of self-awareness but that the use of a mirror does not tap into this ability. Perhaps assessing dogs' responses to different odors, including their own, would yield different results. My own study of a dog's response to his own and to other dogs' "yellow snow" showed that this might be the case. We need to take into account how animals sense their worlds using different sensory modalities that are more or less important to them.

Along with unbridled curiosity, cleverness, and creativity, patience is a virtue when it comes to the study of animal behavior. I well remember many hours spent sitting cold and alone among 250,000 Adélie penguins at the Cape Crozier rookery in Antarctica just waiting for them to do something—anything—besides steal rocks from each other's nests or sleep or stare at me trying to figure out who I was, a curious observer or a new land predator. I also recall falling asleep while waiting for a coyote to wake up and join other pack members who had decided to move to another area in which to hunt and frolic.

Patience is also needed in data analysis. Watching videos over and over and doing the appropriate statistical analyses can try anyone's patience, but these activities are just as important and exciting as collecting reliable data. (Well, maybe they are not all that much fun, but they are essential.) And do not give up on some idea just because others think you are wrong. Sometimes you might be heading in the wrong direction, and sometimes you might not. Be patient, and analyze the arguments of supporters and critics alike. If the late William D. Hamilton III had not been persistent in pursuing his revolutionary ideas about the evolution of social behavior via kin selection, the field of animal behavior would have suffered an enormous loss. Had Jane Goodall not insisted on naming the chimpanzees she studied at Gombe stream in Tanzania, there would have been a delay in our coming to recognize that individuals had distinct personalities. Goodall also was the first researcher to observe chimpanzees use blades of grass as tools to extract a termite meal from a hole, but many other researchers did not believe her until she showed them a video of the activity. Had I given up the study of social play, as some of my colleagues suggested I do when I was a graduate student, I would never have discovered over the next twenty-five years the important connections between social play and the evolution of fairness, trust, and morality. Years of detailed video analysis (which drove some students crazy), discussions with colleagues from different disciplines, and the belief that I was onto something big kept me going. Imagine if Charles Darwin had given in to his critics when he wrote about his theory of natural selection!

One important lesson that I emphasize in my classes is: *does not does not mean cannot*. Just because an animal does not do a particular task does not mean that he or she cannot do it. A wolf might choose not to chase an elk, but this does not mean he cannot do this. A robin might not learn to discriminate friend from foe, but this does not mean she cannot do this. We need to discover why this is so, why individuals often make the choices that they do—and among these choices is the choice not to do anything. Not to do something is to do something. Not to decide is to decide.

As Donna Haraway notes in her book *The Companion Species Manifesto*: "To do biology with any kind of fidelity, the practitioner *must* tell a story, *must* get the facts, and *must* have the heart to stay hungry for the truth and to abandon a favorite story, a favorite fact, shown to be somehow off the mark. The practitioner must also have the heart to stay with a story through thick and thin, to inherit its discordant resonances, to live its contradictions, when that story gets at a truth about life that matters." I could not agree more with her sentiments.

It is important to note that there is ample evidence that compassion begets compassion and that cruelty begets cruelty. There is a close relationship between cruelty to animals and cruelty to humans. Developing an understanding of and a deep appreciation for animals is one way to begin the journey of making this a more compassionate world. In addition, one practical advantage of appreciating animals is that changes of heart might lead to less resistance to preserving critical habitat for many endangered animals whose existence on this earth is seriously imperiled. Habitat loss is considered by most conservation biologists to be the biggest threat to animal and plant biodiversity. Caring might indeed spill over into sharing.

A Brief Road Map for *Animal Passions and Beastly Virtues*

Animal Passions and Beastly Virtues is meant to appeal both to academic and nonacademic ("popular") audiences. As in my other books, I try hard not to compromise solid science to make the major messages accessible to a wide variety of readers. *Animal Passions and Beastly Virtues* is also a strongly interdisciplinary volume that will be attractive to biologists, psychologists, anthropologists, sociologists, philosophers, theologians, lawyers, and the general public. I regularly interact not only with other scientists but also with philosophers, theologians, and religious leaders who are interested in animal behavior, usually focusing on animal cognition, intelligence, emotions, and morality (cooperation, fairness, trust, and forgiveness). Furthermore, while many of the papers present my views, there are also a number of broad review essays that cover a topic from a wide variety of perspectives.

This book is not an exercise in what some might call "recreational ethology" but a blend of hard (data-driven, statistics-laden, experimental) and soft (anecdotal, descriptive, nonexperimental) science, and it shows that what some people call soft science is necessary for learning more about nonhuman animal beings ("animals"). In some essays originally written for professional journals, I have retained the short results sections because some readers will want to see the numbers. But others can easily skip over these and go right to the discussion sections to learn about the major findings for a given study. The introductions to each part of the book summarize the essays that are included in that part, trace the history of the ideas that are presented, and expand on those ideas as necessary to round out the section.

In a variety of ways, *Animal Passions and Beastly Virtues* builds a big-picture view of animals, culture, and society. A brief look at the terrain shows that there are general discussions of such topics as consciousness, self, emotions, and empathy, and a discussion of the social behavior of domestic dogs, coyotes, and wolves. I also consider the nitty-gritty details of social play behavior—what animals do when they play—that after decades of studying play has resulted in my theory of wild justice. I also discuss some aspects of human-animal relationships (the "human dimension") and the ethics of human-animal interactions. Working closely with a number of colleagues in animal behavior, philosophy, and theology has provided me with a broad perspective that makes me think outside the box, but some of these ideas have taken hold only after years of discussion and debate.

Although each section has a unified perspective, some papers are time bound, so there are some inconsistencies in tone, style, and substance. I have not tried to align all my thoughts with my current views, nor have I attempted to resolve all inconsistencies. Ignorance and narrow-mindedness early in my career might show in some places (and may still linger). I made some small changes to some of the papers to correct mistakes and to update references.

Animal Passions and Beastly Virtues is thus also an exposé of how science is done. Science is neither value free nor perfect, and it is our imperfection that drives us to continue to learn about the world in which we live. I believe that the identification of the emergent broad patterns and the dynamic from which they arose from more narrow research will be useful to many colleagues and nonresearchers as examples of the utility of a long-term research career in which challenging ideas originated and were then developed more fully, integrated with others, or discarded or dismissed in frustration, only to arise again later on.

In the opening and closing essays that frame the book, I introduce a wide variety of ideas that have been central to my research, many of which have been marinating in my mind and heart for more than three decades. The threads of thinking and feeling that permeated my research were not always obvious, but compiling *Animal Passions and Beastly Virtues* helped me greatly to elucidate much of what was happening in my head and heart over the past thirty years. In many ways, much of my work was always leading, sometimes directly and sometimes obliquely, to my interests in ethics—how we treat other animals, how they treat one another, that is, wild justice—and the asymmetric nature of human-animal interactions in which arrogant anthropocentrism almost always trumps the animal's view and place in the world.

In Part I, "Emotions, Cognition, and Animal Selves," I consider various aspects of animal cognition and the field of cognitive ethology. I also present material that centers on anthropomorphism, animal emotions, self-awareness, and empathy, hot topics for researchers and nonresearchers alike. In Part II, "The Social Behavior of Dogs and Coyotes," I present essays on various aspects of the behavior of dogs and coyotes—including social organization and behavioral ecology, social communication, and the behavioral biology of feral dogs—that highlight the importance of comparative research in behavior and behavioral ecology.

In Part III, "Social Play, Social Development, and Social Communication," I consider the evolution of social cooperation, fairness, forgiveness, and morality in the context of what animals do when they play and interact with others early in life. The notion of wild justice is introduced to refer to the evolution of social rules of engagement and fairness and forgiveness. I then move on in Part IV, "Human Dimensions," to consider some human (anthropogenic) influences on the lives of other animals.

The material in Part V, "Ethics, Compassion, Conservation, and Activism," deals with the ways in which humans use animals for their own ends and intrude into and redecorate nature. In this section I also raise issues about science, social responsibility, and activism that requires leaving the ivory tower. I believe that it is important for academics to speak their hearts and minds when they are so moved, because the fate of many animals rests more with human attitudes about them and less with how much we know about their social behavior and other habits.

My concluding essay synthesizes my present thoughts and feelings and where I'd like to journey in the future. It draws together themes with which *Animal Passions and Beastly Virtues* is concerned—animal cognition, animal emotions, social play and the evolution of morality and wild justice, cooperation, forgiveness, and general human intrusions into nature. I wrote the original draft for a meeting that was convened by His Holiness the Dalai Lama (in Graz, Austria) and dealt with the wisdom of nature, for his Kalachakra for World Peace 2002.

Many of my colleagues and I know well just how difficult, tedious, frustrating, and challenging it can be to answer the simple question, "What is it like to be a dog or a cat or a chimpanzee or a robin or an ant?" It is the challenge of peeling away the layers of complexity and the mysteries that await us that keeps us going. And so it will for you.

Most of the essays in *Animal Passions and Beastly Virtues* raise more questions than they answer. In my view, this is a good thing, for there can never be enough interest in animal behavior, and this interest will be sparked by paying attention not only to how much we know but also to how much we don't. So, what *is* it like to be a dog or a bat or a praying mantis or an octopus? While neither I nor anyone else can tell you with 100 percent accuracy, I hope you'll get a good feel for the field of animal behavior and just how fascinating and mysterious the minds and lives of other animals are. Please read on.

ACKNOWLEDGMENTS

Many animal beings and human beings have influenced my life, and there is no way to list them all. My parents have always been there for me, tolerating whatever road I chose to travel and always making it clear that they loved me for who I am and not for what I am doing. I am grateful to all my students and others who have worked with me in a wide variety of research situations. Janet Francendese and Clint Sanders provided much support for the production of this book and I'm forever grateful to them for all of their help. Bobbe Needham was a great copy editor. Colin Allen and Dale Jamieson remain my good friends, and I still work closely with them on a variety of projects. Colin and Dale really made me see the light about the incredible importance of cognitive ethology in both academic and practical arenas, and their influence on my research and in other aspects of my life is immeasurable. Jane Goodall also has had a great influence on my thinking about animal behavior and about life in general, and her friendship and support are much appreciated. And last but surely not least, my very best friend, Jan Nystrom, has helped me along in ways far too numerous to count. Jan's critical editing, unwavering support, warmest of warm smiles, and lightness are always abundant, generously shared, and greatly appreciated.

I.

EMOTIONS, COGNITION, AND ANIMAL SELVES: "WOW! THAT'S ME!"

ONE OF THE HOTTEST FIELDS in the study of animal behavior is the study of animal minds—what they are like and what is in them. Researchers in many disciplines are asking questions such as "What is it like to be a specific animal?" "What does it feel like to be that animal?" and "What do animals know about themselves, other individuals, and their environment?"

In this part of the book, "Emotions, Cognition, and Animal Selves," I first consider emotions because there is wide interest in what animals feel and how they express their feelings. To understand why countless people form very close bonds with animals or why we are concerned with how animals are treated, what they *feel* is more important than what they *know*.

The four essays in this section reflect my longtime interest in animal minds, providing a comprehensive and interdisciplinary overview of the important issues in the science of cognitive ethology. Cognitive ethology is the comparative, evolutionary, and ecological study of animal minds, including thought processes, beliefs, rationality, information processing, and consciousness. The essays build on one another thematically, although they are not presented in chronological order. I also present material that centers on the use of what I call the two *a* words, namely *anthropomorphism* (basically, the attribution of human characteristics to nonhuman animals) and *anecdotes*, to inform explanations about the content of animal minds, animal emotions, self-awareness, and empathy. These are all hot topics for researchers and nonresearchers alike.

Parts of this essay are excerpted from Bekoff, M. 1994. "Cognitive Ethology and the Treatment of Non-Human Animals: How Matters of Mind Inform Matters of Welfare. *Animal Welfare* 3: 75–96; Bekoff, M., and C. Allen. 1997. "Cognitive Ethology: Slayers, Skeptics, and Proponents." In R. W. Mitchell, N. Thompson, and L. Miles (eds.), *Anthropomorphism, Anecdote, and Animals: The Emperor's New Clothes?* SUNY Press, Albany, New York. pp. 313–334; and Bekoff, M. 2000. *Strolling with Our Kin: Speaking for and Respecting Voiceless Animals.* Lantern Books, New York.

When I reread the essays in this section, I realized that most of the ideas, if not all, were present in my mind and heart for decades and began to appear in some of my essays in the mid-1970s when I seriously began to ponder the ways in which dogs, coyotes, and foxes communicated their intentions and desires to engage in social play (see Part III). However, I had not yet collaborated with the philosophers Dale Jamieson and Colin Allen, so my thinking was not especially focused or rigorous in some areas. When I met Dale, I was ready for some broad and deep interdisciplinary thinking about animal cognition, animal emotions, and philosophy of mind, and how matters of mind might inform matters of well-being. Dale and I used to get so excited about our joint ventures that we actually outlined the two volumes of our *Interpretation and Explanation in the Study of Animal Behavior* as we stood eating lunch in a parking lot. Much of our work also was done drinking margaritas and taking long hikes with our dogs Grete and Jethro, who seemed bored by our musings but to whom we nonetheless dedicated these books.

What is so very interesting and significant to me is to reflect upon how my own and others' ideas have changed over the years with (1) the accumulation of comparative data for diverse organisms to whom many of my colleagues were loathe to attribute any sort of mind at all, (2) the widespread acceptance of the inevitability of being anthropomorphic, and (3) the infusion of theory with philosophical discourse, common sense, and folk psychological explanations.

THE *A* WORDS: ANECDOTES AND ANTHROPOMORPHISM

Neither of the *a* words is discussed explicitly later on, so I want to consider briefly why anecdotes and anthropomorphism have frequently been used to bash the field of cognitive ethology. There are many different ways of describing what animals do. How one chooses to summarize what they see, hear, or smell depends on the questions in which one is interested. There is not just one correct way to describe or to explain what animals do or feel.

Anecdotes, or stories, always find their way into people's views of animals. Some of my colleagues dislike or ignore anecdotes because they are "merely stories" with little or no substance; they are not hard data. However, although much of our theorizing about the evolution of behavior rests on better or worse stories, few people find this reliance on anecdotes objectionable, perhaps because there is the widely accepted central unifying theory of natural selection.

Anecdotes are central to the study of behavior, as they are to much of science. As we accumulate more and more stories about behavior, we develop a solid database that can be used to stimulate further empirical research and, yes, additional stories. The plural of *anecdote* is data. Stephen J. Gould, in his foreword to *The Smile of a Dolphin*, stressed the importance of case studies in science. Anecdotes, similar to anthropomorphism, can be used to make for better science, if we carefully assess how we are using them.

BIOCENTRIC ANTHROPOMORPHISM: HUMANIZING ANIMALS WITH CARE

In 1908, Professor Margaret Washburn wrote: "We are obliged to acknowledge that *all psychic interpretation of animal behavior must be on the analogy of human experience....* Whether we will or no, we must be anthropomorphic in the notions we form of what takes place in the mind of an animal."

Two years earlier, the naturalist William J. Long wrote in his wonderful book *Brier-Patch Philosophy by "Peter Rabbit"*: "It is possible therefore, that your simple man who lives close to nature and speaks in enduring human terms, is nearer to the truth of animal life than is your psychologist, who lives in a library and to-day speaks a language that is to-morrow forgotten."

Unfortunately, many researchers have ignored what is so very obvious— we are humans and we have, by necessity, a human view of the world. The way we describe and explain the behavior of other animals is limited by the language we use to talk about things in general. By engaging in anthropomorphism, we make other animals' worlds accessible to ourselves and to other human beings. By being anthropomorphic, we can more readily understand and explain the emotions or feelings of other animals. But this is not to say that other animals are happy or sad in the *same* ways in which humans (or even other members of the same species) are happy or sad. Of course, I cannot be absolutely certain that Jethro is happy, sad, angry, upset, or in love, but these words serve to explain what he might be feeling. Referring merely to the firing of different neurons or to the activity of different muscles in the absence of behavioral information and context is insufficiently informative.

Some people argue that anthropomorphism is needless and wrong. The behaviorist psychologist Clive Wynne believes that anthropomorphic explanations are extremely imprecise, but this is really an empirical matter. Nowhere does he cash this out in a scientific way. His view is typical of those who privilege reductionistic stimulus-response explanations over explanations that appeal to such notions as consciousness, intentions, and beliefs, that is, the view that we are right and others are wrong. Many who favor mechanistic explanations have not spent much time watching free-ranging animals. Surely, given the complexity and flexibility of behavior, no explanatory scheme will be correct *all* the time. But more important, Wynne and others ignore the fact that the utility and accuracy of various sorts of explanations have not been assessed empirically. So we really don't know if his flavor of explanation is better for understanding and predicting behavior than the flavors of those he eschews. Until the data are in, we all must be careful in claiming that one sort of explanation is always better than others. It's poor scholarship to take a univocal approach in the absence of supportive data.

To make the use of anthropomorphism and anecdote more acceptable to critics, Gordon Burghardt suggested the notion of "critical anthropomorphism," in which various sources of information are used to generate ideas that may be useful in future research. These sources include natural history, individuals' perceptions, intuitions, feelings, careful descriptions of behavior, identifying with the animal, optimization models, and previous studies.

To help overcome resistance to our tendency to be anthropomorphic, I followed Burghardt's lead and offered the notion of "biocentric anthropomorphism" to stress the point that we can indeed offer reliable explanations of pain, suffering, and behavior without losing our perspective of who animals are in their own world. I also argued that being anthropomorphic is unavoidable because we have to use human languages and experiences to meaningfully describe and explain animal behavior and animal feelings. Describing animal behavior and emotions by referring to the firing of neurons or movement of muscles leaves out context (social and nonsocial), which is essential for us to be able to figure out why animals are doing what they are doing and what they are likely feeling. It seems to me that using various behavior patterns (crouching, hiding, limping, cowering, trembling, running away or avoiding certain situations, closed eyes, gait, posture, urinating, defecating, exuding glandular secretions, changes in respiration, and heart rate, to name a few) along with changes in physiological measures warrants the conclusion, for instance, that many animals do suffer and experience pain in numerous situations to which they are exposed by humans.

Some scientists are freely anthropomorphic outside their laboratories. Bernard Rollin points out that some researchers feel very comfortable attributing human emotions to the companion animals with whom they share their homes, for example. They tell stories of how happy Fido (a dog) is when they arrive at home, how sad Fido looks when they leave him at home or take away a chew bone, how Fido misses his buddies, or how smart Fido is for figuring out how to open a locked door or get around an obstacle. Yet when the same scientists enter their laboratories, dogs (and other animals) become objects, and talking about their emotional lives or how intelligent they are is taboo. One answer to the question of why dogs (and other animals) are viewed differently at work and at home is that at work, dogs are subjected to a wide variety of treatments that would be difficult to administer to one's companion.

I also wonder how some people fail to realize that the food they're savoring, the clothing they're wearing, or the circus act they're enjoying involves sentient beings who have suffered enormously for the person's pleasure. Why are these sorts of extrapolations so difficult to make? I suppose it's because it's very difficult to admit that they're part of the picture of animal abuse, and the picture isn't a pretty one. I frequently hear, "Oh, I didn't know that!" from people who surely know better. Distancing is also a factor, because animal abuse is hidden from most people's daily life, and few people who consume or otherwise use animals abuse them firsthand. Frans de Waal, in his book *The Ape and the Sushi Master*, introduces the notion of "anthropodenial," a practice in which a dualism, or distinct separation between humans and other animals, is suggested. Differences, rather than similarities or evolutionary continuity, are stressed. (Recall Charles Darwin's notion of evolutionary continuity.)

Using anthropomorphic language does not force us to discount the animal's point of view. Anthropomorphism allows other animals' behavior and emotions to be accessible to us. I believe that we can be *biocentrically anthropomorphic* and do rigorous science. Anthropomorphism can help make accessible to us the behavior and thoughts and feelings of the animals with whom we are sharing a particular experience.

THE STUDY OF ANIMAL EMOTIONS: LEARNING ABOUT, APPRECIATING, AND RESPECTING BEASTLY PASSIONS

The first essay in this section, "Beastly Passions," which appeals to the popular taste, considers the nature of animal emotions, a topic of a number of my writings and their secondary sources. This area of research makes some of my colleagues bristle, whereas most nonresearchers readily accept the idea that many animals experience numerous and deep emotions; these people are willing to use common sense, frequently and unknowingly invoking arguments about evolutionary continuity to inform their views and arguments about the nature of animal emotions. Even renowned scientists let their hair down. Frans de Waal was quoted in the *New York Times* as saying: "Sometimes I read about someone saying with great authority that animals have no intentions and no feelings, and I wonder, 'Doesn't this guy have a dog?'"

Stephen Jay Gould notes that there is a lovers' quarrel about the topic of animal emotions. Most people who know animals, including many researchers, believe (some would say they "know") that many animals have deep emotional lives, but it is very difficult to prove the existence of these lives with certainty. It is also very difficult to state categorically that no other animals enjoy themselves when playing, are happy when reuniting, or become sad over the loss of a close friend. Consider wolves when they reunite, their tails wagging loosely to-and-fro and individuals whining and jumping about. Consider also elephants reuniting in a greeting celebration, flapping their ears and spinning about and emitting a vocalization known as a "greeting rumble." Likewise, think about what animals are feeling when they remove themselves from their social group, sulk at the death of a friend, stop eating, and die.

There is now mounting evidence that joy, love, grief, jealousy, and embarrassment, for example, are all experienced by individuals of many species. In *The Smile of a Dolphin*, many well-respected researchers who have spent their lives studying and living with a wide variety of animals share their stories and empirical data about the emotional lives of the animals they know best. Their stories also show that scientists themselves have strong emotional feelings about the animals they study, despite the warnings of some of their colleagues that they should not get attached to their "research subjects," for this connection will taint their science.

In my view, times are changing, and more and more researchers are accepting that many animals do experience emotions—they are not merely acting "as if" they experience feelings. Glib discussions that recall the good old days of behaviorism, in which brains were considered to be black boxes into which we dare not trespass in explanations of behavior, are no longer accepted carte blanche. We can now freely and safely begin our studies by assuming that at least *some* animals experience a variety of emotions and then conduct research to see if our hypotheses are supported, rather than begin by assuming that they do not experience emotions and then have to "prove" that they do. The burden has shifted to the skeptics.

There is ample evidence that for many animals, especially vertebrates, the real question of interest is not *whether* they have emotional lives but rather *why* different emotions have evolved, that is, What are they good for? There is little doubt emotions have a long evolutionary history, as do other behavioral traits. This is not to say that animal emotions are identical to ours, for even among humans, expressions of joy, for example, feel differently to different people, and humans also display fear, bereavement and grief, and anger in a wide variety of ways.

Some skeptics continue to argue that we do not have the tools to study other minds, including those of other humans, because they are private and totally inaccessible. However, we do have the tools to study rigorously animal emotions. Many of the methods used in other areas of behavioral research can be used to study animal emotions. Noninvasive techniques to detect neural activity as measured by firing rates and cell metabolism have proved useful in studies of human cognitive processes and include the measurement of evoked response potentials (ERPs) and the use of positron emission tomography (PET scans) or functional magnetic resonance imaging (fMRI). These techniques can be coupled with others, such as transcranial magnetic stimulation (TMS), that create minidisruptions of neural activities in specific brain regions. The softening and reduction of skepticism is due in great part to new and increasing evidence about the similarities among our brains and those of other animals, and many arguments invoke Darwin's notion of evolutionary continuity.

In "Beastly Passions," I briefly discuss primary and secondary emotions. Let me parse the differences between them a bit more. Primary emotions, considered to be basic inborn emotions, include generalized rapid, reflex-like ("automatic" or hardwired) fear and fight-or-flight responses to stimuli that represent danger. Primary emotions are wired into the evolutionarily old limbic system, especially the amygdala, the "emotional" part of the brain, named by the neurobiologist Paul MacLean in 1952. Animals can perform a primary fear response such as avoiding an object, but they do not have to recognize the object that generates this reaction. Loud raucous sounds, certain odors, and objects flying overhead often lead to an inborn avoidance reaction to all such stimuli that indicate "danger." Natural selection has resulted in innate reactions that are crucial to individual survival. There is little or no room for error when an individual is confronted with a dangerous stimulus.

Secondary emotions—joy, anger, jealousy, resentment, grief, embarrassment, and love—are those that are experienced or felt, those that are evaluated and reflected on. They involve higher brain centers in the cerebral cortex. Thought and reflection allow flexibility of response in changing situations after the individual evaluates which of a variety of actions would be the most appropriate in the specific context. Although most emotional responses appear to be generated unconsciously, consciousness allows an individual to make connections between feelings and action and allows variability and flexibility in behavior.

WHERE TO FROM HERE? NATURALIZING THE STUDY OF ANIMAL EMOTIONS

Field research on animal emotions is of primary importance, for emotions have evolved in specific contexts. Naturalizing the study of animal emotions will provide more reliable data than information collected in unnatural circumstances (although animals raised in extremely impoverished social environments display deep grief), because emotions have evolved just as have other behavioral patterns and organ systems, including stomachs, hearts, kidneys, and brains. Evolution is as private as the minds of other individuals. While we can make better or worse guesses about why a particular behavior pattern evolved, we cannot really know for sure that our reconstruction is *the* correct answer.

Probably the best way to learn about the emotional lives of animals is to conduct comparative and evolutionary ethological, neurobiological, and endocrinological research, and to resist claims that anthropomorphism has no place in these efforts. To claim that we cannot understand elephants, dolphins, or other animals unless we are one of them leaves us nowhere. It is important to try to learn how animals live in their own worlds, to understand their own perspectives. Animals evolved in specific and unique situations, and it discounts their lives if we try to understand them only from our own perspective. Certainly, gathering reliable information on animal emotions is difficult, but it is not impossible.

LEAVING THE TOWER FOR THE FIELD

It is important that researchers in various fields—ethology, neurobiology, endocrinology, psychology, and philosophy—coordinate their efforts to learn about animal emotions. No single discipline will be able to answer *all* the important questions that still need to be dealt with. Laboratory-bound scientists, field researchers, and philosophers must share data and ideas.

Future research must also focus on a broad array of species, and not only on those animals with whom we are familiar (for example, companion animals) or those with whom we are closely related (nonhuman primates), animals to whom many of us freely attribute secondary emotions and a wide variety of moods. Species differences in how emotions are expressed and what they feel like also need to be taken into account. Even if joy and grief in dogs are not the same as joy and grief in chimpanzees, elephants, or humans, this does not mean that there is no such thing as dog joy, dog grief, chimpanzee joy, or elephant grief. Even wild animals—for example, wolves—and their domesticated relatives, dogs, may differ in the nature of their emotional lives.

By remaining open to the idea that many animals have rich emotional lives, even if we are wrong in some cases, little truly is lost. By closing the door on the possibility that many animals have rich emotional lives, even if they are very different from our own or from those of animals with whom we are most familiar, we will lose great opportunities to learn about their lives.

There are many worlds beyond human experience. There are no substitutes for listening to and having direct experiences with other animals. We truly can ask such questions as, Do animals love one another? Do they mourn the loss of friends and loved ones? Do they resent others? Can they be embarrassed? Certainly our own lives will be richer for the effort, and the lives of other animals more understood, appreciated, and respected.

THE SCIENCE OF COGNITIVE ETHOLOGY

The second essay in this section, "Cognitive Ethology," is a general and critical review of cognitive ethology. Topics that are discussed include the naturalizing of animal minds, the importance of Charles Darwin's and Donald Griffin's work in the development and rekindling of scientific interest in cognitive ethology, methods of study, criticisms of the field, and possible future directions—what areas of research would be the most fruitful for us to learn more about the nature of animal minds and what is in them. The third essay, "On Aims and Methods of Cognitive Ethology," written with Dale Jamieson, builds on the important work of Nobel laureate Niko Tinbergen, who published a classic essay in 1963 titled "On Aims and Methods of Ethology" in which he laid out an agenda for ethological investigations. In his paper, Tinbergen defined ethology as "the biological study of behavior" and viewed ethology as an integrated science. He identified four major areas on which ethological research should concentrate—evolution, adaptation (survival value), causation, and ontogeny (development).

Cognitive ethologists want to know how brains and mental abilities evolved—how they contribute to survival—and what selective forces resulted in the wide variety of brains and mental abilities that are observed in various animal species. In essence, cognitive ethologists want to know what it is like to be another animal. Asking what it is like to be other animals requires us to try to think like they do, to enter their worlds. And by engaging in these activities, we can learn much about animal consciousness and animal emotions.

Ethologists, psychologists, anthropologists, and philosophers have weighed in with numerous influential opinions about the nature of animal minds. The significance of an evolutionary biology of mind—the attribution of consciousness and intelligence to other animals—is paramount for informed discussions about animal well-being and animal rights. In another essay, "Reflective Ethology, Applied Philosophy, and the Moral Status of Animals," published in 1991, Dale Jamieson and I developed the notion of "reflective ethology," in which we stress that researchers must be "guided by the injunction to use our own evolutionary position carefully."

SELF-COGNIZANCE: SOME REFLECTIONS ON ANIMAL SELVES

I often wonder if Jethro, my late canine companion, knew who he was. People who know me are not surprised when I ask such questions. I also ponder whether chimpanzees, cats, elephants, dolphins, magpies, mice, salmon, or ants or bees have a sense of self. What do these animals make of themselves when they look in a mirror, see their reflection in water, hear their own or another's bark or howl, or smell themselves and others? Is it possible that exclaiming, "Wow! That's me!" is a uniquely human experience? Some people do not want to acknowledge the possibility of animal self-awareness because then borders between humans and other animals become blurred, and their own narrow, hierarchical anthropocentric view of the world is toppled. Are we really *that* unique? Recall Darwin's ideas about evolutionary continuity—that differences in behavior among various species are differences in degree rather than in kind. Self-cognizance in animals is also a practical matter; what animals might know about themselves is crucial to studies of animal pain and suffering.

Many researchers are eager to discover what animals might know about themselves. Some argue that high levels or degrees of "self-cognizance" have evolved in a wide variety of animals, whereas others believe that only great apes have rich notions of self (knowing who they are or having a theory of mind, which means being able to infer the states of minds of others). Still others argue that it is methodologically too difficult to address this question because animal (like human) minds are subjective and private. Some in this latter category do not attribute any sense of self to animals other than humans and question whether animals are conscious of anything at all.

Do Animals Know Who They Are?

I generally assume that many animals are conscious and have some sense of self. I take an evolutionary approach to the subject and ask why (not if) consciousness and a sense of self evolved in certain animals—that is, what are they good for? To answer such questions, we need to recognize that there are degrees of self and that we need to take into account individuals' social needs and sensory worlds.

In *Minding Animals*, I argue that a sense of bodyness is necessary and sufficient for most animals to engage in social activities that are needed in the social environments in which they live. Many animals know such facts as "This is my tail," "This is my territory," "This is my piece of elk," "This is my mate," and "This is my urine." All Jethro had to know to get along in his dog world was that his was not another's body and some facts about what was his and what wasn't. He, his wild relatives such as wolves, coyotes, jackals, and foxes, and many other animals have a sense of possession or a sense of mineness or bodyness. Their sense of mineness or bodyness is their sense of self. Jethro could communicate a wide variety of messages, socially interact in numerous and varied contexts, and enjoy life as a dog. He showed social self-awareness in that he was aware of the various and different social relationships in which he engaged. He could play, engage in cooperative and deceptive activities, and reciprocate favors.

I also argue in *Minding Animals* (along with colleagues) that studies that rely on vision alone, such as those that use mirrors to track the response of animals to their mirror image to see if they make self-directed movements, are insufficient for studying self-cognizance in a multitude of animals who depend more on olfaction and audition in their daily lives. I also conclude that many animals have a sense of mineness or bodyness but not a sense of "I-ness" (an "I-self"). In order to study animal selves, comparative ethological studies are very useful.

This section's fourth essay, "Reflections on Animal Selves," written with Paul Sherman, argues that there are degrees of self-cognizance, presenting a new scale of animal selves and *self-cognizance* as an umbrella term to cover a continuum ranging from self-referencing to self-consciousness. Perhaps some animals *do* have a sense of "I-ness," one not accessible through methods that do not tap into the neural underpinnings of selfhood. We actually know very little about the distribution of self-cognizance in different groups of animals. Darwin's ideas about evolutionary continuity, along with empirical data and common sense, caution against the unyielding claim that humans and perhaps other great apes and cetaceans are the only species in which some sense of self has evolved.

In no way do Sherman and I believe that we have the final answers. Our paper is meant to stimulate researchers and others to revisit our fundamental assumptions, as well as to foster interdisciplinary discussion.

WHY CARE ABOUT ANIMAL SELF-COGNIZANCE?

As I mentioned earlier, the answers to challenging questions about self-cognizance have wide-ranging consequences, because they are often used by researchers and lawyers as litmus tests for defending the sorts of treatments to which animals can be ethically subjected. However, it is *not* clear that self-awareness or other cognitive capacities should be used for such decisions. Some argue that a sense of "I-ness" is morally relevant and necessary for experiencing pain. However, even if an animal does not know *who* she is, she might feel that "something painful is happening to this body." Even if the experience of pain is not the same across species, individuals of different species might suffer their own type of pain. Self-awareness is not a reliable test for assessing well-being. Jeremy Bentham, a utilitarian philosopher, famously considered animal suffering in these terms: "The question is not, Can they *reason?* nor Can they *talk?* but, Can they *suffer?*"

So, do any animals ever exclaim, "Wow! That's me!"? We really do not know, especially for wild animals. It is time to get out of the armchair and into the field. Speculation does not substitute for the careful study of behavior. The stakes are high. Answers to questions about self-cognizance often inform where humans place themselves in the evolutionary scheme of things and influence how animals are treated. More and careful studies are needed.

1   Beastly Passions

IT STARTED WITH A TOUCH. Soon Butch and Aphro were slowly caressing. Then they rolled together and embraced, locking flippers, before rolling back again. For perhaps three minutes, the two southern right whales lay side-by-side, ejecting water through their blow holes. The cetaceans then swam off, touching, surfacing and diving in unison. As he watched, Bernd Würsig of Texas A&M University became convinced that Butch and Aphro were developing a powerful mutual bond. Could this be leviathan love?

That's a controversial question. Biologists disagree about the nature of emotions in nonhuman animals, and especially whether they consciously experience their emotions. Many would not dare to say that a whale can fall in love, but those like Würsig, who do not dismiss this idea out of hand, can trace their thinking back at least as far as Charles Darwin. In *The Expression of the Emotions in Man and Animals*, he argued that there is continuity between the emotional lives of humans and other animals. Elsewhere, Darwin wrote: "The lower animals, like man, manifestly feel pleasure and pain, happiness and misery."

Despite Darwin's interest in the subject, we still don't know much about which animals have emotional lives and which do not. Perhaps this failure to make much headway can be put down to researchers' fear of being labelled "non-scientific" or too anthropomorphic. But the tide is turning. Nowadays it is permissible to ask such questions as: do animals love one another, do they mourn the loss of friends, and do they feel embarrassment? Current research in animal behaviour and neurobiology is providing compelling evidence that at least some vertebrates feel a full range of emotions from fear and disgust to joy, jealousy, anger and compassion.

Emotions are difficult to pin down. I know they are real because I experience my own every day, but I have no way of knowing exactly how you feel. You might try to describe your emotions using words, but even if you don't, I can deduce something about your emotional state from your body language and behaviour. It is the same with animals—strong clues about what they are feeling can be gleaned from changes in muscle tone, posture, gait, facial expression, pupil size, gaze, vocalisations and odours. You don't have to be an expert to read the signs. People with little experience of observing animals usually agree about what they are seeing. And the subsequent behaviour of animals often suggests they are correct.

Behaviour speaks volumes about animal emotions because emotions are psychological phenomena that help an individual to manage and control its actions. Investigating what is going on in the brain, however, is more tricky. From a neurological perspective, it is useful to divide emotions into two

Reprinted from Bekoff, M. 2000. Beastly Passions. *New Scientist* 166, 32–35, by permission of *New Scientist*.

types. The most basic, or primary emotions, are innate—they do not require conscious thought or feeling. These emotions are likely to be widespread in the animal kingdom, because they tend to increase an individual's chances of survival. More contentious is the idea that animals also have secondary emotions—the ones that require more sophisticated mental processing.

The most obvious example of a primary emotion is the fight-or-flight response, which allows animals to react quickly to danger signs, often with noindication that they feel fear. For instance, a young goose that has never been exposed to predators will run and take cover when it sees a hawk-like silhouette overhead, but will not respond to the outline of a goose. Natural selection favours those individuals who react in this way—and the faster the better. A hawk can swoop down rapidly and pluck a gosling while it is still thinking about what to do, so one that avoids the predator by instinct alone has a greater chance of surviving than one that takes time to decide on a response.

SMELL OF FEAR

Sounds and smells can also trigger primary emotions, including innate fear. Domestic dogs are among the many animals that have hard-wired responses to some odours. My companion dog, Jethro, is normally comfortable visiting the vet, but he will show signs of fear if he goes into an examination room where the previous canine client was afraid. It is an instinctive response to a pungent odour released by the anal glands of the frightened dog. Similarly, lab rats that have never encountered cats or other predators show innate freezing responses to the smell of these animals. Even pieces of cat hair seem to cause anxiety—the rats play and eat less, and are more wary than usual.

Neurobiologists have tracked primary emotions down to an evolutionarily ancient part of the brain called the limbic system, and in particular to a small almond-shaped structure known as the amygdala. This so-called "emotional" brain, which is thought to have evolved to allow sophisticated analysis of smells, is found in fish, amphibians, reptiles, birds and mammals. The amygdala receives raw sensory information from the thalamus—a neural relay station—and is connected by a bundle of nerves to the brainstem, which allows it to prime the body for fast action.

Speed is essential in a survival situation, but the downside of primary emotions is their inflexibility. That's where secondary emotions have the edge. They involve higher brain centres in the cerebral cortex, allowing an individual to reflect and weigh up the relative benefits of different actions in specific circumstances. We don't know which animals other than humans are capable of conscious reflection about their emotions. But the brain structures and biochemistry that are associated with so-called "felt emotions" in our own species are found in others. This has led some researchers to become convinced that secondary emotions are unlikely to be unique to humans.

If we accept that we are not alone in experiencing emotions, where can we draw the line? New findings suggest that reptiles may have been the first animals to experience their emotions. Last year Michel Cabanac from Laval University in Canada showed that iguanas try to maximise sensory pleasure—they prefer to stay warm rather than venture out into the cold to get food. And when basking in a warm environment, they experience physiological changes associated with pleasure in humans and other vertebrates, such as "emotional fever"—a boost in body temperature—and a raised heart rate. Amphibians and fish do not exhibit these behavioural and physiological responses. Cabanac suggests that the first mental event to emerge into consciousness was the ability of an individual to experience the sensations of pleasure or displeasure. His research suggests that reptiles experience basic emotional states, and proposes that such emotions evolved somewhere between amphibians and early reptiles.

Many vertebrates seem to be motivated by pleasure and nowhere is this more apparent than in their play. There's no doubt that animals at play appear to be having fun. Young dolphins often dart about in the water and also seem to enjoy slowly drifting in the current. Buffaloes have been known to go ice-skating, excitedly bellowing "gwaaa!" as they slide across the frozen ground. I once observed a young elk in Rocky Mountain National Park, Colorado, running across a snow field, jumping and twisting its body while in the air, stopping, catching its breath, and doing it again and again. There was plenty of grassy terrain around but the elk chose the snow field.

It certainly looks as though these animals are enjoying themselves, and there are some neurobiological findings that support the inferences. Studies of the chemistry of play indicate that it is fun. Jaak Panksepp from Bowling Green State University, Ohio, has found evidence that rats produce opiates during play. They also have increased dopamine activity in their brains when anticipating play, according to findings made by Steven Siviy from Gettysburg College, Pennsylvania. In humans, both opiates and dopamine are associated with pleasure.

Play is important in development because it teaches a young animal skills that it will require to survive as it becomes independent. If animals play because they enjoy it, then the positive emotions associated with play have an evolutionary advantage just like the fight-or-flight response. A similar argument has been used to explain what looks like romantic love among animals.

BIRDS DO IT

Bees may not do it, but birds certainly seem to. Ravens fall in love, according to renowned biologist Bernd Heinrich from the University of Vermont, Burlington, who has studied and lived with these birds for many years. In his book, *Mind of the Raven*, Heinrich writes: "Since ravens have long-term mates, I suspect that they fall in love like us, simply because some internal reward is required to maintain a long-term pair bond."

In many animals, including southern right whales, romantic love seems to develop during courtship and mating. Often this is protracted, with both parties performing rituals that take time and energy and can be risky. It is as if they need to prove their worth to each other before consummating their relationship. Interestingly, our closest living relatives, chimpanzees, don't appear to fall in love. And male chimps don't spend much time courting, mating, or remaining with the females whose young they have fathered.

Many things have passed for love in humans, yet we do not deny its existence. It is unlikely that romantic love first appeared on the scene in humans with no evolutionary precursors. Many birds and mammals share the brain systems and chemistry that underlie love in humans. Dopamine levels, for example, are elevated in lusting, love-struck humans and in rodents anticipating a sexual encounter. In addition, mammals have the hormone oxytocin, secreted by the pituitary gland, which is associated with courtship and sex. Birds and reptiles have a similar chemical, vasotocin, associated with comparable behaviours. Taken together, these findings suggest that at least some animals are capable of romantic love.

The flip-side of love is grief at the loss of a loved one. Some animals display the characteristic behaviour we associate with grief. Often there is a period of mourning. Grieving animals may withdraw from their group, sit in one place and stare into space as if they were paralysed. They remain unresponsive to attempts by others to interact with them or console them. They may also stop eating, lose interest in sex, or become obsessed with the dead individual. Some even try to revive the corpse or carry it around until it decomposes.

Sea lion mothers, watching their babies being eaten by killer whales, squeal eerily and wail pitifully. Dolphins have been seen struggling to revive a dead infant. At the Gombe Stream National Park in Tanzania, primatologist Jane Goodall observed Flint, an eight-year-old male chimp, withdraw from its group, stop feeding and finally die after the death of his mother, Flo. Elephants may stand guard over a stillborn baby for days maintaining a quiet vigil with their head and ears hung down. And young elephants who witness the death of their mothers often wake up screaming. Joyce Poole, who has spent decades studying elephants in the wild, is convinced the orphans experience grief and depression.

Even birds appear to grieve. "A greylag goose that has lost its partner shows all the symptoms that John Bowlby has described in young human children in his famous book *Infant Grief*," wrote Nobel Prize–winning ethologist Konrad Lorenz. "The eyes sink deep into their sockets, and the individual has an overall drooping experience, literally letting the head hang."

A bereft greylag goose may behave like a bereft human, but does it feel grief in the way that a person does? This question is difficult to address because we don't yet have a biological explanation of how humans experience their emotions. Antonio Damasio from the University of Iowa offers one possibility in his book, *The Feeling of What Happens*, published last year. He suggests that some parts of the brain map both the internal state of our bodies and external objects or situations that are affecting us. Damasio believes that the physiological processes that accompany emotions are not mere by-products, but instead are part of the mechanism that produces feeling. By simultaneously mapping our internal and external environments, we feel our experiences as our own. If Damasio is correct, then his explanation may also apply to some animals, particularly our closest living relatives, the other primates.

Chimpanzees, for example, may not fall in love but they do appear to experience a wide range of emotions, including embarrassment, which requires an individual to wonder what others are thinking about it. Goodall has witnessed embarrassed chimps. She describes a young male showing off by swinging on a sapling in front of a dominant male. When the branch snapped, the youngster fell head first into long grass. He then turned to check that his fall had not been spotted, climbed another tree and began feeding.

Another noted primatologist, Marc Hauser from Harvard University, has observed embarrassment in a rhesus monkey. After copulating, the male strutted away and accidentally fell into a ditch. Hauser recounts how the monkey stood up and quickly looked around. After sensing that no one had seen the tumble, he marched off, back high, head and tail up, as if nothing had happened.

These observations suggest that the differences between human and animal emotions are often differences in degree rather than differences in kind. Even where the similarities with ourselves are not so obvious, if we accept that animals have feelings too, then there are important implications for the way we behave towards them. When animals are seen as automatons with no emotions, it is easy to treat them as mere property with which humans can do as they please. But view them as sentient, feeling individuals and it is more difficult to justify some of our cruel and unthinking practices.

If we close the door on the possibility that many animals have rich emotional lives—which may be very different from our own—we will lose great opportunities to learn about the lives of creatures with which we share this magnificent planet. There are many mental worlds beyond human experience just waiting to be explored.

FURTHER READING

The Smile of a Dolphin: Remarkable Accounts of Animal Emotions edited by Marc Bekoff, Discovery Books (2000)

Minding Animals: Awareness, Emotions, and Heart by Marc Bekoff, Oxford University Press (2002)

"Emotion and phylogeny," by Michel Cabanac, *Journal of Consciousness Studies*, vol 6, p 176 (1999)

The Expression of the Emotions in Man and Animals (third edition) by Charles Darwin, Oxford University Press (1998)

"An exploration of a commonality between ourselves and elephants," by Joyce Poole, *Etica & Animali*, vol 9, p 85 (1998)

Affective Neuroscience by Jaak Panksepp, Oxford University Press (1998)

2 Cognitive Ethology

The Comparative Study of Animal Minds

NATURALIZING ANIMAL MINDS

Cognitive ethology is the comparative, evolutionary, and ecological study of nonhuman animal (hereafter animal) minds, including thought processes, beliefs, rationality, information processing, and consciousness. It is a rapidly growing interdisciplinary field of science that is attracting much attention from researchers in numerous, diverse disciplines, including those interested in animal welfare (Cheney and Seyfarth, 1990; Ristau, 1991; Griffin, 1992; Allen and Bekoff, 1995, 1997; Bekoff and Allen, 1997; Bekoff and Jamieson, 1996). Cognitive ethology can trace its beginnings to the writings of Charles Darwin, an anecdotal cognitivist (Jamieson and Bekoff, 1993), and some of his contemporaries and disciples. Their approach incorporated appeals to evolutionary theory, interests in mental continuity, concerns with individual and intraspecific variation, interests in the worlds of the animals themselves, close associations with natural history, and attempts to learn more about the behavior of animals in conditions that are as close as possible to the natural environment where selection has occurred. They also relied on anecdote and anthropomorphism to inform and motivate more rigorous study. In addition, cognitive ethologists are frequently concerned with the diversity of solutions that living organisms have found for common problems. They also emphasize broad taxonomic comparisons and do not focus on a few select representatives of limited taxa. Many people inform their views of cognitive ethology by appealing to the same studies over and over again (usually those done on nonhuman primates) and ignore the fact that there are many other animals who also show interesting patterns of behavior that lend themselves to cognitive studies.

Comparative cognitive ethology is an important extension of classical ethology, because it explicitly licenses hypotheses about the internal states of animals in the tradition of classical ethologists such as Nobel laureates Niko Tinbergen and Konrad Lorenz. However, although ethologists such as Lorenz and Tinbergen used terms such as *intention movements*, they used them quite differently from how they are used in the philosophical literature. *Intention movements* refers to preparatory movements that might communicate what action individuals are likely to undertake next, and not necessarily to their beliefs and desires, although one might suppose that the individuals did indeed want to fly and believed that if they moved their wings in a certain way they would fly. This distinction is important, because the use of such terms does

Reprinted from Bekoff, M. 1998. Cognitive Ethology: The Comparative Study of Animal Minds. In W. Bechtel and G. Graham (eds.), *Blackwell Companion to Cognitive Science*. Blackwell Publishers, Oxford, England, pp. 371–379, by permission of Blackwell Publishing.

not necessarily add a cognitive dimension to classical ethological notions, although it could.

In his early work Tinbergen identified four overlapping areas with which ethological investigations should be concerned: namely, evolution (phylogeny), adaptation (function), causation, and development (ontogeny), and his framework also is useful for those interested in animal cognition (Jamieson and Bekoff, 1993). The methods for answering questions in each of these areas vary, but all begin with careful observation and description of the behavior patterns that are exhibited by the animals under study. The information provided by these initial observations allows a researcher to exploit the animal's normal behavioral repertoire to answer questions about the evolution, function, causation, and development of the behavior patterns that are exhibited in various contexts.

Donald R. Griffin and Modern Cognitive Ethology

The modern era of cognitive ethology, with its concentration on the evolution and evolutionary continuity of animal cognition, is usually thought to have begun with the appearance of Donald R. Griffin's (1976/1981) book *The Question of Animal Awareness: Evolutionary Continuity of Mental Experience*. Griffin's major concern was to learn more about animal consciousness; he wanted to come to terms with the difficult question of what it is like to be a particular animal (for critical discussion of Griffin's agenda see Jamieson and Bekoff, 1993). While Griffin was concerned mainly with the phenomenology of animal consciousness, it is only one of many important and interesting aspects of animal cognition (Allen and Bekoff, 1997). Indeed, because of its broad agenda and wide-ranging goals, many view cognitive ethology as being a genuine contributor to cognitive science in general. For those who are anthropocentrically minded, it should be noted that studies of animal cognition can also inform, for example, inquiries into human autism.

METHODS OF STUDY

Ethologists interested in animal minds favor research in conditions that are as close as possible to the natural environments in which natural selection occurred or is occurring. When needed, research on captive animals can also inform the comparative study of animal cognition; but cognitive ethologists are resistant to suggestions that (1) field studies of animal cognition are impossible (difficult, yes, but certainly not impossible); (2) they should give up their attempts to study animal minds under natural conditions; and (3) studies of learning and memory are all that are needed to learn about animal cognition. Naturalizing the study of animal cognition and animal minds in the laboratory and in the field should lead to a greater appreciation for the cognitive skills of animals living under natural conditions. Animal minds can be studied rigorously using methods of natural science and will not ultimately have to be reduced or eliminated.

The tractability of cognitive questions involves application of a diverse set of comparative methods in order to draw inferences about cognitive states and capacities. Cognitive research may include staged social encounters, playback of recorded vocalizations, the presentation of stimuli in different modalities, observation of predator–prey interactions, observation of foraging behavior, application of neurobiological techniques, and studies of social and other sorts of learning. Computer analyses are also useful for those who want to learn what kind of information must be represented in an adequate computational model.

There are no large differences between methods used to study animal cognition and those used to study other aspects of animal behavior. Differences lie not so much in what is done and how it is done, as in how data are explained. Thus Allen and Bekoff (1997) argue that the main distinction between cognitive ethology and classical ethology lies not in the types of data collected, but in the understanding of the conceptual resources that are appropriate for explaining those data.

Perhaps one area that will contribute more to the study of animal minds than to other areas of comparative ethology is neurobiology and behavior. Those interested in the cellular or neural bases of behavior and animal cognition and consciousness may use techniques such as positron emission tomography (PET) that are also employed in other endeavors. In general, studies using neuroimaging have provided extremely valuable data for humans engaged in various sorts of activities, whereas the use of these and other imaging techniques on animals has not been pursued rigorously for individuals engaged in activities other than learning or memory in captivity. Furthermore, while neurobiological studies are extremely important to those interested in animal cognition, there remains an explanatory gap between neurophysiological processes and behavior.

Behavioral studies usually start with the observation, description, and categorization of behavior patterns of animals. The result of this process is the development of an ethogram, or behavioral catalog, of these actions. Ethograms present information about an action's form or morphology and its code name. Descriptions can be based on visual information (what an action looks like), auditory characteristics (sonograms, which are pictures of sounds), or chemical constituents (output of chromatographic analyses of glandular deposits or urine or feces, for example). It is essential that great care be given to the development of an ethogram, for it is an inventory that others should be able to replicate without error. Permanent records of observations allow others to cross-check their observations and descriptions against original records. The number of actions and the breadth of the categories that are identified in a behavioral study depend on the questions at hand; but generally it is better to split, rather than lump together, actions in initial stages, and then lump them together when questions of interest have been carefully laid out.

In studies of behavior it is important to know as much as possible about the sensory world of the animals being studied. Experiments should not ask animals to do things that they cannot do because they are insensitive to the experimental stimuli or unmotivated by them. The relationships among normal ecological conditions and differences in the capabilities of animals to acquire, process, and respond to information constitute the domain of a growing field called *sensory ecology*. A good ethologist asks what it is like to be the animal under study and develops an awareness of the senses that the animals use singly or in combination with one another. It is highly unlikely that individuals of any other species sense the world in the same way we do, and it is unlikely that even members of the same species sense the world identically all of the time, so it is important to remain alert to the possibility of individual variation.

Stimulus Control and Impoverished Environments

While carefully conducted experiments in the laboratory and in the field are often able to control for the influence of variables that might affect the expression of behavioral responses, it is usually the case that there is a possibility that the influence of some variable(s) cannot be accounted for. Field studies may be more prone to a lack of control, because the conditions under which they are conducted are inherently more complex and less controllable.

An illustration of the concern for control is found in the excellent cognitive ethological field research of Cheney and Seyfarth (1990) on the behavior (e.g., communication and deception) and minds of vervet monkeys. In their studies of the attribution of knowledge by vervets to each other, Cheney and Seyfarth played back vocalizations of familiar individuals to other group members. These researchers were concerned, however, about their inability to eliminate "all visual or auditory evidence of the [familiar] animal's physical presence" (p. 230). Actually, this inability may not be problematic if the goal is to understand "how monkeys see the world." Typically, in most social situations the physical presence of individuals and access to stimuli from different modalities may be important to consider. Vervets, other nonhumans, and humans may attribute mental states using a combination of variables that are difficult to separate experimentally. Negative or inconclusive experimental results concerning vervets' or other animals' attribution of mind to other individuals may stem from impoverishing their normal environment by removing information that they normally use in attribution. Researchers may also be looking for complex mechanisms involved in the attribution of minds to others and thus overlook relatively simple means for doing so. Just because an animal does not do something does not mean that it cannot do it (assuming that what we are asking the animal to do is reasonable: i.e., within their sensory and motor capacities). Thus, insistence on absolute experimental control that involves placing and maintaining individuals in captivity and getting them accustomed to test situations that may be unnatural may greatly influence results. And the resulting claims, if incorrect, can wreak havoc on discussions of the evolutionary continuity of animal cognitive skills. Cheney and Seyfarth recognize some of these problems in their discussion of the difficulties of distinguishing between alternative explanations, maintaining either that a monkey recognizes another's knowledge or that a monkey monitors another's behavior and adjusts his own behavior to the other.

Although control may be more of a problem in field research than in laboratory work, it certainly is not the case that cognitive ethologists should abandon field work. Cognitive ethologists and comparative or cognitive psychologists can learn important lessons from one another. On the one hand, cognitive psychologists who specialize in highly controlled experimental procedures can teach something about the importance of control to those cognitive ethologists who do not perform such research. On the other hand, those who study humans and other animals under highly controlled and often contrived and impoverished laboratory conditions can broaden their horizons and learn about the importance of more naturalistic methods: they can be challenged to develop procedures that take into account possible interactions among stimuli within and between modalities in more naturalistic settings. For example, among those who are interested in important, *hot* questions about animal minds that are typically studied in controlled captive conditions (e.g., inquiries into the possibility of self-recognition), there is a growing awareness that more naturalistic approaches are needed. The use of single tests relying primarily on one modality—for example, vision—for comparative studies represents too narrow an approach. Ultimately, all types of studies should be used to exploit the behavioral flexibility or versatility of the animals under study.

SOME CRITICISMS OF COGNITIVE ETHOLOGY

A balanced view of cognitive ethology requires consideration of critics' points of view. Criticisms of cognitive ethology come in many flavors but usually center on: (1) the notion that animals do not have minds; (2) the idea that (many, most, all) animals are not conscious, or that so little of their behavior is conscious (no matter how broadly defined) that it is a waste of time to study animal consciousness (cognitive ethology is really a much broader discipline than this suggests, see below); (3) the inaccessibility to rigorous study of animal mental states (they are private) and whatever (if anything) might be contained in them; (4) the assumption that animals do not have any beliefs, because the contents of their beliefs are not similar to the contents of human beliefs; (5) the lack of rigor in collecting data; (6) the lack of large empirical data bases; (7) the nature of the (merely instrumental) soft, nonparsimonious, yet complex explanations that rely heavily on theoretical constructs (e.g., minds, mental states) that are offered for the behavioral phenotype under study (they are too anthropomorphic, too folkpsychological, or too *as if-fy*—animals act *as if* they have beliefs or desires or other thoughts about something); and (8) the heavy reliance on behavior for motivating cognitive explanations (but this is not specific to cognitive inquiries).

While most criticism comes from those who ignore the successes of cognitive ethology, to those who dismiss it in principle because of strong, radical behavioristic leanings, or those who do not understand the basic philosophical principles that inform cognitive ethology, it should be pointed out that more mechanistic approaches to the study of animal cognition are not without their own problems. For example, comparative psychologists often disregard the question of how relevant a study is to the natural existence of the animals under consideration and pay too much attention to the logical structure of the experiments being performed, without much regard for more naturalistic approaches. Noncognitive, mechanistic *rules of thumb* can also be very cumbersome and nonparsimonious and often appeal to hard-to-imagine past coincidences. Furthermore, it is not clear whether the differences between noncognitive rules of thumb and cognitive explanations are differences in degree or differences in kind. Both noncognitive and cognitive explanations can be *just so* stories (just like many evolutionary explanations) that rely on hypothetical constructs, and neither type applies in all situations.

THREE CASE STUDIES

Three case studies that support the application of a broadly comparative cognitive ethological approach can be found in recent field research of antipredator behavior in birds (Ristau, 1991; Bekoff, 1995b) and field and laboratory research on social play behavior in various canids (domestic dogs, wolves, and coyotes; Bekoff, 1995a). Many other examples can be found in Cheney and Seyfarth, 1990; Ristau, 1991: Griffin, 1992; Allen and Bekoff, 1995, 1997; Bekoff and Jamieson, 1996; and references therein. Although Griffin has included the results of many excellent studies of the possibility of language in nonhuman primates, cetaceans, and birds in his broad discussions of animal minds, they do not fall squarely within the primary domain of cognitive ethology as I envision it: the study of natural behaviors in natural settings from an evolutionary and ecological perspective. (Of course, this is not to discount the importance to cognitive ethology of research on captive animals.) Only future research will tell if the behavior of the few captive individuals who have been intensively studied in *language studies* (and those captive individuals observed in other endeavors) is related to the behavior of wild members of the same species, or if the data from captive animals are more a demonstration, admittedly important, of behavioral plasticity and behavioral potential.

Ristau (1991) studied injury feigning in piping plovers (the broken-wing display), wanting to know if she could learn more about deceptive injury feigning if she viewed the broken-wing display as intentional or purposeful behavior ("The plover wants to lead the intruder away from her nest or young") rather than as a hard-wired reflexive response to the presence of a particular stimulus, a potentially intruding predator. She studied the direction in which birds moved during the broken-wing display, how they monitored the location of the predator, and the flexibility of the response. Ristau found that birds usually enacted the display in the direction that would lead an intruder who was following them further away from the threatened nest or young, and also that birds monitored the intruder's approach and modified their behavior in response to variations in the intruder's movements. These and other data led Ristau to conclude that the plover's broken-wing display lent itself to an intentional explanation: that plovers purposely lead intruders away from their nests or young and modify their behavior in order to do so.

In another study of anti-predator behavior in birds, Bekoff (1995b) found that western evening grosbeaks modified their vigilance or scanning behavior in accordance with the way in which individuals were positioned with respect to one another. Grosbeaks and other birds often trade off scanning for potential predators and feeding: essentially (and oversimplified), some birds scan, while others feed, and some birds feed, when others scan. Thus, it is hypothesized that individuals want to know what others are doing and learn about others' behavior by trying to watch them. Bekoff's study of grosbeaks showed that when a flock contained four or more birds, there were large changes in scanning and other patterns of behavior that seemed to be related to ways in which grosbeaks attempted to gather information about other flock members. When birds were arranged in a circular array, so that they could see one another easily, compared to when they were arranged in a line, which made visual monitoring of flock members more difficult, birds who had difficulty seeing one another (1) were more vigilant, (2) changed their head and body positions more often, (3) reacted to changes in group size more slowly, (4) showed less coordination in head movements, and (5) showed more variability in all measures. The differences in behavior between birds organized in circular arrays and birds organized in linear arrays were best explained in terms of individuals' attempts to learn, via visual monitoring, about what other flock members were doing. This may say something about if and how birds attempt to represent their flock, or at least certain other individuals, to themselves. It may be that individuals form beliefs about what others are probably doing and predicate their own behavior on these beliefs. Bekoff argued that cognitive explanations were simpler and less cumbersome than noncognitive rule-of-thumb explanations (e.g., "Scan this way if there are this number of birds in this geometric array" or "Scan that way if there are that number of birds in that geometric array"). Noncognitive rule-of-thumb explanations did not seem to account for the flexibility in animals' behavior as well or as simply as explanations that appealed to cognitive capacities of the animals under study.

Social play behavior is another area that lends itself nicely to cognitive inquiries. The study of social play involves issues of communication, intention, role playing, and cooperation, and the results of this type of research may yield clues about the ability of animals to understand each other's intentions. Play is also a phenomenon that occurs in a wide range of species and affords the opportunity for a comparative investigation of cognitive abilities, extending the all-too-common narrow focus on primates that dominates discussions of nonhuman cognition. A recent study of the structure of play sequences in canids (Bekoff, 1995a) showed that an action called the *bow* (an animal crouches on its forepaws, elevates its hind end, and may wag its tail) is often used immediately before and immediately after an action that can be misinterpreted and disrupt ongoing social play.

The social play of canids (and of other mammals) includes actions, primarily bites, that are used in other contexts (e.g., agonistic or predatory encounters) that do not involve bows. It is important for individuals to tell others that they want to play with them and not fight with them or eat them, and this message seems to be sent by play-soliciting signals, such as the bow, which occur almost only in the context of social play. In canids and other mammals, actions such as biting, accompanied by rapid side-to-side shaking of the head, are used in aggressive interactions and also during predation and could be misinterpreted when used in play. Bekoff hypothesized that if bites accompanied by rapid side-to-side shaking of the head or other behavior patterns could be misread by the recipient and could result in a fight, for example, then the animal who performed the actions that could be misinterpreted might have to communicate to its partner that this action was performed in the context of play and was not meant to be taken as an aggressive or predatory move. On this view, bows would not occur randomly in play sequences: the play atmosphere would be reinforced and maintained by performing bows immediately before or after actions that could be misinterpreted. The results of Bekoff's study of different canids supported the inference that bows served to provide information about other actions that followed or preceded them. In addition to sending the message "I want to play" when performed at the beginning of play, bows performed during social play seemed to carry the message "I want to play despite what I am going to do or just did—I still want to play" when there might be a problem in the sharing of this information between the interacting animals. The noncognitive rules-of-thumb "Play this way if this happens" and "Play that way if that happens" seem to be too rigid an explanation for the flexible behavior that the animals showed.

WHERE TO FROM HERE?

There are other examples that could have been chosen, but these three make the case that chauvinism on either side of the debate as to how to study animal behavior and how to explain animal behavior is unwarranted; a pluralistic approach should result in the best understanding of the nonhumans with whom we share the planet. Sometimes some nonhumans (and some humans) behave as stimulus-response machines, and at other times some nonhumans (and some humans) behave in ways that are best explained using a rich cognitive vocabulary. Methodological pluralism is needed: species-fair methods need to be tailored to the questions and the animals under consideration, and competing hypotheses and explanations must always be considered.

Those interested in animal cognition should resist the temptation to make sweeping claims about the cognitive abilities (or lack thereof) of all members of a given species. A concentration on individuals and not on species should form an important part of the agenda for future research in cognitive ethology. There is a lot of individual variation in behavior within species, and sweeping generalizations about what an individual ought to do because she is classified as a member of a given species must be taken with great caution. Furthermore, people often fail to recognize that in many instances sweeping generalizations about the cognitive skills (or lack thereof) of species, not individuals, are based on small data sets from a limited number of individuals representing few taxa, individuals who may have been exposed to a narrow array of behavioral challenges. The importance of studying animals under field conditions cannot be emphasized too strongly. Field research that includes careful, well-thought-out observation, description, and experimentation that does not result in mistreatment of animals is extremely difficult to duplicate in captivity. While it may be easier to study animals in captivity, they must be provided with the complexity of social and other stimuli to which they are exposed in the field; in some cases this may not be possible.

Cognitive ethologists should also strive to make the study of animal cognition tractable by carefully operationalizing the processes under study. Cognitive ethology can raise new questions that may be approached from various levels of analysis. For example, detailed descriptive information about subtle behavior patterns and neuroethological data may be important for informing further studies of animal cognition and may be useful for explaining data that are already available. Such analyses will not make cognitive ethological investigations superfluous, because behavioral evidence takes precedence over anatomical or physiological data in assessments of cognitive abilities.

To summarize, those positions that should figure largely in cognitive ethological studies include: (1) remaining open to the possibility of surprises concerning animal cognitive abilities; (2) concentrating on comparative, evolutionary, and ecological questions and sampling many different species, including domesticated animals—going beyond primates and avoiding talk of *lower* and *higher* animals, or at least laying out explicit criteria for using these slippery, value-laden terms; (3) naturalizing methods of study by taking the animals' points of view (talking to them in their own languages) and studying them in conditions that are as close as possible to the conditions in which they typically live; often animals do not do what we expect them to (sometimes prey will approach predators), and knowledge of their natural behavior is important in the development of testable, realistic models of behavior; (4) trying to understand how cognitive skills used by captive animals may function in more natural settings; (5) studying individual differences; (6) using all sorts of data, ranging from anecdotes to large data sets; and (7) appealing to different types of explanations as best explanations of the data under scrutiny. Cognitive ethology need not model itself on other fields of science such as physics or neurobiology in order to gain credibility. Hard-science envy is what led to the loss of animal and human minds in the early part of the twentieth century.

We are a long way from having an adequate data base from which claims about the taxonomic distribution of various cognitive skills or about having a theory of mind can be put forth. Consider studies that show that some monkeys cannot perform imitation tasks that some mice can. If the point is to answer the question whether monkeys are smarter than mice, it is misleading, for there is no reason to expect a single linear scale of intelligence. In the world of mice it may be more important to be able to do some things than it is in the world of monkeys, but in other respects a monkey may have a capacity that a mouse lacks. There is also much variation within species, and this too must be documented more fully.

It is unlikely that science will make complete contact with the nature of animal minds at any single point. Both *soft* (anecdotal) information and *hard* (empirical) data from long-term field research are needed to inform and motivate further empirical experimental research. So, questions such as "Do mice ape?" or "Do apes mice?" are premature. Does this mean that many, some, or no animals have a mind or a theory of mind? It would be premature to attempt to answer these questions definitively at this time, given our current state of knowledge.

REFERENCES AND RECOMMENDED READING

Allen, C. and Bekoff, M. 1995: Cognitive ethology and the intentionality of animal behaviour. *Mind and Language*, 10, 313–28.

— 1997: *Species of Mind: The Philosophy and Biology of Cognitive Ethology.* Cambridge, Mass.: MIT Press.

Bekoff, M. 1995a: Play signals as punctuation: the structure of social play in canids. *Behaviour.* 132, 419–29.

— 1995b: Vigilance, flock size, and flock geometry: information gathering by western evening grosbeaks (Aves, Fringillidae). *Ethology.* 99, 150–61.

Bekoff, M. and Allen, C. 1997: Cognitive ethology: slayers, skeptics, and proponents. In R. W. Mitchell, N. Thompson, and L. Miles (eds.), *Anthropomorphism, Anecdote, and Animals: The Emperor's New Clothes?* Albany, NY: SUNY Press, 313–34.

Bekoff, M. and Jamieson, D. (eds.) 1996: *Readings in Animal cognition.* Cambridge, Mass.: MIT Press.

Cheney, D. L. and Seyfarth, R. M. 1990: *How Monkeys See the World: Inside the Mind of Another Species.* Chicago: University of Chicago Press.

Griffin, D. R. 1976/1981: *The Question of Animal Awareness: Evolutionary Continuity of Mental Experience.* New York: Rockefeller University Press.

— 1992: *Animal Minds.* Chicago: University of Chicago Press.

Jamieson, D. and Bekoff, M. 1993: On aims and methods of cognitive ethology. *Philosophy of Science Association*, 2, 110–24.

Ristau, C. (ed.) 1991: *Cognitive Ethology: The Minds of Other Animals. Essays in Honor of Donald R. Griffin.* Hillsdale, NJ: Erlbaum.

DALE JAMIESON AND MARC BEKOFF

3   On Aims and Methods of Cognitive Ethology

1. INTRODUCTION[1]

In 1963 Niko Tinbergen published a paper, "On Aims and Methods of Ethology," dedicated to his friend Konrad Lorenz. This essay is a landmark in the development of ethology. Here Tinbergen defines ethology as "the biological study of behavior" and seeks to demonstrate the "close affinity between Ethology and the rest of Biology" (p. 411). Building on Huxley (1942), Tinbergen identifies four major problems of ethology: causation, survival value, evolution, and ontogeny. Concern with these problems, under different names (mechanism, adaptation, phylogeny, and development), has dominated the study of animal behavior during the last half century (Dawkins, et al. 1991; Dewsbury 1992).

With his emphasis on the importance of innate structures internal to animals, Tinbergen was resolutely antibehaviorist. Yet he remained hostile to the idea that ethology should employ any form of teleological reasoning or make reference to "subjective phenomena" such as "hunger" or the emotions. He wrote that teleological reasoning was "seriously hampering the progress of ethology" and that "[b]ecause subjective phenomena cannot be observed objectively in animals, it is idle to either claim or to deny their existence" (1951, p. 4).[2]

Since the 1976 publication of Donald Griffin's landmark book, *The Question of Animal Awareness*, a growing band of researchers has been attempting to study the cognitive states of nonhuman animals (for samples of this work see Bekoff & Jamieson 1990, and Ristau 1991). Although vigorous debate surrounds this research, cognitive ethology as a field has not yet been clearly delineated, adequately characterized, or sufficiently explained.

Our goal in this paper is to attempt for cognitive ethology what Tinbergen succeeded in doing for ethology: to clarify its aims and methods, to distinguish some of its varieties, and to defend the fruitfulness of the research strategies that it has spawned.

This paper is divided into five main parts. In the first part we briefly sketch the history of ethology and explain the motivation behind the cognitive turn. Next we discuss the groundbreaking work of Donald Griffin and the rise of cognitive ethology. In the third section we distinguish two varieties of cognitive ethology ("weak" and "strong") and provide some reasons for preferring the latter to the former. The fourth part of the paper is a discussion of one area of research in cognitive ethology: social play. Finally we make some concluding remarks.

2. The Story of Animal Behavior

During the third quarter of the nineteenth century, Charles Darwin was the most important contributor to the foundations of animal behavior (Boakes 1984, Richards 1987). Darwin argued for mental continuity between humans and other animals, and claimed that "the lower animals, like man, manifestly feel pleasure and pain, happiness, and misery" (Darwin 1871, p. 448).[3] According to Darwin monkeys are capable of elaborate deceit (1896), insects can solve problems, and many animals can deliberate about what to do (1871, 1896).

Darwin's approach can be characterized as "anecdotal cognitivism." He attributes cognitive states to many animals on the basis of observation of particular cases rather than controlled experiments or manipulations. Darwin's follower, George Romanes, followed in this tradition although he was more critical than Darwin of various cognitive attributions to nonhuman animals. Even Lloyd Morgan, mainly remembered for his canon—"in no case may we interpret an action as the outcome of the exercise of a higher psychical faculty, if it can be interpreted as the outcome of the exercise of one which stands lower in the psychological scale" (Morgan 1894, p. 53)—accepted the Darwin-Romanes view of the continuity of mental states. Indeed, as Rollin (1989) points out, Morgan's canon is not only consistent with the view that animals have mental states, it actually presupposes it.

Behaviorism arose in part as an attempt to overcome the anecdotal approach and to bring rigor to the study of behavior. Controlled experiments rather than field observations provided the primary data, and basic concepts were supposed to be grounded in direct observation. Against this background, animal consciousness came to be seen as "... mystical, unscientific, unnecessary, obscure, and not amenable to study" (Rollin 1989, p. 68).

Jacques Loeb, who was active from about 1890–1915, was an influential forerunner of behaviorism in biology. Although he believed that consciousness was an emergent property of higher organisms, he argued that all animal behavior could be explained nonteleologically in terms of tropisms (Pauly 1987). Throughout the 1920s, with the work of Watson and others, behaviorism became increasingly influential. By 1930 the behaviorist revolution was complete and anecdotal cognitivism had virtually vanished from mainstream science.

Classical ethology developed in Europe with the work of Lorenz and Tinbergen, and arrived in America in the post–World War II period (although as Dewsbury 1992 points out, there were contacts before the war). The roots of classical ethology were in the investigations of Darwin, Charles Otis Whitman, and Oskar Heinroth. Classical ethology signified a return to some of the ideas of Darwin and the early anecdotal cognitivists, especially in its appeals to evolutionary theory, the close association with natural history, and the reliance on anecdote and anthropomorphism in motivating more rigorous study.

Lorenz, who was trained as a physician, comparative anatomist, psychologist and philosopher, did little fieldwork but his knowledge of animal behavior was enormous. His method was to watch various animals, both domestic and wild, who lived near his homes in Austria and Germany. He freely used anecdotes and did very little experimentation. Lorenz thought that empathy, intuition and emotion were important in understanding animals and that science should not be pursued "in the belief that it is possible to be objective by ignoring one's feelings" (Lorenz 1988/1991, p. 7). He attributed to animals such states as love, jealousy, envy, and anger.

Tinbergen complemented Lorenz's naturalistic and anecdotal approaches by doing elegant, simple and usually relatively noninvasive field experiments. Tinbergen also worked with Lorenz on several classical problems, including egg-rolling in geese.

Theoretically what was most important about Lorenz and Tinbergen was the emphasis they placed on internal states such as "instincts," "drives," "motivational impulses" and "outward flowing nervous energy." On their view behavior is typically caused by internal states; external stimuli mainly release or block behavior. This emphasis on internal states was in sharp contrast with the behaviorist tradition.

However by 1973 when Lorenz and Tinbergen were awarded the Nobel Prize (shared with Karl von Frisch), many thought that their grand theory was already in tatters (Kennedy 1992). As early as 1968 Patrick Bateson wrote that "[w]orship of the old gods and the intellectual baggage that went with it still survives quaintly in odd corners. But for the most part proponents of a Grand Theory have either been forced to close their eyes to awkward evidence or modify their ideas to the point of unfalsifiability" (p. 33). Marian Dawkins has written that "[m]ost contemporary textbooks on animal behaviour tend to dismiss 'instinct' altogether and attempt to consign it to honorable retirement" (Dawkins 1986, p. 67).

In recent years no grand theory has arisen to replace the Lorenz-Tinbergen theory of instinct. However the question of adaptation (survival value) has become increasingly central in animal behavior studies. Indeed, many researchers write as if a behavior is completely explained if it can be shown that it might contribute to inclusive fitness. This is surprising since adaptationist explanations are often radically underdetermined by empirical evidence; and when they are not, the availability of a good adaptationist story does not drive out other forms of explanation.

The Lorenz-Tinbergen theory of instinct was meant to be an account of the mechanisms of behavior. With the decline of the "grand theory" some researchers have turned to neuroethology as the replacement for the study of instinct. However, despite great advances in neuroethology, much of what we want to know about animals cannot be explained in these terms alone. If we want to know why Grete (the dog) barked at the postman, an explanation in terms of neural pathways may not be very helpful (Dennett 1987).

Like many of the animals it studies, animal behavior needs all four legs (mechanism, adaptation, phylogeny, and development). And perhaps as never before animal behavior needs to countenance a variety of forms of explanation. Cognitive ethology has the potential to make important contributions to our understanding in a number of areas, for the cognitive vocabulary can help to deliver important insights about animals that may otherwise not be available.

3. GRIFFIN AND THE RISE OF COGNITIVE ETHOLOGY

Many of the same forces that led to the development of cognitive psychology in the 1960s began to gather in animal behavior in the 1970s. Lorenz and Tinbergen had already made appeals to "unobservable" internal states respectable, and philosophers such as Hilary Putnam (1960/1975) and Jerry Fodor (1968) had shown that materialism and mentalism could be made compatible. In addition, Jane Goodall and Dian Fossey were popularizing the idea that the other African apes, including chimpanzees and mountain gorillas (see Cavalieri & Singer 1993), have rich cognitive and emotional lives (Montgomery 1991).

The rise of cognitive ethology can conveniently be dated from the publication of Donald Griffin's *The Question of Animal Awareness* (1976). In view of its historical significance it is surprising that the expression 'cognitive ethology' occurs only twice in the first edition of this landmark book, and then only in the last four pages. By 1978, however, this term figured in the title of Griffin's *Behavioral and Brain Sciences* target article. In each succeeding book (Griffin 1984, 1992) this expression has become more frequent (on Griffin's development see Bekoff 1993, Hailman 1978).

One explanation for Griffin's apparent reluctance to use the term 'cognitive ethology' is his hostility to cognitive psychology. This hostility may be surprising since, as we have suggested, the cognitive turn in ethology can be related to similar developments in psychology. However Griffin appears to think of cognitive psychology as a variety of behaviorism. Indeed, he claims that "conspicuously absent from most of contemporary cognitive psychology is any serious attention to conscious thoughts or subjective feelings" (Griffin 1984, p. 11). Yet it is "conscious thoughts" and "subjective feelings" that Griffin is most interested in exploring. Griffin writes that the challenge of cognitive ethology "is to venture across the species boundary and try to gather satisfactory information about what other species may think or feel" (Griffin 1984, p. 12).

Griffin's picture is of a world of creatures with different subjectivities leading their own individual lives. Trying to learn about the minds of other animals involves trying to get "a window" on their minds (Griffin 1984, Chapter 8).

Griffin seems to think that communication offers such a window, and in his writings he focuses on the communication systems of various animals.

Griffin's cognitive ethology has been attacked from several directions. Scientists, especially those of a behaviorist persuasion, often argue that cognitive or mental concepts cannot be operationally defined, thus there are no researchable questions in cognitive ethology. On this view cognitive ethology should be banished from the citadel of science and consigned to the scrapheap of idle speculation (for discussion see Bekoff & Allen 1997).

Griffin seems to be of two minds about this objection. In much of his work he has been concerned to satisfy his critics by framing definitions. Yet he seems impatient with the demand for definition and sometimes dismissive of it. In his early work (1976, 1981) Griffin is concerned to define such terms as "conscious awareness" and "mental experience." In Griffin (1982, 1984) he tries to define "mind," "aware," "intend," "conscious," "feeling," and "think;" but he is most concerned to define "consciousness." Although Griffin seems to think that it is important to define these key terms, he never seems completely happy with the definitions that he gives. In 1981 he writes that "almost any concept can be quibbled to death by excessive insistence on exact operational definitions" (p. 12). By 1991 he is claiming that "it is therefore neither necessary nor advisable to become so bogged down in quibbles about definitions that the investigation of animal cognition and consciousness is neglected altogether" (pp. 4–5). But despite his interest in getting on with it, even if the central terms cannot precisely be defined, Griffin returns again and again to the problem of definition.

In our view classical definitions cannot be given for key terms in cognitive ethology but it is not necessary to give them in order to have a viable field of research. Classical definitions preserve meaning and provide necessary and sufficient conditions for the application of a term. An area in which there is controversy is likely to be one in which the definitions of key expressions are contested. It is not only the application of cognitive terms that is contested, there are also competing definitions of such terms as 'fitness', 'recognition', communication', 'play', 'choice', 'dominance', 'altruism', and 'optimality'. With respect to mental concepts, a huge literature has developed over the years about whether or not it is part of the meaning of mental terms that what they refer to is private, introspectable, incorrigible, and so on. One result of scientific inquiry is to help fix and refine definitions. As science advances, definitions change and become more precise and entrenched. In order to get an area of inquiry going, what is needed is some common understanding of the domain to be investigated, not agreement about the meaning of key terms. Key terms in cognitive ethology are well enough understood to begin inquiry, even if classical definitions are difficult to come by.

Griffin's cognitive ethology is not sunk by the failure of definition. Yet it should be clear from this discussion that Griffin is tempted by some key assumptions of his critics. It is another assumption, one that Griffin shares with some of his critics, that is especially problematical for his version of cognitive ethology.

Griffin appears to accept a fundamentally Cartesian notion of the mind, at least with respect to its epistemological status. Although he formulates his central question in different ways, what Griffin really wants to know is whether animals are conscious. He assimilates the question of consciousness to the question of whether animals have subjective states. When the question is posed in this way, the link between mind and behavior seems highly contingent: two creatures may be in the same subjective (i.e. mental) state, but in only one does this have any objective (i.e. behavioral) consequence; two creatures may be in the same objective (i.e. behavioral) state, but in only one is the behavior caused by a subjective (i.e. mental) state. Knowledge of the minds of others is, on this view, inferential and probabilistic (Griffin 1992, p. 260). From our observations of objective states we make inferences to unobservable, subjective states. But since the connections between observable, objective states and unobservable, subjective states are weak and contingent, these inferences can be incorrect. On this view the passage from behavioral observations to the attribution of mentality is always uncertain and possibly treacherous. Nevertheless Griffin believes that many animals are conscious and he appeals to three sorts of evidence in support of his view.

The first sort of evidence can be viewed as a generalization of an argument given by Mill (1884) for the existence of other human minds. It involves noting that in my own case various forms of consciousness are associated with various behaviors, physical states and structures; and inferring that these behaviors, states, and structures are probably associated with various forms of consciousness in other creatures as well. It has often been pointed out that this argument fails in its goal of establishing the existence of other human minds; for generalizing to countless cases from my own involves a very large generalization from a very small sample (Rosenthal 1991, Part II.A.). When the analogies are weaker, as they are when drawn between humans and nonhumans, the induction is even more suspect.

Other arguments that Griffin gives involve appeals to novel or flexible behaviors. These appeals often have the rhetorical power of "gee whiz" stories. When people hear about the neat things that animals do they are often inclined to infer consciousness. But such inferences are open to the following objection. If flexible and novel behaviors can fully be explained by reference to noncognitive states or processes whose existence is relatively uncontroversial, then it is reasonable to explain them in these noncognitive terms. In many cases such behavior can be explained in such noncognitive terms (e.g. see Galef 1990). In other cases it cannot, but Griffin's critics say that cognitive explanations are just temporary placeholders for the "real" explanations of which we are currently ignorant. Put in these terms, the dispute appears to be a standoff.

In the light of these difficulties with other forms of argument, it is not surprising that the evidence that Griffin most relies on involves communication.

Just as Descartes placed a great deal of weight on the importance of language, so Griffin views communication as providing a window on other minds.

Communication can provide important evidence for various views about the nature of animal minds (see Cheney & Seyfarth 1990; Smith 1990, 1991). But this concept as it is used in the ethological literature has its problems (Philips & Austad 1990). Communication is not a transparent window that permits us to see into another "subjectivity." Thus facts about animal communication do not always provide support for views about the kinds of minds that Griffin believes that animals have.

So the objectors are right (in a way) but for the wrong reasons. They point out that the existence of Griffin-style minds in nonhuman animals is highly speculative and cannot convincingly be demonstrated by inferences from behavioral data. From this they conclude that animals do not have minds, or that if they do, they cannot systematically be studied. Instead the correct conclusion is that animals do not have Griffin-style minds, but for that matter neither do we. Our minds are closely tied to behavior and so are the minds of other animals. However our knowledge of other minds is not generally a matter of inference from behavior.

We agree with Griffin that many animals have mental states and that this belief is supported by close observations of their behavior. As we shall suggest in section four, minds that are closely tied to behavior can systematically be studied. In our view cognitive ethology is not only possible, but it is an active field of ongoing research.

In summary, Griffin's great contributions are to insist that questions about animal minds be addressed, to argue that what we say about animal minds must be continuous with our views about human minds, to bring a fully comparative perspective to bear on these questions, and to have motivated empirical research in a neglected area. However, despite his contributions and his immensely important historical role, cognitive ethology must develop more sophisticated conceptions of the mind and its relation to behavior, and develop research programs that are capable of answering some very specific questions. In the next two sections we will take some initial steps towards discharging these obligations.[4]

4. TWO CONCEPTS OF COGNITIVE ETHOLOGY[5]

Cognitive ethology is an area that is undergoing growth and expansion. Among the different sorts of practices, two kinds of cognitive ethology can be distinguished. We will refer to them as "weak cognitive ethology" and "strong cognitive ethology," and discuss them in turn.

A. Weak Cognitive Ethology (WCE)

WCE is the most common form of cognitive ethology. WCE countenances the use of a cognitive vocabulary for the explanation of behavior, but not its description. The following passage is a characteristic expression of WCE (although in this passage it is offered as a "definition" of cognitive psychology).

[I]t is the study of the mental processes that result in behavior. These internal processes act on sensory input: transforming, reducing, elaborating, storing, retrieving, and combining. Because these processes are usually not directly observable, their characteristics and the information upon which they act are inferred from behavior. Hypotheses about internal events (i.e. cognitive theories) generate predictions of how environmental inputs will be transformed in the production of behavior. (Yoerg 1991, p. 288)

WCE is an advance over behaviorism because it takes information processing seriously. Behaviorists typically treated organisms as "black boxes" whose internal states were irrelevant to the real job of science which involves mapping environmental inputs onto behavioral outputs. WCE pries the lid off the black box and treats its contents as important.

However the description of the contents of the black box often relies on fashionable computer metaphors. Indeed, one might say that WCE simply replaces the mechanical metaphors of the behaviorist tradition with the computer metaphors of cognitive science. It may be, as many think, that the computer metaphor marks a real advance over mechanical ones. Digital computers have impressive formal powers that old-fashioned machines that rely on gears and pulleys do not. But Griffin and others (e.g. Searle 1992) remain unimpressed. They say that something is left out even in these very sophisticated models (e.g. "consciousness," "intrinsic intentionality").

Whether or not something has been left out, there appears to be a double-standard between humans and nonhumans that is implicit in much work that is done in WCE. Nonhumans are often assimilated to computers in a way in which humans are not. But the significant border, if there is one, is not between animals and computers on the one hand and humans on the other; but between biological creatures and nonbiological entities. Both may process information but they seem importantly different. The capacity for having affective states is a feature of many biological creatures, but one that computers do not seem to share. Many biological creatures suffer pain, distress, fear, and can be happy or contented. WCE leaves out the affective states of biological organisms. Cognition may play a role in emotion, but emotional and affective states cannot simply be reduced to cognitive states.

Another weakness of WCE is that it attempts to protect the description of behavior from the cognitive vocabulary. Researchers in the tradition of WCE seem to share the behaviorist presumption that the behavior that is to be explained can and should be described in a cognitive-free language that makes reference only to bodily movements. Appeals to cognitive states enter only with attempts at explanation. We believe that a great deal of animal behavior cannot meaningfully be described without using cognitive and affective vocabularies. What distinguishes strong cognitive ethology from WCE (in part) is the willingness to deploy these vocabularies in the interpretation of behavior as well as in its explanation.

B. Strong Cognitive Ethology (SCE)

SCE underwrites a range of research programs in which both cognitive and affective vocabularies are willingly employed for purposes of interpretation and explanation. We will explain these concepts of interpretation and explanation in turn.

One important function of ethological investigation is to describe the behavior of animals. This role is not as highly prized as it was in the early days of ethology and is often dismissed as a hangover from natural history and sometimes likened to stamp collecting. Yet any science must provide a description of its domain and it is important to know what animals do if we are to explain why they do it.

In recent animal behavior studies there has been a search for canonical descriptions that reflect the basic categories of behavior (e.g. Golani 1992; see also Purton 1978). The idea is that for any behavior it is possible to produce a description in a common vocabulary that is solely based on what is observable. Other descriptions of behavior, though they may be useful, involve "reading into the behavior" and are ultimately eliminable. This view is untenable for a number of reasons.

First, although we cannot argue the point in detail here, we believe that the search for basic nonhuman behaviors is doomed for the same reasons that the search for basic human actions is doomed. At time T1 Kelly presses the button, rings the doorbell, and displaces some molecules. Did Kelly do one thing or many things? If one thing, which thing? If many things, which thing is basic? Grete (the dog) may simultaneously engage in a play behavior, bow, bend her front legs, kick up some dust, and displace some molecules. The same questions arise about how many things Grete did and which they are. We believe that no plausible answers to these questions can be given that are independent of pragmatic factors. What an animal does and how this is conceptualized is a contextual matter.

A second reason why this approach is untenable is related to this point. In our view descriptions of behavior are intrinsically plural and multidimensional. What counts as "the best" description is relative to the questions being asked and the interests of the interrogator. It would be unfruitful and perhaps impossible to constrain all descriptions of animal behavior by a set of basic categories (Mason 1986). This point is perhaps most obvious with respect to primates. Primatologists virtually always describe the behavior of their subjects in highly abstract and functional terms. Later, often for purposes of publication, they may try to translate these descriptions into the vocabulary of bodily movements. But if primatologists were forbidden to use abstract, functional vocabularies, one wonders if they could describe the behavior of their subjects at all (Bekoff 1995). Indeed, what would be the title, or the subject for that matter, of a classic book like De Waal's *Peacemaking Among Primates.*

A third problem with this approach is that in many cases descriptions of an animal's behavior in the canonical language would deprive us of insights into the meaning of the behavior. Predator-avoidance may take many forms, and since nonhuman animals are no more infallible than human animals, such behavior may fail, or occur when no predator is within striking distance. In many cases we might be disposed to say that the animal is trying to avoid a predator, yet a description of the animal's behavior just in terms of her observable bodily movements would not allow this insight.

Finally, an animal's behavioral repertoire is organized functionally as well as in other ways. The same bodily movements may have different meanings; and the same behavior, defined in functional terms, may involve different bodily movements. For example, the same bodily movements involved in canid play are also involved in aggression and reproduction (see section 4). And the same behavior from a functional point of view, for example predator avoidance, may involve tree climbing in one case and running in another.

For these reasons we believe that the search for canonical descriptions of animal behavior fails. This approach is rooted in the positivist dream of a value-free observation language that can be used to characterize the phenomena that covering laws are supposed to explain. Whatever the plausibility of this model for the physical sciences, it is highly implausible for ethology.

Because the attempt to describe behavior in a canonical vocabulary that reflects basic categories is unsuccessful, we favor the use of the term "interpretation" where others use the term "description." This acknowledges the fact that describing what animals do involves interpreting their behavior.

A central role of explanation is to specify why something happened. Although we cannot tell the story here, we would defend a view of explanation that is similar to our account of interpretation: explanations can be plural, noncompetitive, and occur at different levels of abstraction. In our view appeal to generalizations that involve cognitive and affective states can genuinely be explanatory.

However a word of caution is in order. We have tried to defeat a picture of ethology that leaves no room for cognitive and affective interpretations and explanations. But even if what we have said is correct, no one is compelled to employ such vocabularies. It is still open to someone to object that such vocabularies are illegitimate—neither suitable for interpretation nor explanation. The rejection of the "canonical description view" does not imply the legitimacy—much less the fruitfulness—of the SCE alternative. A second objection is weaker. It may be admitted that although cognitive and affective vocabularies can be employed legitimately in interpretation and explanation, we are not compelled to use them and indeed would do better if we did not.

With respect to the second objection, we concede that no one is driven to apply cognitive and affective vocabularies to animals on pain of logical contradiction. Quine and Skinner could write their autobiographies as narratives of their bodily movements without falling into logical inconsistency. No doubt the same would be true of Digit and Koko. But Quine's autobiography is boring: it lacks insight and inspiration. One has the feeling that much of what is important has been left out. In our view the same is true with respect to interpreting and explaining the behavior of many nonhuman animals: one can avoid cognitive and affective vocabularies, but as we will try to show in the next section, in many cases one does this on pain of giving up interesting and insightful perspectives.

With respect to the first objection, this charge most plausibly comes either from those who espouse a double standard with respect to humans and non-humans (or languageless creatures and those with language [e.g. Carruthers 1989]), or eliminativists with respect to cognitive and affective vocabularies. We have argued elsewhere, as have many others, that a principled double standard cannot be maintained, so we will not repeat those arguments here (Bekoff & Jamieson 1991; Jamieson & Bekoff 1992). With respect to eliminativism, if it is true that cognitive and affective vocabularies will one day bite the dust, then SCE would cease to exist. But SCE is not singularly vulnerable. The elimination of cognitive and affective vocabularies would fell other scientific enterprises as well and be part of a radical revision of the way that we think about the world. It is enough here to defend SCE against those who are more modest in their claims.[6]

In this section we have distinguished two concepts of cognitive ethology, spoken in favor of one, and defended it against two objections. The heart of the case for SCE, however, rests with its fruitfulness as a conceptual guide to empirical research. In the next section we will discuss one area of research in cognitive ethology.

5. SOCIAL PLAY

Space does not allow us to cover the many areas of research (e.g. mate choice, habitat selection, individual recognition and discrimination, injury-feigning, assessments of dominance, foraging for food, caching food, various types of social communication, observational learning, tool use, imitation, teaching) in which cognitive ethological approaches have been useful in gaining an understanding of the behavior of animals (for examples see Griffin 1984, 1992; Mitchell & Thompson 1986; Byrne & Whiten 1988; Cheney & Seyfarth 1990; Bekoff & Jamieson 1990, 1991; Ristau 1991; Bekoff 1995). Here we will discuss only one area: social play.

Social play is a behavior that lends itself to cognitive studies, and poses a great challenge to researchers (Mitchell 1990; Bekoff & Allen 1992). In particular, the question of how mammals communicate their intention to engage in social play presupposes cognitive states, without which it would be difficult or impossible to describe the social encounter (Bekoff 1995).

The canid "play bow" is a highly stereotyped movement that seems to function to stimulate recipients to engage (or continue to engage) in social play (Bekoff 1977). When an animal performs a play bow she crouches on her forelimbs, leaves her hind legs fairly straight, and may wag her tail and bark.

Such play-soliciting signals appear to transmit the message that "what follows is play." Play-soliciting signals are used to communicate to others that actions such as biting, biting and shaking of the head from side-to-side, and mounting are to be taken as play and not as aggressive, predatory, or reproductive behavior.

Play-soliciting signals appear to foster cooperation between players so that each responds to the other in a way consistent with play and different from the responses that the same actions would elicit in other contexts (Bekoff 1975). This cooperation may occur because each of the participants has a belief about the intentions of the other animals who are involved in the social encounter. For example, in coyotes the response to a threat gesture is very different if it is immediately preceded by a play signal or if a play signal is performed at the beginning of the interaction (Bekoff 1975). The play signal can be viewed as altering the meaning of a threat signal by establishing (or maintaining) a "play mood." When a play signaler bites or mounts the recipient of a play signal, the recipient is not disposed to injure or to mate with the signaler.

It is difficult to describe canid play behavior without using a cognitive vocabulary. One and the same bodily movement can be aggression or play. The difference between a movement that is aggressive and one that is playful is naturally described in terms of one animal's intention and another animal's appreciation of the intention.

Similarly the cognitive vocabulary appears to provide the resources for explaining some play behavior. For example, suppose that we want to know why Grete permitted Jethro to nip at her ears. One explanation may be that Grete believes that Jethro is playing. This gives rise to further questions, such as whether Jethro believes that Grete believes that Jethro is playing. One of the challenges of research in cognitive ethology is to investigate the extent to which such questions are well-formed and what the possible answers to them might be.

In this section we have been able to provide only a brief summary of some questions about social play. Because of the brevity of this account, we have not been able to discuss behaviors in which the affective vocabulary gains a foothold. Nor did we discuss what might be reasonable empirical constraints on cognitive interpretations and explanations.

It is important to remember that we are pluralists with respect to both explanation and interpretation. Cognitive explanations do not exclude other causal ones, nor do they rule out explanations that are adaptationist, phylogenetic, or developmental. In our view we need to employ a large range of conceptual resources in order to understand behavior.

6. Concluding Remarks

We have argued that cognitive ethology can be defended against its critics. In addition, we have discussed some of its varieties and forms and briefly sketched one area of research in cognitive ethology. Before closing, it is worth mentioning what cognitive ethology can contribute to cognitive studies generally.

Cognitive ethology can help to broaden the perspective of cognitive studies in two ways. First, cognitive ethology can help to situate the study of cognition in an evolutionary framework. It should be a necessary condition for postulating a cognitive state in a human that the existence of this state is at least consistent with evolutionary history. Although lip service is sometimes given to this constraint, talk of evolution in cognitive science is too often metaphorical. Cognitive ethology has the potential to make cognitive science take evolution seriously. Second, the fact that cognitive ethology is fully comparative can help to make cognitive science less parochial. Although there has been a great deal of concern about parochialism with respect to nonbiological systems, this concern has often coexisted with a surprising degree of "chimpocentrism" (Beck 1982). Many people are more willing to countenance cognition in computers or space aliens than in rodents, amphibians, or insects. Even in cognitive studies there is a tendency to view cognition as "essential" to humans and instantiated in various (lesser) degrees only in those who are phylogenetically close to humans. With its view of cognition as a strategic evolutionary response to problems that might have been faced by a variety of diverse organisms, cognitive ethology can help to overcome this form of parochialism.

There is no question but that the issue of animal minds is difficult and complex. Like questions about the human mind, it is tangled in issues of definition, conception, relation to behavior and so on. Yet in our view cognitive ethology is here to stay. For the adoption of cognitive and affective vocabularies by ethologists opens up a range of explanations, predictions, and generalizations that would not otherwise be available. As long as there are animals to behave and humans to wonder why, cognitive interpretations and explanations will be offered. In our view this is not only permissible, it is often enlightening. Sometimes it is even science.

NOTES

1. We are grateful to all those who participated in discussions of this material at the University of Wyoming and the 1992 Philosophy of Science Association meetings. We especially thank Colin Allen, Marc Hauser, David Resnik and Carolyn Ristau.

2. However Tinbergen seems to suggest only a page later that "the study of subjective phenomena" is "consistent in the application of its own methods" but that this study should be kept distinct from the study of causation (1951, p. 5).

3. However there is a passage in Darwin (1871, Chapter 2) where he seems to suggest discontinuity between humans and other animals. Humans are dominant, according to Darwin, because of language, and language in part depends on human intellectual faculties. This suggests that discontinuities in power between humans and other animals may reflect discontinuities in intellect.

4. There is an important strand in Griffin's work that we have not addressed: He wants to understand creatures from "the inside out;" he wants to know what it is like to be a bat (for example), and he assumes (following Nagel 1974) that such knowledge does not consist in knowing some set of "objective" facts about bats (for a contrary view see Akins 1990). If Griffin is right in supposing that such radical subjectivity exists, cognitive ethology as we understand it will not deliver a deep appreciation of it. Griffin's concerns about radical subjectivity may be of profound importance, but they go beyond the boundaries of science as it is currently understood.

5. In what follows we make several simplifying assumptions including these: first, that cognitive ethology is directed towards explaining behavior rather than cognitive competencies; second, that for many organisms in many cases intentional interpretations and explanations count as cognitive ones; and third, that information processing in many organisms counts as cognitive activity. All of these assumptions warrant further discussion.

6. As suggested in the text, the existence of a cognitive vocabulary is a necessary condition for the persistence of cognitive ethology. However cognitive ethology is not committed to "folk psychology." Cognitive ethology is committed to the view that the behavior of nonhuman animals can usefully be interpreted or explained in ways consistent with our best understanding of cognitive states, whether these involve folk psychological concepts or not. If our best understanding of cognitive states involves some alternative to folk psychology, then cognitive ethology should embrace the alternative.

REFERENCES

Akins, K. (1990), "Science and Our Inner Lives: Birds of Prey, Bats, and the Common Featherless Bi-ped", in Bekoff & Jamieson (1990), volume 1, pp. 414–27.

Bateson, P. (1968), "Ethological Methods of Observing Behavior", in *Analysis of Behavioral Change*, L. Weiskrantz (ed.). New York: Harper and Row, pp. 389–99.

Beck, B. (1982), "Chimpocentrism: Bias in Cognitive Ethology", *Journal of Human Evolution* 11:3–17.

Bekoff, M. (1975), "The Communication of Play Intention: Are Play Signals Functional?", *Semiotica* 15:231–9.

—. (1977), "Social Communication in Canids: Evidence for the Evolution of a Stereotyped Mammalian Display", *Science* 197:1097–9.

—. (1993), Animal minds. *Ethology*. 95:166–170.

—. (1995), "Cognitive Ethology and the Explanation of Nonhuman Animal Behavior", in *Comparative Approaches to Cognitive Science*, J.-A. Meyer & H. Roitblat (eds.). Cambridge, MA: MIT Press, pp. 119–150.

Bekoff, M. & Allen, C. (1992), "Intentional Icons: Towards an Evolutionary Cognitive Ethology", *Ethology* 91:1–16.

Bekoff, M. & Allen, C. (1997), "Cognitive Ethology: Slayers, Skeptics, and Proponents", in *Anthropomorphism, Anecdotes, and Animals: The Emperor's New Clothes?*, R. Mitchell, N. Thompson, & L. Miles (eds.). Lincoln: University of Nebraska Press, pp. 313–334.

Bekoff, M. & Jamieson, D. (eds.) (1990), *Interpretation and Explanation in the Study of Animal Behavior*, two volumes. Boulder, CO: Westview Press.

Bekoff, M. & Jamieson, D. (1991), "Reflective Ethology, Applied Philosophy, and the Moral Status of Animals", in *Perspectives In Ethology 9: Human Understanding and Animal Awareness*, P. Bateson & P. Klopfer (eds.). New York: Plenum Press, pp. 1–47.

Boakes, R. (1984), *From Darwin to Behaviorism: Psychology and the Minds of Animals.* New York: Cambridge University Press.

Byrne, R. & Whiten, A. (eds.) (1988), *Machiavellian Intelligence: Social Expertise and the Evolution of Intellect in Monkeys, Apes, and Humans.* Oxford: Oxford University Press.

Carruthers, P. (1989), "Brute Experience", *Journal of Philosophy* 86:258–69.

Cavalieri, P. & Singer, P. (eds.) (1993), *The Great Ape Project.* London: Fourth Estate.

Cheney, D. & Seyfarth R. (1990), *How Monkeys See the World: Inside the Mind of Another Species.* Chicago: The University of Chicago Press.

Darwin, C. (1871), *The Descent of Man, and Selection in Relation to Sex*, two volumes. London: Murray.

—. (1896), *The Variation of Animals and Plants Under Domestication*, two volumes. New York: Appleton.

Dawkins, M. (1986), *Unraveling Animal Behavior.* Essex, England: Longman Group.

Dawkins, M., Halliday, T., and Dawkins, R. (eds.) (1991), *The Tinbergen Legacy.* London: Chapman & Hall.

Dennett, D. (1987), *The Intentional Stance.* Cambridge, MA: The MIT Press.

Dewsbury, D. (1992), "On the Problems Studied in Ethology, Comparative Psychology, and Animal Behavior", *Ethology* 92:89–107.

Fodor, J. (1968), *Psychological Explanation.* New York: Random House.

Galef B. (1990), "Tradition in Animals: Field Observations and Laboratory Analyses", in Bekoff & Jamieson (1990), volume 1, pp. 74–95.

Golani, I. (1992), "A Mobility Gradient in the Organization of Vertebrate Movement", *The Behavioral and Brain Sciences* 15:249–308.

Griffin, D. (1976), *The Question of Animal Awareness.* New York: The Rockefeller University Press.

—. (1978), "Prospects for a Cognitive Ethology", *The Behavioral and Brain Sciences*", 4:527–38.

—. (1981), *The Question of Animal Awareness: Evolutionary Continuity of Mental Experience*, revised and enlarged edition. New York: The Rockefeller University Press.

—. (ed.) (1982), *Animal Mind–Human Mind.* New York: Springer-Verlag.

—. (1984), *Animal Thinking.* Cambridge, MA: Harvard University Press.

—. (1991), "Progress Towards Cognitive Ethology", in Ristau (1991), pp. 3–17.

—. (1992), *Animal Minds.* Chicago: The University of Chicago Press.

Hailman, J. (1978), Review of Griffin (1976). *Auk* 95:614–5.

Huxley, J. (1942), *Evolution: The Modern Synthesis.* New York: Harper.

Jamieson, D. & Bekoff, M. (1992), "Carruthers on Nonconscious Experience," *Analysis* 52:23–8.

Kennedy, J. (1992), *The New Anthropomorphism.* Cambridge: Cambridge University Press.

Lorenz, K. (1988/1991), *Here Am I—Where Are You? The Behavior of the Greylag Goose.* New York: Harcourt, Brace, Jovanovich, Publishers.

Mason, W. (1986), "Behavior Implies Cognition", in *Science and Philosophy: Integrating Scientific Disciplines*, W. Bechtel (ed.). Boston: Kluwer, pp. 297–307.

Mill, J. (1884), *An Examination of Sir William Hamilton's Philosophy.* New York: Henry Holt.

Mitchell, R. (1990), "A Theory of Play", in Bekoff & Jamieson (1990), volume 1, pp. 197–227.

Mitchell, R. & Thompson, N. (eds.) (1986), *Deception: Perspectives on Human and Nonhuman Deceit.* Albany: State University of New York Press.

Morgan, L. (1894), *Introduction to Comparative Psychology.* London: Scott.

Montgomery, S. (1991), *Walking With the Great Apes.* Boston: Houghton Mifflin Company.

Nagel, T. (1974), "What is it Like to be a Bat?", *Philosophical Review*, 83:435–50.

Pauly, P. (1987), *Controlling Life: Jacques Loeb and the Engineering Ideal in Biology.* Berkeley: University of California Press.

Philips, M. & Austad, S. (1990), "Animal Communication and Social Evolution", in Bekoff & Jamieson (1990), volume 1, pp. 254–68.

Purton, A. (1978), "Ethological Categories of Behavior and Some Consequences of Their Conflation", *Animal Behaviour* 26:653–70.

Putnam, H. (1960/1975), "Minds and Machines", in *Mind, Language and Reality, Philosophical Papers*, Volume 2. New York: Cambridge University Press, pp. 362–85.

Richards, R. (1987), *Darwin and the Emergence of Evolutionary Theories of Mind and Behavior.* Chicago: The University of Chicago Press.

Ristau, C. (ed.) (1991), *Cognitive Ethology: The Minds of Other Animals.* Hillsdale, NJ: Erlbaum.

Rollin, B. (1989), *The Unheeded Cry: Animal Consciousness, Animal Pain and Science.* New York: Oxford University Press.

Rosenthal D. (ed.) (1991), *The Nature of Mind.* New York: Oxford University Press.

Searle, J. (1992), *The Rediscovery of the Mind.* Cambridge, MA: MIT Press.

Smith, W. (1990), "Communication and Expectations: A Social Process and the Cognitive Operations It Depends Upon and Influences", in Bekoff & Jamieson (1990), volume 1, pp. 234–53.

—. (1991), "Animal Communication and the Study of Cognition", in Ristau (1991), pp. 209–30.

Tinbergen, N. (1963), "On Aims and Methods of Ethology", *Zeitschrift fur Tierpsychologie* 20:410–29.

—. (1991), *The Study of Instinct.* Oxford: Oxford University Press.

Yoerg, S. I. (1991), "Ecological Frames of Mind: The role of cognition in behavioral ecology", *Quarterly Review of Biology* 66:287–301.

Marc Bekoff and Paul W. Sherman

4   Reflections on Animal Selves

Is SELF-COGNIZANCE a uniquely human attribute, or do other animals also have a sense of self? Although there is considerable interest in this question, answers remain elusive. Progress has been stymied by misunderstandings in terminology, a focus on a narrow range of species, and controversies over key concepts, experimental paradigms and interpretations of data. Here, we propose a new conceptual and terminological framework, emphasizing that degrees of self-cognizance differ among animals because of the cognitive demands that their species-specific social structures and life-history characteristics have placed upon them over evolutionary time. We suggest that the self-cognizance of an organism falls at a point on a continuum of social complexity and conscious involvement.

Although laypersons and researchers from many disciplines have long been interested in animal self-knowledge (or self-cognizance) [1–3], and a large amount of information has accumulated, few unambiguous conclusions are available. This is mainly because of the difficulty of objectively assessing self-knowledge and quantifying its neurobiological substrates among organisms whose patterns of communication we only partially understand. Progress has also been limited by inconsistencies in terminology, and by experimental paradigms that concentrate on visual rather than on chemical or auditory cues. Moreover, relatively few species have been examined in detail, and all were vertebrates, mostly primates.

Here, we suggest that it is appropriate and useful to consider knowledge of self, or 'self-cognizance', as a continuum ranging from self-referencing to self-awareness to self-consciousness (Box 1). We argue that degrees of self-cognizance are better predicted by the behavioral ecology of a species rather than by its relative brain size or phylogenetic closeness to humans. In social animals, cognitive demands imposed by selection for cooperation, maintenance of pair bonds, nepotism, and reciprocity on the one hand, and avoidance of being cheated and effectiveness in competition on the other hand, have resulted in the evolution of increased mental complexity [1–3]. Studies of self-cognizance will benefit from capitalizing on this diversity, and also from considering self-cognizance in invertebrates and vertebrates. We argue that the degree of self-cognizance of individuals in any species can be represented as a point on a continuum of complexity and conscious involvement.

Reprinted from Bekoff, M., and P. W. Sherman. 2004. Reflections on Animal Selves. *Trends in Ecology and Evolution* 19, 176–180, with permission from Elsevier.

However, documenting degrees of self-cognizance is difficult. Ideally, individuals should be studied in their natural environments when they are making decisions about how to modify their behavior toward other individuals of their social group in light of the previous responses of those group members to them. Thus, it will be useful to combine field observations of dynamic changes in the behavior of an individual in social situations requiring self-cognizance, such as deciding how long or hard to fight over a resource [4] or responding to being cheated in a social contract [5,6], with noninvasive neural techniques to determine whether the target behaviors are linked to electrophysiological responses of the types, and in the specific brain regions, that are active in self-cognizant humans.

Currently, technical difficulties preclude applying certain neural techniques to field situations. However, relevant techniques are being developed and, in the meantime, cleverly designed laboratory experiments [5,7,8] might enable

---

BOX 1. CATEGORIES (DEGREES) OF SELF-COGNIZANCE

In our scheme, 'self-cognizance' is used as an umbrella term to cover the continuum from self-referencing to self-consciousness. We hypothesize that species exhibit different degrees of self-cognizance, which reflect variations in their social environments and life histories. The position of an individual on the self-cognizance continuum is based on the degree to which members of its species or group engage in repetitive competitive or cooperative interactions with the same conspecifics over their lifetimes and benefit from changing their responses in light of outcomes of those previous interactions (see also [1,7,23]).

Self-Referencing

(also referred to as self-referent phenotype matching and the 'armpit effect': [17,31,42–45]). Self-referencing is a perceptual process involving matching phenotypic characteristics of a target individual against the phenotype of the discriminator. Discriminators compare labels of the target (such as of odor or appearance) against labels learned from their own phenotype, and accept or reject that target based on the degree of similarity [42,46]. Self-referencing can be reflexive and noncognitive, even occurring in the immune system and in creatures without brains, such as tunicates and plants [13,14,17]. If a brain is present, it might be used in deciding, consciously or nonconsciously, what behavioral action to take once recognition occurs [47].

Self-Awareness

(also referred to as 'perceptual consciousness' [1] and 'body-ness' or 'mine-ness' [9,10]). Self-awareness is the cognitive process that enables an individual to discriminate between its own body and those of others, or to discriminate possessions such as 'my bone' or 'my territory' from the similar possessions of others. A sense of 'body-ness' is necessary for most animals to function in their social and ecological milieus (i.e. to find mates, to evade predators, or to avoid

Box 1 (continued)

bumping into each other). A brain is required for this level of self-cognizance, although the actual discrimination can be conscious or unconscious. Being self-aware does not imply that individuals use self-referent phenotype matching or vice versa.

Self-Consciousness

(analogous to 'reflective consciousness' [1], 'sense of self' [7], 'self-reflection' [35], 'I-ness' [9] and 'I-self' [34]; having 'sympathy, empathy and a theory of mind' [27] also are included). Self-consciousness involves having a sense of one's own body as a named self, knowing that 'this body is me' and thinking about one's self and one's own behavior in relation to the actions of others. A brain is required and the underlying processes are conscious. Being self-conscious implies that an individual is self-aware, and that it can use self-referent phenotype matching. We hypothesize that self-consciousness evolves when individuals benefit from analyzing and revising their own behavior in light of how specific members of their social group, including actual or potential mates, responded to their behavior in the past. Self-consciousness leads to dynamic and finely graded behavioral outputs, ranging from cooperation to selfishness, depending on the costs and benefits of previous responses of conspecifics to the focal individual.

us to infer what is happening within the brains of animals as they make decisions requiring self-cognizance.

ANIMAL SELVES: WHAT IS THE PROBLEM?

Although there is considerable interdisciplinary interest in animal self-cognizance [1–3,7–11], few unequivocal answers are available. Individuals of most species behave as if they 'know' that they are similar to, but distinct from, others of the same species [12]. For example, they seldom mate with the wrong species; they position their body parts in space so that they do not collide with nearby conspecifics as they move, or travel as a coordinated hunting unit or flock; and, they discriminate members of their social group from foreign group members, relatives from nonrelatives, and close from distant kin [13–16]. However, there is presently no agreed-upon objective way to assess the degree of self-cognizance of an individual.

Here, we address five specific questions, namely: (i) what does it mean to say that an animal is self-cognizant?; (ii) is self-cognizance a dichotomous phenomenon or a continuum?; (iii) does the occurrence of self-referent phenotype matching [17] imply that an animal is self-cognizant?; (iv) is knowledge of the neural mechanisms underlying self-cognizance in humans useful for inferring self-cognizance in other animals?; and (v) what are the promising directions for future research?

Is Self-Cognizance a Continuum?

In 1871, Darwin [18] asserted that 'the difference in mind between man and the higher animals, great as it is, certainly is one of degree and not of kind'. By contrast, Hauser [7] recently suggested that 'our own species may be on its own in having the capacity to understand what it's like to have a sense of self, to have unique and personal mental states and experiences'. So, is self-cognizance best characterized as a dichotomous variable (either an animal has it or it doesn't) or as a continuum?

We argue for characterizing self-cognizance as a continuum. First, too few species have been studied in sufficient detail to support empirically the claim that a general cognitive discontinuity exists between humans and all other animals [1,2,7,11]. Second, even if there were discontinuities between humans and other animals in some cognitive capacities (e.g. language abilities [19]), we are not forced to accept that discontinuities therefore exist in all cognitive capacities [1,20–22]. We hypothesize that species exhibit different degrees of self-cognizance (Box 1), which reflect variations in their social environments and life histories. The position of an individual on the self-cognizance continuum is determined, ultimately, by natural selection, based on the degree to which members of its species or group (e.g. males or females) repeat competitive or cooperative interactions with the same conspecifics over their lifetimes and benefit from changing their responses in light of outcomes of those previous interactions (see also [1,7,23]).

We suggest that self-cognizance is favored to the degree that individuals benefit from reflecting on their own behaviors in light of the previous responses of conspecifics, and dynamically and adaptively adjusting their future behaviors accordingly. These are differences in degree, rather than in kind, among species and individuals, and they should be reflected in a continuum of self-cognizance.

Methodological Issues

It is obvious to most pet owners that their companion animals are self-cognizant to some degree [certainly self-aware, and perhaps even self-conscious (Box 1)]. Initially, it also seemed reasonable to suppose that our closest primate relatives, such as chimpanzees, gorillas and orangutans, share a human-like capacity for self-consciousness (i.e. the highest degree of self-cognizance). However, none of these conjectures can be proven, because there is no agreed upon objective way to quantify self-cognizance.

Research on this topic has been conducted on a few captive individuals, some of which received extensive training [1,7,12,22,24–26]. We actually know very little about degrees of self-cognizance among companion animals, less still about free-living nondomesticated species and essentially nothing about interindividual variation in degrees of self-cognizance in nature, for example between males and females, juveniles and adults, or dominants and subordinates. Most importantly, we do not know how variations in expression of self-cognizant behaviors affect the survival and reproductive success of their bearers [10].

Thirty years ago, Gallup [25,27] proposed using the mirror test to infer self-consciousness. This test was based on the observation that some captive chimpanzees would gaze into a mirror and then touch a colored spot that had been placed on their forehead whilst they were sedated. This response became the gold standard for inferring animal self-consciousness.

Recently, however, many authors [7,22,26,28,29] have highlighted problems with interpreting the results of the mirror test. Most importantly, it can yield false negatives: if an individual fails the test, it does not necessarily mean that the animal is not self-conscious. For example, an individual might fail the test because vision is not the primary sensory modality of recognition in that species; chemical cues often are more important [30–32]. Even in animals that primarily use vision in recognition, the mirror test can yield false negatives; for example, if an individual recognized itself but did not give a detectable behavioral response [13,14]. This might account for some of the well known variability in mirror-test results [7]. Finally, some species or individuals (e.g. male canids and primates) tend to avoid eye contact with same-sex conspecifics, because it is a threatening gesture. These individuals are hesitant about gazing directly into a mirror.

If failing the mirror test does not prove that an individual lacks self-consciousness, what does passing the test mean? Some researchers [3,7,9,10] believe that it indicates only that chimpanzees are self-aware (Box 1). Others offer a richer interpretation. Thus, Gallup [27] concluded that 'not only are some animals aware of themselves but such self-awareness enables these animals to infer the mental states of others. In other words, species that pass the mirror test are also able to sympathize, empathize and attribute intent and emotions in others—abilities that some might consider the exclusive domain of humans'. Gallup believes that passing the mirror test implies self-consciousness and having a 'theory of mind'.

However, too little is known about the behavioral ecology of animal self-awareness to support either the rich or the impoverished interpretation of passing (or failing) the mirror test. Moreover, results from a few captive individuals might not reflect the capacities for self-cognizance of an entire species in nature. By itself, the mirror test is therefore neither necessary nor sufficient to infer where species or individuals lie along the continuum of self-cognizance.

BRINGING TOGETHER ETHOLOGY, BEHAVIORAL ECOLOGY AND NEUROBIOLOGY

The foregoing discussion about degrees of self-cognizance poses more questions than it answers. For example, do the great apes have a special, refined sense of self-cognizance that is similar to self-consciousness in humans but which is lacking in the other creatures? To what degree are other social animals, including insects, spiders, rodents, herpestids (mongooses), canids, birds or fish self-cognizant? How would we find out? Addressing these issues requires objective criteria for recognizing degrees of self-cognizance, criteria that take into account the sensory capabilities and behavioral ecology of each species. Given the diversity of animal social and sensory systems, no single technique is likely to provide an acid-test for determining degrees of self-cognizance across all taxa.

However, a relatively new and potentially promising general approach to designing tests of self involves the use of noninvasive techniques to detect neural activity, as measured by firing rates and cell metabolism. These methods include the measurement of evoked response potentials (ERPs) and the use of positron emission tomography (PET scans) or functional magnetic resonance imaging (fMRI). These techniques can be coupled with others, such as transcranial magnetic stimulation (TMS), that create mini-disruptions of neural activities in specific brain regions.

Neural imaging has recently been used on humans to identify brain areas involved in certain perceptual and emotional processes [33,34], including what Johnson *et al.* [35] termed 'self-reflection' (our self-consciousness: Box 1). Based on results of neuroimaging studies, Keenan *et al.* [36] suggested that "there may be a bias for the processing of 'self' within the right prefrontal cortex in humans and other primates".

We eagerly anticipate the broader application of neuroimaging and other neurobiological techniques, perhaps eventually to free-living animals in their native ecological and social environments. However, there are major technical hurdles that must first be overcome, because current methods require the confinement of subjects, and even then artifacts resulting from their movements can lead to confusion in the interpretation of data.

Nonetheless, we are optimistic. Technical solutions are emerging, such as being able to capture brain activities during socially relevant situations in a highly restrictive scanner. Until appropriate technology is available, it might be possible to design relevant laboratory experiments [5,7,8] that, when coupled with existing technology, enable us to infer where and when activity is occurring in the brains of animals that are only loosely restricted.

If so, the next step would be to visualize the neural processes that occur in humans when we engage in tasks requiring mobilization of self-consciousness, such as thinking about our own thoughts and actions [1] or considering how to respond to being cheated in a social contract. If neural imaging studies yield a baseline profile of what brain activities are associated with behaviors requiring self-consciousness in humans, it would be a place to begin the search for objective evidence of self-consciousness in non-humans. For example, to investigate the degrees of self-cognizance enlisted in the mirror test, it would be valuable to map the brain regions and neural activity profiles that occur in chimpanzees that are passing the test, as well as in those that are failing it. Results could be compared with neural imaging data from humans who were taking the mirror test or otherwise were behaving self-consciously [35,36]. If active brain regions and neural profiles of chimpanzees that pass the mirror test were similar to those of humans engaged in tasks known to involve self-consciousness, but different from chimpanzees that do not pass, then, by analogy, the mirror test has revealed probable self-consciousness in chimpanzees. However, if brain regions and neural profiles of chimpanzees that pass the test are very different from those of self-conscious humans, then either chimpanzees are self-aware but not self-conscious (Box 1) or else chimpanzee brains and neural processes are quite different from those of humans.

Thus, neurobiological studies of other social species that are engaged in relevant behavioral tasks, although currently technically impossible, are likely to be rewarding in the future. Neural correlates that are associated with various degrees of human self-cognizance might differ from those in other species because of variations in neuroanatomy (e.g. the presence or absence of a prefrontal cortex) or because of the use of different sensory modalities. However, this is more of a caution than a deterrent to such investigations.

We predict that species will exhibit various degrees of self-cognizance, reflecting differences in their social environments and life-history characteristics [1,2,7,9,10]. In particular, greater degrees of self-cognizance (Box 1) are expected in species in which individuals benefit most from reflecting upon and revising their own behavior in light of how particular conspecifics have responded to them previously. Self-cognizance should thus be most developed in long-lived, group-living animals, in which individuals have repeated interactions, both cooperative and competitive, with the same suite of conspecifics [23]. The putative self-consciousness of chimpanzees and gorillas [7,25,26] supports this hypothesis, but that of orangutans [7,37] might not, because they are relatively nonsocial on Borneo. However, orangutans are more social elsewhere in their range (e.g. on Sumatra). It would be interesting to compare the self-cognizance of individual orangutans living in these different areas.

It also will be illuminating to investigate degrees of self-cognizance in social vertebrates and invertebrates, such as honey bees *Apis mellifera*, paper wasps *Polistes fuscatus*, damp-wood termites *Zootermopsis nevadensis*, gray wolves *Canis lupus*, naked mole-rats *Heterocephalus glaber*, lions *Panthera leo*, meerkats *Suricata suricata*, gray parrots *Psittacus erithacus*, Florida scrub jays *Aphelocoma coerulescens* and acorn woodpeckers *Melanerpes formicivorus* [6,37–40]. In each species, mated pairs and other group members interact repeatedly over their lifespans, groups comprise close and distant kin, and intra-group dynamics can involve nepotism, reciprocity, competition and selfishness [40]. The abilities of individuals to reflect upon and modify their own behaviors in response to previous responses of members of their social group would presumably enhance cooperation and group coordination in finding food (honey bees, wolves and lions), maintenance of food stores (woodpeckers and naked mole-rats) and pair bonds (damp-wood termites and parrots), and avoidance of predators (paper wasps, meerkats and jays).

We hypothesize that degrees of self-cognizance evolved along with cooperative breeding and sociality. Moreover, we expect highly social species to be self-conscious because if individuals only were self-aware (Box 1), they would be unable to respond adaptively to the previous responses of group-mates to them. Lack of self-consciousness could thus restrict the ability of individuals to cooperate and to compete effectively, which, in turn, could compromise group cohesion and stability, and limit the reproductive opportunities of the individuals concerned.

WHERE TO FROM HERE?

Studies of self-cognizance as a continuum will undoubtedly lead to bold programs of interdisciplinary research and forge new links among animal behaviorists, evolutionary biologists, cognitive ethologists and neuroscientists. Future studies must pay attention to the behavioral ecology of each species as well as to basic and well accepted biological ideas, such as evolutionary continuity and the comparative method.

It is useful to return to basics. We must revise our definitions and refocus our questions, and an agreed-upon terminology is a good place to begin. Defining what self-cognizance means, what behavioral abilities accompany different degrees of it, and what neural activities are diagnostic of each degree, are essential (e.g. Box 1). In particular, if we can agree on objective criteria that characterize human self-consciousness [36], for example based on behavioral and neural responses to perceived cheating on social contracts [41], we might then be able to apply those same criteria to infer self-consciousness in other animals.

Although there are major methodological hurdles, we are optimistic that researchers and technological innovations can meet these challenges. Our goal should be to quantify and compare degrees of self-cognizance among animals in natural or semi-natural ecological and social settings, and also to investigate how different sensory modalities contribute to enabling different degrees of self-cognizance.

Finally, and in light of Darwin's principle of evolutionary continuity [18], we urge abandonment of the anthropocentric view that only big-brained creatures, such as great apes, elephants and cetaceans have sufficient mental capacities for the most complex degree of self-cognizance: self-consciousness. We hope the current conventional wisdom that only a few species are self-conscious will become a historical curiosity and that, in its place, will arise an empirical understanding of where the minds of various social vertebrates and invertebrates lie on a continuum of self-cognizance.

ACKNOWLEDGEMENTS

We thank Colin Allen, Mark Hauber, Jan Nystrom, Judith Scarl, Janet Shellman and three anonymous referees for helpful comments. Financial support was provided to P.W.S. by the College of Agriculture and Life Sciences at Cornell through the kindness of Daniel J. Decker and the Hatch Grant program. M.B. was supported by a sabbatical leave from the University of Colorado, Boulder. We dedicate this article to the memory of Donald R. Griffin (1915–2003), the founder of cognitive ethology.

REFERENCES

1. Griffin, D.R. (2001) *Animal Minds*, University of Chicago Press

2. Dawkins, M.S. (1998) *Through Our Eyes Only?* Oxford University Press

3. Bekoff, M. *et al.*, eds (2002) *The Cognitive Animal*, MIT Press

4. Taylor, P.W. and Elwood, R.W. (2003) The mismeasure of animal contests. *Anim. Behav.* 65, 1195–1202

5. Hauser, M.D. (1992) Costs of deception: cheaters are punished in rhesus monkeys (*Macaca mulatta*). *Proc. Natl. Acad. Sci. U.S.A.* 89, 12137–12139

6. Reeve, H.K. and Nonacs, P. (1992) Social contracts in wasp societies. *Nature* 359, 823–825

7. Hauser, M.D. (2000) *Wild Minds: What Animals Really Think*, Henry Holt

8. Brosnan, S. and De Waal, F.B.M. (2003) Monkeys reject unequal pay. *Nature* 425, 297–299

9. Bekoff, M. (2002) Animal reflections. *Nature* 419, 255

10. Bekoff, M. (2003) Consciousness and self in animals: some reflections. *Zygon* 38, 229–245

11. Keenan, J. P. (2003) *The Face in the Mirror: The Search for the Origins of Consciousness*, HarperCollins

12. Allen, C. (2003) Animal Consciousness. In *The Stanford Encyclopedia of Philosophy* (Zalta, E.N., ed.), (http://plato.stanford.edu/archives/sum2003/entries/consciousnessanimal/)

13. Sherman, P.W. *et al.* (1997) Recognition systems. In *Behavioural Ecology* (4th edn) (Krebs, J.R. and Davies, N.B., eds), pp. 69–96, Oxford University Press

14. Holmes, W.G. (2001) The development and function of nepotism. In *Handbook of Behavioral Neurobiology* (Vol. 13) (Blass, E., ed.), pp. 281–316, Plenum Press

15. Griffin, A.S. and West, S.A. (2003) Kin discrimination and the benefit of helping in cooperatively breeding vertebrates. *Science* 302, 634–636

16. Buchan, J.C. *et al.* (2003) True paternal care in a multi-male primate society. *Nature* 425, 179–181

17. Hauber, M.E. and Sherman, P.W. (2001) Self-referent phenotype matching: theoretical considerations and empirical evidence. *Trends Neurosci.* 24, 609–616

18. Darwin, C. (1871/1936) *The Descent of Man and Selection in Relation to Sex*, Random House

19. Hauser, M.D. *et al.* (2002) The faculty of language: what is it, who has it, and how did it evolve? *Science* 298, 1569–1579

20. Allen, C. and Bekoff, M. (1997) *Species of Mind*, MIT Press

21. Shettleworth, S.J. (1998) *Cognition, Evolution, and Behavior*, Oxford University Press

22. Bekoff, M. (2002) *Minding Animals: Awareness, Emotions, and Heart*, Oxford University Press

23. Gallup, G.G., Jr (1998) Self-awareness and the evolution of social intelligence. *Behav. Proc.* 42, 239–247

24. Pepperberg, I.M. (1999) *The Alex Studies: Cognitive and Communicative Abilities of Grey Parrots*, Harvard University Press

25. Gallup, G.G., Jr *et al.* (2002) The mirror test. In *The Cognitive Animal* (Bekoff, M. *et al.*, eds), pp. 325–333, MIT Press

26. Shumaker, R.W. and Swartz, K.B. (2002) When traditional methodologies fail: cognitive studies of great apes. In *The Cognitive Animal* (Bekoff, M. *et al.*, eds), pp. 335–343, MIT Press

27. Gallup, G.G., Jr (1998) Can animals empathize? Yes. *Sci. Am.* 9, 66–71

28. Heyes, C.M. (1994) Reflections on self-recognition in primates. *Anim. Behav.* 47, 909–919

29. de Veer, M.W. and van den Bos, R. (1999) A critical review of methodology and interpretation of mirror self-recognition research in nonhuman primates. *Anim. Behav.* 58, 459–468

30. Mateo, J.M. (2002) Kin recognition abilities and nepotism as a function of sociality. *Proc. R. Soc. Lond. Ser. B* 269, 721–727

31. Todrank, J. and Heth, G. (2003) Odor-genes covariance and genetic relatedness assessments: rethinking odor-based 'recognition' mechanisms in rodents. *Adv. Stud. Behav.* 32, 77–130

32. Wyatt, T.D. (2003) *Pheromones and Animal Behavior: Communicating by Smell and Taste*, Cambridge University Press

33. Keenan, J.P. *et al.* (2001) Self-recognition and the right hemisphere. *Nature* 409, 305

34. Damasio, A. (2001) Fundamental feelings. *Nature* 413, 781

35. Johnson, S.C. *et al.* (2002) Neural correlates of self-reflection. *Brain* 125, 1808–1814

36. Keenan, J.P. *et al.* (2000) Self-recognition and the right prefrontal cortex. *Trends Cogn. Sci.* 4, 338–344

37. Miles, H.L.W. (1994) Me Chantek: the development of self-awareness in a signing orangutan. In *Self-awareness in Animals and Humans: Developmental Perspectives* (Parker, S.T. *et al.*, eds), pp. 254–272, Cambridge University Press

38. Sherman, P.W. *et al.* (1995) The eusociality continuum. *Behav. Ecol.* 6, 102–108

39. Shellman-Reeve, J.S. (1997) The spectrum of eusociality in termites. In *The Evolution of Social Behavior in Insects and Arachnids* (Choe, J.C. and Crespi, B.J., eds), pp. 52–93, Cambridge University Press

40. Pusey, A.E. and Packer, C. (1997) The ecology of relationships. In *Behavioural Ecology* (4th edn) (Krebs, J.R. and Davies, N.B., eds), pp. 254–283, Oxford University Press

41. Sugiyama, L.S. *et al.* (2002) Cross-cultural evidence of cognitive adaptations for social exchange among the Shiwiar of Ecuadorian Amazonia. *Proc. Natl. Acad. Sci. U.S.A.* 99, 11537–11542

42. Sherman, P.W. (1991) Multiple mating and kin recognition by self-inspection. *Ethol. Sociobiol.* 12, 377–386

43. Petrie, M. *et al.* (1999) Peacocks lek with relatives even in the absence of social and environmental cues. *Nature* 401, 155–157

44. Hauber, M.E. and Sherman, P.W. (2003) Designing and interpreting tests of self-referent phenotype matching. *Anim. Cogn.* 6, 69–71

45. Mateo, J.M. and Johnston, R.E. (2000) Kin recognition and the 'armpit effect': evidence of self-referent phenotype matching. *Proc. R. Soc. Lond. Ser. B* 267, 695–700

46. Reeve, H.K. (1989) The evolution of conspecific acceptance thresholds. *Am. Nat.* 133, 407–435

47. Neff, B.D. and Sherman, P.W. (2002) Decision making and recognition mechanisms. *Proc. R. Soc. Lond. Ser. B* 269, 1435–1441

II.

THE SOCIAL BEHAVIOR OF DOGS AND COYOTES

THE ESSAYS IN PART II are concerned with various aspects of the social behavior and behavioral ecology of coyotes and dogs, apart from social play, which is the subject of the next section. They highlight the importance of comparative research, covering such topics as social organization and behavioral ecology, social communication, behavioral flexibility, the behavioral biology of feral dogs, scent marking, and the processes of domestication and feralization. Dogs are fascinating beasts on their own, independent of the wonderful traits which we impute to them. I have learned much from the dogs—Moses, Mishka, Sky, Inukpuk, Sasha, and Jethro—with whom I have shared my home, and I always love to recall John Allen Boone's lovely stories about his canine friend Strongheart, and John Muir's beautiful prose about his beloved dog-buddy Stickeen. Muir wrote: "Stickeen was more than just a clever dog, he was a messenger, a harbinger of good news about the natural world."

There are numerous examples of the close bonds that develop between dogs and people, and because of this, there are numerous opportunities to learn not just about dogs but about how their behavior is similar to and different from that of their wild relatives, and about ourselves. Dogs are relatively easy to study, and knowledge of their behavior can add to our enjoyment as we watch them romp about in our homes and at dog parks. We can also learn much about dog behavior by studying shelter dogs, a point well made in Leslie Irvine's book *If You Tame Me*.

My graduate work at Washington University focused on comparative aspects of behavioral development and detailed analyses of the dynamics of social play in various canids. I had longed to conduct field research, and when an opening for an ethologist became available at the University of Colorado in Boulder, I applied for the position and was hired in fall 1974.

Shortly thereafter I was fortunate enough to have two superb graduate students join me—Joel Berger and John Byers—who have gone on to enjoy stellar careers. Both Joel and John conducted fieldwork on various aspects of behavioral development and social organization in bighorn sheep and peccaries, and their field experiences kindled my desire to get out into the field.

In September 1977, I began a seven-year field project on the social behavior and ecology of coyotes (*Canis latrans*) who lived around Blacktail Butte in the Grand Teton National Park. The main focus at the start was on differences in behavioral development among individual coyote littermates and how these differences influence later patterns of social behavior, especially social play and aggression. The fieldwork in the Grand Tetons was absolutely wonderful, often tedious and frustrating but also incredibly rewarding in numerous ways.

My interest in coyotes also had a practical side, stemming from a wide variety of horrific techniques that were used to control—kill—them, methods that did not work then and still do not work. I wanted to try to bridge the gap between those "wildlifers" who wanted to control coyotes despite the lack of knowledge about their behavior and those who wanted to learn more about them from a more academic perspective that could have practical implications. In 1974, I organized a symposium on coyotes and later edited a book on their biology, behavior, and management. In the late 1970s, data were published that suggested that coyotes were major predators on livestock and other animals, but much of that information was not subjected to statistical analysis. Indeed, when I did some statistical analysis, it turned out that coyotes were not as devastating to livestock as were, for example, other predators and disease. Interestingly, my paper was accepted and then temporarily rejected for what I learned were political reasons. Some influential people weren't happy with what the statistical analyses showed.

COYOTES: TIRELESS TRICKSTERS, PROTEAN PREDATORS

The first essay in this section, "The Social Ecology of Coyotes," appeared as a cover story in *Scientific American*. In this paper, Mike Wells and I presented data that showed that the social organization of coyotes—whether they lived alone, with a mate, or in a pack that resembled a wolf pack—was influenced by the nature of their food supply, especially elk carrion. We also showed that for the most part, a coyote pack was an extended family of parents and young from various years.

Coyotes are genuine masters of behavioral flexibility. Talking about "the" coyote is misleading. The moment one begins making broad generalizations, one is proven wrong. Coyotes show great variation in their social organization. In some areas, coyotes live like typical gray wolves, in resident packs of four to eight individuals that are close-knit extended families consisting of overlapping generations of parents, the young of the year, and adult helpers who do not reproduce but could if they left the group. In other habitats, they live either as mated pairs or as roaming single individuals, showing little or no attachment to a particular site. During our study, we discovered that coyotes living as few as 1.5 kilometers apart showed variations in social organization.

In a nutshell, coyotes are quintessential and resourceful opportunists who defy profiling as individuals who predictably behave this way or that. Because of their slyness and behavioral flexibility, they are fascinating and challenging to study. Coyotes are a model animal for learning about adaptability and success by nonhuman individuals striving to make it in a human-dominated world. Coyotes, like Proteus the Greek, who could change his form at will and avoid capture, are truly protean predators. They are a success story, and perhaps hapless victims of their very success.

WHERE DID DOGS COME FROM?

I loved studying coyotes because of their uncanny ability to adapt to myriad different and highly variable situations. I also found myself becoming increasingly interested in the behavior of domestic dogs, in light of what my colleagues and I were learning about wild canids.

Though incredibly special to me, the dogs with whom I shared my home were just a few of more than hundreds of millions of dogs worldwide. We are surrounded by these amazing and lovable creatures. In 2001, there were about than sixty-eight million dogs in forty million households in the United States.

But where did dogs come from? There is a lot of interest in the origin of dogs among researchers and down-home dogophiles. It is well accepted that all dogs descended from gray wolves, but there is still some debate about precisely where and when dogs originated. Archeological and genetic evidence suggest that they appeared about twelve to fifteen thousand years ago, but other evidence suggests a more ancient origin, perhaps as long as a hundred thousand years ago. Early dogs were indistinguishable from small wolves, which is one reason they might not show up in the archeological record.

Peter Savolainen and his colleagues at the Department of Biotechnology at the Royal Institute of Technology in Stockholm, Sweden, searching with his colleagues for what he calls the "dog Eve," analyzed mitochondrial DNA (DNA from cellular structures called mitochondria that provide the power for life's processes) from the hair of 654 dogs representing all populations worldwide. They discovered a common origin for all populations of dogs, a single gene pool in East Asia (Thailand, Cambodia, Tibet, China, Japan, and Korea) about fifteen thousand years ago, but it is possible that dogs differentiated as many as forty thousand years ago.

Jennifer Leonard, working at the University of California in Los Angeles along with an international team of five colleagues, discovered that native American lineages of dogs originated from about five different lineages of dogs that accompanied humans across the Bering Strait in the late Pleistocene (the "ice age," about ten thousand years ago) as they colonized the New World. Ancient American and Eurasian domestic dogs share a common origin, Old World gray wolves. Ancient New World dogs are more similar to Old World dogs than they are to New World wolves. All in all, it is well accepted that dogs were domesticated in the Old World and brought to the New World.

Most modern breeds formed in the last two centuries. And although there is a lot of variability in behavior, size, color, coat, tail length, and ears, a recent study by Scandinavian researchers Kenth Svartberg and Björn Forkman on more than fifteen thousand dogs of 164 breeds showed that, despite individual and breed differences, dogs share five personality traits. These can be boiled down to playfulness, curiosity/fearlessness, chase proneness, sociability, and aggressiveness. Earlier research on wolves showed comparable results, suggesting that personality traits were little affected by domestication.

Dogs live in a wide variety of habitats, and they are able to adjust to novel situations by being flexible rather than locked into a single or a few modes of behaving. But is Fido smarter than Kitty, or not as smart as Jane Goodall's chimpanzee friend Fifi? This question can be misleading. As a biologist, I do not get much out of these comparisons, but I am interested in why some individuals of the same species are smarter—more adaptable—than others. I can put this question to rest by saying there is not a clear linear scale of intelligence on which it is easy to place some species above others. This is not to say that dogs are not smarter than mosquitoes, but I really do not know this for a fact, since mosquito intelligence has not been studied, and mosquitoes seem to fare quite well in their world.

Are Dogs Merely Dumbed-Down Wolves?

Dogs are domesticated animals. Domestication is an evolutionary process that involves varying degrees of human control, takes place over long periods of time, and involves genetic changes. It is important to emphasize that animals can be socialized but not domesticated—*domesticated* and *socialized* are not synonyms, because domestication does not take place during an individual's lifetime. Thus, the phrase "domesticated wolf" is misleading, although dogs are domesticated wolves, from an evolutionary perspective. Even a feral dog is a domesticated individual. Obviously, there are no genetic changes in an individual during the transition from the feral to the socialized state; however, it remains possible that over time and a significant period of reproductive isolation, genetic changes in a population of feral animals might occur.

People often wonder if dogs are dumbed-down wolves, because dogs have been domesticated and selectively bred (or "artificially selected," according to Charles Darwin) by humans for whatever traits we desired. But they are not. It is important to emphasize that there is a big difference between "being domesticated" and "being socialized." A tame wolf is not domesticated, but rather she is socialized to humans. Likewise, an unsocialized and aggressive dog is still a domesticated animal. Again, domestication is a long-term evolutionary process, whereas socialization occurs during the lifetime of an individual.

Domesticated dogs have retained various juvenile characteristics, an effect called *neoteny*. Such features include changes in head and body size, rounder foreheads that are more attractive to caregivers, smaller canine teeth, and drooping ears. Selection for more docile individuals has also changed dog behavior to be more infantile—dogs are usually more solicitous and deferential than are their wild relatives. While domestication has resulted in floppy ears, tails of all shapes and sizes, the loss of antipredatory responses, reduced head (around 20 percent) and brain size (about 10–15 percent, when dogs are compared to wolves of similar body size), and smaller teeth, the close association of dogs with humans has also had an effect on their ability to think. So, as it turns out, dogs can do things that wolves cannot. Wolves are impressive, but so are dogs.

Harvard University researcher Brian Hare and his colleagues conducted a series of experiments in Massachusetts and Germany to see if dogs and human-reared wolves could take cues from a human's gaze or pointing to locate food that was out of sight. Hare and his team performed what are called "ecologically relevant" experiments that take into account the dog's ecological niche, one that includes humans. Their results are very interesting and important. None of the seven wolves scored higher than chance could account for with any of the cues, but all seven dogs did. Furthermore, wolves who were raised by humans did not follow human signals, but young puppies who had little human contact did. Dogs could also follow the human eye and hand but would not follow the eye if it conflicted with the hand movement. Even great apes have trouble with this. Adam Miklosi and his colleagues discovered that dogs could learn to negotiate a detour faster if they watch a human do it first. They also learned that dogs could use their gaze to direct humans' attention to various aspects of dogs' environment. A nice two-way street it is, and it is not so surprising, given the close and enduring connections between dogs and people.

Now, this does not mean that dogs are necessarily or always smarter than wolves, but it does point out that domesticated animals are smart and can adapt to what they need to do to live in their human-dominated worlds. Dogs are constantly attending to human gazing and pointing, whereas wolves are not. Dogs have learned to understand us, and we have learned to understand them. Wolves have no need to develop these skills.

Dogs can also make tools. Lenny Frieling, whom I met at a meeting near Boulder, Colorado, told me that his dog, Grendel, made a tool so that she could scratch her back. Grendel, a small mutt who had a long torso and short legs, couldn't reach the center of her back to scratch it. When Frieling gave Grendel a cylindrical bone that had parallel flat sides, Grendel chewed one side of the bone so that it had raised ridges. She would place the bone on the floor, flat side down, and roll over onto the two raised ridges, using the protrusions to scratch the center of her back. What's very interesting is that Grendel did this with two different bones.

THE TRUTH ABOUT DOGS—OH, REALLY?

Of course, there are always killjoys. Stephen Budiansky, in his book *The Truth about Dogs* and in an op-ed essay in the *New York Times* in December 2002, tried to argue that dogs exploit their relationship with humans selfishly, that they "play us like accordions," and that they chose us during domestication and became master manipulators. Perhaps Budiansky should meet Jackie Tresize and ask this homeless man about his best friend, Champion (see the Introduction to this volume); Omar Eduardo Rivera, a blind man who was rescued from the seventy-first floor of the North Tower on 9/11 by his guide dog, Salty; prisoners who care for dogs; and the millions of other people who have enjoyed mutually cooperative relationships with dogs, have gotten much solace from them, and in turn offered them much comfort. Dogs are complex beings whose psyches and behavior are not easily understood or teased apart.

Budiansky also eschews anthropomorphism, but he uses it freely. He claims too that dogs most likely do not have a "theory of mind,... an ability to imagine what others are thinking, perceiving, and feeling." Instead, they are driven by having formed "fairly simple associations." Once again, no one has truly studied whether dogs have a theory of mind, and until we have sufficient data, we need to keep the door open to the possibility that they do, like other animals, especially some nonhuman primates. The data of Hare and his colleagues and my own data on social play (Part III) argue strongly against Budiansky's claim.

One of Budiansky's concerns is that dogs do not have language, or at least a humanlike language, and some people believe that an organism without language cannot be conscious. The criterion of language is extremely anthropocentric—very self-serving for humans who want to separate humans from other animals—and it can easily be used to deny dogs and all animals conscious thought. Dogs do not have a humanlike language, but they have their own sorts of complex communication systems and their own consciousness, which may or may not resemble human consciousness. Perhaps dogs have sound or odor representations or "pictures" in their minds, and while some of these mental activities might be incredibly foreign to us, they are no less real to the dogs, and our canine buddies do not need any language at all to make conscious decisions.

FERAL DOGS

Now that it is clear that we can learn much from studying dogs—as if you needed more convincing—I want to discuss various aspects of dog behavior, beginning with studies of the social biology of free-ranging dogs living in Ciudad Juarez, Mexico, and on the Navajo Reservation near the communities of Window Rock, Arizona, and Navajo, New Mexico. Tom Daniels, who had done extensive research on free-roaming dogs in Newark, New Jersey, was the perfect person to do this research.

In the second essay in Part II, "Population and Social Biology of Free-Ranging Domestic Dogs, *Canis familiaris*," Tom and I show that urban and rural dogs were less social than expected and that feral dogs usually lived in packs. A pack was defined as "a group of animals that traveled, rested, foraged, and hunted together." Little advantage was conferred on group-living dogs, because the scarce resources that were available could be more easily exploited by lone individuals. What was very significant about this research is that it showed that we need to be careful about making broad generalizations about the behavior of "dogs"—there is great variability in their behavior and social organization, as there is for many other animals, and trying to figure out why there is this variability is extremely challenging and begs for more detailed research. What is also clear is that we can earn much from studying dogs and that in many ways their behavior—how they respond to variations in food resources and exploitation by humans—is the same as that of their wild relatives.

WHY DO DOGS SCRATCH THE GROUND AFTER PEEING? IT'S MORE COMPLEX THAN IT SEEMS

Everyone who has watched dogs knows that not only do they like to urinate as they move around, but also on occasion they vigorously scratch the ground after they pee. I always wanted to know more about ground scratching, so I decided to study it and see if I could add some "hard data" to the discussion. As I report in the third essay of this section, "Ground Scratching by Male Domestic Dogs: A Composite Signal?" I discovered that ground scratching occurred more when there were other dogs around to see it, and that it likely is a visual signal that carries the message, "I just peed." Ground scratching might also serve to deposit scent from the interdigital glands in dog's paws and to indicate "There's pee here" with the visible slash it leaves on the ground. However, dogs also scratch the ground after they raise their leg but do not deposit any obvious urine (called *dry marking*), a sequence that calls attention to the idea that on some occasions dogs might want to deceive other dogs into thinking they just urinated. Thus, ground scratching is a composite signal that combines visual and chemical components and is more complex than it appears at first glance.

DON'T EAT YELLOW SNOW—MOVE IT!

It's a cold winter morning and I'm following my late companion dog, Jethro, on a snowy trail near my home outside Boulder, Colorado, eager for him to pee so I can scoop up the yellow snow to learn more about what he knows about himself and others. He readily complies, again and again. "Observations of Scent-Marking and Discriminating Self from Others by a Domestic Dog (*Canis familiaris*): Tales of Displaced Yellow Snow," the final essay in

Part II, reports on my discoveries on this day and throughout a five-year project that some have called weird, especially people who watched me follow Jethro and other dogs waiting for them to pee. I frankly thought it rather normal to begin my day by moving yellow snow to see how Jethro would respond to the olfactory symphonies emanating from it—a new-fashioned method by which to study what dogs think about and what they know. I discovered that Jethro discriminated his own urine from other dogs' urine and that while interest in his own urine waned over time, it remained constant for other dog's urine. Jethro also discriminated between the urine from males and that from non-estrus—out of heat—females. While some of these results are not surprising, there have been few experimental studies, and only one of free-roaming dogs, that have investigated questions about dogs' responses to their own and others' scents. In this case, some of our intuitions turned out to be correct, but there is more to the story. Clearly, we can learn much from living with and studying dogs. And it's a lot of fun to do so.

MARC BEKOFF AND MICHAEL C. WELLS

5   The Social Ecology of Coyotes

MOTION-PICTURE FILMS about the American West almost always depict coyotes in the same way, as solitary animals howling mournfully on the top of a distant hill. In reality, coyotes are protean creatures that display a wide range of behavior. They are characterized by highly variable modes of social organization, ranging from solitary (except for the breeding season) and transient individuals to gregarious and stable groups that may live in the same area over a long period of time. Between the two extremes are single individuals and mated pairs that tend to remain in one area. Indeed, a single coyote may in its lifetime experience all the different grades of sociality. This remarkable flexibility in the ways coyotes interact with one another can best be understood by examining their ecology, or the ways they interact with their environment.

It is generally accepted that most animal characteristics are the product of an interaction between inherited predispositions and the environment. In other words, although the cumulative passing of genes by successfully reproducing individuals establishes certain tendencies in each animal, many observable traits are subject to modification by proximate, or immediate, factors in the animal's environment. Thus many of an animal's traits, in particular behavioral ones, can be viewed as adaptations to the environments in which the animal has lived or is living. For example, the Dutch ethologist Hans Kruuk, who has done intensive studies of hyenas, has concluded that for many large carnivores, which typically have few predators (other than man), the nature of food resources is an important proximate factor that influences social behavior. More precisely, it appears that variations in the sociality of carnivores of the same species can often be traced to differences in their food supply.

For the past three years we have been observing the behavior of coyotes in the wild, mostly in Grand Teton National Park near the town of Jackson in northwestern Wyoming. Our studies indicate that the social organization of coyotes is indeed a reflection of their food resources and that three variables have a direct and significant impact in this regard: the size of the available prey, the prey's spatial distribution and its temporal, or seasonal, distribution. We shall report on our findings about both the specific behavioral adaptations coyotes seem to make to different types of food supply and the advantages these adaptations seem to confer. Before we undertake to sort out this aspect

Reprinted from Bekoff, M., and M. C. Wells. 1980. The Social Ecology of Coyotes. *Scientific American* 242, 130–148. Reprinted with permission. Copyright © 1980 by Scientific American, Inc. All rights reserved.

of the complex relation between coyotes and their environment we shall briefly describe the animals and the setting in which we are studying them.

COYOTES (*Canis latrans*) belong to the same mammalian family as jackals, foxes, wolves and domestic dogs. There are 19 recognized subspecies of coyotes, but because the animals are currently more mobile than they used to be and crossbreed to a greater extent there seems little reason to retain the more refined classification. Coyotes mate once a year and are generally monogamous, so that the same pair may mate in the same area over long periods, often returning to the same den site year after year. (Coyotes bear their young in holes in the ground, which they may or may not dig for themselves; the coyotes we observed generally made use of holes that had already been excavated by badgers.)

In a study of coyotes in the Canadian province of Alberta, Donald Bowen of the University of British Columbia noted that coyotes living in packs not only eat, sleep and travel in close association with one another but also tend to exhibit dominance relations. Franz J. Camenzind, who has studied coyotes on the National Elk Refuge adjoining the town of Jackson, has made similar observations. In general pack members are more sociable with one another than they are with outsiders, such as single coyotes living in the same area or passing through. It appears that most members of a coyote pack are genetically related. Indeed, the basis of coyote social structure is probably the mated pair supplemented by those offspring that do not leave the pack when they are old enough to care for themselves.

Typically only one male and one female breed in each pack. Some of the nonbreeding individuals may help to raise other members of the pack, most probably their younger siblings, and to defend food supplies, mainly against other coyotes. Packs may also include nonbreeding hangers-on, probably also offspring of the mated pair in the pack, that continue to live in the vicinity of the pack but interact very little with it. (It is possible that these individuals benefit from such a minimal association by "inheriting" a breeding area after a parent leaves it or dies.)

Coyotes are found in diverse habitats in Canada, Central America and most of the states of the continental U.S., but even within a single geographical setting their social behavior can vary dramatically. Our primary site for the long-term observation of wild coyotes is the area around Blacktail Butte in the southeastern corner of Grand Teton National Park. This is a particularly good place for a study of behavior and ecology because the animals that live in the park are relatively unaffected by man. Moreover, from Blacktail Butte, which rises some 300 meters from the surrounding valley floor, it is easy to observe coyotes going about their normal activities. Our findings for the Blacktail Butte area have been supplemented by observations of coyotes one of us (Bekoff) made with the aid of several students in Rocky Mountain National Park in Colorado. In the Moraine Park section of that park, where the study was carried out, the environmental conditions were quite different from those found at Blacktail Butte, and so in many cases comparing data from the two locations has helped us to identify variables influencing social behavior. We have also done experiments with animals in captivity, so that relevant competing variables could be more closely controlled.

For studies such as ours it is important to be able to identify various members of wild populations, but in the case of coyotes distinguishing characteristics such as size (ranging from eight to 20 kilograms for males) and coat color (a highly variable blend of white, gray, brown and rust) may change with time. As a result it has been necessary to capture and mark individual coyotes, and for this purpose we generally rely on foot traps, the jaws of which are wrapped with thick cotton padding to reduce the likelihood of injury to the trapped animal. To keep the coyote from thrashing around in the trap we frequently attach a tranquilizer pellet, which the animal usually swallows. The tranquilizer sedates the trapped coyote but does not render it unconscious. The trap lines are covered on foot, on skis or by automobile every six to eight hours so that the coyotes are restrained no longer than is necessary.

Once a coyote has been captured it becomes extremely docile, and so when we find a coyote in one of our traps, we immediately release it and then proceed to weigh it, note its sex, make an assessment of its physical condition and estimate its age. Next we attach a colored identification tag to each ear and fit it with a collar bearing a small radio transmitter. In this way after the coyote is released we can identify it even when it is out of sight, and we can always tell which coyotes are associating with one another. Because the area around Blacktail Butte is quite open, however, we are usually able to see the coyotes (with binoculars or a spotting telescope if not with the eye), and the radio transmitters serve primarily for the gathering of data on wide-ranging movements of individuals and groups.

THERE ARE MANY WAYS in which the nature of food resources might influence the social behavior of coyotes. For example, when large prey animals such as ungulates (hoofed mammals) are available, several carnivores (including lions, wolves, jackals and African wild dogs) have been seen to band together in packs for cooperative hunting. Pack living may also be an adaptation for the defense of major food supplies such as caches of carrion. The observations of David Macdonald of the Animal Behavior Research Group at the University of Oxford indicate that this is the case for golden jackals (*Canis aureus*) found in Israel. We have observed that for coyotes, at least in the conditions under which we are observing them, group hunting is a rare and generally unsuccessful undertaking. In fact, from our vantage on Blacktail Butte we have never seen either a group of coyotes or a single coyote attacking a large live ungulate. On the other hand, our findings and Bowen's indicate that coyotes do group together to defend certain food resources.

In the area around Blacktail Butte there is a significant seasonal fluctuation in the food items that sustain coyotes. In "summer" (the period from May through October) the coyotes feed mainly on rodents such as pocket gophers, field mice and Uinta ground squirrels. In "winter" (the period from November through April) the major food supply is the carrion of ungulates such as deer, moose and in particular elk that have died from causes other than coyote predation. To put it another way, in summer the coyotes hunt and kill small prey that are generally distributed widely over the area in which the coyotes live and in winter they feed on large dead prey (mainly elk) that because of the formation of herds and legal hunting by human beings during a limited season generally tend to be distributed as isolated clumps of carrion. The increased availability of carrion in winter is a widespread phenomenon, largely as a result of the higher ungulate mortality in that season.

Our basic hypotheses about the role that the size of food items and their spatial and seasonal distribution play in molding coyotes' social behavior suggest that it should be possible to see variations in the sociality not only of populations of coyotes with access to different food resources but also within a single population from season to season. To determine the effects of the seasonal fluctuation of prey at Blacktail Butte we compared the sizes of the coyote groups we found there in summer and in winter. Between September, 1977, and August, 1979, we made more than 1,000 sightings of 35 marked coyotes and about 15 unmarked ones and found that in the summer months, when rodents were the major food resource, the average group size was 1.3 individuals and that in winter the average rose to 1.8. Hence the availability of large, clumped prey items did seem to be correlated with heightened sociability in these coyotes.

Moreover, we made another interesting discovery when we compared our findings with Camenzind's for coyotes on the National Elk Refuge. Camenzind's observation site is only about seven kilometers from our own, but since many more elk winter there, the supply of ungulate carrion is larger and denser. Camenzind found that on the elk refuge the coyote groups were also larger, with an average group size of 1.6 individuals in summer and three in winter. This finding suggests that the increased availability of ungulate carrion in winter not only serves to increase sociability in that season but also may have a cumulative effect, resulting in increased gregariousness the following summer. It is also interesting to note that in the Moraine Park area of Rocky Mountain National Park, where for three successive winters there was virtually no ungulate carrion, the situation was quite different. The coyotes were forced to depend on small rodents throughout the year, and the average group size in both summer and winter was 1.1.

We also compared the frequency with which three coyote social groupings—single individuals, mated pairs and packs of three or more individuals—were sighted at the various observation areas over an entire year. For example, at Blacktail Butte 35 percent of our sightings were of packs and about 50 percent were of single individuals, either transients passing through an area occupied by a pack (or by a mated pair) or solitary coyotes living on the edges of the area. On the carrion-rich elk refuge, however, only about 15 percent of Camenzind's observations were of single coyotes and about 60 percent were of packs.

It would appear that in the vicinity of Blacktail Butte, where ungulate carrion is scarcer and is clumped in only a few small areas, fewer individuals can live in packs that defend these resources. The remaining coyotes, which are generally excluded from the clumped carrion, must forage widely for food, either alone or as a mated pair. This conclusion is supported by the fact that at the Rocky Mountain National Park site, where there was almost no carrion, 97 percent of the sightings were of single individuals.

IN ORDER TO GAIN a better understanding of the nature of coyote groupings and the advantages of the adaptation to defendable resources we did not have to cover a large area. Indeed, the observation over the past three years of two groups of coyotes with contiguous home ranges in the vicinity of Blacktail Butte has provided us with ample evidence of the ways in which food supply can influence social behavior. (An animal's home range is defined as the area it covers routinely in the course of its daily activities.)

For example, in the winter of 1978–79 there was a significant difference in the quantity of elk carrion found on the two home ranges. Completely by chance (no attempt was made to control the distribution of carrion in the Blacktail Butte area) Group A had about 17 percent of the available carrion and Group B about 83 percent. As might be expected, Group A was the smaller one, consisting from November, 1978, through April, 1979, of only a single mated pair. All the young of the pair from previous years had dispersed. In the same period Group B had four members: a mated pair, an adult male born to them in 1977 and a male yearling born to them in 1978. (The older nonbreeding male helped to raise its siblings born in 1978.) The group also included two female hangers-on, one that was born to the mated pair in 1978 and another that we believe was born to them in 1977; these individuals rarely interacted with the members of the pack but were allowed to remain in their vicinity. From November, 1978, through the following May (and beyond) the four main members of Group B were highly cohesive: eating, sleeping, traveling and defending carrion in close association with one another. In this period only 6 percent of the sightings of pack members were of single individuals and more than 50 percent were of all four pack members together. From November through April the male and female of Group A were observed together 71 percent of the time, and on the remaining occasions each animal was seen in the vicinity of other coyotes, although not in close association with them.

It has been observed that when coyotes other than a mated pair spend a winter together, there is an increased probability they will also spend the summer together. Our observations of the two groups in the area of Blacktail Butte indicate that when winter food is in good supply, older pups may continue to share at least a part of their parents' home range, and that if the pups remain in association with their parents throughout their first winter, there is a good chance that as yearlings they will remain through the following summer and perhaps beyond. It is interesting to note that two of the young that left the home range of Group *A* (the mated pair) in the fall of 1978 returned to it (from the National Elk Refuge, where they had spent the winter) the following spring, their return coinciding with the seasonal increase in rodents on the parental home range. These yearlings have remained solitary, not helping to raise their younger siblings, and in general they appear to be less closely bonded to their parents than the yearlings in Group *B*, which never left the pack.

During the past winter (1979–80) there has been another interesting development in the relation between food availability and social organization in the coyote groups living in the vicinity of Blacktail Butte. In the previous two winters heavy snows fell in our study area in December, but this year snow did not blanket the home ranges of Group *A* (the mated pair) and Group *B* (the pack) until late January. As a result rodents were available in greater number and for a longer period than they had been in the preceding winters, supplementing the usual winter supply of elk carrion. In the previous two winters all the young from Group *A* had dispersed by November, but this year a juvenile born in April, 1979, was still with its parents in February. (In Group *B* three juveniles born in April, 1979, still remained with the pack in February.) Thus it appears that a naturally occurring change in the coyotes' food resources resulted in a change in their social organization, at least over a short period of time. The consequences of this change will be investigated in the future.

SOCIAL BONDING is not the only aspect of coyotes' social behavior that is affected by variations in the food supply. Such variations also have a strong influence on how the animals make use of space. For the purposes of this discussion it is important to understand the distinction between a home range, the area an animal or a group of animals covers routinely in the course of its daily activities, and a territory. A home range has a flexible, undefended boundary, so that the home ranges of different individuals or groups may overlap considerably. A territory, on the other hand, is defined as the area that an individual or group occupies to the almost complete exclusion of other animals of the same species and that it will actively defend against them. In some geographical areas coyotes clearly defend their territory against other animals, but in other areas there is no evidence that they are territorial. Our own findings indicate it is only coyotes in packs that are territorial; individuals with a fixed home range but living alone or in mated pairs are not. Consider the two coyote groups we observed in the area of Blacktail Butte.

The four members of Group *B* maintained as a group a territory with rigorous boundaries between themselves and Group *A*, the mated pair. They also repelled many other coyotes from their territory, sometimes chasing an intruder for as much as two or three kilometers. (In April, 1979, we saw the breeding female of the pack chase an intruding coyote for a kilometer only a few days after she had given birth to a litter, and when she returned to the den, her mate chased the intruder for three more kilometers.) On the other hand, the two members of Group *A* were never seen defending a part of their home range against any other coyote. These findings, which are confirmed by those of other workers, indicate that the intensity with which an area is defended by individuals or groups is related to the presence of a large, clumped food resource.

We also found that a shortage of food clearly brings about increased trespassing into neighboring home ranges and territories, particularly those in which desired food items can be found. For example, although Group *A*, the mated pair, made frequent forays into the territory defended by Group *B*, no member of Group *B* was ever observed intruding onto the home range of Group *A*. In fact, the members of the pack rarely left their own territory, which is not surprising considering the wealth of ungulate carrion in it.

The sizes of coyotes' home ranges and territories vary markedly, although not consistently, with the locale, the season and the year and also with the age and the sex of the individuals. When we measured the home ranges of 10 adults in the Blacktail Butte area, we found that the average size was 21.1 square kilometers, with no discernible differences according to sex. When we classified the home-range sizes according to the coyotes' social groupings, however, we found that solitary individuals and mated pairs, which are excluded from carrion in winter, have a larger home range, with an average size of 30.1 square kilometers. Pack members, which defend a food resource in winter and tend to remain in their own territory, have an average home range of only 14.3 square kilometers. The sizes of pack members' home ranges also show considerably less variation, probably because of the clumped distribution of ungulate carrion.

PACK LIVING CONFERS advantages not only in the defense of food resources against competitors but also in reproductive activities. Coyotes generally mate in the period from January to April, the date varying from one locale to another. The female coyote's pregnancy rate, her productivity and her pups' rate of survival are clearly related to the general state of her health, which in turn is closely linked to the quantity and quality of the food available to her before and during pregnancy, that is, to the winter food supply. Therefore the increased ease with which pack members are often able to locate food items may represent an important reproductive advantage. Moreover, when we examined the amounts of time coyotes invest in other types of activity in winter and summer, we made an interesting discovery.

Coyotes typically are active in the early morning and early evening, but when we compared the time 50 coyotes (35 of them marked) devoted to hunting and resting, we found that in winter, when carrion is available but the food supply is usually low, much less time is spent hunting and considerably more is spent resting than is the case in summer, when small rodents are readily available but must be found, caught and killed. The higher ratio of resting time to hunting time may be generally beneficial for pregnant females, which must conserve energy for the nutritional demands placed on them during the nine-week gestation period and afterward. (There are six pups in an average coyote litter, and they are altricial, or dependent, at birth, requiring feeding and protection for the first few months of their life.) If females living in packs are able to spend more time resting than females living alone with their mate, then the pack-living females might reproduce more successfully. Moreover, as we have mentioned, females living in packs are more likely to receive help in raising their offspring.

Our findings about the pack-living adaptation of coyotes are supported by data gathered for golden jackals and hyenas, and we have been able to draw some general conclusions that should be tested with other species of carnivores. We have found that in situations where there are "haves" and "have-nots" with respect to the winter food supply (that is, individuals living in an area where a food resource is large and clumped as opposed to individuals living in one where the resource is scarce) the haves (1) are more social and cohesive than the have-nots, (2) are territorial and will defend the food resources, (3) have a more compressed home range, (4) are subject to higher rates of intrusion by members of the same species on the areas where the food is clumped and (5) in winter are able to travel less and so rest more. And the advantages of pack living can include any of the following: (1) food can be more successfully defended, particularly in winter; (2) food items can be more readily located; (3) individuals, particularly sexually mature females, can conserve energy needed for reproduction and care of the young; and (4) help, in the form of feeding and protection, can be provided for the young by individuals other than parents (most likely older siblings). Whether or not pack living confers an advantage in the acquisition of large prey remains an open question.

SO FAR WE HAVE MAINLY discussed the pack-living adaptation to defendable food resources, but solitary living is also an adaptation to a particular food resource. For the coyotes we observed from Blacktail Butte the resource is rodents: prey items that coyotes cannot defend against other coyotes and that are difficult to share except with pups. Our studies have shown that even coyotes living in cohesive groups become temporarily solitary when they are hunting rodents. Hence just as it is important to study the various patterns of behavior associated with the group defense of territory and food, so it is important to study the various patterns of behavior associated with solitary predation. Not much is known about how wild coyotes locate and capture prey, but we have done several experiments to throw some light on this type of behavior.

To begin with, the process by which any predator locates prey is complex, and different species of carnivores go about the task quite differently. Visual, auditory and olfactory stimuli are all clearly important and in nature probably interact to elicit the predator's response to the prey. It is interesting, however, to try to determine the relative importance of these three types of stimuli for coyotes and to try to relate such findings to the natural history of the species. The experiments required for the purpose are best done with captive coyotes, under conditions in which external stimuli can be rigorously controlled.

In the first set of experiments, conducted at Colorado State University in collaboration with Philip N. Lehner, coyotes were placed in a small room 30 meters square with a hidden rabbit. The time individual coyotes needed to find the rabbit with all possible combinations of the three types of stimuli was measured. Visual stimuli were suppressed by eliminating all light from the room (in which case the coyotes were tracked by means of infrared motion-picture photography), auditory stimuli by using a dead rabbit as prey and olfactory stimuli by either blowing a masking odor into the room (the odors from a rabbit colony) or by irrigating the coyote's nasal mucous membranes with a zinc sulfate solution.

The results of the experiments showed that when visual cues were present, the absence of auditory or olfactory ones led to only minor changes in the duration of the coyote's search for its prey. For example, with all three stimuli available the average search time was 4.4 seconds; with nothing but visual cues available the figure rose only to 5.6 seconds. With visual cues removed and only olfactory and auditory ones present, the average search time rose to about 36.1 seconds, or eight times the duration with all three types of stimuli. When auditory cues alone were present, the search time decreased slightly, to an average of 28.8 seconds; when olfactory cues alone were present, it went up to 81.1 seconds. With all three types of stimuli suppressed, it took the coyotes an average of 154.8 seconds, or more than 2.5 minutes, to find the prey by means of touch.

Thus under these experimental conditions the senses that facilitate the location of prey for the coyote are, in decreasing order of their importance, sight, hearing and smell. The fact that vision is of primary importance is confirmed by the results of another series of experiments in which coyotes were presented simultaneously with a hidden rabbit making sounds (breathing, rustling and so on) and a visible rabbit making no sound. The visible rabbits were without exception captured first. The coyote probably evolved on open plains covered with low-growing grasses, where prey would be highly visible, and its heavy reliance on vision is presumably the result of adaptation to this habitat.

In order to replicate the coyote's natural hunting environment more closely a similar set of experiments was run outdoors in a large fenced-in area (6,400 square meters) at the Maxwell Ranch, owned by Colorado State University. With the larger search area and the larger number of distracting factors outdoors the average search times were all higher, but once again vision proved to be the most important sense in locating prey. Here, however, smell proved to be more important than hearing: the coyotes could find the rabbits faster with visual and olfactory cues present (when they needed an average of 34.5 seconds) than with visual and auditory cues present (when they needed an average of 43.7 seconds). Similarly, with only olfactory stimuli present the coyotes took an average of 72.7 seconds to locate the prey, and with only auditory stimuli the average search time rose to 208.8 seconds. When all three types of stimuli were present, the average search time was 30.1 seconds; when all three were suppressed, the average rose to about 22.2 minutes.

The differences between the results of the indoor experiments and those of the outdoor ones can be explained by taking into account the effects of the wind. Airborne olfactory stimuli are clearly important directional cues to a hunting coyote, as is indicated by the fact that outdoors, where smell was more important than hearing, 83.9 percent (47 out of 56) of the approaches to the rabbit were made from the downwind side. Similarly, at our study site in Grand Teton National Park we found that 74.9 percent of all the approaches we observed to mice by wild coyotes were from the downwind side. In addition, in the outdoor experiments where only olfactory cues were available to the coyotes, a significant correlation was observed between wind velocity and approach distance, or the distance at which a hunting coyote becomes aware of the location of its prey. More precisely, as the wind velocity increased the approach distance increased as well, so that when the wind was 10 kilometers per hour, the approach distance was about two meters, whereas when the wind rose to 40 kilometers per hour, the approach distance increased to about five meters.

Hence although the coyote seems to depend most heavily on vision when it is hunting, it appears to have effective backup systems that can be relied on when certain types of sensory cues are absent or inadequate. When prey are visible, pursuit based on visual cues is most likely to start before olfactory or auditory cues can come into play, but when the prey is well hidden, the coyote probably relies on some combination of olfactory and auditory cues. (The exact combination probably depends on the wind conditions and the amount of noise made by the prey.) Coyotes are highly efficient predators and can clearly switch back and forth between these various hunting modes in order to take maximum advantage of whatever the environmental conditions are at the time.

How does the coyote actually kill the prey it locates? Information on the subject may be useful not only to biologists interested in the comparative and evolutionary aspects of predatory behavior but also to those concerned with the control and management of predators. Here it will be most convenient to distinguish between prey animals that are smaller than the coyote and those that are larger. (Coyotes do occasionally prey on large live animals, although as our observations of the coyotes in the area of Blacktail Butte indicate, this form of predation is rare.)

To begin with, we have observed seven distinct activities that can be included in the predatory behavior of a coyote when its prey is a small animal such as a rodent. In sequence they are long-distance searching (in which the coyote traverses large areas and scans the ground cover for a sign of prey), close searching (in which the coyote pokes around in the ground cover), orientation (in which the coyote assumes an alert posture, perhaps sniffing or pricking its ears to determine the exact location of detected prey), stalking (in which the coyote slowly and stealthily approaches its prey), pouncing (in which the coyote first rears up on its hind legs and then falls forward on its front legs to pin the prey to the ground), rushing (in which the coyote makes a rapid dash toward the prey) and finally killing. A coyote generally kills a rodent by biting it in the area of the head, and in many cases the coyote will also shake the prey vigorously from side to side.

It is important to understand that not all these activities are always included in a single predatory sequence. For example, we found that if the prey is a smaller rodent such as a field mouse, a coyote does not usually rush the rodent but simply stalks it and then pounces on it, pinning it to the ground so that a killing bite can be delivered. When the prey is a larger rodent such as a Uinta ground squirrel or a Richardson's ground squirrel, however, the coyotes we observed rushed it in more than 90 percent of the cases and pounced only rarely.

The success of the coyote's predatory sequences in catching and killing rodents varies considerably. Our data indicate that coyotes are successful between 10 and 50 percent of the time. We have not yet identified all the variables that influence the rate of success, but ground squirrels seem to be easier to catch than mice. The hunger level of a coyote may also be important. Observations in captivity reveal that satiated coyotes often play with a rodent before killing and eating it, and frequently the rodent escapes. Similar observations have been made in the field.

We also wondered whether the predatory skills of coyotes improve with age, and so we compared the time that nine young coyotes from three to six months old and 15 adults spent in the activities of searching, orienting and stalking when they were hunting mice or ground squirrels. The adults, it turned out, spent less time searching and orienting, and in addition the times adults devoted to these activities were much less variable than those of the pups. There was no difference in the time spent stalking, however, an activity to which coyotes in both age groups devoted an average of about 5.5 seconds. Therefore it would appear that the pups are less effective than the adults in locating their prey, but once the prey has been located coyotes in either age group will stalk briefly and then go in for the kill. Studies of coyotes in captivity also reveal that pups only 30 days old are capable of carrying out a successful predatory sequence on a mouse. In other words, although coyotes of that age rarely have an opportunity to kill a small rodent in the wild, they clearly have the ability.

Turning to the subject of how coyotes kill large wild prey, such as sheep, deer, elk and moose, there are for a number of reasons few observations from which useful generalizations can be drawn. To begin with, coyote kills are often indistinguishable from those of other wild predators or even domestic dogs. Moreover, it has been noted that most healthy ungulates living in the same locale as coyotes are able to defend themselves against a single coyote, so that instances of such predation are rare and hence difficult to observe. The few data that do exist indicate that two or more coyotes are usually required to take down, say, a healthy adult deer. In most cases coyotes appear to kill either young ungulates or weak ones, typically by attacking the head, neck, belly and rump. It is generally believed coyotes do not have any significant detrimental effect on wild ungulate populations.

THE EFFECTS OF COYOTE predation on domestic sheep are less clear-cut, which brings us to a more controversial aspect of coyote biology, namely the management and control of coyotes. Coyotes are said to have a significant detrimental effect on the sheep industry, and as a result for a century coyotes have been a particular target of predator-control programs. At present large amounts of time, energy and money (in many cases from public funds) are being devoted to such efforts. The returns on the investment are small, in terms both of reducing coyote populations and of preventing livestock losses and damage. The failure of the control and management programs is due essentially to the lack of sufficient background information on the behavioral and population dynamics of coyotes.

Indeed, very little is known about the predatory habits of wild coyotes with regard to domestic sheep. Guy Connolly and his colleagues at the United States Fish and Wildlife Service have found that even when coyotes are confined with sheep, their predatory behavior is surprisingly inefficient. In these experiments coyotes killed sheep in only 20 out of 38 encounters. Moreover, both the average time that elapsed before the coyotes attacked the sheep (47 minutes) and the average time that elapsed before the sheep were killed (13 minutes) were quite long, totaling an hour. The defensive behavior of the sheep deterred the coyotes in only 31.6 percent of the cases, and so it is understandable that the coyotes would take their time before killing the sheep. Of course, there are no instances of such inefficient predation in natural predator-prey interactions, where the prey either flees or actively fights off the predator as long as it can. It is clear, however, that sheep, which have been subjected to artificial selection by the great domesticator *Homo sapiens*, have been left virtually defenseless against predation.

Coyotes do kill sheep, then, as well as other livestock and poultry. Many studies have shown, however, that factors other than coyote predation can cause considerably heavier losses. For example, it was reported in a recent study that in the early 1970's the value of the losses of ewes and lambs in the state of Idaho amounted to $2,343,438. Of this total 36 percent could be attributed to disease, 30 percent to unspecified causes and 34 percent to predation; only 14.3 percent of the losses could be attributed to predation by coyotes. Moreover, there are data to indicate that not all coyotes are sheep killers and that the indiscriminate killing of coyotes in areas where sheep are being killed is an ineffective method of control. A recent study of livestock predation in 15 Western states issued by the Animal Damage Control Program of the Department of the Interior concluded that the relation between such predation and the population dynamics of coyotes is obscure.

In a sense the coyote is victimized by success: it is threatened because it takes advantage of livestock that have been robbed of most of their defenses by shortsighted practices of domestication. It is to be hoped that in the future defensive behavior will be bred back into livestock. For the present one can only assume that the failure of predation control is due to a lack of basic knowledge about predatory species, a problem that can be remedied by further studies of behavior and ecology of the kind we have described here.

WE HAVE FOUND the coyote to be a particularly good subject for such investigations. Further field study will be needed to determine to what extent our findings can be applied to other coyote populations, to closely related species and to carnivores in general. In the meantime coyotes should be appreciated as animals that have adapted remarkably well to the pressures exerted by their environment, including harassment by man and the severe restriction of their natural habitats.

Thomas J. Daniels and Marc Bekoff

6 Population and Social Biology of Free-Ranging Domestic Dogs, *Canis familiaris*

Social organization refers to the spatial relationships, group composition, and patterns of social interaction among individuals, and the overall manner in which these variables interact to characterize a population (Bekoff and Wells, 1986). Among carnivores, intraspecific variation in social organization often is a response to the quantity and distribution of local food resources (Bekoff et al., 1984), and the strategy for acquiring those resources (Caraco and Wolf, 1975; Nudds, 1978).

Few detailed data on the social organization of free-ranging domestic dogs (*Canis familiaris*), (those having unrestricted access to public property—Beck, 1973), have been reported (Beck, 1973; Daniels, 1983a, 1983b; Fox, 1978), and no comparative studies of populations in different habitats have been conducted previously. Likewise, factors that influence patterns of social behavior have remained largely unexamined despite the 10,000–14,000-year (Davis and Valla, 1978; Fox and Bekoff, 1975; Scott, 1967) association between dogs and humans. However, dogs provide an excellent model to study comparative aspects of canid ecology and behavioral plasticity (Daniels, 1987a); they are found in every terrestrial habitat in which humans reside and may be the most abundant extant land carnivore.

In this paper, we present data on survivorship patterns, population size and density, age structure, and sex ratios for urban, rural, and "wild" or feral dogs. In addition, we describe the social organization of three populations of free-ranging dogs and factors that influence it.

Materials and Methods

Dogs were observed between June 1983 and December 1984 on the Navajo reservation in the southwestern United States and in Ciudad (Cd.) Juarez, Chihuahua, Mexico. Three habitat types were selected: urban, rural, and wild. Urban sites were defined as areas with a human population density $\geq 386/km^2$ (U.S. Bureau of the Census, 1982). Urban dogs were studied in Cd. Juarez (1,200 m elev.), on the United States-Mexico border directly across the Rio Grande from El Paso, Texas. Cd. Juarez is the largest Mexican border city, with a human population approaching 1 million and an area of 4,854 km².

Reprinted from Daniels, T. J., and M. Bekoff. 1989. Population and Social Biology of Free-Ranging Domestic Dogs, *Canis familiaris*. *Journal of Mammalogy* 70, 754–762, by permission of Alliance Communications Group.

The city is located in the northernmost reaches of the Chihuahuan desert (Schmidt, 1979), with a mean annual precipitation of about 20 cm. Two study sites were selected in poorer sections of Cd. Juarez because of the high correlation between economically depressed areas and the occurrence of free-ranging dogs (Beck, 1973; Daniels, 1983a). Site 1 was 0.91 km² and site 2, about 12 km ESE of site 1, was 0.67 km².

Study sites in rural and wild areas were located on the Navajo reservation, a 64,750-km² area located primarily in Arizona, and extending into New Mexico and Utah. Rural sites were less populated and more isolated geographically (surrounded by broad expanses of sparsely inhabited land) than urban areas. Wild sites were uninhabited or sparsely inhabited by humans. Mean human density was 1.7/km² although most people lived at higher densities in the approximately 110 communities that compose the reservation. Field work was conducted in and near the communities of Window Rock, Arizona and Navajo, New Mexico, on the Arizona-New Mexico border. Reservation communities typically have ≤2,000 residents distributed among several small housing areas. Virtually every reservation community was rural in that it provided habitat intermediate between the urban and wild areas. Rural dogs came in contact with people at a greater rate than feral animals, although not as frequently as dogs in urban areas, and had access to more isolated areas free of human residents. Thus, rural dogs had resources available within the community and the potential to roam beyond community boundaries and to encounter wildlife and feral dogs.

Efforts to locate feral dogs were centered on a dump on the outskirts of Navajo, New Mexico. Dumps provided locally abundant food resources that attracted feral dogs (Daniels, 1988).

The reservation habitat is dominated by a mix of piñon pine (*Pinus edulis*) and Rocky Mountain juniper (*Juniperus scopulorum*) trees (Brown, 1982). Major subdominant shrub species were big sagebrush (*Artemisia tridentata*), cliffrose (*Cowania neomexicana*) and snakeweed (*Gutierrezia sarothrae*). Mean annual precipitation is between 25 and 50 cm, and the sites were at 1,500–2,300 m elevation. The numerous sandstone canyons may be 2.0–3.5 km long, bordered by walls reaching 30 m or more high. Natural depressions in these walls provided cave-like shelters that served as dens for litters of pups.

To estimate dog populations, the same route through a study site was traveled by auto for 5 mornings, when dogs were most active (Daniels, 1983a); every free-ranging dog within about 70 m of the vehicle was photographed. Descriptions of each dog were recorded on cassette tapes to complement the photographs. Photos of dogs taken on successive days were compared and the number of "recaptures" noted (Beck, 1973). This is a modification of Schnabel's (1938) technique that had the advantage of avoiding incidents of trap-shy and trap-prone animals. Further marking of dogs was unnecessary because of their distinctive coat colors and patterns. Confidence limits were calculated for the population estimates (Overton, 1971).

Feral dogs were censused by enumeration of all individuals observed during the study. The number of feral dogs reported is the minimum number present (Davis and Winstead, 1980). However, live trapping was conducted (Daniels and Bekoff, 1989) to fit several feral dogs with radio collars (AVM Instrument Co., Dublin, CA). Telemetry permitted estimation of home-range use (Daniels and Bekoff, 1989) and aided in locating uncollared animals. Sex of dogs generally was determined easily by observation of the animal and its behavior, especially patterns of urination (Bekoff, 1979).

Visual observation was used to distinguish pups (birth–4 months), juveniles (4 months–1 year), adults (1–7 years), and old adults (>7 years). Interviews of area residents were conducted as necessary to determine a dog's age, if it was owned. Age classification of feral dogs also was based on visual estimates of tooth wear (Gier, 1968; Kirk, 1977) when possible, and the animal's general appearance.

All occurrences of single dogs, pairs, or groups of three or more animals were recorded during daily auto surveys through study sites. Frequency data were compared to expected values in a zero-truncated Poisson distribution to determine if grouping patterns were random (Beck, 1973; Cohen, 1960). Details of statistical methods may be found in Beck (1973) and Daniels (1987a).

RESULTS

A population of 376 ± 53 (95% confidence interval) free-ranging dogs was estimated in Cd. Juarez study site 1, whereas 556 ± 70 free-ranging dogs were estimated in study site 2. Study site 1 was larger (0.91 km²) than site 2 (0.67 km²), thus the estimated density of dogs was 534 dogs/km² at site 1 and 936 dogs/km² at site 2.

Dog populations were estimated to be 228 ± 29 in the St. Michael's housing area of Window Rock, Arizona and 431 ± 56 in Navajo, New Mexico. Because of the disjunct pattern of small. concentrated housing areas surrounded by large expanses of uninhabited land, population estimates could not be extrapolated reliably to areas larger than the sampling area itself. However, the Window Rock sampling area was approximately 0.52 km², whereas the Navajo site measured 1.94 km². Thus, Window Rock supported approximately twice the density of free-ranging dogs as Navajo.

Population estimates based on mark-recapture techniques were not calculated for feral dogs because of problems associated with repetitive live trapping (e.g., trap shyness, trap proneness) and the difficulty of otherwise locating dogs. Enumeration of individuals indicated a minimum population of 12 dogs (three juveniles. nine adults), excluding pups, in the immediate vicinity of Navajo dump.

The frequency distribution of groups composed of 1, 2, or ≥3 dogs, when compared to a zero-truncated Poisson distribution (Beck, 1973), was significantly different from expected for both urban site 1 ($\chi^2 = 30.87$, $d.f. = 1$, $P < 0.001$) and site 2 ($\chi^2 = 29.59$, $d.f. = 1$, $P < 0.001$). There were more singles,

TABLE 6.1 Summary statistic of mean group sizes of domestic dogs for two rural and two urban sites.

Site	Group size (X)	Groups observed (n)	Variance	Sites compared	t
Window Rock	1.32	2,586	0.65	Window Rock–Cd. Juarez 1	–2.96*
Navajo	1.29	749	0.68	Navajo–Window Rock	–0.88
Cd. Juarez 1	1.24	1,596	0.78	Cd. Juarez 1–Cd. Juarez 2	5.19**
Cd. Juarez 2	1.10	2,517	0..61	Cd. Juarez 2–Window Rock	10.0**

The test statistic, t, is based on a test of means when variances are unequal.
* $P < 0.01$.
** $P < 0.001$.

fewer pairs, and slightly more large groups than expected at both sites. Overall, there was a stronger tendency for dogs to avoid conspecifics than to group. A total of 1,987 dogs in 1,596 groups resulted in a mean group size of 1.24 dogs at site 1, and 2,781 dogs in 2,517 groups resulted in mean group size of 1.10 dogs at site 2. The difference in mean size of groups was significant (Table 6.1) when compared using a test of means when variances were unequal (Sokal and Rohlf, 1981).

The frequency distribution of different-sized dog groups differed significantly from the expected zero-truncated Poisson for both Window Rock ($\chi^2 = 75.26$, $d.f. = 3$, $P < 0.001$) and Navajo ($\chi^2 = 104.58$, $d.f. = 3$, $P < 0.001$) populations, indicating that grouping patterns were not random. As with the urban population, dogs in the reservation communities were observed more frequently as singles, less often in pairs, and somewhat more frequently in large groups than expected.

Mean sizes of groups were 1.29 and 1.32 dogs for Navajo and Window Rock, respectively, and comparison of the means indicated that they were not significantly different (Table 6.1). Data from Window Rock thus were considered representative of rural dog populations on the reservation and were compared individually to each of the two urban sites. In both instances the mean size of groups was significantly larger for the rural population than for either urban site (Table 6.1), indicating a trend toward greater sociality on the reservation.

A pack was defined as a group of animals that traveled, rested, foraged, and hunted together. Although canid packs usually are groups of related individuals (Bekoff et al., 1984; Mech, 1970), the criterion of relatedness was not applied to dog groups because these data could not be collected. Most feral dogs were members of either the Canyon or Corral pack, designated by homesite location.

The Canyon pack consisted of a core of four adults. Adult membership occasionally varied, however, as transients ($n = 4$) joined the pack temporarily, remaining with them for 1 day to 1 week. The Corral pack consisted of a core of one adult female and a juvenile female; their relationship could not be determined. A third pack, consisting of two juvenile males and an adult female, was observed infrequently.

Pack composition changed in both the Corral and Canyon packs with parturition in late autumn (November 1983; Corral pack) and early winter (January 1984; Canyon pack). Two pups in the Corral pack were discovered when they were approximately 4 weeks old but litter size may have been higher at birth; domestic dogs typically produce six to 12 pups per breeding period (Palmer and Fowler, 1975). Ten pups were born in the Canyon pack and all were discovered in a sandstone cave along a canyon wall when 2–3 weeks old. However, subsequent capture of a female from the Canyon pack shortly after the pups were discovered, and observations of the dominant female in the pack, indicated that both were lactating. It is likely that the 10 pups actually composed two litters and that both females gave birth at nearly the same time; there was no discernible difference in age of the pups and all were being reared communally. Pups from both litters remained together into early summer 1984, when observations of surviving young ceased.

In addition to communal denning, feral dogs also may employ a strategy of pack splitting. Pack splitting refers to the temporary emigration from the pack of one or more individuals that travel and feed on their own (Burkholder, 1959; Jordan et al., 1967; Mech, 1966). Behavior data collected from two solitary females, neither of which moved far from established packs, strongly suggest that these dogs previously were part of the Corral and Canyon packs, respectively.

Both females reared their young apart from the packs for approximately 2 months after parturition, although regular contact between the females and other pack members was observed. At the end of this period, none of the three pups of the first female could be found (initial litter size was not known) and interactions of the female with the Corral pack increased, including joint foraging trips to the dump. Pups of the second female actively left the den-site cave by 10 February 1984, approximately 5 weeks after birth, and briefly interacted with the pups of the Canyon pack by 24 February 1984. The litters again separated as the solitary female and its pups moved farther up the canyon, away from the Canyon pack, in early March 1984. Subsequent observations indicated that the female had rejoined the pack fully by late May 1984 and traveled with it through the summer. A single observation of the female on 24 October 1984 indicated that it was still with the Canyon pack.

The distributions of different-aged dogs at urban sites 1 and 2 were not significantly different (Kolmogorov-Smirnov two-sample test, $D = 0.6$, $p > 0.05$); pups and juveniles each represented 7–9% of the population, adults composed 73–75% of the population, and old adults approximately 1.5–2.5% of the population. Individuals of unknown age accounted for approximately 7.5% of the total population in each site.

Age distributions of dogs surveyed ($n = 45$) in Window Rock and Navajo did not differ significantly from that at either Cd. Juarez site 1 (Kolmogorov-Smirnov two-sample test, $D = 0.2$, $P > 0.05$) or site 2 ($D = 0.2$, $P > 0.05$). The proportion of pups in the feral population ranged from none in September–October to approximately 70% ($n = 30$) in December–February. Only one (8.3%) old dog, a member of the Canyon pack, was observed during this study.

The relative success of feral dogs in maintaining population levels by reproduction remains undetermined. Weaning begins when pups are about 5 weeks old (Scott and Fuller, 1965) and by the age of 4 months juveniles essentially are independent. Juveniles then may disperse to another part of the home range of the pack, and much mortality probably occurs during this period of early independence. Dogs commonly disappeared even though they had been relatively easy to observe earlier. The initiation of pup independence coincided with an increase in pack movement (Daniels and Bekoff, 1989), and pups simply may have dispersed from the pack as it expanded its home range.

A difficulty in estimating mortality was that carcasses of dogs seldom were found, particularly if the animals had initiated movement away from den sites and no longer were restricted to small areas. In addition, golden eagles, *Aquila chrysaetos* ($n = 2$), coyotes ($n = 3$), common crows, *Corvus brachyrhynchos* ($n = 10$), ravens, *Corvus corax* ($n = 2$), and even other dogs ($n = 6$; Daniels, 1987b) were observed to feed on dog remains during the study. Thus, the likelihood of finding carcasses was reduced further.

Observations of 18 wild-born pups suggested that mortality was relatively high early in life. Three (17%) of the pups were known to have died and remains were recovered. Necropsy results indicated that one probably died of distemper, a common viral infection of young canids, but the cause of death could not be determined for two others. Both of these dogs had been dead for at least several days when the remains were recovered and further examination revealed little more. Only six (33%) pups were observed past 4 months of age, the age of independence. Of these, two sibling pairs remained together during the study and one pair was found in the company of an abandoned pup adopted (Daniels, 1987b) into the Canyon pack. The remaining pups were observed infrequently past 3 months of age and most, if not all, probably did not survive. Thus, the overall survival rate to 4 months of age was 34% for the litters of five females.

In Cd. Juarez, the sex ratio was estimated to be 1.6:1 in favor of males at site 1, and 2:1 in favor of males at site 2. On the reservation, males outnumbered females 4:1 in Window Rock and 3:1 in Navajo. In contrast, the sex ratio of the feral population living beyond the Navajo community borders favored females by about 3.5:1. The predominance of males in Navajo may have been maintained by removal of females from the community. However, there were few places to bring unwanted animals on the reservation and abandonment at dumps was a common practice. During this study, 54 dogs were known to have been abandoned. Abandoned dogs predominantly were pups (69%), and females outnumbered males two to one for those dogs for which sex could be determined.

DISCUSSION

Densities of free-ranging dogs in Cd. Juarez were 2–5 times greater than those reported in urban areas of the United States (ca. 232 dogs/km^2 in Baltimore, Maryland—Beck, 1973; ca. 154 dogs/km^2 in Newark, New Jersey—Daniels, 1983a). The high overall density of dogs in Cd. Juarez may partly reflect beliefs of owners that many dogs help provide adequate protection of family and property in areas with high crime rates (J. G. Rodríguez Torres, pers. comm.). Differences in the population density of dogs between the two sites in Cd. Juarez may reflect variations in density of human populations or the local crime rate at each site, rather than differences in reproduction. The absence of an effective dog control program that encompasses removal of free-ranging dogs from the streets, leash laws that restrict abilities of dogs to wander, and spay and neuter programs to limit reproduction may contribute to the high density of dogs.

By comparison, dog densities in the relatively small patches of housing within the rural communities of Window Rock and Navajo were nearly as high as those in Cd. Juarez. Furthermore, urban and rural dogs in this study were predominantly solitary. Data from urban dog populations in Baltimore, Maryland (Beck, 1973) and Newark, New Jersey (Daniels, 1983a) indicate the same general pattern of avoidance of conspecifics. Thus, similar factors may influence social organization in all of these sites. The net effect of such urban-like "islands" on the reservation was that rural dogs behaved much like dogs in an urban population (Daniels, 1986).

The inverse relationship between mean group size and population density at the Cd. Juarez sites suggests that dog density may influence the observed social system. Site 2 contained approximately twice as many dogs per unit area as site 1, indicating that as density increased, the tendency for positive social interactions within the population decreased.

The effects of population density on social behavior are well documented (Alexander, 1974; Crook, 1965; Eisenberg et al., 1972; Wilson, 1975; Wynne-Edwards, 1962), although population density alone is not the most significant proximate influence on social organization. Rather, the distribution of local shelter and food resources, and the magnitude and direction of change in those resources as population density changes, more precisely define social organization. Urban and rural dogs, for example, exhibited territorial behavior restricted to the homesite. Food also was provided at these sites by the owner, thus, homesites represented relatively small (approximately 600 m^2), easily defended areas of local resource abundance.

In addition, dogs probably were not as social as expected because little advantage was conferred on group-living animals. Scarce resources beyond those provided by human residents at both the urban and rural site would be exploited more efficiently by individuals than by larger groups (Beck, 1973). Further, individual differences in behavior among dogs largely accounted for the presence of those few groups that formed in urban areas (Daniels, 1983a).

Dogs that did not share the homesite with a conspecific, typically because the owner cared for and fed only one dog, spent little time engaged in social activities with conspecifics. Dogs that shared the homesite with one or more conspecifics were social most of the time, although predominantly with only a few individuals. Observed patterns of social organization at urban and rural sites, therefore, were based largely on dog-ownership practices.

Feral dogs were the most social of the three populations examined. Of the 12 juvenile and adult feral dogs known living near Navajo dump, nine (75%) lived in packs year-round and two (17%) others apparently were seasonal pack members.

Mechanisms of pack formation in feral dogs remain unclear. Two packs observed in this study were formed before initiation of field work, so factors influencing selection of pack members are not known. However, the nucleus of a new pack may consist of siblings that disperse together (Bekoff, 1977). For instance, the two male offspring of the Corral pack female formed a new pack with an older female near the natal den site of the males. Because nursing females often leave their pups for long periods between feedings, stronger social relationships develop among littermates than between offspring and parent (Scott and Fuller, 1965). Familiarity resulting from regular interactions between conspecifics that live in close proximity (Daniels, 1983a, 1983b, 1987a) may be a prerequisite to group formation because of the development of strong social bonds (Bekoff, 1977, 1981).

Pack composition (adult members) essentially was stable during the study. However, variations in pack size associated with the presence of dependent pups suggest that packs also may be maintained by assimilation of nondispersing young into the pack (Bekoff et al., 1984). Observations of the Canyon pack in late spring–early summer indicated that several pups >4 months of age were traveling with the pack. Further data are needed on the frequency of dispersal by juveniles and the role this has in determining pack size and stability.

There may be several advantages of pack living for feral dogs, including enhanced vigilance resulting in greater protection from potential predators (e.g. humans) and increased ability to gain access to higher-quality food resources (Daniels and Bekoff, 1989). However, pack living may at times be disadvantageous. Breeding by a second female in the pack might induce it to leave and establish a new homesite temporarily. In wolves (*Canis lupus*), for example, breeding generally is restricted to a single dominant female (Harrington et al., 1982: Mech, 1970), and pack splitting may reduce the burden of alloparental care on the pack. Pack splitting also may protect a subordinate female's pups from the threat of infanticide by the dominant female (Corbett, 1988; Macdonald, 1980; Van Lawick and Van Lawick-Goodall, 1971). Overt aggression by the dominant female might increase as parturition approaches. (e.g., in wolves— Fox, 1971), which could facilitate pack splitting. In this study, both females resumed living with their respective packs after pup rearing was complete (either because the young died or became independent), suggesting that the benefits of pack splitting were temporary. Presently, it is not understood why a second subordinate female in the Canyon pack reared its pups with those of the dominant female, whereas one female left to rear its pups alone.

The timing of reproduction is an important aspect of the biology of free-ranging dogs with respect to the number of breeding periods and the time of year breeding occurs. Dogs average breeding twice yearly but nondomestic canids have a single annual breeding cycle (Kleiman, 1968). Although only one litter was observed from each of four females in this study, a second litter by a female in the Corral pack indicates that feral dogs maintain two cycles per year. Although domestic dogs generally are thought not to exhibit seasonal patterns of breeding (Engle, 1946) because of artificial selection for faster reproductive rates, the relative synchrony of breeding among females suggests that breeding may be seasonal. Gipson (1972) also noticed an increase in breeding in spring and fall for dogs in Arkansas, though breeding occurred throughout the year. No pattern of seasonal breeding was noted for urban and rural populations, but further data are necessary to determine the degree of synchrony of breeding at specific times of the year.

Feral dogs differed in reproductive timing from coyotes (*Canis latrans*), their sympatric nondomestic congeners, which typically breed in January and February and give birth in March or April, about 63 days after fertilization (Kennelly, 1978). Feral dogs gave birth 2 months earlier, in midwinter, possibly contributing to early mortality of their pups.

In general, mortality early in life appears to be high in all three habitats. Although the proportion of adults in the Cd. Juarez population was high, the population appeared to be relatively young. Free-ranging dog populations in Baltimore, Maryland and St. Louis, Missouri also were young, with an average adult age of about 2.5 years (Beck, 1974) and a mortality rate estimated at 50% in the 1st year of life for the Baltimore population (Beck, 1973). This indicates a relatively high turnover rate, therefore, high mortality.

The likelihood of surviving to old age was low at both Cd. Juarez sites; only about 2% of the urban population was composed of old dogs. By comparison, populations of confined pets often have a higher mean age (Beck, 1973) reflecting lower early mortality. Thus, a free-ranging existence, despite a dog's ownership status, may reduce survival markedly.

Furthermore, the demands of gestation and lactation require that a breeding female increase its energy intake from 1.5 to 3 times the average nonbreeding rate (Gessaman, 1973; National Research Council, 1974). which may be difficult under conditions of scarce resources. A high density of dogs also increases the probability of disease transmission. Frequently lethal illnesses such as distemper and canine hepatitis (Carbyn, 1982; Choquette and Kuyt, 1974; Mongeau, 1961; Trainer and Knowlton, 1968) generally are contagious to conspecifics. Rabies, an important canid disease in Cd. Juarez (Rodríguez Torres, 1982), also may have a severe impact on pup survival (Chapman, 1978; Rausch, 1958). The relative importance of each of these factors and the roles they play in shaping social organization vary from one site to another and merit further investigation.

The sex ratio of the feral population differed markedly from those of the urban and rural populations. Sex ratios of dog populations in urban areas tend to be skewed for males. Beck (1973) found a ratio of 1.8:1 in favor of males in Baltimore, Maryland, and Daniels (1983a) reported a ratio of 3:1 in favor of males in each of three Newark, New Jersey study sites. Because most urban dogs are owned, the sex ratio probably results from selection of males as pets (Beck, 1973). Also, females may be removed selectively from the population during breeding periods to avoid unwanted matings and pups. Although the sex ratio may reflect higher mortality of females than males, this is unlikely in the absence of preferential treatment of males. A similar case may be made for the rural population observed in this study. Although male-biased sex ratios have been reported in several nondomestic canid species (Crespo, 1975; Egoscue, 1975; Mech, 1975; Storm et al., 1976; Trapp and Hallberg, 1975), the same factors (e.g. declining population in a saturated habitat, hunting pressure) are not at work on these dog populations.

The female-skewed sex ratio of feral dogs does not result from a bias in the production of female pups at birth, based on litters observed in this study. Likewise, there is no evidence of differential survival between sexes within a litter. Thus, an important source of feral dogs may be the abandonment of females in the vicinity of established packs. Although the probability of survival is low for abandoned animals (Daniels, 1987a), the continued addition of abandoned females to the area as a potential source of pack members may be critical to maintaining feral populations.

ACKNOWLEDGEMENTS

We thank R. Falco, A. Moore, and an anonymous reviewer for helpful comments on previous drafts of this paper. The help of E. Olson, Bureau of Indian Affairs, J. Antonio and the Navajo Fish and Wildlife Department, S. Linhart, U.S. Fish and Wildlife Service, J. G. Rodrguez Torres, Pan American Health Organization, and Drs. Rauda and Bernes of the Cd. Juarez Antirabies, all of whom provided logistical support, and R. Loken, Navajo Community College, who performed the necropsies, is gratefully acknowledged. This work was supported partially by National Science Foundation grants BNS 78-27616, BNS 79-23463, and BNS 79-05770 awarded to MB, and a University of Colorado Doctoral Research Fellowship, University of Colorado Graduate Student Foundation Fund Award, and a Sigma Xi Grant awarded to TJD.

LITERATURE CITED

Alexander, R. D. 1974. The evolution of social behavior. Ann. Rev. Ecol. Syst., 5:325–383.

Beck, A. M. 1973. The ecology of stray dogs: a study of free-ranging urban animals. York Press, Baltimore, 98 pp.

—. 1974. Ecology of unwanted and uncontrolled pets. Pp. 31–39, *in* Proceedings of the national conference on the ecology of the surplus dog and cat problem. Amer. Humane Assoc., Denver, Colorado, 128 pp.

Bekoff, M. 1977. Mammalian dispersal and the ontogeny of individual behavioral phenotypes. Amer. Nat., 111:715–732.

—. 1979. Scent-marking by free-ranging domestic dogs. Biol Behav., 4:123–139.

—. 1981. Mammalian sibling interactions: genes, facilitative environments, and the coefficient of familiarity. Pp. 307–346, *in* Parental care in mammals (D. J. Gubernick and P. H. Klopfer, eds.). Plenum Press, New York, 459 pp.

Bekoff, M., and M. C. Wells. 1986. Social ecology and behavior of coyotes. Adv. Study Behav., 16: 251–338.

Bekoff, M., T. J. Daniels, and J. L. Gittleman. 1984. Life history patterns and the comparative social ecology of carnivores. Ann. Rev. Ecol. Syst., 15:191–232.

Brown, D. E. 1982. Biotic communities of the American Southwest—United States and Mexico. Desert Plants, 4:1–342.

Burkholder, B. L. 1959. Movements and behavior of a wolf pack in Alaska. J. Wildl. Mgmt., 23:1–11.

Caraco, T., and L. L. Wolf. 1975. Ecological determinants of group sizes of foraging lions. Amer. Nat., 109:343–352.

Carbyn, L. N. 1982. Incidence of disease and its potential role in the population dynamics of wolves in Riding Mt. National Park, Manitoba. Pp. 106–116, *in* Wolves of the world: perspectives of behavior, ecology, and conservation (F. H. Harrington and P. C. Paquet, eds.). Noyes Publ., Park Ridge, New Jersey, 474 pp.

Chapman, R. C. 1978. Rabies: decimation of a wolf pack in arctic Alaska. Science, 201:365–367.

Choquette, L. P. E., and E. Kuyt. 1974. Serological indication of canine distemper and of infectious canine hepatitis in wolves (*Canis lupus* L.) in northern Canada. J. Wildl. Dis., 10:321–324.

Cohen, A. C. 1960. Estimating the parameters in a conditional Poisson distribution. Biometrics, 16: 203–211.

Corbett, L. K. 1988. Social dynamics of a captive dingo pack: population regulation by dominant female infanticide. Ethology, 78:177–198.

Crespo, J. A. 1975. Ecology of the Pampas gray fox and the large fox (Culpeo). Pp. 179–191, *in* The wild canids: their systematics, behavioral ecology, and evolution (M. W. Fox, ed.). Van Nostrand Reinhold and Co., New York, 508 pp.

Crook, J. H. 1965. The adaptive significance of avian social organization. Symp. Zool. Soc. London, 14:181–218.

Daniels, T. J. 1983*a*. The social organization of free-ranging urban dogs. I. Non-estrous social behavior. Appl. Anim. Ethol., 10:341–363.

—. 1983*b*. The social organization of free-ranging urban dogs. II. Estrous groups and the mating system. Appl. Anim. Ethol., 10:365–373.

—. 1986. A study of dog bites on the Navajo Reservation. Public Health Rept., 101:50–59.

—. 1987*a*. The social ecology and behavior of free-ranging dogs. Unpubl. Ph.D. dissert., Univ. Colorado, Boulder, 303 pp.

—. 1987*b*. Conspecific scavenging by a young domestic dog. J. Mamm., 68:416–418.

—. 1988. Down in the dumps. Nat. Hist., 97: 8–12.

Daniels, T. J., and M. Bekoff. 1989. Spatial and temporal resource use by feral and abandoned dogs. Ethology, 181:300–312.

Davis, D. E. and R. L. Winstead. 1980. Estimating the numbers of wildlife populations. Pp. 221–245, in Wildlife management techniques manual. Fourth ed. (S. D. Schemnitz, ed.). Wildl. Soc. Washington, D.C., 686 pp.

Davis, S. J., and F. R. Valla. 1978. Evidence for domestication of the dog 12,000 years ago in the Natufian of Israel. Nature. 276:608–610.

Egoscue, H. J. 1975. Population dynamics of the kit fox in western Utah. Bull. S. California Acad. Sci., 74:122–127.

Eisenberg, J. F., N. A. Muckenhirn, and R. Rudran. 1972. The relation between ecology and social structure in primates. Science, 176:863–874.

Engle, E. T. 1946. No seasonal breeding cycle in dogs. J. Mamm., 27:79–81.

Fox, M. W. 1971. Behaviour of wolves, dogs, and related canids. Harper and Row, New York, 220 pp.

—. 1978. The dog: its domestication and behavior. Garland Press, New York, 276 pp.

Fox, M. W., and M. Bekoff. 1975. The behavior of dogs. Pp. 370–409, in The behaviour of domestic animals. Third ed. (E. S. E. Hafez, ed.). Bailliere Tindall, London, 532 pp.

Gessaman, J. A. 1973. Methods of estimating the energy cost of free existence. Pp. 6–31, in Ecological energetics of homeotherms (J. A. Gessaman, ed.). Utah State Univ. Press, Logan, 567 pp.

Gier, H. 1968. Coyotes in Kansas. Kansas State Univ., Agric. Exp. Sta. Bull., 393:1–118.

Gipson, P. S. 1972. The taxonomy, reproductive biology, food habits, and range of wild Canis (Canidae) in Arkansas. Unpubl. Ph.D. dissert., Univ. Arkansas, Fayetteville, 196 pp.

Harrington, F. H., P. C. Paquet, J. Ryon, and J. C. Fentress. 1982. Monogamy in wolves: a review of the evidence. Pp. 209–222, in Wolves of the world: perspectives of behavior, ecology, and conservation (F. H. Harrington and P. C. Paquet, eds.). Noyes Publ., Park Ridge, New Jersey, 474 pp.

Jordan, P. A., P. C. Shelton, and D. L. Allen. 1967. Numbers, turnover, and social structure of the Isle Royale wolf population. Amer. Zool., 7:233–252.

Kennelly, J. J. 1978. Coyote reproduction. Pp. 73–93, in Coyotes: biology, behavior, and management (M. Bekoff. ed.). Academic Press, New York, 384 pp.

Kirk, R. W. 1977. Current veterinary therapy. Vol. VI: small animal practice. W. B. Saunders Co., Philadelphia, 1418 pp.

Kleiman, D. G. 1968. Reproduction in the Canidae. Internat. Zoo Yearb., 8:1–7.

MacDonald, D. W. 1980. Rabies and wildlife: a biologist's perspective. Oxford Univ. Press, New York, 151 pp.

Mech, L. D. 1966. The wolves of Isle Royale. U.S. Natl. Park. Serv. Fauna Ser., 7:1–210.

—. 1970. The wolf: the ecology and behavior of an endangered species. Nat. Hist. Press, New York, 384 pp.

—. 1975. Disproportionate sex ratios of wolf pups. J. Wildl. Mgmt., 39:737–740.

Mongeau, N. 1961. Hepatic distomatosis and infectious canine hepatitis in northern Manitoba. Canadian Vet. J., 2:33–38.

National Research Council. 1974. Nutrient requirements of dogs. Natl. Acad. Sci., Washington, D.C., 71 pp.

Nudds, T. D. 1978. Convergence of group size strategies by mammalian social carnivores. Amer. Nat., 112:957–960.

Overton, W. S. 1971. Estimating the numbers of animals in a wildlife population. Pp. 403–456, *in* Wildlife management techniques. Third ed. (R. H. Giles, Jr., ed.). Wildl. Soc., Washington, D.C., 623 pp.

Palmer, E. L., and H. S. Fowler. 1975. Fieldbook of natural history. McGraw-Hill Book Co., New York, 778 pp.

Rausch, R. L. 1958. Some observations on rabies in Alaska, with special reference to wild Canidae. J. Wildl. Mgmt., 22:246–260.

Rodrguez Torres, J. G. 1982. Rabies on Mexico's northern border, 1969–1980. Bull. Pan Amer. Health Organ., 16:111–116.

Schmidt, R. H., Jr. 1979. A climatic delineation of the real Chihuahuan desert. J. Arid Environ., 2:243–250.

Schnabel, Z. E. 1938. The estimation of the total fish population in a lake. Amer. Math. Monthly, 45:348–352.

Scott, J. P. 1967. The evolution of social behavior in dogs and wolves. Amer. Zool., 7:373–381.

Scott, J. P., and J. L. Fuller. 1965. Genetics and the social behavior of the dog. Univ. Chicago Press, Chicago, 468 pp.

Sokal, R. R., and F. J. Rohlf. 1981. Biometry: the principles and practice of statistics in biological research. Second ed. W. H. Freeman and Sons, San Francisco, 859 pp.

Storm, G. L., R. D. Andrews, R. L. Phillips, D. B. Siniff, and J. R. Tester. 1976. Morphology, reproduction, dispersal, and mortality of midwestern red fox populations. Wildl. Monogr., 49:1–82.

Trainer, D. O., and F. F. Knowlton. 1968. Serologic evidence of diseases in Texas coyotes. J. Wildl. Mgmt., 32:981–983.

Trapp, G., and D. L. Hallberg. 1975. Ecology of the gray fox (*Urocyon cinereoargenteus*): a review. Pp. 164–178, *in* The wild canids: their systematics, behavioral ecology, and evolution (M. W. Fox, ed.). Van Nostrand Reinhold and Co., New York, 508 pp.

U.S. Bureau of the Census. 1982. User's guide, parts A and B: 1980 census of the population and housing. U.S. Dept. Commerce, Washington, D.C., 143 pp.

Van Lawick, H., and J. Van Lawick-Goodall. 1971. Innocent killers. Houghton Mifflin Co., Boston, 222 pp.

Wilson, E. O. 1975. Sociobiology: the new synthesis. Harvard Univ. Press, Cambridge, Massachusetts, 697 pp.

Wynne-Edwards, V. C. 1962. Animal dispersion in relation to social behaviour. Oliver and Boyd, Edinburgh, Scotland, 653 pp.

7   Ground Scratching by Male Domestic Dogs

A Composite Signal?

WHILE MAMMALIAN SCENT marking and the significance of various chemical deposits (e.g., urine, feces, saliva, glandular secretions) in social communication has generated considerable interest (Birch, 1974; Eisenberg and Kleiman, 1972; Johnson, 1973; Müller-Schwarze and Mozell, 1977), much less emphasis has been placed on visual components of behaviors used to deposit scent. Hediger (1949) coined the term "demonstration marking" to refer to conspicuous marking behaviors that also might function as visual social displays. However, that a particular behavior associated with scent (urine) deposition also might have evolved to serve as a visual display has been demonstrated only once. In male domestic dogs (*Canis familiaris*), raised leg urination (RLU) (Peters and Mech, 1975) postures occurred in the absence of urine expulsion as a raised leg display (RLD) (Bekoff, 1979). Data were collected that support the idea that the raised leg posture might function as a visual display and that the motor patterns of leg lifting and urine expulsion were separate acts. Another aspect of scent marking sequences performed by a variety of mammals is ground scratching (GS), during which the individual slashes at the ground with one or more paws and usually leaves a visible sign (Bekoff, 1979; Peters and Mech, 1975; Seidensticker et al., 1973; Sprague and Anisko, 1973; von Uexküll and Sarris, 1931). Ground scratching might result in dispersing scent (von Uexküll and Sarris, 1931). However, scent dispersion does not seem to have played a significant role in the evolution of GS because the deposited substance (at least in dogs and wolves, *C. lupus*) rarely is hit directly (Bekoff, 1979; Peters and Mech, 1975). Additional scent from inter-digital glands may be deposited by GS (Ewer, 1973; Mykytowycz, 1972; Peters, 1974; Peters and Mech, 1975). Yet another function of GS may involve the visual, rather than the olfactory, aspects of the behavior. Two visual effects are possible: 1) visible scratches on the substrate may convey some message; 2) the act of GS might serve as visual display to other individuals who see it performed. Male dogs in the act of GS are frequently avoided by other dogs during and shortly thereafter, but a urine deposit (Bekoff, 1979; Scott, 1967) or a slash on the ground does not necessarily repel other individuals.

In the present study, the hypothesis that GS by male domestic dogs might serve as a visual display was tested. Specifically, I determined if GS was performed more frequently when it could be observed by other dogs.

Reprinted from Bekoff, M. 1979. Ground Scratching by Male Domestic Dogs: A Composite Signal? *Journal of Mammalogy* 60, 847–848, by permission of Alliance Communications Group.

Thirteen free-ranging, individually identified male dogs were observed either on the campus of Washington University (St. Louis, Missouri) or in the vicinity of Nederland, Colorado from 1971 to 1976. The frequencies of occurrence of marking by RLUs, the performance of the RLD (the dog assumed the RLU posture but no detectable urine was expelled), and simple urination (Bekoff, 1979; Kleiman, 1966) were noted as was the occurrence of GS either preceding, following, or in the absence of one of these behaviors. In addition, I noted whether other dogs (1) could be seen by the individual doing the GS and (2) could see the GS as well (the dogs clearly were in one another's visual field). This situation was referred to as "dog in sight." All data were recorded by hand or dictated directly into a cassette audio recorder and later transcribed.

Urine marking (n = 361), the RLD (n = 180), and simple elimination of urine (n = 251) occurred 792 times. GS occurred 121 times, 52 times after marking (14.4%), 30 times after the RLD (16.7%), and 39 times after simple elimination (15.5%). Sprague and Anisko (1973) also reported relatively low frequencies of GS in dogs. Females (n = 11) performed GS at approximately the same relative percentage as males (9.13%) but only 38 scratches were observed. There were no significant differences among the relative frequencies of occurrence of GS after RLU marking, RLD's, or simple urination ($\chi^2 = 0.54$, d.f. = 2, $P > 0.05$) (Snedecor, 1956:227). GS occurred only once before and three times in the absence of these behaviors. Dogs scratched only on grass or dirt. There was no relationship between GS and prior sniffing of the ground or of a known (to the observer) urine deposit. A 2×2 analysis indicated that GS was nonrandomly distributed when other dogs were in sight ($\chi^2 = 51.6$, d.f. = 1, $P < 0.001$). Of 121 times that GS occurred, dogs were in sight on 93 (76.9%) occasions and only in 28 (23.1%) instances dogs were not in sight ($t_s = 5.27$, $P < 0.001$) (Sokal and Rohlf, 1969:607). Also, when no other individuals were in sight dogs failed to scratch 393 (93.3%) of 421 times, significantly more often than they scratched ($t_s = 10.71$, $P < 0.001$).

These data suggest that GS by male dogs after RLU marking, RLD, or simple urination was influenced by the presence of other dogs. Because GS did not invariably follow these behaviors even in the presence of other dogs, it does not seem to be essential to convey the message "urine was just deposited." However, GS most likely conveys this information, because it rarely occurred before, or in the absence of, these behaviors. GS after the RLD might communicate an erroneous message, since no urine was deposited. However, scent from interdigital glands also might have been deposited and a visible slash produced.

Ground scratching may be viewed as a composite signal (Smith, 1977; Wickler, 1978) combining chemical and visual components that carry information over different distances at different speeds. For example, GS may serve to communicate immediately, over long distances, that urine was deposited, thereby extending the more limited range of the urine scent, the visible slash on the substrate, or scent from interdigital glands. GS may also be an intimidation display (Ewer, 1968). Visual aspects of scent deposition must be studied as well as the olfactory effects of various chemicals. In many species, selection for conspicuous marking behaviours that were not required for deposition of a particular scent (e.g., male canids urinate without performing the raised leg posture) is obvious (Hediger, 1949).

I thank A. Bekoff, J. Byers, D. Duvall, and V. Lipetz for comments on an earlier draft of this paper and all of the students who helped on this project. This study was supported in part by the Department of Biology at the University of Missouri (St. Louis), Washington University, and by the Department of EPO Biology at the University of Colorado. Additional support was provided by BRSG grants RR 07013–09, 10, and 11, awarded by the Biomedical Research Support Grant Program, Division of Research Resources, National Institutes of Health, to the University of Colorado (Boulder).

LITERATURE CITED

Bekoff, M. 1979, Scent marking by free ranging domestic dogs; olfactory and visual components. Biol. Behav., 4:123–139.

Birch, M. 1974. Pheromones. Elsevier, New York, 495 pp.

Eisenberg, J. F., and D. G. Kleiman. 1972. Olfactory communication in mammals. Ann. Rev. Ecol. Syst., 3:1–32.

Ewer, R. F. 1968. Ethology of mammals. Plenum Press, New York, 418 pp.

—. 1973. The carnivores. Cornell Univ. Press, Ithaca, New York, 494 pp.

Hediger, H. 1949. Saugetierterritorien und ihre Markierungen. Bilds. tot de Dierdke, 28:172–184.

Johnson, R. P. 1973. Scent marking in mammals. Anim. Behav., 21:521–535.

Kleiman, D. G. 1966. Scent marking in the Canidae. Symp. Zool. Soc. Lond., 18:167–177.

Müller-Schwarze, D., and M. M. Mozell. 1977. Chemical signals in vertebrates. Plenum Press, New York, 609 pp.

Mykytowycz, R. 1972. The behavioural role of the mammalian skin glands. Die Naturwiss., 59:133–139.

Peters, R. P. 1974. Wolf sign: scents and space in a wide-ranging predator. Unpubl. Ph.D. dissert., Univ. Michigan, Ann Arbor, 227 pp.

Peters, R. P., and L. D. Mech. 1975. Scentmarking in wolves. Amer. Sci., 63:628–637.

Scott, J. P. 1967. The evolution of social behavior in dogs and wolves. Amer. Zool., 7:373–381.

Seidensticker, J. C. IV, M. G. Hornocker, W. V. Wiles, and J. P. Messick. 1973. Mountain lion social organization in the Idaho primitive area. Wildl. Monogr., 35:1–60.

Smith, W. J. 1977. The behavior of communicating. Harvard Univ. Press, Cambridge, Massachusetts, 545 pp.

Snedecor, G. W. 1956. Statistical methods. Iowa State Univ. Press, Ames, 534 pp.

Sokal, R. R., and F. J. Rohlf. 1969. Biometry: the principles and practice of statistics in biological research. W. H. Freeman, San Francisco, California, 776 pp.

Sprague, R. H., and J. J. Anisko. 1973. Elimination patterns in the laboratory beagle. Behaviour, 47:257–267.

von Uexküll, J., and G. E. Sarris. 1931. Das dutfeld des Hundes. Z. Hundesforschung, 1:55–68.

Wickler, W. 1978. A special constraint on the evolution of composite signals. Z. Tierpsychol., 48:345–348.

8 Observations of Scent-Marking and Discriminating Self from Others by a Domestic Dog (*Canis familiaris*)

Tales of Displaced Yellow Snow

1. INTRODUCTION

Despite much interest in scent-marking by carnivores (Bekoff 1979a,b; Bekoff and Wells 1986; Gese and Ruff 1997; Allen et al. 1999 and references therein), there have been few experimental field studies of the phenomenon, and none such as the one described here in which clumps of urine-saturated snow ('yellow snow') were moved from one place to another to compare the responses of an individual to his own and other conspecific urine. Thus, little is known about urinating and marking behavior despite popular accounts that suggest otherwise, and there are few detailed field data concerning how free-ranging animals respond to their own and other conspecific urine.

The purpose of the present study was to investigate the role of urine in eliciting urinating and scent-marking in a male domestic dog, *Canis familiaris*, by using a new approach for free-ranging individuals (others have used 'yellow snow' experiments to investigate reproductive conditions and individual discrimination of urine in captive canids (Brown and Johnston 1983; Mech et al., 1987; McCleod et al., 1996)). Tinbergen (1951/1989) stressed the importance of conducting simple field experiments. Moving yellow snow from place-to-place falls into this category. This type of experiment can also be used for other animals, and would yield important data concerning individual discrimination of their own and others' scents and its influence on urinating, scent-marking, and territorial behavior.

2. METHODS

Data were collected from October to April 1995 and from October to April 1997–2000 between 06:00 and 09:00 when there was snow on the ground. Jethro, a 35 kg neutered male mix (predominantly German Shepherd and Rottweiler castrated at 9 months of age) who has never mated, was observed as he sniffed his own and other dogs' urine while he walked freely along a bicycle path paralleling Boulder Creek, just west of Boulder, Colorado (USA). Jethro was 5.5–10.5 years of age during the course of this experiment. Immediately after Jethro or other dogs (known males and females) urinated on

Reprinted from *Behavioural Processes* 55. Bekoff, M. Observations of Scent-Marking and Discriminating Self from Others by a Domestic Dog (*Canis familiaris*): Tales of Displaced Yellow Snow, 75–79, 2001, with permission from Elsevier.

snow, I scooped up the clump of yellow snow (about 4 cm × 4 cm) in gloved hands while Jethro was elsewhere and did not see me pick it up or move it. Before picking up urine the gloves were cleaned thoroughly using clean snow to minimize odor cues. I kept track of which other dogs were present and did not use the urine of the same dogs for at least 1 week, and Jethro had not previously sniffed the other dogs' urine during a given session. After being moved, yellow snow was matted by hand into other snow to minimize visual cues.

It was impossible to know whether all dogs were intact (not castrated), but when I was able to gather this information by observing males or by asking the human(s) accompanying the dogs I learned that all but three males and five females were neutered. The urine of two females in heat was not used.

Yellow snow was moved so that Jethro arrived at the displaced urine: (i) within about 10 s (about 5–10 m down trail) of my placing it down; (ii) 10–120 s later (usually 10–50 m down trail); or (iii) 120–300 s later (more than 50 m down the trail). These intervals were chosen arbitrarily and might have to be changed for different experimental conditions. I also recorded the duration of sniffing (less than or greater than 3 s) using a stopwatch, whether Jethro urinated over the displaced yellow snow using the typical male raised-leg urination (RLU) posture, and whether or not he sniffed and then immediately urinated over the displaced yellow snow using the RLU posture. Sniffing immediately followed by directing urine towards a target is generally referred to as 'scent-marking' (Wells and Bekoff, 1981).

Data were analyzed using proportions tests (Bruning and Kintz, 1977, p. 222ff) that generate the z statistic. I used $P < 0.05$ (two-tailed test: $Z_{crit} > 1.96$) to indicate significant differences between two percentages. The phrase 'no significant difference' or similar terms means that $Z < 1.96$ and $P > 0.05$. Critical values of Z for other levels of statistical significance are 2.58 ($P < 0.010$) and 3.30 ($P < 0.001$).

3. RESULTS

There were no differences in Jethro's behavior (the percentage of time he responded to different conditions) from year-to-year so data were pooled ($Z < 1.96$, $P = 0.05$). Data were also pooled for Jethro's responses to neutered and intact dogs for there were no differences in his response to the urine from dogs in either condition.

3.1. Jethro Arrived at Displaced Yellow Snow Within 10 s

For this situation, Jethro's urine was moved 57 times, that of other males 38 times, and that of females 49 times (Table 8.1). Jethro paid significantly less attention ($Z > 3.30$, $P < 0.001$) to his own displaced urine (89.5% of his sniffs were < 3 s) than he did to the displaced urine of other males (18.8% of his sniffs were < 3 s). There was no significant difference between the proportion of sniffs that lasted for fewer than 3 s that were directed to the urine of other males or to the urine of females. Jethro urinated over or sniffed and then

TABLE 8.1 A summary of the percentage of times in which Jethro sniffed his own ('own'), other males' ('males'), or females' ('females') displaced urine (yellow snow) for fewer than 3 s, urinated over it, or sniffed and immediately urinated (scent-marked) over it

	Sniff < 3 s			Urinate over			Sniff and urinate over		
Arrives[a]	Own	Males	Females	Own	Males	Females	Own	Males	Female
Less 10s	89.5	18.8	16.3	21.1	86.8	77.6	8.8	26.8	24.2
N	57	38	49						
10–120s	54.3	22.6	16.8	43.8	67.7	55.8	0	41.7	23.5
N	73	31	43						
120–150s	44.3	22.9	15.4	14.8	86.4	77.0	3.8	31.6	11.5
N	61	22	26						

[a] The times listed under the column labeled 'Arrives' refer to the length of time it took for Jethro to arrive at displaced urine.

immediately urinated over (scent-marked) his own displaced urine significantly less ($Z > 3.30$. $P < 0.001$) than he did in response to the urine of other males or females. There were no significant differences between his marking over the urine of other males or females.

3.2. Jethro Arrived at Displaced Yellow Snow 10–120 s Later

For this situation, Jethro's urine was moved 73 times, that of other males 31 times, and that of females 43 times. Jethro paid more attention to his own urine than he did when he arrived sooner (a significant decrease in the proportion of sniffs that lasted $Z > 3.30$. $P < 0.001$), but there were no differences in his response to the displaced urine of other males or that of females in this situation when compared to his arriving sooner. He urinated over or sniffed and then immediately urinated over (scent-marked) his own displaced urine significantly less ($Z > 3.30$. $P < 0.001$) than he did in the other two situations (there were no significant differences between his response to the urine of other males or females).

However, Jethro sniffed at and then immediately urinated over (scent-marked) the displaced urine of other males significantly more than he did the displaced urine of females ($Z > 3.30$, $P < 0.001$). Jethro never marked over his own urine in this situation.

3.3 Jethro Arrived at Displaced Yellow Snow Between 120 and 300 s Later

For this situation, Jethro's urine was moved 61 times, that of other males 22 times, and that of females 26 times. Jethro paid slightly more attention to his own urine than he did when he arrived at the displaced urine within 10–120 s. but he continued to pay less attention to his own displaced urine than to others' urine. There were no differences in his response to the displaced urine of other males or that of females in this situation when compared to his arriving sooner. Jethro's pattern of urinating over the displaced urine of other males or that of females was very similar to that observed when he arrived at the displaced urine within about 10 s. However, he sniffed at and then immediately urinated over (scent-marked) the displaced urine of other males significantly more than he did the displaced urine of females ($Z > 3.30$, $P < 0.001$) although he did so in both instances less than he did when he arrived at the displaced urine within 10–120 s. Jethro rarely marked over his own urine in this situation.

4. Discussion

Moving yellow snow from one place to another was a useful method for learning about Jethro's patterns of urinating and scent-marking and how they were influenced by the presence of his own or other dogs' urine. Whether intact males or females would respond similarly is not known. Although Jethro was the only dog whose response to displaced urine was analyzed, this study is the first of its kind for a free-ranging animal and provided answers to questions that have previously not been studied experimentally in canids or other carnivores. In their pilot study of individual discrimination of urine in captive dogs and wolves, Brown and Johnston (1983) did not investigate the response of an individual to her or his own urine.

4.1 Self and Others: Sniffing and Urination Patterns

It is not surprising that Jethro clearly discriminated his own urine from other dogs' urine. There were notable differences in his behavior following his arrival at displaced urine that were influenced by the latency of his arrival and whether the displaced urine was his, that of other males, or that of females. Jethro paid less attention to his own displaced urine than he did to displaced urine from other males or females. In their study of the response of captive 6–11-year-old uncastrated male beagles to urine from other males, Dunbar and Carmichael (1981) reported that they spent almost twice as much time sniffing the urine from colony males (mean=6.2 s) compared to their own urine (mean=3.5 s). When Jethro arrived at 'yellow snow' within 10 s. about 90% of his sniffs directed to his own urine lasted less than 3 s. Brown and Johnston (1983) reported much longer sniffing durations by captive female beagles (as long as 30–40 s) and captive male and female wolves to conspecific urine (mean=21 s to familiar urine and 46 s to unfamiliar urine). Sniffing durations of this magnitude were not observed in this study nor were they reported by Dunbar (1978) or Dunbar and Carmichael (1981) for the beagles they studied.

Jethro showed about the same amount of interest in displaced urine from other males and displaced urine from females as determined by sniffing duration. Jethro urinated over his own urine most frequently when he arrived at displaced yellow snow 10–120 s later. However, he urinated over the displaced urine from other males and that from females the least when he arrived within 10–120 s when compared to when he arrived within 10 or 120–300 s later.

Regardless of when he arrived at the displaced urine. Jethro urinated over others' urine significantly more than over his own. Although there were no statistically significant differences between the percentage of time that he urinated over the urine of other males and the urine of females, in all instances he urinated over other males' urine more frequently than females' urine.

4.2 Scent-Marking Behavior

The differences in Jethro's response to the displaced urine from other males or from females are worth noting, especially when considering scent-marking behavior. Scent-marking is differentiated from merely urinating by a number of criteria that include sniffing before urinating followed by directing the stream of urine at urine that is already known to be present or at another target (where there might be urine; Wells and Bekoff, 1981). The behavior pattern that best differentiated Jethro's response to the urine of other males from his response to the urine of females was marking: sniffing and immediately urinating over the yellow snow. When Jethro arrived at the displaced urine either within 10 or 120–300 s later, he sniffed and then immediately scent-marked the displaced urine significantly more when it was from other males than when it was from females. Dunbar (1978) reported that captive male beagles spent more time investigating female urine than male urine.

Of course, more data are needed for additional individuals. It is not known whether wild canids show these patterns, but it usually is assumed that males are more responsive to the urine of other males than to the urine of females especially during territory acquisition and maintenance (Wells and Bekoff 1981 and references therein). Although this is a pilot study, the method used can be applied as a model for other species and modified as needed. For example, the use of naive observers who did not know from which individuals urine was taken could remove possible biases (perhaps unconscious cues) due to information to which knowledgeable observers were privy. Nonetheless, future research that involves relocating urine-soaked snow or dirt, combined with detailed observations of sniffing, urinating, and marking sequences, will help to elucidate what stimulates other animals to urinate or to scent-mark. This information can help us learn more about such topics as territorial behavior and sex differences in territory acquisition and maintenance.

ACKNOWLEDGEMENTS

I thank Thomas Daniels, Carron Meaney, and two anonymous reviewers for comments on an ancestral version of this manuscript.

REFERENCES

Allen, J. J., Bekoff, M., Crabtree, R. L., 1999. An observational study of coyote (*Canis latrans*) scent-marking and territoriality in Yellowstone National Park. Ethology 105, 289–302.

Bekoff, M., 1979a. Ground scratching by male domestic dogs: a composite signal. J. Mammal. 60, 847–848.

Bekoff, M., 1979b. Scent-marking by free-ranging domestic dogs: olfactory and visual components. Biol. Behav. 4, 123–139.

Bekoff, M., Wells, M. C., 1986. Social ecology and behavior of coyotes. Adv. Study Behav. 16, 252–338.

Brown, D. S., Johnston, R. E., 1983. Individual discrimination on the basis of urine in dogs and wolves. In: Muller-Schwarze, D. (Ed.), Chemical Signals in Vertebrates 3. Plenum Press. New York, pp. 343–346.

Bruning, J. L., Kintz, B. L., 1977. Computational Handbook of Statistics. Scott, Foresman and Company. Glenview, Illinois, p. 308.

Dunbar, I., 1978. Olfactory preferences in dogs: the response of male and female beagles to conspecific urine. Bio. Behav. 3, 273–286.

Dunbar, I., Carmichael, M., 1981. The response of male dogs to urine from other males. Behav. Neural Bio. 31, 465–470.

Gese, E. M., Ruff, R. L., 1997. Scent-marking by coyotes, *Canis latrans*: the influence of social and ecological factors. Anim. Behav. 54, 1155–1166.

McCleod, P. J., Moger, W. H., Ryon. J., Gadbois, S., Fentress, J. C., 1996. The relation between urinary cortisol levels and social behavior in captive timber wolves. Canad. J. Zool. 74, 209–216.

Mech, L. D., Seal, U. S., Delgiudice, G. D., 1987. J. Wildl. Manage. 51, 10–13.

Tinbergen, N., 1951/1989. The Study of Instinct. Oxford University Press. New York, p. 228.

Wells, M. C., Bekoff. M., 1981. An observational study of scent-marking in coyotes. Anim. Behav. 29, 332–350.

III.

SOCIAL PLAY, SOCIAL DEVELOPMENT, AND SOCIAL COMMUNICATION: COOPERATION, FAIRNESS, AND WILD JUSTICE

IN PART II, we saw that dogs are extraordinary animals from whom we can learn much about comparative and evolutionary aspects of social behavior, social organization, and behavioral ecology. Dogs also are wonderful animals to study in our quest to learn more about the details and complexity of social play, as well as to develop a more complete understanding of, and appreciation for, fascinating topics such as cooperation, fairness, and morality—"wild justice," as I call it—to refer to the evolution of social rules of engagement and fairness and forgiveness.

Playing is about being fair, being nice, and minding manners. Social play is a foundation of fairness. I argue that we need to go beyond primates and study social carnivores who live in large extended family groups in which it is essential that the integrity and smooth functioning of the group is retained. I have been much influenced by the views of His Holiness the Dalai Lama on the importance of cooperation and compassion in our and another animal's daily interactions, and the ideas of the Russian anarchist Petr Kropotkin about the importance of cooperation in the evolution of behavior. The seminal research of the neurobiologist Antonio Damasio on the evolution of emotions and morality has also greatly influenced my thinking.

I often find myself wondering why some humans are so arrogant as to think that our behavior should be the standard against which the ethics of other animals is evaluated. A glimpse at the headlines of any major newspaper cautions us to carefully take stock of who we are and how we behave, with abundant humility and considerably less hubris. I'm reminded of a conversation between Groucho Marx (Firefly) and a Mr. Trentino in the movie *Duck Soup*.

> Firefly: Maybe you can suggest something. As a matter of fact, you do suggest something. To me you suggest a baboon.
> Trentino: What!
> Firefly: I'm sorry I said that. It isn't fair to the rest of the baboons.

As we go about celebrating our moral superiority, let's also remember to be fair to other animals.

THE FIRST PENGUIN: KEEPING OPEN MINDS

In this section, the central topics on which I concentrate are social play and social development. While I am not the first person to attempt to argue for a moral sense in animals, I often feel like that first penguin who jumps into the water while others wait to see if there are any predators around, an event I witnessed when I studied Adélie penguins in Antarctica. I say this not to toot my own horn but because I have endured some harsh criticism from colleagues who think that some of my ideas are outlandish. Nonetheless, in the spirit of science and scientism, which require an open mind as data are collected, I felt someone had to jump in and test ideas. Nothing is to be gained by impregnating science with preformed ideas and risking the loss of potentially fruitful ones. While science is not value free, we should try as hard as we can to lessen the impact of our own views of who we are and where we stand in comparison with other animals. As the papers in Part III show, studying play was not a waste of time.

In many of these papers, I discuss aspects of the evolution of social cooperation, fairness, forgiveness, and morality in the context of what animals *do* when they play and interact with others. Taking videos of the animals and then watching the tapes in slow motion or one frame at a time is very helpful for learning about the subtleties of social communication and for appreciating, for instance, how rapidly messages can be sent even when dogs are running here and there. To discern the details of what animals *do* when they play, my students and I have filmed animals playing and watched the videos countless times, finding something new almost every time we study the play sequences.

What Is Play?

One of my graduate students, John Byers, studied wild pigs (peccaries) while I studied various canids (members of the dog family, including domestic dogs, wolves, coyotes, jackals, and foxes). Like some other researchers, we discovered many features in common in the play of these (and other) mammals. Although a consensus on the definition of play has eluded researchers for many years, John and I defined social play as an activity directed toward another individual in which actions from other contexts are used in modified forms and in altered sequences. Some actions also are performed during play for a different length of time than when animals are not playing. Our definition centers on what animals do, or the structure of play.

When animals play, they use actions drawn from other activities such as predation (hunting), reproduction (mating), and aggression. Full-blown threatening and submitting only rarely, if ever, occur during play. Behavior patterns used in antipredatory behavior also show up in play. This is especially so in prey animals such as ungulates (deer, elk, moose, gazelles), who run about in unpredictable zigzag patterns during play. These actions change in form and intensity and combine in a wide variety of unpredictable sequences. For example, when polecats, coyotes, and American black bears bite in play fighting, they hold back as compared to biting in real fighting. This holding back is called *self-handicapping*. Play clawing in bears is also inhibited and less intense, and biting and clawing are directed to more parts of the body of another individual during play than during aggression. Play in bears also is nonvocal.

Play sequences may be more variable and less predictable because individuals are mixing actions from a number of different contexts. Because there are more actions for individuals to choose from, it is not surprising that sequences are more variable. "More variable" simply means that it is more difficult to predict which actions will follow one another during play than, for example, during predation or aggression. During play in dogs, coyotes, or wolves, one might see the following sequence: biting, chasing, wrestling, body slamming, wrestling, mouthing, chasing, lunging, biting, and wrestling, whereas during aggression one would be more likely to see threatening, chasing, lunging, attacking, biting, wrestling, and then one individual submitting to the other.

Because play is a hodge-podge of lots of different activities, it takes time to identify the details of what is happening. In my own studies, I can spend hours conducting frame-by-frame analyses of five minutes of play caught on video.

The Joys of Playing Cooperatively, Fairly, and with Forgiveness

It is clear that animals love to play. The drive to play is very powerful, and normal animals do not usually intentionally seek out activities they do not enjoy. Studies of brain chemistry—called *neurochemistry*—support the idea that play is pleasurable and fun. Most of this research has been done on rats, in whom Jaak Panksepp, at Bowling Green State University, discovered a close association between opiates and play—an increase in the activity of neurochemicals called *opioids* facilitates rats' playfulness; opioids may thus enhance pleasure and rewards associated with playing. (Panksepp also discovered that rats enjoy being tickled.) Following Darwin's ideas about evolutionary continuity, there's little reason to believe that the neurochemical basis of joy in dogs would differ substantially from that in rats, cats, chimpanzees, or humans.

Dogs are not the only animals relentless about seeking out play. Young cats, chimpanzees, foxes, bears, and rats love to play to exhaustion. When a potential playmate does not respond to a play invitation, these wired kids often turn to another individual or to their own tails. My companion-dog Jethro once whirled around so fast as he chased his tail that he fell over, spilling a glass of great merlot. Only then did his buddy Zeke get up and honor Jethro's request to play. The rhythm, dance, and spirit of animals at play are also incredibly contagious; just seeing animals playing can stimulate play in others.

Play is also a cooperative and voluntary activity. Individuals who do not want to play do not play. Individuals of different species fine-tune ongoing play sequences to maintain a play mood and to prevent play from escalating into real aggression. Detailed analyses of film show that in canids there are subtle and fleeting movements and rapid exchanges of eye contact that suggest that players are exchanging information on the run, from moment to moment, to make certain that everything is all right, that this is still play. Dogs and their wild relatives communicate with one another (and with us) using their face, eyes, ears, tail, body, and various gaits and vocalizations. They combine facial expressions and tail positions with different types of barks to produce a large number of detailed messages about what they want or how they feel. Dogs and wolves have more than a dozen facial expressions, a wide variety of tail positions, and numerous vocalizations, postures, and gaits, so the number of possible combinations of all of these modes of communication is staggering.

To sum up, it is premature to dismiss the possibility that social play has some role in the evolution of fairness and social morality, or that animals other than primates are unable intentionally to choose to behave fair because they lack the necessary cognitive skills or emotional capacities. We really have very little information that bears on these questions.

WHERE MIGHT HUMAN MORALITY COME FROM?
DO JETHRO, ZEKE, SUKI, FERD, AND JEROME
HOLD THE ANSWER?

> Jethro bounds toward Zeke, stops immediately in front of him, crouches on his forelimbs, wags his tail, barks, and immediately lunges at him, bites his scruff and shakes his head rapidly from side-to-side, works his way around to his back-side and mounts him, jumps off, does a rapid bow, lunges at his side and slams him with his hips, leaps up and bites his neck, and runs away. Zeke takes off in wild pursuit of Jethro and leaps on and off his back and bites his muzzle and then his scruff, and shakes his head rapidly from side to side. Suki bounds in and chases Jethro and Zeke and they all wrestle with one another. They part for a few minutes, sniffing here and there and resting. Then Jethro walks slowly over to Zeke, extends his paw toward Zeke's head, and nips at his ears. Zeke gets up and jumps on Jethro's back, bites him, and grasps him around his waist. They then fall to the ground and mouth wrestle. Then they chase one another and roll over and play. Suki decides to jump in, and the three of them frolic until they're exhausted. Never did their play escalate into aggression.

This description of dog play comes from some of my field notes taken on a clear and cool morning in August 1998. Jethro, Zeke, and Suki were at it again, and Parker and Izzy had not even arrived. I wanted to jump right in, wouldn't you? It is observations of animal play—the sheer joy of their wrestling, running about with abandon, and chasing one another while maintaining the rules of the game: "this is play"—that led me to ponder whether or not animals could be moral beings.

I recall with a smile that a few years ago one of my students, Josh, called and, between excited pants, told me this story in disbelief: "Hey, I saw the most amazing thing today at Mount Sanitas. Jerome [Josh's 120-pound malamute] wanted to play with a strange dog [named Ferd] who was about a quarter his size. Jerome bowed, barked, wagged his tail, rolled over on his back, leapt up, and bowed again, all to no avail—Ferd just stood there with surprising indifference. But about a minute later, while Jerome was sniffing a bush where a large mutt had just peed, Ferd strolled over and launched onto Jerome's neck and bit him hard and was sort of hanging in midair, legs off the ground. I thought, 'This is it, Jerome will kill this little monster.' And you know what? Jerome shrugged Ferd off like a fly on his back, turned around and bowed and then took the little guy's head into his mouth and gently mouthed him. They then played for about a half-hour, during which Jerome never ever was very assertive or unfair. He would bite Ferd softly, roll over and paw at his friend's face, swat him lightly, and then when things got rough and Ferd backed off with his tail down and cocking his head from side to side trying to figure out if he was a goner, Jerome would bow again and they would play some more. Jerome seemed to know that he had to be nice—fair—in order to play with his little buddy. Ferd knew what Jerome wanted, and Jerome knew what Ferd wanted, and they worked together to get it. Man, dogs are smart. I couldn't believe it."

Josh's story points to the evolution of fairness and social play, an idea that I have been pondering for years. And he isn't the only person to relate such a story to me.

All the essays in Part III raise big and challenging questions that have remained unanswered for many years. I have always emphasized how important it is to listen carefully to the stories that animals tell us about who they are and how and why they do the things they do. Now let me tell you why I have come to firmly believe that some animals can have a moral sense of right and wrong in certain social situations, and why studies of play are central to my ideas. To do this, I need to consider such "human virtues" as trust, apology, forgiveness, and honesty, and even the possibility that there are public sanctions for animals who breach a friend's trust. My musings have helped me wrap my views into a coherent package that brings together science and religion and asks such questions as, "Just where do humans fall in the great scheme of things, but specifically in the moral arena?" I ponder questions like this while keeping within the bounds of respectable science. I see my role as a scientist as putting ideas out there for discussion without removing my scientific hat, and I take my role seriously. While stepping onto thin ice can be risky, total risk aversion doesn't usually lead to novel discoveries.

To some people, the idea that animals can be moral beings is preposterous, bordering on blasphemy. Surely, they say, it is human morality that defines "human nature," and morality sets us apart from, and above, other animals. To propose that play is important in the evolution, development, and practice of morality adds fuel to the fire of this controversy, but I contend that animals can be moral beings in specific social situations such as play.

If we keep open minds, the idea of animal morality is not any more silly then the well-accepted idea that many animals are thinking and feeling beings. The naysayers are on the run, for as we have seen, their arguments ignore what we now know to be true for many different species. Surprises are always in store as we continue to learn about the intelligence and the cognitive and emotional capacities of animals. We need to be careful that our expectations do not lead us down the wrong path, especially in the absence of information.

But it is abundantly clear that we do not have to ascribe to animals far-fetched cognitive and emotional capacities to reach the conclusion that they can make moral decisions in certain situations. Neither should we deny that some cognitive and emotional capacities are well within their grasp. Our place in the grand scheme of beings is not at risk, and we do not have to worry that we're not special or unique. All animals are special and unique.

The study of animal play demands an interdisciplinary approach to make sense of why play develops and evolves as it does. These essays were chosen to present a general picture of social play, its possible functions, and the details of how animals communicate their intentions to play. Testable hypotheses (some of which have been confirmed in canids and other species) are offered for future investigation. All these essays show not only how my own and others' thinking about the importance of studying social play has evolved, but also that many fields of inquiry intersect in an analysis of play.

As I conducted my doctoral research on social play in infant dogs, coyotes, wolves, and wolf-dog hybrids, I became especially interested in how animals communicate their intentions to play—how they tell others, "I want to play with you." I wrote a review article titled "The Development of Social Interaction, Play, and Metacommunication in Mammals: An Ethological Perspective," whose main message centered on the importance of social play in behavioral development. The article analyzed why play evolved, that is, why it is an adaptive behavioral phenotype, and what functions it might serve; showed that there are close relationships between patterns of social play and patterns of social organization across species; and discussed the importance of "metacommunication"—communication about communication—(following Gregory Bateson's ideas) when individuals told others that they wanted to play with them. Little did I know that I would continue this line of research for more than three decades, that I would wind up working with philosophers on these topics, and that right now, in 2005, I am writing a book that deals with the same topics.

WHY PLAY? TRAINING FOR THE UNEXPECTED

One of the joys of studying play goes beyond the fun and the challenge of trying to figure out what animals are doing when the play—it is the joy of working with colleagues who are as passionate as I am to learn about a given topic. In the fall of 1998, my colleague Marek Spinka came from the Czech Republic to Boulder to study play with me. Marek had been studying play in pigs for many years and had also collaborated with Ruth Newberry at

Washington State University. Marek and Ruth chose to study pigs because pigs are not only very playful but also extremely intelligent, passionate, and sensitive.

Several answers have been proposed to the question, Why has play evolved, or why is play adaptive? Despite, in their play, risking injury and using energy that they might need for growth or to get food (these are called "costs of play"), many individuals, especially youngsters, persistently seek out play and play to exhaustion. What benefits might outweigh the costs of play? Evolutionary (or functional) explanations are often tied to analyses of what individuals do when they play. Although many researchers agree that play is important in the development of social skills, locomotor skills, or cognitive skills that support motor performance, solid evidence is scant and opinions are divided.

One important theme from recent comparative research is that play does not appear to serve only a single function across the diverse species in which individuals play. It serves different functions not only in individual species but also among animals who differ in age and sex. For example, play fighting was once considered important in learning fighting skills that would be used in adulthood or for physical training. While in some species, play may be important for the development of certain skills and physical aerobic and anaerobic training, in other species this might not be the case. Thus, play fighting does not appear to be important in the development of motor training for fighting skills in laboratory rats, but research has shown that play may be important in the development of motor training, cognitive/motor training, or other social skills in other mammals, including humans. Play also may serve a number of functions simultaneously, for example, socialization, exercise, practice, or cognitive development. Play is not a waste of time.

No matter what its functions may be, many researchers think that play is "brain food," because it provides important nourishment for brain growth and helps rewire the brain, increasing the connections between neurons in the cerebral cortex. A number of researchers have suggested that play hones cognitive skills, including logical reasoning and behavioral flexibility—the ability to make appropriate choices in changing and unpredictable environments. Marek, Ruth, and I suggested that play allows animals to develop flexible responses to unexpected events. Play increases the versatility of movement used to recover from sudden shocks such as a loss of balance and falling over and to enhance the ability of animals to cope emotionally with unexpected stressful situations. The jury is still out about why most animals play. But our theory about behavioral flexibility fits in nicely with my ideas about wild justice.

Play Begins with a Bow, and Then Something Happens

The first essay in Part III, "Social Communication in Canids," reports observations of the form and duration of play bows. Play bows appear to be highly stereotyped social signals, but no one had ever tried to measure them to determine just how stereotyped they are. I decided to do just that, and in the process I came to realize why no one had done it previously—viewing a movie or videotape one frame at a time to measure the body movements that are used in social signals is incredibly time-consuming. The data showed that play bows are indeed highly stereotyped in duration and form so that they message they send—"I want to play with you"—is an unambiguous and reliable indicator of an individual's intention and desire to play. Ethologists refer to play bows as fixed or modal action patterns that are ritualized signals, the evolution of which is driven by a need for clarity and reliability in social signaling.

In addition to demonstrating that play bows are highly ritualized signals, I was also interested in whether they were used strategically—that is, nonrandomly—during social play. To learn about the dynamics of play, it is essential to pay attention to the subtle details that are lost in superficial analyses. Dogs and other animals keep track of what is happening, so we need to do this also.

Perseverance and good eyesight paid off, and eighteen years after the first essay was published, I concluded that play bows were not used randomly but were placed (with care and intent) to communicate an intention to play when it was not clear that play was the name of the game. The dogs, coyotes, and wolves who used play bows had a purpose in mind. For example, biting accompanied by rapid side-to-side shaking of the head is performed during serious aggressive and predatory encounters and can easily be misinterpreted if its meaning is not modified by a bow. I was surprised to learn that bows are used not only at the very beginning of play to tell another dog, "I want to play with you," but also right before biting accompanied by rapid side-to-side head shaking as if to say, "I'm going to bite you hard, but it's still in play," and right after vigorous biting as if to say, "I'm sorry I just bit you so hard, but it was play." I concluded that bows serve as punctuation—exclamation points—to call attention to what the dog wants to tell her friend. Bows also reduce the likelihood of aggression in African wild dogs.

Dogs and their wild relatives rapidly learn how to play fair, and their response to play bows seems to be innate. There is little evidence that play signals are used to deceive others. Cheaters who bow and then attack are unlikely to be chosen as play partners and have difficulty getting others to play. There are sanctions, so if a dog doesn't want to play, she shouldn't bow.

You too can easily observe much of what I have been writing about. Visit your local dog park and watch play groups of dogs and how they go about having fun with their friends, how they dance in play. And join in! Get down on all fours and bow and lunge; there's no need for words, but maybe a bark will help. Dogs know what play signals given by humans mean. Nicola Rooney and her colleagues at the University of Southampton in the United Kingdom discovered that bowing and lunging by humans increased play in dogs, but that lunging was more effective. But be careful with dogs you do not know; some dogs are not very tolerant of unfamiliar humans who want to play with them and who get in their face without the proper introduction or greeting.

WILD JUSTICE AND FAIR PLAY: THE BIGGEST QUESTION OF THEM ALL

The second essay in Part III, "Virtuous Nature," lays out the general framework for the section's final essay, which in many ways tackles the biggest question of them all. My ideas result from more than three decades of trying to figure out why play has evolved as it has and whether the big-picture view places social play squarely in the center of the interdisciplinary arena in which questions about the evolution of morality are discussed by biologists, psychologists, anthropologists, theologians, and religious leaders. I have no doubt that by studying the details of what animals do when they engage in social play, we can learn much about the evolution of social morality; furthermore, recent data show that it does indeed feel good to be nice.

Explanations of social play rely on such notions as trusting, being nice, playing fair, forgiving, apologizing, and perhaps being just, behavioral attributes that underlie human social morality and moral agency. Dogs and other animals can be just—democratic—and honest. Recent research on nonhuman primates has shown that punishment and apology play important roles in cooperative interactions. Given what we know about play, I do not find this at all surprising. During play, animals need to cooperate with one another and play fair. Individuals have to trust that others will play by the rules and not cheat or try to beat them up after "telling" them that they want to play.

I believe that social morality—in this case, behaving fair, being nice, and minding one's manners—is an adaptation that is shared by many mammals. Behaving fair evolved because it helped young animals acquire social and other skills needed as they matured into adults. Without social play, individuals and social groups would lose out. Morality evolved because it is adaptive, because it helps animals, including humans, survive and thrive in particular environments. This idea might sound radical or outlandish, but there is no reason to assume that social morality is unique to humans. Uncooperative play is in fact impossible, an oxymoron, and so it is likely that natural selection weeds out cheaters, those who do not play by the accepted and negotiated rules.

Agree or not, I hope that my (and others') essays will change your views of animals (if they needed to be changed) so that informed debate will replace the arrogant and anthropocentric view that animals cannot possibly be moral beings and so have nothing to do with the roots of human morality.

9   Social Communication in Canids

Evidence for the Evolution of a Stereotyped Mammalian Display

DESPITE A HISTORY of considerable interest in animal social communication (*1–3*), few data are available on the "anatomy" or form of signals that are used. Indeed, one of the basic concepts of classical ethology, the "fixed" action pattern, rarely has been studied quantitatively (*4–7*). The form of visual displays has been studied quantitatively in invertebrates, lizards, and birds (*4–7*); however, there are very few data for mammalian displays (*8, 9*). In addition, little is known about the ontogeny of mammalian displays (*2, 8, 10*). Available evidence has demonstrated clearly that some social signals show phenotypic plasticity and that selection can shape various components (for example, duration, inter-act interval, form, sequence) of a signal or set of signals (*1–7, 11–13*). In cases in which it would be important to reduce ambiguity in the communicated message, selection could operate on signal structure (as with any other morphological structure) to reduce variability. Furthermore, it also is possible for certain signals to be restricted to specific contexts. Below I report the results of an analysis of a specific canid "play invitation" signal, the bow (*14, 15*), that shows marked stereotypy both in duration and form.

The bow is an easily recognized canid social display. When performing this motor act, the animal crouches on its forelimbs and remains standing on its hind legs. The bow is infrequently observed outside the context of play (*15*). The bows of the following groups of animals were analyzed: 12 infant coyotes, *Canis latrans*; 4 infant wolves, *C. lupus*; 4 infant wolf-malamute hybrids; 13 infant beagles, *C. familiaris*; and 16 free-ranging domestic dogs over 1 year of age (age verified by owners). Infants were observed from about 20 to 90 days of age in a variety of situations. Some of the infants were hand-reared, and periods of social interaction with conspecific age-mates were limited only to times when observers were present. For these infants, it was possible to record the first occurrence of the bow during social interaction. Other infants were mother-reared in semi-natural conditions, and observations commenced when they emerged from the den that their mother had dug or from the den box that I provided. The free-ranging dogs were observed on the campus of Washington University (St. Louis, Missouri) and in and around Nederland, Colorado.

Reprinted with permission from Bekoff, M. 1977. Social Communication in Canids: Empirical Studies of the Evidence for the Evolution of a Stereotyped Function of Play Bows Mammalian Display. *Science* 197, 1097–1099. Copyright 1977 AAAS.

Animals were photographed with a super-8 or 16-mm movie camera (film speed, 64 frames per second). Films were analyzed with a single-frame analyzer. Camera speed was checked prior to each analysis to correct for possible error. Both duration and form were measured for bows that occurred in the beginning of a sequence (that is, the first act) and during a sequence. Duration was measured by counting the number of frames during which the individual remained crouched. The number of frames was then multiplied by 0.0156 second (= 1 frame) to convert to a measure of time. Means, standard deviations, and coefficients of variation were then calculated. Form was measured as declination of the shoulders relative to standing height on a grid system. In order to standardize for individual differences in size as well as for changes in size with age, the height of the body at the shoulders was divided by 10, and a grid system of ten equal segments was used. Each grid unit was divided into fourths. Two observers independently took measures for each data point, and measurements were taken only when vertical displacement of the shoulders could be observed unambiguously. Interobserver agreement was consistently between 90 and 95 percent. For each group of animals, data from different rearing conditions were lumped because *no* significant differences were detected. In addition, data for the wolves and wolf-malamute hybrids were combined because the two groups were indistinguishable.

The mean duration of bows performed at the beginning of sequences for the infant coyotes, wolves (and hybrids), beagles, and adult free-ranging dogs was 0.31, 0.38, 0.33, and 0.32 second, respectively. Only the wolves differed significantly from the other groups ($F = 2.93$, d.f. = 3,436, $P < .05$). Mean duration of bows performed during play bouts was on the average 0.03 to 0.07 second shorter than mean duration of bows at the beginning of play sequences, and there were no significant differences between the groups, although the bows performed by the wolves were slightly longer. The longer duration of the wolf bows may simply be due to the greater body weight of young wolves when compared to coyotes and beagles of the same age (*16*). For coyotes, beagles, and adult dogs, bows performed during an interaction showed significantly higher variability in duration than bows performed at the beginning of sequences (Table 9.1). The greater variation in duration for bows performed during a sequence can be explained by the fact that these bows were preceded by a variety of different acts from which the individual went into the bow. On the other hand, the bows that occurred at the beginning of sequences almost always took place after the individual had been standing upright for a few seconds or as part of an approach.

All groups showed significantly less variability ["c" statistic (*17*), $P < .02$] in form when compared to duration. Furthermore, there were no significant differences in form between bows performed at the beginning of and during sequences, although in all cases bows performed during sequences were slightly more variable.

In addition to there being a high degree of stereotypy, especially in the form of the bow, it is important to stress two other findings: (i) there were no

TABLE 9.1 The variability, expressed as the coefficient of variation (%), of bows performed at the beginning of and during play bouts by three canid species. Form was measured on a grid system (see text). The number on the left of the slash (/) refers to bows that were performed at the beginning of play bouts, and the number on the right of the slash refers to bows that were performed during an on-going interaction. The differences between the coefficients of variation for bows per-formed at the beginning of and during play bouts were tested for statistical signifi-cance by using the "c" statistic (17); see footnotes. The bows performed by the infant coyotes showed significantly less variability in form than those performed by the other groups. For example, when the bows of the coyotes were compared with those of the wolves, the differences were highly significant (for bows performed at the beginning of a bout, c = 3.46, d.f. = 169, P < .001; for bows performed during a bout, c = 3.04, d.f. = 119, P <.01). The significance of play signals for highly aggres-sive infant coyotes when compared with less aggressive infant wolves and beagles is discussed in (15) and (23).

		Coefficient of variation (%)	
Species	Number of bows	Duration of bows	Form of bows
Coyotes ($N = 12$)	73/57	9.68/13.79*	5.49/6.55†
Wolves + wolf-dog hybrids ($N = 8$)	98/64	10.53/11.43†	8.02/9.77†
Beagles ($N = 13$)	116/81	15.15/18.75\?\	9.71/10.57†
Adult dogs ($N = 16$)	153/114	21.87/28.13§	10.87/12.70†

*c = 2.70, d.f. = 128, P < .01. \?\c = 2.20, d.f. = 195, P < .05, §c = 2.79, d.f. = 265, P < .01.

significant changes in the variability of bows performed by infants of differ-ent ages (18), and (ii) the first bows performed by individuals who had been hand-reared (19), and who had not previously interacted with another indi-vidual or seen a bow, did not differ either from subsequent bows performed by that "isolate" or from the first observed bows performed by individuals who had been group-reared. The observed stereotypy when coupled to these obser-vations (and also to the lack of differences between older animals reared in different conditions) provides evidence that there is a strong genetic compo-nent underlying this behavioral pattern.

The data presented herein are the first (to my knowledge) of their kind for a mammalian display. When compared to data on invertebrates and other ver-tebrates (5–7, 13), the bow is seen to be an equally stereotyped display, even for the adult free-ranging dogs. That is, the bow is a "relatively fixed" or "modal" action pattern (4, 5). Indeed, there have been no analyses of signal form that have resulted in coefficients of variation equal, or nearly equal, to zero, and the implication of absolute (invariant) morphological rigidity in the term "fixed action pattern" is misleading (4–7) and apparently was not intended when the term was coined (20).

It has been suggested that the most stereotyped motor coordinations are those that are important in locomotion and communication (7, 13). The bow is a locomotor intention movement which also has signal value. Many factors may select for stereotypy in signal form. Certainly, anatomical constraints may be operating (9, 21). In addition, if one analyzes the situations in which bows (and other play signals in other species) are used (15, 22–24), it is entirely plausible that the signal value of the bow was increased via selection for stereotypy. When animals engage in social play, actions from different contexts [for example, sexual, predatory, aggressive (14, 15, 22–24)] are used. If play signals, such as the bow, are important in communicating play intention [that is, announcing that "what follows is play" (14, 15, 22–24)] and overriding the "meaning" of an aggressive signal (23), for example, then one would expect the play signal to be different from other types of signals and to be stereotyped so as to reduce ambiguity in meaning. Furthermore, there can also be a reduction in the number of contexts in which a signal is used (2, 12). In many mammals, signals that appear to function in the communication of play intent (i) are observed almost solely in the context of play (15, 22–24), (ii) are different from other types of social signals (22–24), and (iii) *appear* to be highly stereotyped. With respect to the canid play bow, these three criteria apply fully. In addition, it has been demonstrated in coyotes and other infant canids that signals that are used to solicit social play do function to reduce the likelihood of play grading into aggression (23, 25). In these (and possibly other) animals, there has been selection for signals that serve to communicate play intention, signals that have a "tonic" (26) effect in that they serve to change the probability distribution of subsequent responses by the recipient of the signal (23).

An analysis of the variability of individual motor acts does not provide any information about the ways in which these behaviors, stereotyped or not, are linked together to form continuous chains of behavior. It is possible for selection to operate on individual motor acts as well as on the order in which they are performed (27), and it has been suggested that behavioral sequences can serve display functions (28). That is, a sequence may function as a composite signal. For the infant canids used in this study, play sequences were more variable than nonplay sequences (6, 25). Therefore, it is possible that there are two sets of signals that are used in play. The first would be a play signal itself and the second would be the sequencing of the acts. In this way, the play intention of an individual could be communicated initially, and then the "play mood" could be maintained either by repeating play soliciting signals or by using the ongoing sequence as a play signal. In canids, play signals occur either in the beginning of play sequences or are randomly distributed throughout (23, 25). The proposed signal value of variable canid play sequences may be one reason for the observation that canid play signals seem to be more important in the initial soliciting of social play and less so for the maintenance of the "play mood" (23).

REFERENCES AND NOTES

1. For reviews see T. A. Sebeok, Ed., *Animal Communication* (Indiana Univ. Press, Bloomington, 1968); *How Animals Communicate* (Indiana Univ. Press, Bloomington, 1977).

2. W. J. Smith, *The Behavior of Communicating: An Ethological Approach* (Harvard Univ. Press, Cambridge, Mass., 1977).

3. E. O. Wilson, *Sociobiology: The New Synthesis* (Harvard Univ. Press, Cambridge, Mass., 1975).

4. G. Barlow, in *The Central Nervous System and Fish Behavior*, D. Ingle, Ed. (Univ. of Chicago Press, Chicago, 1968), p. 217.

5. —, in *How Animals Communicate (1)*, p. 94.

6. M. Bekoff, in *Quantitative Methods in the Study of Animal Behavior*, B. A. Hazlett, Ed. (Academic Press, New York, 1977), p. 1.

7. W. Schleidt, *Z. Tierpsychol.* 36, 184 (1974).

8. G. Hausfater, *Folia Primatol.* 27, 41 (1977).

9. I. Golani [*Perspect. Ethol.* 2, 69 (1976)] has proposed a variety of methods for measuring displays but has not studied variability in the form of "fast movements." He wrote that "their systemetic description is essential for the understanding of the actual genesis of agonistic and play sequences" (p. 125).

10. S. Chevalier-Skolnikoff, *Contrib. Primatol.* 2, 1 (1974); G. M. Burghardt, in *How Animals Communicate (1)*, p. 67; J. P. Hailman, *Optical Signals: Animal Communication and Light* (Indiana Univ. Press, Bloomington, 1977).

11. O. Heinroth, *Verh. 5th Int. Ornithol. Kongr. Berlin* 5, 589 (1911); J. S. Huxley, *Proc. Zool. Soc. London* (1914), p. 491; J. S. Huxley, Ed., *Philos. Trans. R. Soc. London, Ser. B* 251 (1966); C. O. Whitman, *Carnegie Inst. Washington Publ. 257* (1919); K. Z. Lorenz, *J. Ornithol. Suppl.* 89, 194 (1941); P. Marler, *Behaviour* 11, 13 (1957); in *Growing Points in Ethology*, P. P. G. Bateson and R. A. Hinde, Eds. (Cambridge Univ. Press, New York, 1976), p. 239; N. Tinbergen, *Behaviour* 15, 1 (1959); D. Otte, *Adv. Ecol. Syst.* 5, 385 (1974); F. McKinney, in *Function and Evolution in Behaviour*, G. Baerends, C. Beer, A. Manning, Eds. (Oxford Univ. Press, New York, 1975), p. 331; C. G. Beer, in *ibid.*, p. 16; *Am. Zool.* 17, 155 (1977).

12. T. D. Johnston, *J. Theor. Biol.* 57, 43 (1976).

13. R. H. Wiley, *Behaviour* 47, 129 (1973).

14. M. Bekoff, thesis, Washington University, St. Louis (1972).

15. —, *Am. Zool.* 14, 323 (1974).

16. — and R. Jamieson, *J. Mammal.* 56, 685 (1975).

17. See R. Dawkins and M. Dawkins, *Behaviour* 45, 83 (1973) for formula for "c."

18. W. Schleidt and M. D. Shalter [*Z. Tierpsychol.* 33, 35 (1973)] and Wiley (*13*) also found no changes in variability with age in the birds that they studied [see also (*6*)].

19. The mean day of age for the first occurrence of bows was 26 for coyotes, 24 for wolves and wolf-dog hybrids, and 23 for beagles.

20. I. Eibl-Eibesfeldt, *Ethology* (Holt, Rinehart, & Winston. New York, 1975).

21. A. Portmann, *Animal Forms and Patterns* (Faber & Faber, London, 1952); D'Arcy Thompson, *On Growth and Form* (Cambridge Univ. Press, New York, 1961); R. B. Stein, K. G. Pearson, R. S. Smith, J. B. Redford, Eds., *Control of Posture and Locomotion* (Plenum, New York, 1974); R. E. Talbott, in *ibid.*, p. 273; P. Lehner, in *Coyotes: Behavior, Ecology, and Management*, M. Bekoff, Ed. (Academic Press, New

York, in press). The greater variability observed in the bows of the adult dogs may be due to the fact that a heterogeneous population (different breeds and crosses) was studied. Since the vertical displacement of the shoulders is somewhat related to the length of the humerus, and in different breeds the length of this bone and its articulation with the scapula vary [M. Lyon, *The Dog in Action* (Howell, New York, 1952), pp. 102–103], greater variation would be expected when comparing a heterogeneous population to more homogeneous ones.

22. D. S. Sade, *Am. J. Phys. Anthropol.* 38, 537 (1973); M. Bekoff, *Q. Rev. Biol.* 47, 412 (1972); *Perspect. Ethol.* 2, 165 (1976); D. Symons, *Am. Zool.* 14, 317 (1974).

23. M. Bekoff, *Semiotica* 15, 231 (1975).

24. S. A. Altmann, in *Social Communication Among Primates*, S. A. Altmann, Ed. (Univ. of Chicago Press, Chicago, 1967), p. 325.

25. M. Bekoff and J. Moran, in preparation.

26. W. Schleidt, *J. Theor. Biol.* 42, 359 (1973).

27. D. J. McFarland, in *Growing Points in Ethology (11)*, p. 55; R. M. Sibly and D. J. McFarland, *Am. Nat.* 110, 601 (1976); C. G. Beer, *Ann. N.Y. Acad. Sci.* 280, 413 (1976).

28. F. McKinney, *Behaviour, Suppl.* 7 (1961).

29.   I thank numerous colleagues for reading an earlier draft of this report and the students in the Animal Behavior Laboratory who helped with filming and analysis. J. Moran helped with data compilation. This work was supported in part by PHS grants GM-01900 and Es-00139 and Biomedical Grant Support from the University of Colorado.

10   Virtuous Nature

IF YOU THINK that we are the only creatures on Earth with a moral sense, then you're in good company. Most experts in behaviour believe that morality is a uniquely human trait, without which our complex social life would never have emerged. I disagree. Accuse me of anthropomorphising if you like, but I'm convinced that many animals can distinguish right from wrong. Decades spent watching wild and captive animals have persuaded me that species living in groups often have a sense of fair play built on moral codes of conduct that help cement their social relationships. Nature isn't always ruthlessly and selfishly competitive.

That's not all. I suspect that herein lies the origin of our own virtue. Biologists have had real problems trying to explain why humans are frequently inexplicably nice to each other. It just doesn't make sense in evolutionary terms, unless there are ulterior motives behind our seemingly altruistic actions. Perhaps we expect a payback somewhere down the line, or maybe our good deeds are directed only towards kin, with whom we share genes and hence a biological heritage. Nobody has really considered the possibility that being considerate to your neighbours might sometimes be the best way to survive. But I'm starting to find evidence that a well-developed sense of fair play helps non-human animals live longer, more successful lives. In other words, virtue is its own reward—fairer is fitter.

It's an understatement to say that looking for the roots of morality in animals is very difficult, but at least we can start to break the problem down. The first question to answer is, are animals capable of the empathy and feelings that underlie morality? We know that in humans the neural basis for these feelings lies in the brain's amygdalae and hypothalamus, and they are mediated by neurotransmitters such as dopamine, serotonin and oxytocin. We also know that many animals, especially mammals, possess the same neurological structures and brain chemicals as we do. Of course, this doesn't necessarily mean they share our feelings, but careful observation of animals in action suggests that at least some of them do.

Recent overviews of research by Stephanie Preston and Frans de Waal from the Yerkes Primate Center in Atlanta and Stanley Kuczaj's group at the University of Southern Mississippi in Hattiesburg show that empathy is more widespread among animals than science has so far been willing to recognise. They point to research that suggests non-human primates, dolphins, whales, elephants and hippopotamuses, and even some rodents, behave in ways that support the claim that empathy has deep evolutionary roots.

In one classic study published in 1964, Stanley Wechlin and his team at the Northwestern University Medical School in Illinois showed that a hungry

Reprinted from Bekoff, M. 2002. Virtuous Nature. *New Scientist* 13 July, 34–37, with permission from *New Scientist*.

rhesus monkey would not take food if doing so meant another monkey got an electric shock. In similar situations rats will also hold back when they know their actions would cause pain to another individual.

Then there's the study published two decades ago by Hal Markowitz from San Francisco State University. He reported that after training Diana monkeys to insert a token into a slot to get food, he observed a male helping the oldest female who had failed to learn the task. On three occasions the male picked up the tokens she had dropped, put them into the machine, and allowed her to have the food.

We'll probably never know whether these rats and monkeys were feeling empathy as we do. But what we can do is start comparing what's going on in animal brains with what happens in our own. Neuroimaging techniques such as PET scans and functional MRI are starting to shed new light on human emotions, and I hope that it won't be long before we start doing similar studies with non-human primates and other animals.

In the meantime, watching animals in action has convinced many researchers, myself included, that they possess the emotions upon which a moral sense is built. Chimps and monkeys, for example, seem to feel embarrassment, whales and ravens show signs of falling in love, and even iguanas register pleasure (*New Scientist*, 29 April 2000, p 32). In my own research I have taken this one step further—looking for evidence of fair behaviour. I'm particularly interested in social play—the joyful rough and tumble common to many mammals, especially youngsters—because it has its own special rules of engagement, allowing participants to reinterpret acts that might otherwise seem aggressive or sexual. The fact that play rarely escalates into all-out fighting is a strong indication that animals do indeed abide by the rules and that they expect others to do likewise.

My studies of infant dogs, wolves and coyotes based on careful observation and analysis of video playbacks reveal that they use a special signal to prevent misinterpretation of playful actions. They perform a "bow"—which entails crouching on the forelimbs while keeping the rear upright—when initiating play, or in association with aggressive actions such as biting, to modify their meaning. I've also found that players often use self-imposed handicaps to limit the force they use against a weaker playmate when body slamming or biting. And role reversal is common, so that during play a dominant animal will often allow a subordinate to have the upper hand. Such behaviours reduce inequalities in size, strength and dominance between playmates, fostering the cooperation and reciprocity that are essential for play to occur. Indeed, on the rare occasions when a canid says "let's play" and then beats up an unsuspecting animal, the cheat usually find itself ostracised by its erstwhile playmates.

Similar cooperative behaviour has been found in many animals at play. For example, Sergio Pellis from the University of Lethbridge in Alberta found that rats will constantly monitor and fine-tune their behaviour to keep play going. But while there has been much talk about animal cooperation, no one has considered the role that social play may have had in the evolution of morality. Yet what could be a better atmosphere in which to learn the rights and wrongs of social interaction—the moral norms that can then be extended to other situations such as sharing food, defending resources, grooming and giving care?

My belief is that a sense of fairness is common to many animals, because there could be no social play without it, and without social play individual animals and entire groups would be at a disadvantage. If I'm right, morality evolved because it is adaptive. It helps many animals, including humans, to survive and flourish in their particular social environment. This may sound like a radical idea, particularly if you view morality as uniquely human and a sort of mystical quality that sets us apart from other animals. But if you accept my argument that play and fairness are inextricably linked, you're halfway there. The challenge then is to show that individual animals benefit from these behaviours.

It's hardly radical these days to suggest that play is essential food for the brain. Recent research shows that the more animals play, the bigger their brains grow (*New Scientist*, 9 June 2001, p 28). Social play seems to rewire the brain, increasing connections between neurones in the cortex. It hones an individual's cognitive skills, including logical reasoning, learning and behavioural flexibility. And it helps perfect survival skills such as hunting and mating, which will be essential in later life. Quantifying these benefits of play is extraordinarily difficult, but the more we learn about the way play affects the brain the more apparent it becomes that the activity is far from idle time-wasting.

My own fieldwork has uncovered one of the penalties paid by animals that fail to engage fully in play. I've found that coyote pups who don't play much are less tightly bonded to other members of their group and are more likely to strike out on their own. And life outside the group is much more risky than within it. In my seven-year study of coyotes living in the Grand Teton National Park outside Moose, Wyoming, I found that about 60 per cent of the yearlings who drifted away from their social group died, whereas fewer than 20 per cent of their stay-at-home peers did. I'm sure that close scrutiny of other social animals will reveal more evidence that having a sense of fairness benefits individuals.

More controversially, I also believe that a moral sense may benefit groups as a whole. That's because group members learn rules of engagement during social play that influence their decisions about what is acceptable behaviour when dealing with each other. Recent research by Kyoko Okamoto and Shuichi Matsumura at Kyoto University suggests that we are not the only primates to use punishment and apology to help reinforce the rules of social engagement. And sticking to the rules is essential if individuals are to work in harmony to create a successful group that can outcompete other groups. My observations of coyotes confirm that members of a pack who work together are more successful at driving off intruders than are single individuals, and I'm sure that if other researchers looked they would find similar evidence for the benefits of group living in other animals.

I'm not arguing that there is a gene for fair or moral behaviour. As with any behavioural trait, the underlying genetics is bound to be complex, and environmental influences may be large. No matter. Provided there is variation in levels of morality among individuals, and provided virtue is rewarded by a greater number of offspring, then any genes associated with good behaviour are likely to accumulate in subsequent generations. And the observation that play is rarely unfair or uncooperative is surely an indication that natural selection acts to weed out those who don't play by the rules.

What does all this tell us about human morality? First, we didn't invent virtue—its origins are much more ancient than our own. Secondly, we should stop seeing ourselves as morally superior to other animals. True, our big brains endow us with a highly sophisticated sense of what's right and wrong, but they also give us much greater scope for manipulating others to cheat and deceive and try to benefit from immoral behaviour. In that sense, animal morality might be "purer" than our own.

We should accept our moral responsibility towards other animals, and that means developing and enforcing more restrictive regulations governing animal use. There is growing evidence that while animal minds vary from one species to another, they are not so different from our own, and only when we accept this can we be truly moral in our relations with other creatures and with nature as a whole.

11   Wild Justice, Cooperation, and Fair Play

Minding Manners, Being Nice, and Feeling Good

IN THIS PAPER I argue that we can learn much about "wild justice" and the evolutionary origins of social morality—behaving fairly—by studying social play behavior in group-living animals, and that interdisciplinary cooperation will help immensely. In our efforts to learn more about the evolution of morality we need to broaden our comparative research to include animals other than nonhuman primates. If one is a good Darwinian, it is premature to claim that only humans can be empathic and moral beings. By asking the question "What is it like to be another animal?" we can discover rules of engagement that guide animals in their social encounters. When I study dogs, for example, I try to be a "dogocentrist" and practice "dogomorphism." My major arguments center on the following "big" questions: Can animals be moral beings or do they merely act as if they are? What are the evolutionary roots of cooperation, fairness, trust, forgiveness, and morality? What do animals do when they engage in social play? How do animals negotiate agreements to cooperate, to forgive, to behave fairly, to develop trust? Can animals forgive? Why cooperate and play fairly? Why did play evolve as it has? Does "being fair" mean being more fit—do individual variations in play influence an individual's reproductive fitness, are more virtuous individuals more fit than less virtuous individuals? What is the taxonomic distribution of cognitive skills and emotional capacities necessary for individuals to be able to behave fairly, to empathize, to behave morally? Can we use information about moral behavior in animals to help us understand ourselves? I conclude that there is strong selection for cooperative fair play in which individuals establish and maintain a social contract to play because there are mutual benefits when individuals adopt this strategy and group stability may also be fostered. Numerous mechanisms have evolved to facilitate the initiation and maintenance of social play to keep others engaged, so that agreeing to play fairly and the resulting benefits of doing so can be readily achieved. I also claim that the ability to make accurate predictions about what an individual is likely to do in a given social situation is a useful litmus test for explaining what might be happening in an individual's brain during social encounters, and that intentional or representational explanations are often important for making these predictions.

Reprinted and slightly modified from Bekoff, M. 2004. Wild Justice, Cooperation, and Fair Play: Minding Manners, Being Nice, and Feeling Good. In R. Sussman and A. R. Chapman (eds.), *The Origins and Nature of Sociality.* Copyright © 2004 Walter de Gruyter, Inc. Published by Aldine de Gruyter, Hawthorne, NY. pp. 53–80.

WILD JUSTICE: SOCIAL MORALITY, MANNERS, AND COOPERATION IN ANIMALS

> Those communities which included the greatest number of the most sympathetic members would flourish best and rear the greatest number of offspring.
>
> —Charles Darwin 1871/1936, p. 163

> I believe that at the most fundamental level our nature is compassionate, and that cooperation, not conflict, lies at the heart of the basic principles that govern our human existence ... By living a way of life that expresses our basic goodness, we fulfill our humanity and give our actions dignity, worth, and meaning.
>
> —His Holiness the Dalai Lama 2002, p. 68

> Different as they are from language-using human beings, they are able to form relationships not only with members of their own species, but also with human beings, while giving expression to their own intentions and purposes. So that the relationships are far more clearly analogous to human relationships than some of the philosophical theorizing that I have discussed would allow. Some human beings indeed and some nonhuman animals pursue their respective goods in company with and in cooperation with each other. And what we mean by 'goods' in saying this is precisely the same, whether we are speaking of human or dolphin or gorilla.
>
> —Macintyre 1999, p. 61

> Now he worships at an altar of a stagnant pool; And when he sees his reflection, he's fulfilled; Oh, man is opposed to fair play; He wants it all and he wants it his way.
>
> —Bob Dylan 1983

The behavior of nonhuman animal beings ("animals") fascinates people of all ages and of all cultures. People around the world are interested in what animals do, either because they are interested in the animals themselves or because they want to know more about the origins of human behavior. There also is much interdisciplinary interest in questions about animal behavior—what available data mean, what methods are the best for answering questions that are frequently at once important, challenging and frustrating, and what role representatives of each discipline play in helping us to gain a better understanding of the behavior of our nonhuman kin. Interdisciplinary discourse is essential. I also want to stress that all sorts of information, including anecdotes, intuitions, philosophical musings, and "hard" data, are important as we try to understand "wild justice" and the origins of moral behavior (Allen, this volume, argues that there are many levels of abstraction that inform explanations of animal behavior). "Real world" examples—data from careful studies of animal behavior—are critical for furthering our understanding. Anecdotes, intuitions, and philosophical musings along with empirical data all drive further empirical research. I also want to emphasize the importance of adopting a broad comparative approach to the study of animal behavior and for coming to terms with what available information has to say about the cognitive abilities of other animals in the context of what we know about them in terms of their own evolutionary and natural histories.

Of course some people want to learn more about animals to make the case for human uniqueness, usually claiming that humans are "above" and "better" than other animals. But the more we study animals and the more we learn about "them" and "us" we frequently discover there is not a real dichotomy or non-negotiable gap between animals and humans because humans are, of course, animals. There is evolutionary continuity. Art, culture, language, and tool use and manufacture can no longer be used to separate "them" from "us" (but perhaps cooking food is uniquely human; Wrangham and Conklin-Brittain 2003). Line-drawing can be very misleading especially when people take the view that nonhuman animals are "lower" or "less valuable" than "higher" animals, where "higher" means human. In many ways "we are them" and "they are us" (Bekoff 2002a).

Charles Darwin (1859, 1872/1998) emphasized that there is evolutionary *continuity* among different species. His ideas about evolutionary continuity, that behavioral, cognitive, emotional, and moral variations among different species are differences in *degree* rather than differences in *kind*, are often invoked in trying to answer questions about the evolution of various behavioral phenotypes. On this view there are shades of gray among different animals and between non-humans and humans; the differences are not black and white with no transitional stages or inexplicable jumps (Gruen 2002; Güzeldere and Nahmias 2002; see also many other essays in Bekoff, Allen, and Burghardt 2002). Current work in evolutionary biology and anthropology suggests that linear scales of evolution in which there are large gaps between humans and at least some animals are simplistic views of the evolutionary process.

There is no doubt that we can learn much about humans by carefully studying our animal kin and also by listening to their stories. One reason I find the study of animal behavior, and in particular questions centering on animal cognition, animal emotions, and animal morality to be so fascinating, exciting, and also frustrating and challenging, is because I want to learn more about why both the similarities and differences have evolved.

One area that will surely benefit from a meeting of interdisciplinary minds concerns the evolution of social morality and the negotiation and maintenance of cooperation, fairness, kindness, generosity, trust, respect, and social norms. Researchers from many disciplines have debated the evolutionary origins of social morality, asking if some animals have codes of social conduct that regulate their behavior in terms of what is permissible and what is not permissible during social encounters (for wide ranging discussion see Kropotkin 1902; de Waal 1996, 2001; Solomon 1995; Hurd 1996; Ridley 1996, 2001;

Mitchell 1998; Macintyre 1999; Sober and Wilson 1998, 2000; *Journal of Consciousness Studies*, Volume 7, No. 1/2, 2000; Field 2001; Hinde 2002; Jamieson 2002; Wilson 2002; de Waal and Tyack 2003). These scientists and philosophers want to know what are the moral capacities of animals, can they be moral agents with a moral sense who are able to live in moral communities? In a recent issue of the *Journal of Consciousness Studies* (Volume 7, No. 1/2, 2000) researchers from many disciplines debated the evolutionary origins of morality. These scholars were interested in discussing animal roots on which human morality might be built, even if human morality is not identical to animal morality, which it likely is not.

Recently there also has been a resurgence of interest in the notion of fairness and altruism in humans (Sober and Wilson 1998, 2000; Douglas 2001; Riolo, Cohen, and Axelrod 2001; Sigmund and Nowak 2001; Bowles and Gintis 2002; Fehr and Gächter 2002; Jamieson 2002; Sigmund, Fehr, and Nowak 2002; Bewley 2003; Fehr and Rockenbach 2003). Researchers are interested in learning about how individuals from different cultures share resources, and if they share them equitably even if they are not compelled to do so. Despite Bob Dylan's lament (above) much research shows that human beings are more generous and more fair than game-theory and other models predict. There seems to be a set of core values that are learned through social interactions with others, and these values influence moral decisions. There also is evidence that people will punish free-riders in the absence of personal gain, and that cooperation is sustained by such "altruistic punishment" (Bowles and Gintis 2002; Fehr and Gchter 2002). Taken together, cross-cultural data suggest that there may be an innate drive to be fair. Of course, much more comparative work still needs to be done.

But what about animals? Can there be "wild justice?" Is "being fair, nice, and moral" doing what comes naturally? I will return to these questions below. Charles Darwin argued this case and also considered the development and the intellectual and moral faculties that are important in cooperative social encounters.

Many animals live in fairly stable social groups that resemble those of ancestral humans. There are divisions of labor, food sharing, communal care of young, and inter- and intrasexual dominance hierarchies. Many animals, especially mammals, also share with humans neuroanatomical structures in the amygdala and hypothalamus and neurochemicals (dopamine, serotonin, oxytocin) that form the neural bases for the expression and experience of emotions and empathy (Panksepp 1998; Preston and de Waal 2002). A wide variety of social behavior patterns in animals have also been influenced by living in groups of various sizes. If one is a good Darwinian and believes in evolutionary continuity, it seems premature to claim that *only* humans can be empathic and moral beings. As we increasingly come to recognize that animals share their emotions with us it becomes increasingly difficult to deny their existence.

SOCIAL PLAY: A FOUNDATION OF FAIRNESS

In this essay I consider various aspects of the evolution of cooperation and fairness using social play behavior in animals, especially mammals, as my exemplar of an activity in which one would expect to see on-going negotiations of cooperation and agreements to behave fairly because the social dynamics of play require that players agree to play and not to fight or to mate with one another. I am specifically concerned with the notion of "behaving fairly." I touch on many topics that are considered elsewhere in this volume, including what is cognitive ethology, anthropomorphism, the importance of broadening our taxonomic horizons in studies of animal cognition beyond non-human primates, levels of selection, and the role that anecdotes, intuitions, and common sense play in doing "hard" science, and generating data that may be called "science sense" (Bekoff 2002a).

By "behaving fairly" I use as a working guide the notion that animals often have social expectations when they engage in various sorts of social encounters the violation of which constitutes being treated unfairly. By studying the details and dynamics of social play behavior one can test some of these ideas. Also tied into the notion of expectation is the element of surprise. Often, animals seem surprised by what happens to them in a given social interaction. For example, a dog or wolf may cock her head from side-to-side and squint, as if she is wondering what went "wrong" when a play-mate becomes too assertive or too aggressive. Perhaps they feel indignant when they are wronged, when their expectations or sense of justice is violated, when they feel they are not being treated "right."

I will conclude that social play is a "foundation of fairness." I argue that it is through social cooperation that groups (communities) are built from individuals agreeing to work in harmony with other individuals. Further, based on recent research on the neurobiology of human cooperation, I argue that "being fair" may feel good for animals as well. Lastly, I stress that in our efforts to learn more about the evolution of social morality we need to broaden our comparative research to include animals other than nonhuman primates.

THE SCIENCE OF COGNITIVE ETHOLOGY: NATURALIZING THE STUDY OF ANIMAL MINDS

> There are two kind of biologists: those who are looking to see if there is one thing that can be understood, and those who keep saying it is very complicated and nothing can be understood.
> —Pigliucci 2002, p. 92

Basically, the interdisciplinary science of cognitive ethology is concerned with claims about the evolution of cognitive processes. Since behavioral abilities have evolved in response to natural selection pressures, ethologists favor observations and experiments on animals in conditions that are as close as possible to the natural environment where selection occurred. Often a double-standard is used to criticize cognitive ethology for being too "soft." For example, levels of statistical significance and data bases that are acceptable in other branches of science are not accepted in cognitive ethological studies (Griffin 2001; Bekoff 2002a). Why is this so? Reasons offered include lack of control of observations and experiments and also the fact that mental experiences are private affairs and hypotheses about mental experiences are not falsifiable. I have little to say about this other than that it is clear that cognitive ethology *is* a field of science, that we have the tools to learn much about mental processes and mental states in animals, and that falsifiable hypotheses can be offered and tested (Allen and Bekoff 1997; Griffin 2001; Bekoff 2002a; Bekoff, Allen, and Burghardt 2002). We also now really do know quite a lot about animal minds (Hauser 2000; Griffin 2001; Bekoff 2002a; essays in Bekoff, Allen, and Burghardt 2002). Skeptics need to offer more motivated reasons for bashing cognitive ethology. (It is important to note that the atmosphere at the meeting at which the papers in this volume were presented was very pro-animal cognition. Nonetheless, critical and skeptical questions were asked but the discussion did not get bogged down nor was it deflected by an insistence that the lack of absolute certainty means that no or little progress can be made on the questions at hand. I will return to this topic later on in my brief discussion of the notion of prediction.)

No longer constrained by psychological behaviorism, cognitive ethologists are interested in comparing thought processes, consciousness, beliefs, and rationality in animals. In addition to situating the study of animal cognition in a comparative and evolutionary framework, cognitive ethologists also argue that field studies of animals that include careful observation and experimentation can inform studies of animal cognition, and that cognitive ethology will not have to be brought into the laboratory to make it respectable (Allen and Bekoff 1997). Furthermore, because cognitive ethology is a *comparative* science, cognitive ethological studies emphasize broad taxonomic comparisons and do not focus on a few select representatives of limited taxa. Cognitive psychologists, in contrast to cognitive ethologists, usually work on related topics in laboratory settings, and do not emphasize comparative or evolutionary aspects of animal cognition. When cognitive psychologists do make cross-species comparisons, they are typically interested in explaining different behavior patterns in terms of common underlying mechanisms. Ethologists, in common with other biologists, are often more concerned with the diversity of solutions that living organisms have found for common problems.

Many different types of research fall under the term "cognitive ethology" and it is pointless to try to delimit the boundaries of cognitive ethology; because of the enormous amount of interdisciplinary interest in the area, narrow definitions of cognitive ethology are likely to become rapidly obsolete. There also seems to be little difference between methods used to study animal cognition and those used to study other aspects of animal behavior. Differences lie not so much in what is done and how it is done, but rather how data are explained. Colin Allen and I, in our book, *Species of mind: The Philosophy and biology of cognitive ethology* (1997), have argued that the main distinction between cognitive ethology and classical ethology lies not in the types of data collected, but in the understanding of the conceptual resources that are appropriate for explaining those data.

CLASSICAL ETHOLOGY AND COGNITIVE ETHOLOGY: WHAT IS IT LIKE TO BE A ____?

Nobel Laureate Niko Tinbergen (1963) identified four overlapping areas with which ethological investigations should be concerned, namely, evolution (phylogeny), adaptation (function), causation, and development (ontogeny). Tinbergen's framework is also useful for those interested in animal cognition (Jamieson and Bekoff 1993; Allen and Bekoff 1997; Smuts 2001). Burghardt (1997) suggested adding a fifth area, *private experience*. He (p. 276) noted that "The fifth aim is nothing less than a deliberate attempt to understand the private experience, including the perceptual world and mental states, of other organisms. The term private experience is advanced as a preferred label that is most inclusive of the full range of phenomena that have been identified without prejudging any particular theoretical or methodological approach."

Burghardt's suggestion invites what he calls "critical anthropomorphism," carefully used anthropomorphism, an approach with which many agree. I have suggested that we be "biocentrically anthropomorphic" and that by doing so we do not necessarily lose the animal's point of view. We are humans and we have by necessity a human view of the world (Bekoff 2000b).

The way we describe and explain the behavior of other animals is influenced and limited by the language we use to talk about things in general. By engaging in anthropomorphism we make the world of other animals accessible to ourselves and to other human beings. By being anthropomorphic we can more readily understand and explain the emotions or feelings of other animals. But this is not to say that other animals are happy or sad in the *same* ways in which humans (or even other members of the same species) are happy or sad. Of course, I cannot be absolutely certain that my late dog, Jethro, was happy, sad, angry, upset, or in love, but these words serve to explain what he might have been feeling. Merely referring to the firing of different neurons or to the activity of different muscles in the absence of behavioral information and context is insufficiently informative because we do not know about the specific situation in which the animal finds herself.

BEING A DOG-O-CENTRIST

My research and that of others begins with the question "What is it like to be a specific animal?" So, when I study dogs, for example, I try to be a dog-o-centrist and practice dogomorphism. Thus, when I claim that a dog is happy, for example when playing, I am saying it is dog-joy, and that dog-joy may be different from chimpanzee-joy. While I will not go into it any further, this is a very important stance for it stresses that there are important species and individual differences in behavior, cognitive capacities, and emotions, and that it is wrong and simplistic to claim that if animal joy is not like our joy then they do not have it.

What it basically comes down to is that as humans studying other animals, we cannot totally lose our anthropocentric perspective. But we can try as hard as possible to combine the animals' viewpoints to the ways in which we study, describe, interpret, and explain their behavior.

THE EVOLUTION OF SOCIAL MORALITY: CONTINUITY, PROTO-MORALITY, AND QUESTIONS OF HUMAN UNIQUENESS

Evolutionary reconstructions of social behavior often depend on educated guesses (some better than others) about the past social (and other) environments in which ancestral beings lived. In the same sense that others' minds are private, so is evolution (Bekoff 2002a). Often it is difficult to know with a great deal of certainty very much about these variables and how they may have figured into evolutionary scenarios. It is an understatement to note that it is extremely difficult to study the evolution of morality in any animal species, and the very notion of animal morality itself often makes for heated discussions. Bernstein (2000) claims that "morality in animals might lie outside of the realm of measurement techniques available to science" (p. 34). *Nonetheless, it seems clear that detailed comparative analyses of social behavior in animals can indeed provide insights into the evolution of social morality.* Certainly, these sorts of studies are extremely challenging, but the knowledge gained is essential in our efforts to learn more about the evolution of sociality and social morality and to learn more about human nature and perhaps human uniqueness.

Many discussions of the evolution of morality center on the development of various sorts of models (e.g. Axelrod 1984; Ridley 1996, 2001; Skyrms 1996; Dugatkin 1997; Sober and Wilson 1998, 2000; essays in *Journal of Consciousness Studies*, 2000, volume 7, No. 1/2). While these models are very useful for stimulating discussion and further research, they do not substitute for available data (however few) that may bear on animal morality (see, for example, some essays in Aureli and de Waal (2000) for additional comparative information and also Dugatkin and Bekoff 2003).

The study of the evolution of morality, specifically cooperation and fairness, is closely linked to science, religion, theology, spirituality and perhaps even different notions of God, in that ideas about continuity and discontinuity (the possible uniqueness of humans and other species), individuality, and freedom need to be considered in detail. Furthermore, it is important to discuss relationships among science, religion, and God because spirituality and the notion of one form of God or another had strong influences on the evolution of our ancestors, their cognitive, emotional, and moral lives.

Gregory Peterson (2000; see also Peterson 1999) has discussed the evolutionary roots of morality (stages that he refers to as "quasi-morality" and "proto-morality" in animals) and religion in relation to the roles played by cognition and culture. He also stresses the importance of recognizing continuities and discontinuities with other animals, arguing ultimately (and speciesistically) that while some animals might possess proto-morality (they are able "to rationally deliberate actions and their consequences", p. 475) none other than humans is "genuinely moral" because to be able to be genuinely moral requires higher emergent levels of cognition as well as culture and the world view that culture provides, namely, religion. Peterson (2000, p. 478) claims that "Quasi-moral and proto-moral systems do not require a global framework that guides decision making. They are always proximate and pragmatic. In these systems, there is no long-term goal or ideal state to be achieved. Yet, genuine morality is virtually inconceivable without such conceptions."

Peterson also claims that any sociobiological account (based on selfishness or combativeness) of human morality is incomplete. I agree and also argue that this is so for some non-human animals as well. When animals are studied in their own worlds they may indeed have their own form of genuine morality, there might indeed be long-term goals and ideal states to be achieved. Our anthropocentric view of other animals, in which humans are so taken with themselves, is far too narrow. The worlds and lives of other animals are not identical to those of humans and may vary from species-to-species and even within species. The same problems arise in the study of emotions (Bekoff 2000a, 2002a, 2004) if we believe that emotions in animals are going to be identical to or even recognizably similar among different species. There is also variability among humans in what some might view as long-term goals and ideal states, and it would be premature to conclude that there is one set of long-term goals and ideal states that characterize, or are essential to, the capacity to be genuinely moral. To cash out stages of moral evolution as does Peterson, it looks like quasi-morality and proto-morality are less than genuine morality.

COOPERATION AND FAIRNESS ARE NOT BY-PRODUCTS OF AGGRESSION AND SELFISHNESS

> ... my thesis is that justice is first of all a natural sentiment, an inborn sense of our connectedness with others and our shared interests and concerns.
>
> —Solomon 1995, p. 153

My arguments center on the view that cooperation is not merely always a by-product of tempering aggressive and selfish tendencies (combating Richard

Dawkins' selfish genes) and attempts at reconciliation. Rather, cooperation and fairness can evolve on their own because they are important in the formation and maintenance of social relationships (Solomon 1995 also forcefully argues this point). This view contrasts with those who see aggression, cheating, selfishness, and perhaps amorality as driving the evolution of sociality, fairness, and justice. The combative Hobbesian world in which individuals are constantly at one another's throat is not the natural state of affairs. Nature is not always red in tooth and claw. Dawkins (2001) himself has been quoted as saying "A pretty good definition of the kind of society in which I don't want to live is a society founded on the principles of Darwinism."

DOES IT FEEL GOOD TO BE FAIR?

> It will be only after we have established the facts of mutual aid in different classes of animals and their importance for evolution, that we shall be able to study what belongs in the evolution of sociable feelings, to parental feelings, and what to sociability proper ... Mutual Aid [is] an argument in favour of a pre-human origin of moral instincts, but also as a law of Nature and a factor of evolution.
> —Petr Kropotkin 1902, pp. x–xii

> Justice begins with our emotional engagement in the world, not in philosophical detachment or in any merely hypothetical situation.
> —Solomon 1995, 199

Studies of the evolution of social morality need to pay close attention to the rich cognitive, intellectual, and deep emotional lives of animals (Bekoff, 2000a,b, 2002a,b) and how these capacities figure into moral sensibility and the ability to make moral judgments. Truth be told, we really do not know much about these capacities even in our primate relatives despite claims that we do (Bekoff 2002c, 2003a, 2005). We know that animals and humans share many of the same emotions and same chemicals that play a role in the experience and expressions of emotions such as joy and pleasure. If being nice feels good then that is a good reason for being nice. It is also a good reason for a pattern of behavior to evolve and to remain in an animal's arsenal.

Are some animals capable of the emotions and empathy that might underlie morality? We know that in humans the amygdala and hypothalamus are important in emotional experiences and that they are mediated by neurotransmitters such as dopamine, serotonin and oxytocin. We also know that many animals, especially mammals, share with humans the same neurological structures and chemicals (Panksepp 1998; Bekoff 2002a) . Of course, this does not necessarily mean animals share our feelings, but careful observation of individuals during social encounters suggests that at least some of them do. While their feelings are not necessarily identical to ours this is of little or no concern because it is unlikely that they should be the same as ours.

Empathy is also important to consider. Preston and de Waal (2002) argue that empathy is more widespread among animals than has previously been recognized (see also Kuczaj, Tranel, Trone, and Hill 2001). In a classic study, Wechlin, Masserman, and Terris (1964) showed that a hungry rhesus monkey would not take food if doing so subjected another monkey to an electric shock. In similar situations rats will also restrain themselves when they know their actions would cause pain to another individual (Church 1959). In another study, Diana monkeys were trained to insert a token into a slot to obtain food (Markowitz 1982). A male was observed helping the oldest female who had failed to learn the task. On three occasions he picked up the tokens she had dropped, put them into the machine, and allowed her to have the food. His behavior seemed to have no benefits for him at all; there did not seem to be any hidden agenda.

Along these lines, de Waal observed Kuni, a captive female bonobo, capture a starling and take the bird outside and place it on its feet (Preston and de Waal 2002). When the bird did not move Kuni tossed it in the air. When the starling did not fly Kuni took it to the highest point in her enclosure, carefully unfolded its wings and threw it in the air. The starling still did not fly and Kuni then guarded and protected it from a curious juvenile.

Elephants also may show concern for others. Joyce Poole (1998), who has studied African elephants for decades, was told a story about a teenage female who was suffering from a withered leg on which she could put no weight. When a young male from another group began attacking the injured female, a large adult female chased the attacking male, returned to the young female, and touched her crippled leg with her trunk. Poole argues that the adult female was showing empathy and sympathy.

While good stories alone are not enough to make a compelling argument, when there are many such anecdotes they can be used to provide a solid basis for further detailed empirical research. Ignoring them is to ignore a rich data base. I have argued elsewhere that "the plural of anecdote is data" (Bekoff 2002a).

We will probably never know whether these rats, monkeys, and elephants were feeling empathy as we do. But there are ways in which we can begin comparing what is going on in animal brains to what happens in our own. Neuroimaging techniques are shedding new light on human emotions, and it likely will not be long before we begin doing similar studies with other animals.

It is important to consider the possibility that it feels good to be fair to others, to cooperate with them and to treat them fairly, to forgive them for their mistakes and shortcomings. Recent neural imaging research on humans by Rilling and his colleagues (Rilling et al. 2002) has shown that the brain's pleasure centers are strongly activated when people cooperate with one another, that we might be wired to be fair or nice to one another. (I do not want to argue here that "being fair" always means "being nice.") This is extremely significant research for it posits that there is a strong neural basis for human cooperation and that it feels good to cooperate, that being nice is rewarding in social interactions and might be a stimulus for fostering cooperation and fairness. Despite challenging technical difficulties, this sort of noninvasive research is just what is needed on other animals.

ANIMAL PLAY AND SOCIAL CONTRACTS: LESSONS IN COOPERATION, JUSTICE, FAIRNESS, AND TRUST

> What is justice? Justice is fairness, so they say. But, what is fair?
> —Bradie 1999, p. 607

"Happiness is never better exhibited than by young animals, such as puppies, kittens, lambs, &c., when playing together, like our own children." So wrote Charles Darwin in *The Descent of Man and Selection in Relation to Sex* (Darwin 1871/1936, p. 448).

Animal play is obvious and few if any people would argue that play is not an important category of behavior (for definitions of social play see Bekoff and Byers 1981, 1998; Fagen 1981; Power 2000; Burghardt 2005). Animal social morality, however, is a more slippery concept. Cognitive ethological approaches are useful for gaining an understanding of social play for various reasons including (Allen and Bekoff 1997): (1) it exemplifies many of the theoretical issues faced by cognitive ethologists; (2) empirical research on social play has and will benefit from a cognitive approach, because play involves communication, intention, role-playing, and cooperation; (3) detailed analyses of social play may provide more promising evidence of animal minds than research in many other areas, for it may yield clues about the ability of animals to understand one another's intentions; and (4) play occurs in a wide range of mammalian species and in a number of avian species, and thus it affords the opportunity for a comparative investigation of cognitive abilities extending beyond the narrow focus on primates that often dominates discussions of non-human cognition. For example, during social play, many animals engage in self-handicapping and role-reversals, two behavior patterns that are often used to make inferences about intentionality (and consciousness and self-consciousness).

Social play in animals is an exhilarating activity in which to engage and to observe. The rhythm, dance, and spirit of animals at play is incredibly contagious. Not only do their animal friends want to join in or find others with whom to romp, but I also want to play when I see animals chasing one another, playing hide-and-seek, and wresting with reckless abandon. My body once tingled with delight as I watched a young elk in Rocky Mountain National Park, Colorado, running across a snow field, jumping in the air and twisting his body while in flight, stopping to catch his breath, and then jumping and twisting over and over and again. There was plenty of grassy terrain around but he chose the more challenging snow field in which to romp (supporting Byers' (1977, 1998) idea that play may be very important in physical training). Buffaloes will also follow one another and playfully run onto and slide across ice, excitedly bellowing "Gwaaa" as they do so. And, of course, we all know that dogs and cats love to play, as do many other mammals. I and many others have observed birds also playfully soar across the sky chasing, diving here and there, and frolicking with one another.

Consider also some of my field notes of two dogs at play:

> Jethro bounds towards Zeke, stops immediately in front of him, crouches on his forelimbs, wags his tail, barks, and immediately lunges at him, bites his scruff and shakes his head rapidly from side-to-side, works his way around to his backside and mounts him, jumps off, does a rapid bow, lunges at his side and slams him with his hips, leaps up and bites his neck, and runs away. Zeke takes wild pursuit of Jethro and leaps on his back and bites his muzzle and then his scruff, and shakes his head rapidly from side-to-side. Suki bounds in and chases Jethro and Zeke and they all wrestle with one another. They part for a few minutes, sniffing here and there and resting. Then, Jethro walks slowly over to Zeke, extends his paw toward Zeke's head, and nips at his ears. Zeke gets up and jumps on Jethro's back, bites him, and grasps him around his waist. They then fall to the ground and mouth wrestle. Then they chase one another and roll over and play. Suki decides to jump in and the three of them frolic until they're exhausted. Never did their play escalate into aggression.

The unmistakable emotions associated with play—joy and happiness—drive animals into becoming at one with the activity. One way to get animals (including humans) to do something is to make it fun, and there is no doubt that animals enjoy playing. Studies of the chemistry of play support the claim that play is fun. Dopamine (and perhaps serotonin and norepinephrine) is important in the regulation of play. Rats show an increase in dopamine activity when anticipating the opportunity to play (Siviy 1998) and enjoy being playfully tickled (Panksepp 1998, 2000). There is also a close association between opiates and play (Panksepp 1998).

Neurobiological data are essential for learning more about whether play truly is a subjectively pleasurable activity for animals as it seems to be for humans. Siviy's and Panksepp's findings suggest that it is. In light of these neurobiological ("hard") data concerning possible neurochemical bases for various moods, in this case joy and pleasure, skeptics who claim that animals do not feel emotions might be more likely to accept the idea that enjoyment could well be a motivator for play behavior.

IT BEGINS WITH A "BOW": "I WANT TO PLAY WITH YOU"

To learn about the dynamics of play it is essential to pay attention to subtle details that are otherwise lost in superficial analyses. During play there are continuous rapid exchanges of information "on the run." Dogs and other animals keep track of what is happening when they play so we also need to pay attention to details. My studies of play are based on careful observation and analyses—some might say obsessive analyses—of video-tape. I watch tapes of play one frame at a time to see what the animals are doing and how they exchange information about their intentions and desires to play. This is tedious work and some of my students who were excited about studying dog play had second thoughts after watching the same video frames over and over again. But when they then were able to go out and watch dogs play and understand what was happening they came to appreciate that while studying play can be hard work it's well-worth the effort.

So, a typical scene might go as follows. "Would you care to play" asks one wolf of another? "Yes, I would" says the other. After each individual agrees to play and not to fight, prey on, or mate with the other, there are on-going rapid and subtle exchanges of information so that their cooperative agreement can be fine-tuned and negotiated on the run, so that the activity remains playful. Incorporated into many explanations of social play are such notions as making a deal, trusting, behaving fairly, forgiving, apologizing, and perhaps justice, behavioral attributes that underlie social morality and moral agency (Bekoff 2002a). Recent research by Okamoto and Matsumara (2000) suggests that punishment and apology play a role in maintaining cooperation between individual non-human primates.

When individuals play they typically use action patterns that are also used in other contexts, such as predatory behavior, antipredatory behavior, and mating activities. Behavior patterns that are observed in mating may be intermixed in flexible kaleidoscopic sequences with actions that are used during fighting, looking for prey, and avoiding being eaten. These actions may not vary much across different contexts, or they may be hard to discriminate even for the participants. So, how do animals know that they are playing? How do they communicate their desires or intentions to play or to continue to play? How is the play mood maintained?

Because there is a chance that various behavior patterns that are performed during on-going social play can be misinterpreted, individuals need to tell others "I want to play," "this is still play no matter what I am going to do to you," or "this is still play regardless of what I just did to you." An agreement to play, rather than to fight, mate, or engage in predatory activities, can be negotiated in various ways. Individuals may use various behavior patterns— play markers—to initiate play or to maintain (prevent termination of) a play mood (Bekoff 1975, 1977a, 1995; Bekoff and Allen 1992, 1998; Allen and Bekoff 1997; Flack, Jeannotte, and de Waal 2004) by punctuating play sequences with these actions when it is likely that a particular behavior may have been, or will be, misinterpreted (it is also possible that there are auditory, olfactory, and tactile play markers; Bekoff and Byers 1981; Fagen 1981).

One action that is very common in play among canids (members of the dog family) is the "bow." Bows occur almost exclusively in the context of social play. The "bow," a highly *ritualized* and *stereotyped* movement that seems to function to stimulate recipients to engage (or to continue to engage) in social play, has been extensively studied in various canids in this context. Bows (the animal crouches on her forelimbs and elevates her hindlimbs) occur through-out play sequences, but most commonly at the beginning or towards the middle of playful encounters. In a detailed analysis of the form and duration of play bows (Bekoff 1977a) I discovered that duration was more variable than form, and that play bows were always less variable when performed at the beginning, rather than in the middle of, ongoing play sequences. Three pos-sible explanations for this change in variability include: (1) fatigue, (2) the fact that animals are performing them from a wide variety of preceding postures, and (3) there is less of a need to communicate that "this is still play" than there is when trying to initiate a new interaction. These explanations are not exclu-sive alternatives.

In a long-term and continuing study of social play I also found that play signals in infant canids (domestic dogs, wolves, and coyotes) were used *non-randomly*, especially when biting accompanied by rapid side-to-side shaking of the head was performed (Bekoff 1995). Biting accompanied by rapid side-to-side shaking of the head is performed during serious aggressive and predatory encounters and can easily be misinterpreted if its meaning is not modified by a play signal. Following the work of Bateson (2000), Neuman (2003, p. 1) argues that in certain situations such as play "meaning is a form of coordination between interacting agents, and that this form of coordina-tion is orchestrated through context markers..." He refers to this process as "meaning-in-context."

Play signals are an example of what ethologists call "honest signals." There is little evidence that social play is a manipulative or "Machiavellian" activ-ity. Play signals are rarely used to deceive others in canids or other species. There are no studies of which I am aware that actually look at the relative frequencies of occurrence of honest and deceptive play signaling, but my own long-term observations indicate that deceptive signaling is so rare that I cannot remember more than a few occurrences in thousands of play sequences. Cheaters are unlikely to be chosen as play partners because oth-ers can simply refuse to play with them and choose others. Limited data on infant coyotes show that cheaters have difficulty getting other young coyotes to play (personal observations). It is not known if individuals select play partners based on what they have observed during play by others.

In domestic dogs there is little tolerance for non-cooperative cheaters. Cheaters may be avoided or chased from play groups. There seems to be a sense of what is right, wrong, and fair. While studying dog play on a beach in San Diego, California, Alexandra Horowitz (2002) observed a dog she called Up-ears enter into a play group and interrupt the play of two other dogs, Blackie and Roxy. Up-ears was chased out of the group and when she returned Blackie and Roxy stopped playing and looked off toward a distant sound. Roxy began moving in the direction of the sound and Up-ears ran off following their line of sight. Roxy and Blackie immediately began playing once again. Even in rats fairness and trust are important in the dynamics of playful interactions. Sergio Pellis (2002), a psychologist at the University of

Lethbridge in Canada, discovered that sequences of rat play consist of individuals assessing and monitoring one another and then fine-tuning and changing their own behavior to maintain the play mood. When the rules of play are violated, when fairness breaks down, so does play.

Detailed analyses show that individual actions may change their form and duration during play. Individuals might also know that they are playing because the actions that are performed differ when they are performed during play when compared to other contexts (Hill and Bekoff 1977), or the order in which motor patterns are performed differs from, and might be more variable than, the order in which they are performed during the performance of, for example, serious aggressive, predatory, or reproductive activities (Bekoff and Byers 1981).

Individuals also engage in role-reversing and self-handicapping (Bekoff and Allen 1998; Bauer and Smuts 2002; Horowitz 2002) to maintain social play. Each can serve to reduce asymmetries between the interacting animals and foster the reciprocity that is needed for play to occur. Self-handicapping happens when an individual performs a behavior pattern that might compromise herself. For example, a coyote might not bite her play partner as hard as she can, or she might not play as vigorously as she can. Watson and Croft (1996) found that red-neck wallabies adjusted their play to the age of their partner. When a partner was younger, the older animal adopted a defensive, flat-footed posture, and pawing rather than sparring occurred. In addition, the older player was more tolerant of its partner's tactics and took the initiative in prolonging interactions.

Role-reversing occurs when a dominant animal performs an action during play that would not normally occur during real aggression. For example, a dominant animal might voluntarily not roll-over on his back during fighting, but would do so while playing. In some instances role-reversing and self-handicapping might occur together. For example, a dominant individual might roll over while playing with a subordinate animal and inhibit the intensity of a bite.

From a functional perspective, self-handicapping and role-reversing, similar to using specific play invitation signals and gestures, or altering behavioral sequences, might serve to signal an individual's intention to continue to play. In this way there can be mutual benefits to each individual player because of their agreeing to play and not fight or mate. This might differentiate cooperative play from the situation described above in which a male Diana monkey helped a female get food when she could not learn the task that would bring her food. There seemed to be no benefit to the male to do so. (I thank Jan Nystrom for marking this distinction.)

CAN ANIMALS FORGIVE?

Even for the behavior of forgiving, which is often attributed solely to humans, the renowned evolutionary biologist David Sloan Wilson (2002) shows that forgiveness is a complex biological adaptation. In his book *Darwin's cathedral: Evolution, religion, and the nature of society*, Wilson concludes that "... forgiveness has a biological foundation that extends throughout the animal kingdom." (p. 195) And further, "... Forgiveness has many faces—*and needs to*—in order to function adaptively in so many different contexts." (p. 212) While Wilson concentrates mainly on human societies his views can easily be extended—and responsibly so—to nonhuman animals. Indeed, Wilson points out that adaptive traits such as forgiveness might not require as much brain power as once thought. This is not to say that animals aren't smart but rather that forgiveness might be a trait that is basic to many animals even if they don't have especially big and active brains. Perhaps if we try to learn more about forgiveness in animals and how it functions in play we will also learn to live more compassionately and cooperatively with one another.

FINE-TUNING PLAY: WHY COOPERATE AND PLAY FAIRLY?

Why do animals carefully use play signals to tell others that they really want to play and not try to dominate them, why do they engage in self-handicapping and role-reversing? Why do they plan play? During social play, while individuals are having fun in a relatively safe environment, they learn ground rules that are acceptable to others—how hard they can bite, how roughly they can interact—and how to resolve conflicts. There is a premium on playing fairly and trusting others to do so as well. There are codes of social conduct that regulate actions that are and are not permissible, and the existence of these codes likely speaks to the evolution of social morality. What could be a better atmosphere in which to learn social skills than during social play, where there are few penalties for transgressions? Individuals might also generalize codes of conduct learned in playing with specific individuals to other group members and to other situations such as sharing food, defending resources, grooming, and giving care. (Social morality does not mean other animals are behaving unfairly when they kill for food, for example, for they have evolved to do this.)

Playtime generally is safe time. Transgressions and mistakes are forgiven and apologies are accepted by others especially when one player is a youngster who is not yet a competitor for social status, food, or mates. There is a certain innocence or ingenuousness in play. Individuals must cooperate with one another when they play—they must negotiate agreements to play (Bekoff 1995). Fagen (1993, p. 192) noted that "Levels of cooperation in play of juvenile primates may exceed those predicted by simple evolutionary arguments ..." The highly cooperative nature of play has evolved in many other species (Fagen 1981; Bekoff 1995; Bekoff and Allen 1998; Power 2000; Drea and Frank 2003; Burghardt 2005). Detailed studies of play in various species indicate that individuals trust others to maintain the rules of the game (Bekoff and Byers 1998). While there have been numerous discussions of cooperative behavior in animals (e.g. Axelrod 1984; de Waal 1996; Ridley 1996; Dugatkin 1997; Hauser 2000; essays in *Journal of Consciousness Studies*, Volume 7, No. 1/2, 2000 and references therein), none has considered the details of social play, the requirement for cooperation and reciprocity and its possible role in the evolution of social morality, namely behaving fairly.

Individuals of different species seem to fine-tune on-going play sequences to maintain a play mood and to prevent play from escalating into real aggression. Detailed analyses of film show that in canids there are subtle and fleeting movements and rapid exchanges of eye contact that suggest that players are exchanging information on the run, from moment-to-moment, to make certain everything is all right, that this is still play. Aldis (1975) suggested that in play, there is a 50:50 rule so that each player "wins" about 50% of their play bouts by adjusting their behavior to accomplish this (for further discussion and details on rodent play, see Pellis 2002).

Why might animals fine-tune play? Why might they try hard to share one another's intentions? While play in most species does not take up much time and energy (Bekoff and Byers, 1998; Power 2000), and in some species only minimal amounts of social play during short windows of time early in development are necessary to produce socialized individuals (two 20 minute play sessions with another dog, twice a week, are sufficient for domestic dogs from three–seven weeks of age (Scott and Fuller 1965)), researchers agree that play is very important in social, cognitive, and/or physical development, and may also be important for training youngsters for unexpected circumstances (Spinka, Newberry, and Bekoff 2001). While there are few data concerning the actual benefits of social play in terms of survival and reproductive success, it generally is assumed that short-term and long-term functions (benefits) vary from species-to-species and among different age groups and between the sexes within a species. No matter what the functions of play may be, there seems to be little doubt that play has *some* benefits and that the absence of play can have devastating effects on social development (Spinka, Newberry, and Bekoff 2001; Power 2000; Burghardt 2005).

During early development there is a small time window when individuals can play without being responsible for their own well-being. This time period is generally referred to as the "socialization period" for this is when species-typical social skills are learned most rapidly. It is important for individuals to engage in at least *some* play. All individuals need to play and there is a premium for playing fairly if one is to be able to play at all. If individuals do not play fairly they may not be able to find willing play partners. In coyotes, for example, youngsters are hesitant to play with an individual who does not play fairly or with an individual whom they fear (Bekoff 1977b). In many species individuals also show play partner preferences and it is possible that these preferences are based on the trust that individuals place in one another.

Fairness and Fitness: Coyotes, Play, and Dispersal

One big question of interest to biologists is how differences in the performance of a given behavior influence an individual's reproductive success. It is extremely difficult to show with great certainty that the performance of a specific behavior is directly and *causally* coupled to reproductive success, especially under field conditions, so in many instances we have to rely on guesswork.

With respect to the topic at hand the question is "Do differences in play and variations in fair play influence an individual's reproductive fitness?" I am not arguing that there is a gene for social morality but I am claiming that it is reasonable to ask if there are differences among individuals and that perhaps more virtuous individuals are more fit and have more offspring than less virtuous individuals. A sense of fairness is common to many animals, and without it social play would be difficult to maintain. And without social play I and others have argued individual animals and entire groups would be at a disadvantage (Bekoff 2002a). If I am correct, morality evolved because it is adaptive in its own right not because it is merely an antidote to competition or aggression. Behaving fairly helps many animals, including humans, to survive and flourish in their particular social environment. I fully realize that this may sound like a radical idea, particularly if one views morality as uniquely human (and a sort of puzzling capacity) that sets us apart from other animals. But if you accept my argument that play and fairness may be linked then we need to demonstrate that individual animals might benefit from these behaviors.

Dogs, coyotes, and wolves are fast learners when it comes to fair play and I bet that other animals are as well. There are serious sanctions when they breach the trust of their friends and these penalties might indeed become public information if others see an individual cheating his companions. Biologists call these penalties "costs," which means that an individual might suffer some decline in his or her reproductive fitness if they do not play by the expected and accepted rules of the game.

My fieldwork on coyotes has revealed one direct cost paid by animals who fail to engage in fair play or who do not play much at all. I found that coyote pups who don't play as much as others because they are avoided by others or because they themselves avoid others are less tightly bonded to other members of their group and more likely to strike out on their own (Bekoff 1977b). But life outside the group is much more risky than within it. In a seven year study of coyotes living in the Grand Teton National Park outside Moose, Wyoming, we found that more than 55 per cent of yearlings who drifted away from their social group died, whereas fewer than 20 per cent of their stay-at-home peers did (Bekoff and Wells 1986). Was it because of play? We are not sure, but information that we collected on captive coyotes suggested that the lack of play was a major factor in individuals spending more time alone, away from their littermates and other group members.

The Evolution of Fairness:
A Game-Theoretical Model

Much research on the evolution of cooperation has been modeled using game-theoretic approaches. Lee Dugatkin and I (Dugatkin and Bekoff 2003) used a similar technique to analyze four possible strategies that an individual could adopt over time (for species in which fairness can be expressed during two different developmental stages), namely, being fair (*F*) and at a later date being fair (*F/F*), being fair and then not fair (*F/NF*), being not fair and then fair (*NF/F*), and being not fair and then not fair (*NF/NF*). Of these, only *F/F* was an Evolutionarily Stable Strategy (ESS) that could evolve under the conditions of the model. None of the other three strategies were ESSs, and when no strategy was an ESS all four could coexist. There are two clear predictions from our results. First, always acting fairly should be more common than never acting fairly in species in which fairness can be expressed during two different developmental stages. Second, there should be many more cases in which none of the strategies we modeled would be an ESS, but all four could coexist at significant frequencies. That F/NF is not an ESS is of interest because this strategy could be conceived as a form of deceit. This finding fits in well with what is known about play signals, for as I mentioned above, there is little evidence that play signals are used to deceive others at any stage of development (Bekoff 1977a; Bekoff and Allen 1998). Our ideas are certainly testable in principle by following identified individuals and recording how they distribute fairness across different activities as they mature.

Neurobiological Bases of Sharing Intentions and Mind-Reading: Possible Connections Among Acting, Seeing, Feeling, and Feeling/Knowing

Detailed observations and descriptions are mandatory. We need to know what animals are doing when they interact with one another in order to learn more about the neural correlates of their social activities. This work is tedious and time-consuming.

How might a play bow (or other action) serve to provide information to its recipient about the sender's intentions? Is there a relationship among acting, feeling, seeing, and feeling/knowing? Perhaps one's own experiences with play can promote learning about the intentions of others. Perhaps the recipient shares the intentions (beliefs, desires) of the sender based on the recipient's own prior experiences of situations in which she performed play bows. Recent research suggests a neurobiological basis for sharing intentions. "Mirror neurons," found in macaques, fire when a monkey executes an action and also when the monkey observes the same action performed by another monkey (Gallese 1998; Gallese and Goldman 1998; Motluk 2001).

Research on mirror neurons is truly exciting and the results of these efforts will be very helpful for answering questions about which species of animals may have "theories of mind" or "cognitive empathy" about the mental and emotional states of others. Gallese and Goldman (1998) suggest that mirror neurons might "enable an organism to detect certain mental states of observed conspecifics ... as part of, or a precursor to, a more general mind-reading ability." Laurie Carr and her colleagues at The University of California at Los Angeles, discovered, by using neuroimaging in humans, similar patterns of neural activation both when an individual observed a facial expression depicting an emotion and when they imitated the facial expression. This research suggests a neurobiological underpinning of empathy (Laurie Carr, personal communication). Frith and Frith (1999) report the results of neural imaging studies in humans that suggest a neural basis for one form of "social intelligence," understanding others' mental states (mental state attribution).

More comparative data are needed to determine if mirror neurons (or functional equivalents) are found in other taxa and if they might actually play a role in the sharing of intentions or feelings—perhaps keys to empathy— between individuals engaged in an on-going social interaction such as play. Neuroimaging studies will also be especially useful.

LEVELS OF SELECTION

I am sure that close scrutiny of social animals will reveal more evidence that having a sense of fairness benefits individuals. More controversially, I also believe that a moral sense benefits groups as a whole because during social play group members learn rules of engagement that influence their decisions about what is acceptable behavior when dealing with each other. Such an understanding is essential if individuals are to work in harmony to create a successful group able to out compete other groups. Following the lines of Sober and Wilson's (1998, pp. 135ff) discussion concerning the choice of social partners, it may be that behaving fairly is a group adaptation, but once a social norm evolves it becomes individually advantageous to behave fairly for there are costs to not doing so (Elliott Sober, personal communication). We still need somehow to figure out how to test rigorously ideas about levels of selection—group selection "versus" individual selection—and studies of the evolution of social morality are good places to focus for expanding our views (e.g. Boehm 1999; Leigh 1999; see also Aviles 1999; Bradley 1999; Gould and Lloyd 1999; Kitchen and Packer 1999; Mayr 2000).

THE IMPORTANCE OF PREDICTION: A LITMUS TEST FOR KNOWING?

The ability to make accurate predictions about what an individual is likely to do in a given social situation may be closely linked with one's having extensive experience with those individuals. Of course, extensive formal ("scientific") experience watching animals is not necessary for being able to make accurate predictions. Also, while I cannot know with absolute certainty that any of the animals about whom I have written (or others) have beliefs, desires, or intentions, I also cannot know with absolute certainty if they have a sense of "right" or "wrong" or if they are merely acting "as if" they are moral beings. They perform what can be called "moral behavior" but it might have no bearing on what they are thinking or feeling. However, the inescapable uncertainty associated with these claims does not mean that I do not know quite a lot about what is happening in their minds. It seems fair to ask skeptics to do more than say "'as if' is not enough" and to assume some responsibility for studying these questions in more rigorous ways (Bekoff 2000b).

In *Species of Mind*, Colin Allen and I (1997) argued that there are a number of reasons that cognitive explanations that entail beliefs, desires, or intentions may be the best explanations to which to appeal because they help us come to terms with questions centering on the comparative and evolutionary study of animal minds. First, the explanatory power of our theorizing is increased. Second, it is obvious that a cognitive approach can generate new ideas that can be tested empirically, help in evaluations of extant explanations, lead to the development of new predictive models, and perhaps, lead to the reconsideration of old data, some of which might have resisted explanation without a cognitive perspective. Third, cognitive explanations account for observed flexibility in behavior better than do less flexible stimulus-response accounts that stipulate do "this" in "this" situation or "that" in "that" situation (Bekoff 1996). Fourth, cognitive explanations might help scientists come to terms with larger sets of available data that are difficult to understand. Fifth, cognitive explanations may also be more parsimonious and less cumbersome than explanations that require numerous and diverse stimulus-response contingencies (Bekoff 1996; Allen and Bekoff 1997; Bekoff and Allen 1997; see also de Waal 1991).

The ability to predict what an individual is likely to do next in a social encounter might be a useful litmus test for what is happening in that individual's brain. This is not to say that the ability to predict on-going behavior will ever be as accurate as, say, astronomical predictions concerning the position of stars in the sky. Nonetheless, researchers and others who have spent much time watching individual animals are rather good at predicting their behavior, and many of these predictions are tied in with attributions of beliefs, desires, or intentions. This is the case for my own extensive experience of watching canids signal their intentions to engage in and to maintain social play. Intentional or representational explanations are important to my making accurate predictions about future behavior.

All I want to put out on the table here is the idea that the ability to predict behavior with a high degree of accuracy might also be a good reason to favor cognitive explanations in certain situations. Accurate prediction might be used as one measure of what a human observer "knows" about the behavior of the animals he or she is studying.

THERE *IS* WILD JUSTICE, FAIRNESS, AND SOCIAL COOPERATION: DOING WHAT COMES NATURALLY

> Justice presumes a personal concern for others. It is first of all a sense, not a rational or social construction, and I want to argue that this sense is, in an important sense, natural.
>
> —Solomon 1995, p. 102

> It is not difficult to imagine the emergence of justice and honor out of the practices of cooperation.
>
> —Damasio 2003, p. 162

> More than any other species, we are beneficiaries and victims of a wealth of emotional experience.
>
> —Dolan, 2002, 1191

> Our evaluative conceptions from the nature and ideals of right-living are drawn from vast networks of social activities that have transpired over enormous reaches of time: models of conduct and character have been established, assayed, rejected, confirmed, revised, redrawn, shown unfit.
>
> —Hudson 1986, p. 121

To learn more about the evolution of cognitive capacities and morality we need to broaden our taxonomic studies to include species other than non-human primates. We need to go beyond primatocentrism which usually is "great ape-o-centrism." Some authors have been more resistant to this idea than others. Consider the following claims by Richard Byrne (1995, my emphases added) from his book *The Thinking Ape.*

> It *seems* that the great apes, especially the common chimpanzee, can attribute mental states to other individuals; but no other group of animals can do so—apart from ourselves, and perhaps cetaceans. (p. 146)
>
> This contrasts with the findings on understanding of beliefs, attribution of intentions, and how things work—where a sharp discontinuity is *implied* between great apes and all other animals. (p. 154)
>
> Of course, until similar painstaking work is done with monkeys, we *cannot* argue that only apes have such abilities ... and no-one has yet risked the huge expenditure of time and money to find out. (p. 172)

We simply do not have enough data to make hard and fast claims about the taxonomic distribution among different species of the cognitive skills and emotional capacities necessary for being able to empathize with others, to behave fairly, or to be moral agents. Marler (1996, p. 22) concluded a review of social cognition in non-human primates and birds as follows: "I am driven to conclude, at least provisionally, that there are more similarities than differences between birds and primates. Each taxon has significant advantages that the other lacks." Tomasello and Call (1997, pp. 399–400) summarized their comprehensive review of primate cognition by noting that "The experimental foundation for claims that apes are 'more intelligent' than monkeys is not a solid one, and there are few if any naturalistic observations that would substantiate such broad-based, species-general claims." While Flack and de Waal's (2000) and others' focus is on non-human primates as the most likely animals to show precursors to human morality, others have argued that we might learn as much or more about the evolution of human social behavior by studying social carnivores (Schaller and Lowther 1969; Tinbergen 1972; Thompson 1975; Drea and Frank 2003), species whose social behavior and organization resemble that of early hominids in a number of ways (divisions of labor, food sharing, care of young, and inter- and intrasexual dominance hierarchies).

What we really need are long-term field studies of social animals for which it would be reasonable to hypothesize that emotions and morality have played a role in the evolution of sociality, that emotions and morality are important in the development and maintenance of social bonds that allow individuals to work together for the benefit of all group members (see also Gruen 2002).

To stimulate further comparative research (and the development of models) on a wider array of species than has previously been studied, I offer the hypothesis that social morality, in this case behaving fairly, is an adaptation that is shared by many mammals, not only by non-human and human primates. Behaving fairly evolved because it helped young animals acquire social (and other) skills needed as they mature into adults. A focus on social cooperation is needed to balance the plethora of research that is devoted to social competition and selfishness (for further discussion see Boehm 1999; Singer 1999; Wilson 2002).

I also wonder if our view of the world would have been different had Charles Darwin been a female, if some or many of the instances in which competition is invoked were viewed as cooperation. Women tend to "see" more cooperation in nature than do men. Adams and Burnett (1991) discovered that female ethologists working in East Africa use a substantially different descriptive vocabulary than do male ethologists. Of the nine variables they studied, those concerning cooperation and female gender were the most important discriminating women's and men's word use. They concluded (p. 558) that "The variable COOPERATION demonstrates the appropriateness of feminist claims to connection and cooperation as women's models for behaviour, as divergent from the traditional competitive model." Why women and men approach the same subject from a different perspective remains largely unanswered. Perhaps there is more cooperation than meets the eye.

Group-living animals in which there is a variety of complex social interactions among individuals and in which individuals assess social relationships may provide many insights into animal morality (Bekoff 2002a,b, 2003b; Drea and Frank 2003). In many social groups individuals establish social hierarchies and develop and maintain tight social bonds that help to regulate social behavior. Individuals coordinate their behavior—some mate, some hunt, some defend resources, some accept subordinate status—to achieve common goals and to maintain social stability. Consider briefly, pack-living wolves, exemplars of highly developed cooperative and coordinated behavior. (Solomon (1995, pp. 139ff) also considers the importance of learning more about wolves in his discussion of justice, emotions, and the origins of social contracts.)

For a long time researchers thought pack size was regulated by available food resources. Wolves typically feed on such prey as elk and moose, each of which is larger than an individual wolf. Hunting such large ungulates successfully takes more than one wolf, so it made sense to postulate that wolf packs evolved because of the size of wolves' prey. Defending food might also be associated with pack-living. However, long-term research by Mech (1970) showed that pack size in wolves was regulated by *social* and not food-related factors. Mech discovered that the number of wolves who could live together in a coordinated pack was governed by the number of wolves with whom individuals could closely bond ("social attraction factor") balanced against the number of individuals from whom an individual could tolerate competition ("social competition factor"). Codes of conduct and packs broke down when there were too many wolves. (Colin Allen, personal communication, notes that it is possible that social factors might be proximate influences after long periods of selection for hunting prey of a certain size favoring packs of a certain size.) Whether or not the dissolution of packs was due to individuals behaving unfairly is unknown, but this would be a valuable topic for future research in wolves and other social animals. Solomon (1995, p. 143) contends that "A wolf who is generous can expect generosity in return. A wolf who violates another's ownership zone can expect to be punished, perhaps ferociously, by others." These claims can easily be studied empirically. (For interesting studies of the "social complexity hypothesis" that claims "that animals living in large social groups should display enhanced cognitive abilities" when compared to those who do not, see Bond, Kamil, and Balda 2003 (p. 479) and Drea and Frank 2003).

In social groups, individuals often learn what they can and cannot do, and the group's integrity depends upon individuals agreeing that certain rules regulate their behavior. At any given moment individuals know their place or role and that of other group members. As a result of lessons in social cognition and empathy that are offered in social play, individuals learn what is "right" or "wrong"—what is acceptable to others—the result of which is the development and maintenance of a social group that operates efficiently. The absence of social structure and boundaries can produce gaps in morality that lead to the dissolution of a group (Bruce Gottlieb, personal communication).

In summary, I argue that mammalian social play is a useful behavioral phenotype on which to concentrate in order to learn more about the evolution of fairness and social morality. (While birds and individuals of other species engage in social play, there are too few data from which to draw detailed conclusions about the nature of their play.) There is strong selection for playing fairly because most if not all individuals benefit from adopting this behavioral strategy (and group stability may be also be fostered). Numerous mechanisms (play invitation signals, variations in the sequencing of actions performed during play when compared to other contexts, self-handicapping, role-reversing) have evolved to facilitate the initiation and maintenance of social play in numerous mammals—to keep others engaged—so that agreeing to play fairly and the resulting benefits of doing so can be readily achieved.

Ridley (1996) points out that humans seem to be inordinately upset about unfairness, but we do not know much about others animals reaction to unfairness. Brosnan and de Waal, (2003) have recently shown that captive brown capuchin monkeys who were trained to exchange a token for cucumber would no longer do so when they saw another monkey receive a grape, a more favored reward. The monkey's response to unequal reward distribution was interpreted as their having a sense of fairness.

Ridley also suggests that perhaps behaving fairly pays off in the long run. Dugatkin's and my model of the development and evolution of cooperation and fairness (Dugatkin and Bekoff 2003) suggests it might. Hauser (2000) concluded that there is no evidence that animals can evaluate whether an act of reciprocation is fair. However, he did not consider social play in his discussion of animal morality and moral agency. De Waal (1996) remains skeptical about the widespread taxonomic distribution of cognitive empathy after briefly considering social play, but he remains open to the possibility that cognitive empathy might be found in animals other than the great apes (see Preston and de Wall 2002). It is premature to dismiss the possibility that social play plays some role in the evolution of fairness and social morality or that animals other than primates are unable intentionally to choose to behave fairly because they lack the necessary cognitive skills or emotional capacities. We really have very little information that bears on these questions.

Let me emphasize again that I am not arguing that there is a gene for fair or moral behavior. As with any behavioral trait, the underlying genetics is bound to be complex, and environmental influences may be large and difficult to pin down. Nonetheless, provided there is variation in levels of morality among individuals and the trait is highly heritable, and provided virtue is rewarded by a greater number of offspring, then genes associated with good behaviour are likely to accumulate in subsequent generations. The observation that play is rarely unfair or uncooperative is surely an indication that natural selection acts to weed out those individuals who do not play by the rules.

Future comparative research that considers the nature and details of the social exchanges that are needed for animals to engage in play—reciprocity and cooperation—will undoubtedly produce data that bear on the questions that I raise in this brief essay and also help to "operationalize" the notion of behaving fairly by informing us about what sorts of evidence confirm that animals are behaving with some sense of fairness. In the absence of this information it is premature to dismiss the possibility that social play plays some role in the evolution of fairness and social morality or that animals other than primates are unable intentionally to choose to behave fairly because they lack the necessary cognitive skills or emotional capacities. These are empirical questions for which the comparative data base is scant.

Gruen (2002) also correctly points out that we still need to come to terms with what it means to be moral. She also suggests that we need to find out what cognitive and emotional capacities operate when humans perform various moral actions, and to study animals to determine if they share these capacities or some variation of them. Even if it were the case that available data suggested that non-human primates do not seem to behave in a specific way, for example, playing fairly, in the absence of comparative data this does not justify the claim that individuals of other taxa cannot play fairly. (At a meeting in Chicago, Illinois in August 2000 dealing with social organization and social complexity (see de Waal and Tyack 2003), it was hinted to me that while my ideas about social morality are interesting, there really is no way that social carnivores could be said to be so decent—to behave (play) fairly—because it was unlikely that even non-human primates were this virtuous.)

Learning about the taxonomic distribution of animal morality involves answering numerous and often difficult questions. Perhaps it will turn out that the best explanation for existing data in some taxa is that some individuals do indeed on some occasions modify their behavior to play fairly.

Play may be a unique category of behavior in that asymmetries are tolerated more so than in other social contexts. Play cannot occur if the individuals choose not to engage in the activity and the equality (or symmetry and kindness) needed for play to continue makes it different from other forms of seemingly cooperative behavior (e.g. hunting, care-giving). This sort of egalitarianism is thought to be a precondition for the evolution of social morality in humans. From whence did it arise? Truth be told, we really do not know much about the origins of egalitarianism. Arm-chair discussions, while important, will do little in comparison to our having direct experiences with other animals. In my view, studies of the evolution of social morality are among the most exciting and challenging projects that behavioral scientists (ethologists, geneticists, evolutionary biologists, neurobiologists, psychologists, anthropologists), theologians, and religious scholars face. We need to rise to the *extremely* challenging (and frustrating) task before us rather than dismiss summarily and unfairly, in a speciesistic manner, the moral lives of other animals. *Fair is fair.*

MORALITY AND HUMAN NATURE: THE PRECAUTIONARY PRINCIPLE

Just what role does human morality play in defining "human nature"? We do not really know despite strong claims to the contrary. Using animal models to rationalize cruelty, divisiveness, warfare, territoriality, and selfishness, is a disingenuous use of much available information on animal social behavior. While animals surely can be nasty this does not explain much of the behavior that is expressed to other individuals. I have argued that animals make choices to be nice and to be fair.

Ecologists and environmentalists have developed what they call the "precautionary principle" that is used for making decisions about environmental problems. This principle states that a lack of full scientific certainty should not be used as an excuse to delay taking action on some issue. The precautionary principle can be easily applied in studies of the evolution of social morality. To wit, I claim that we know enough to warrant further comparative studies of the evolution of social morality in animals other than nonhuman primates, and that until these data are available we should keep an open mind about what individuals of other taxa can and cannot do.

It is important for us to learn more about the evolution of social morality and how this information can be used to give us hope for the future rather than our accepting a dooms-day view of where we are all heading "because it's in our nature." Accepting that competition, selfishness, and cheating are what drive human and animal behavior leaves out a lot of the puzzle of how we came to be who we are. Cooperation and fairness can also be driving forces in the evolution of sociality.

The importance of interdisciplinary collaboration and cooperation in studies of animal cognition, cooperation, and moral behavior cannot be emphasized too strongly. It is clear that morality and virtue did not suddenly appear in the evolutionary epic beginning with humans. While fair play in animals may be a rudimentary form of social morality it still could be a forerunner of more complex and more sophisticated human moral systems. It is self-serving anthropocentric speciesism to claim that we are the *only* moral beings in the animal kingdom. It is also a simplistic and misleading view to assume that humans are merely naked apes.

The origins of virtue, egalitarianism, and morality are more ancient than our own species. Humans also are not necessarily morally superior to other animals. But, we will never learn about animal morality if we close the door on the possibility that it exists. It is still far too early to draw the uncompromising conclusion that human morality is different in kind from animal morality and walk away in victory.

REFERENCES

Adams, E. R. and Burnett, G. W. 1991. Scientific vocabulary divergence among female primatologists working in East Africa. *Social Studies of Science* 21, 547–560.

Aldis, O. 1975. *Play fighting.* Academic Press, New York.

Allen, C., and Bekoff, M. 1997. *Species of Mind: The Philosophy and Biology of Cognitive Ethology.* MIT Press, Cambridge, Massachusetts.

Aureli, F. and de Waal, F. B. M. (ed.) 2000. *Natural Conflict Resolution.* Berkeley, University of California Press.

Aviles, L. 1999. Cooperation and non-linear dynamics: An ecological perspective on the evolution of sociality. *Evolutionary Ecology Research*, 1: 459–477.

Axelrod, R. 1984. *The Evolution of Cooperation.* New York, Basic Books.

Bateson, G. 2000. *Steps to an ecology of mind.* University of Chicago Press, Chicago.

Bauer, E. B. and Smuts, B. B. 2002. Role reversal and self-handicapping during play-fighting in domestic dogs, *Canis familiaris.* Paper presented at the meetings of the Animal Behavior Society, University of Indiana.

Bekoff, M. 1975. The communication of play intention: Are play signals functional? *Semiotica*, 15, 231–239.

Bekoff, M. 1977a. Social communication in canids: Evidence for the evolution of a stereotyped mammalian display. *Science* 197, 1097–1099.

Bekoff, M. 1977b. Mammalian dispersal and the ontogeny of individual behavioral phenotypes. *American Naturalist* 111, 715–732.

Bekoff, M. 1995. Play signals as punctuation: The structure of social play in canids. *Behaviour*, 132, 419–429.

Bekoff, M. 1996. Cognitive ethology, vigilance, information gathering, and representation: Who might know what and why? *Behavioural Processes* 35: 225–237.

Bekoff, M. (ed.) 2000a. *The Smile of a Dolphin: Remarkable Accounts of Animal Emotions* (New York, Discovery Books/Random House).

Bekoff, M. 2000b. Animal Emotions: Exploring passionate natures. *BioScience* 50, 861–870.

Bekoff, M. 2001a. Social play behaviour, cooperation, fairness, trust and the evolution of morality. *Journal of Consciousness Studies* 8 (2), 81–90.

Bekoff, M. 2001b. The evolution of animal play, emotions, and social morality: On science, theology, spirituality, personhood, and love. *Zygon (Journal of Religion and Science)* 36, 615–655.

Bekoff, M. 2002a. *Minding animals: Awareness, emotions, and heart.* New York, Oxford University Press.

Bekoff, M. 2002b. Virtuous nature. *New Scientist* 13 July, 34–37.

Bekoff, M. 2002c. Self-awareness. *Nature* 419, 255.

Bekoff, M. 2003a. Consciousness and self in animals: Some reflections. *Zygon Journal of Religion and Science)* 38, 229–245.

Bekoff, M. 2003b. Empathy: Common sense, science sense, wolves, and well-being. *Behavioral and Brain Sciences* 25, 26–27.

Bekoff, M. 2005. The question of animal emotions: An ethological perspective. In F. McMillan (ed.), *Mental Health and Well-Being in Animals*, Iowa State University Press, Ames, Iowa.

Bekoff, M., and Allen, C. 1992. Intentional icons: towards an evolutionary cognitive ethology. *Ethology* 91, 1–16.

Bekoff, M., and Allen, C. 1997. Cognitive ethology: Slayers, skeptics, and proponents. In R. W. Mitchell, N. Thompson, and L. Miles (eds.), *Anthropomorphism, Anecdote, and Animals: The Emperor's New Clothes?* SUNY Press, Albany, New York. pp. 313–334.

Bekoff, M., and Allen, C. 1998. Intentional communication and social play: How and why animals negotiate and agree to play. In *Animal Play: Evolutionary, Comparative, and Ecological Perspectives*, ed. by M. Bekoff and J. A. Byers. Cambridge University Press, Cambridge and New York. Pp. 97–114.

Bekoff, M., Allen, C., and Burghardt, G. M. (eds.) 2002. *The cognitive animal.* MIT Press, Cambridge, Massachusetts.

Bekoff, M., and Byers, J. A. 1981. A critical reanalysis of the ontogeny of mammalian social and locomotor play: An ethological hornet's nest.' In *Behavioral Development: The Bielefeld Interdisciplinary Project*, ed. by K. Immelmann, G. W. Barlow, L. Petrinovich, and M. Main, Cambridge University Press, New York. Pp. 296–337.

Bekoff, M. and Byers, J. A. (eds.) 1998. *Animal Play: Evolutionary, Comparative, and Ecological Approaches* (New York, NY: Cambridge University Press).

Bekoff, M. and M. C. Wells. 1986. Social behavior and ecology of coyotes. *Advances in the Study of Behavior* 16, 251–338.

Bernstein, I. S. 2000. The law of parsimony prevails: Missing premises allow any conclusion. *Journal of Consciousness Studies* 7, 31–34.

Bewley, T. 2003. Fair's fair. *Nature* 422, 125–126.

Boehm, C. 1999. *Hierarchy in the Forest: The Evolution of Egalitarian Behavior.* Cambridge: Harvard University Press.

Bond, A., A. C. Kamil, and R. P. Balda. 2003. Social complexity and transitive inference in corvids. *Animal Behaviour* 65, 479–487.

Bowles, S. and Gintis, H. 2002. *Homo reciprocans. Nature* 415, 125–128.

Bradie, M. 1999. Evolutionary game theory meets the social contract. *Biology and Philosophy* 14, 607–613.

Bradley, B. J. 1999. Levels of selection, altruism, and primate behavior. *Quarterly Review of Biology* 74: 171–194.

Brosnan, S. F. and F. B. M. de Waal. 2003. Monkeys reject unequal pay. *Nature* 425, 297–299.

Burghardt, G. M. 2005. *The genesis of play.* MIT Press, Cambridge, Massachusetts.

Byers, J. A. 1977. Terrain preferences in the play of Siberian ibex kids (*Capra ibex sibirica*). *Zeitschrift fr Tierpsychologie* 45, 199–209.

Byers, J. A. 1998. Biological effects of locomotor play: getting into shape or something else? Pages 205–2 in Bekoff M, Byers JA, eds. *Animal Play: Evolutionary, Comparative, and Ecological Perspectives.* New York: Cambridge University Press.

Byrne, R. 1995. *The thinking ape.* Oxford University Press, New York.

Church, F. 1959. Emotional reactions of rats to the pain of others. *Journal of Comparative and Physiological Psychology* 52, 132–134.

Damasio, A. 2003. *Looking for Spinoza: Joy, sorrow, and the feeling brain.* Harcourt, New York.

Darwin C. 1859. *On the Origin of Species By Means of Natural Selection.* London: Murray.

Darwin, C. 1871/1936. *The Descent of Man and Selection in Relation to Sex.* New York: Random House.

Darwin, C. 1872/1998. The *Expression of the Emotions in Man and Animals*, Third edition. New York: Oxford University Press (with an Introduction, Afterword, and Commentaries by Paul Ekman).

Dawkins, R. 1976. The selfish gene. New York, Oxford University Press.

Dawkins, R. 2001. Sustainability doesn't come naturally: A Darwinian perspective on values. <www.environmentfoundation.net/richard-dawkins.htm>.

de Waal, F. 1991. Complementary methods and convergent evidence in the study of primate social cognition. *Behaviour* 18, 297–320.

de Waal, F. 1996. *Good natured: The origins of right and wrong in humans and other animals.* Harvard University Press, Cambridge, Massachusetts.

de Waal, F. 2001. *The ape and the sushi master: Cultural reflections of a primatologist.* New York, Basic Books.

de Waal, F., and P. L. Tyack (eds.) 2003. *Animal social complexity: Intelligence, culture, and individualized societies.* Harvard University Press, Cambridge, Massachusetts.

Dolan, R. J. 2002. Emotion, cognition, and behavior. Science 298: 1191–1194.

Douglas, K. 2001. Playing fair. *New Scientist* 10 March (No. 2281), 38–42.

Drea, C. M. and L. G. Frank. 2003. The social complexity of spotted hyenas. In de Waal, F. and P. L. Tyack (eds.), *Animal social complexity: Intelligence, culture, and individualized societies.* Harvard University Press, Cambridge, Massachusetts, pp. 121–148.

Dugatkin, L. A. 1997. *Cooperation Among Animals: An Evolutionary Perspective.* New York: Oxford University Press.

Dugatkin, L. A. and Bekoff, M. 2003. Play and the evolution of fairness: A game theory model. *Behavioural Processes* 60:209–214.

Dylan, B. 1983. *Infidels.* CBS Inc.

Fagen, R. 1981. *Animal Play Behavior.* New York: Oxford University Press.

Fagen, R. 1993. Primate juveniles and primate play. In *Juvenile Primates: Life History, Development, and Behavior*, ed. by M. E. Pereira and L. A. Fairbanks, Oxford University Press, New York. Pp. 183–196.

Fehr, E. and Gächter, S. 2002. Altruistic punishment in humans. *Nature* 415, 137–140.

Fehr, E. and B. Rockenbach. 2003. Detrimental effect of sanctions on human altruism. *Nature* 422, 137–140.

Field, A. 2001. *Altruistically inclined? The behavioral sciences, evolutionary theory, and the origins of reciprocity.* Ann Arbor, The University of Michigan Press.

Flack, J. C. and de Waal, F. 2000. Any animal whatever: Darwinian building blocks of morality in monkeys and apes. *Journal of Consciousness Studies* 7: 1–29.

Flack, J. C., L. A. Jeannotte, and F. de Waal. 2004. Play signaling and the perception of social rules by juvenile chimpanzees. *Journal of Comparative Psychology.*

Frith, C. D. and Frith, U. 1999. Interacting minds—a biological basis. *Science* 286: 1692–1695.

Gallese, V. 1998. Mirror neurons, from grasping to language. *Consciousness Bulletin* Fall, Pp. 3–4.

Gallese, V. and Goldman, A. 1998. Mirror neurons and the simulation theory of mind-reading. *Trends in Cognitive Science* 2: 493–501.

Gould, S. J. and Lloyd, E. A. 1999. Individuality and adaptation across levels of selection: How shall we name and generalize the unit of Darwinism. *Proceedings of the National Academy of Sciences* 96: 11904–11909.

Griffin, D. R. 2001. *Animal minds.* University of Chicago Press, Chicago.

Gruen, L. 2002. The morals of animal minds. In Bekoff, Allen, and Burghardt (2002).

Güzeldere, G., and Nahmias, E. 2002. Darwin's continuum and the building blocks of deception. In Bekoff, Allen, and Burghardt, *The cognitive animal.*

Hauser, M. 2000. *Wild minds.* New York, Henry Holt.

Hill, H. L. and Bekoff, M. 1977. The variability of some motor components of social play and agonistic behaviour in Eastern coyotes, *Canis latrans* var. *Animal Behaviour*, 25, 907–909.

Hinde, R. A. 2002. *Why good is good: The sources of morality.* New York,. Routledge.

His Holiness the Dalai Lama. 2002. Understanding our fundamental nature. In R. J. Davidson and A. Harrington (eds.), *Visions of Compassion: Western Scientists and Tibetan Buddhists Examine Human Nature.* Oxford University Press, New York. pp. 66–80.

Horowitz, A. C. 2002. The behaviors of theories of mind, and a case study of dogs at play. Ph.D. dissertation, University of California, San Diego.

Hudson, S. D. 1986. *Human character and morality: Reflections from the history of ideas.* Routledge & Kegan Paul, Boston.

Hurd, J. P. 1996. (ed.) *Investigating the biological foundations of human morality.* The Edwin Mellen Press, Lewiston, New York.

Jamieson, D. 2002. Sober and Wilson on psychological altruism. *Philosophy and Phenomenological Research.* LXV, 702–710.

Jamieson, D. and Bekoff, M. 1993. On aims and methods of cognitive ethology. *Philosophy of Science Association* 2, 110–124.

Kitchen, D. M. and Packer, C. 1999. Complexity in vertebrate societies. In *Levels of Selection in Evolution*, ed. by L. Keller, Princeton University Press, Princeton, New Jersey. Pp. 176–196.

Kropotkin, P. 1902. *Mutual aid: A factor of evolution.* New York, McClure, Philips & Co.

Kuczaj, S., Tranel, K., Trone, M., and Hill, H. 2001. Are animals capable of deception or empathy? Implications for animal consciousness and animal welfare. *Animal Welfare* 10, S161–173.

Leigh, Jr., E. G. 1999. Levels of selection, potential conflicts, and their resolution: Role of the "Common good". In *Levels of Selection in Evolution*, ed. by L. Keller, Princeton University Press, Princeton, New Jersey. Pp. 15–30.

Macintyre, A. 1999. *Dependent rational animals: Why human beings need the virtues.* Open Court, Chicago.

Markowitz, H. 1982. *Behavioral enrichment in the zoo.* New York, Van Reinhold Company.

Marler, P. 1996. Social cognition: Are primates smarter than birds? In *Current Ornithology* Volume 13, ed. by V. Nolan, Jr. and E. D. Ketterson, Plenum Press, New York. Pp. 1–32.

Mayr, E. 2000. Darwin's influence on modern thought. *Scientific American* 283: 67–71.

Mech, L. D. 1970. The *Wolf.* Garden City, New York: Doubleday.

Mitchell, L. E. 1998. *Stacked deck: A story of selfishness in America.* Philadelphia, Pennsylvania, Temple University Press.

Motluk, A. 2001. Read my mind. *New Scientist* 169:22–26.

Neuman, Y. 2003. The logic of meaning-in-context. *American Journal of Semiotics* (special issue: Gregory Bateson).

Okamoto, K. and Matsumara, S. 2000. The evolution of punishment and apology: an iterated prisoner's dilemma model. *Evolutionary Ecology* 14, 703–720.

Panksepp J. 1998. *Affective Neuroscience.* New York: Oxford University Press.

Panksepp, J. 2000. The rat will play. In Bekoff M, ed. *The smile of a dolphin: Remarkable accounts of animal emotions.* New York: Random House/Discovery Books. Pp. 146–147.

Pellis, S. 2002. Keeping in touch: Play fighting and social knowledge. In Bekoff, Allen, and Burghardt, 2002.

Peterson, G. R. 1999. The evolution of consciousness and the theology of nature. *Zygon* 34:283–306.

Peterson, G. R. 2000. God, genes, and cognizing agents. *Zygon* 35:469–480.

Pigliucci, M. 2002. Are ecology and evolutionary biology "soft" sciences? *Annals Zoologica Fennici* 39, 87–98.

Poole, J. 1998. An exploration of a commonality between ourselves and elephants. *Etica & Animali.* 9/98, 85–110.

Power, T. G. 2000. *Play and Exploration in Children and Animals.* Hillsdale, New Jersey: Lawrence Erlbaum Associates.

Preston, S. D., and de Waal, F. B. M. (2002). Empathy: Its ultimate and proximate bases. *Behavioral and Brain Sciences.* 25, 1–72.

Ridley, M. 1996. *The Origins of Virtue: Human Instincts and the Evolution of Cooperation.* New York, Viking.

Ridley, M. 2001. *The cooperative gene.* New York, The Free Press.

Rilling, J. K., Gutman, D. A., Zeh, T. R., Pagnoni, G., Berns, G. S., and Kitts, C. D. 2002. A neural basis for cooperation. *Neuron* 36, 395–405.

Riolo, R. L., Cohen, M. D., and Zelrod, R. 2001. Evolution of cooperation without reciprocity. *Nature* 414, 441–443.

Schaller, G. B. and Lowther, G. R. 1969. The relevance of carnivore behavior to the study of early hominids. *Southwestern Journal of Anthropology* 25, 307–341.

Scott, J. P. and Fuller, J. L. 1965. *Genetics and the Social Behavior of the Dogs.* Chicago, Illinois: University of Chicago Press.

Skyrms, B. 1996. *Evolution of the Social Contract.* New York: Cambridge University Press.

Sheets-Johnstone M. 1998. Consciousness: A natural history. *Journal of Consciousness Studies* 5: 260–294.

Sigmund, K., Fehr, E., and Nowak, M. A. 2002. The economics of fair play. *Scientific American* 286 (1), 83–87.

Sigmund, K. and Nowak, M. A. 2001. Evolution: Tides of tolerance. *Nature* 414, 403–405.

Singer, P. 1999. *A Darwinian Left: Politics, Evolution, and Cooperation.* New Haven: Yale University Press.

Siviy S. 1998. Neurobiological substrates of play behavior: Glimpses into the structure and function of mammalian playfulness. Pages 221–242 in Bekoff M, Byers JA, eds. *Animal Play: Evolutionary, Comparative, and Ecological Perspectives.* New York: Cambridge University Press.

Smuts, B. B. 2001. Encounters with animal minds. *Journal of Consciousness Studies* 8, 293–309.

Sober, E. and Wilson, D. S. 1998. *Unto Others: The Evolution and Psychology of Unselfish Behavior.* Cambridge, Massachusetts: Harvard University Press.

Sober, E. and Wilson, D. S. 2000. Summary of: *Unto Others: The Evolution and Psychology of Unselfish Behavior, Journal of Consciousness Studies* 7: 185–206.

Solomon, R. 1995. A passion for justice: Emotions and the origins of the social contract. Lanham, Maryland, Rowman & Littlefield Publishers, Inc.

Spinka, M., Newberry, R. C., and Bekoff, M. 2001. Mammalian play: Training for the unexpected. *Quarterly Review of Biology* 76, 141–168.

Thompson, P. R. 1975. A cross-species analysis of carnivore, primate, and hominid behavior. *Journal of Human Evolution* 4, 113–124.

Tinbergen, N. 1972. Introduction to Hans Kruuk, *The Spotted Hyena.* Chicago: University of Chicago Press.

Tomasello, M., and Call, J. 1997. *Primate Cognition.* New York: Oxford University Press.

de Waal, F. 1996. *Good-natured: The origins of right and wrong in humans and other animals.* Cambridge, Massachusetts, Harvard University Press.

Watson, D. M., and Croft, D. B. 1996. Age-related differences in playfighting strategies of captive male red-necked wallabies (*Macropus rufogriseus banksianus*). *Ethology* 102, 33–346.

Wechlin, S., Masserman, J. H., and Terris, W. Jr. 1964. Shock to a conspecific as an aversive stimulus. *Psychonomic Science* 1, 17–18.

Wilson, D. S. 2002. *Darwin's cathedral: Evolution, religion, and the nature of society.* Chicago, University of Chicago Press.

Wrangham, R., and N. Conklin-Brittain. 2003. Cooking as a biological trait. *Comparative Biochemistry and Physiology*, Part A.

IV.

HUMAN DIMENSIONS: HUMAN-ANIMAL INTERACTIONS

OUR RELATIONSHIPS with other animals raise numerous and complicated issues about who we are in the grand scheme of things, and big questions about how we should treat the other animal beings with whom we share Earth. As we intrude here and there, are we guardians, responsible researchers, responsible stewards, or conquerors? Our relationships with other animals range from fairly straightforward and symmetrical, especially with companion animals with whom we share our homes and our hearts, to rather complicated and asymmetrical, as with animals with whom we do not feel especially close or individuals whom we call pests because they interfere with our own often narrow and arrogant interests. (Some of these issues will also be discussed in Part V, "Ethics, Compassion, Conservation, and Activism: Redecorating Nature."). Human effects on other animals and the environment are called *anthropogenic* effects.

The essays in Part IV speak to some issues concerning the nature of human-animal interactions, namely, how our behavior influences the behavior of other animals and the attitudes we hold toward them. Serious and inevitable conflicts arise that need to be understood and resolved.

SOME OF THE THINGS WE DO TO OTHER ANIMALS: *CAN* DOES NOT MEAN *MUST*

Not only do we influence the lives of other animals in an immediate sense, but also we effect long-lasting and enduring changes in their behavior and physiology. For instance, global warming influences the distribution and behavior of animals, as well as the resources on which they depend, such as food, water, and resting spots. Depending on the pace of warming, it has been predicted that between 15 and 37 percent of species could become extinct between now and 2050 as a result of global warming. Traces of the human-made toxin deca-BDE, a flame retardant widely used in televisions and plastic toys, are now found in polar bears and seagulls in the Arctic, and it will take years to know what its effects will be.

Another human activity, hunting, not only results in the death of individual animals but also affects entire populations in unforeseen ways. For example, trophy hunting is reducing the average size of horns among bighorn sheep, because hunters selectively pick off large rams with big horns. As a result, there is less head butting among males for access to females. In addition to this change in mating behavior, there might be an effect on population genetics among these mountain monarchs. We just don't know yet.

Other studies have shown that humans can also rapidly change the feeding habits of bears who live around dumpsters; to avoid humans, they become active during the night rather than during the day. These bears become obese and lazy—fast food makes them fat. There also is a change in their natural activity patterns: they enter dens later in the fall and remain in them for shorter periods of time than do bears who do not forage at dumps. Hormones from cattle feedlots can demasculinize males and defeminize wild fish. Our fishing can induce sex changes in fish. Animals such as cougars, coyotes, foxes, and deer can become so habituated to humans that rather than flee from us they become bold and curious and intrude into our neighborhoods. The predators are regarded as endangering children and domestic animals, so they are often themselves in danger. Deer who forage among expensive suburban foliage are regarded as pests that ought to be eliminated. It's almost trite to say that humans are all over the place, but we are. And we need to be very careful how we intrude into the lives of other animals, because we *do* make a big difference.

The first essay in Part IV summarizes some of the ways in which we influence the behavior of animals, either intentionally or unintentionally. Knowledge of how we affect animals' behavior will help us make more informed and intelligent choices about whether we should interfere in their lives or just let them be. We influence animals not only when we attempt to coexist with them but also when we study them. Thus, when we interfere in the lives of other animals, we often cannot answer the questions in which we are interested because of our very intrusions.

There are many ways in which our research methods can influence the behavior of the animals in whom we are interested, and as a result we may form misleading inferences from data that are tainted from the start. I have long been interested in how researchers interfere in the lives of the animals they study and whether in doing so they make it impossible to answer the very questions that motivated their research. Among animal behaviors that are sensitive to mere human presence or intrusive research techniques are nesting and reproductive patterns, dominance relationships, mate choice, use of space, vulnerability to predators, feeding, and caregiving. Thus, models generated from animal-behavior studies can be misleading, because they assume human intrusions to be neutral. There is a sort of double bind here, because often what we learn about other animals is useful for developing guidelines for the types of research that are permissible and those that are not permissible. Thus, *some* research is needed, but what sorts of research do not compromise the animals' lives and the data we wish to collect?

When behavior and activity patterns are used as the litmus test for what we call "normal species-typical behavior," we need to be sure that the behavior patterns truly are an indication of who the *individual* is in terms of its age, gender, and social status. If the information used to make assessments of well-being is invalid, then it is likely that the conclusions that are reached and the animal models that are generated are also unreliable and can mislead current and future research programs. And, of course, our errors can have horrific effects on the lives of the animals being studied.

Our research ethic should require that we learn about the normal behavior and natural variation of these activities so that we learn just what we are doing to the animals we are trying to study. We must continue to investigate in more detail the validity of animal models in behavioral and behavioral ecological studies.

Habituation to Humans by Black-Tailed Prairie Dogs and Other Wild Animals

Like many other animals, black-tailed prairie dogs are affected by the presence of humans. In the mid-1980s, two undergraduate students (Rick Adams and Brad Lengas) and I showed how human presence influences the behavior of these rodents, specifically the threshold of their avoidance responses to intruding humans. Habituation of wild animals to the presence of humans is a major problem worldwide. Many species are known to habituate to the presence of humans rather than flee from them. They become less wary, less secretive, and more visible. For example, we discovered the black-tailed prairie dogs we studied in and around Boulder were less wary and more tolerant in urban areas where they had a lot of contact with humans than in more remote habitats where there were fewer human intrusions. Urban prairie dogs showed reduced flight distances to humans; they allowed people to get closer to them and generally were less disturbed by human presence. Other mammals, including coyotes, foxes, mountain lions, and birds such as great crested grebes, ospreys, greylag geese, and great blue herons also show high levels of habituation in areas of high human activity.

THE EFFECTS OF MOVING PRAIRIE DOGS FROM HERE TO THERE: REDECORATING NATURE

The second paper in Part IV reports the first attempt to learn about the consequences of moving individual prairie dogs from one place to another. Often animals have to be moved around, a process that involves trapping, handling, and moving individuals to a new habitat. John Farrar, Karin Coleman, Eric Stone, and I discovered that translocated prairie dogs have a greater sensitivity to human disturbance than do prairie dogs who were not moved. Whether or not the increased sensitivity of individual prairie dogs influences their survival and reproduction is not known. Nonetheless, this novel study, which began as a class project, had a very useful practical aspect. Before this study was conducted, very little was known about what happens to individual animals when they are moved around, and our results have been used to call attention to the fact that we do indeed influence the behavior of translocated animals and we need to know what effects we have on their behavior, reproduction, and survival.

HUMAN-ANIMAL CONFLICTS: IT'S THE PEOPLE WHO ARE THE PROBLEM, NOT THE DOGS

The next two essays in Part IV center on people and their dogs. In "Interactions among Dogs, People, and the Environment in Boulder, Colorado," Carron Meaney and I studied behavioral disturbance of off-leash dogs who were accompanied by a person. We wanted to determine, among other things, just who was the problem when dogs were considered to be the problem. The people in the study and dog owners and non–dog owners alike agreed that people were more disruptive to the environment than dogs and that unruly people were more a problem than were unruly dogs. This study has been widely cited and used as a model for other locales in which dogs and people compete for limited spatial resources.

In the last essay, "Interactions Among Dogs, People, and Nature in Boulder, Colorado," Robert Ickes and I show that people are a problem in another respect. This study demonstrates that prairie dogs who were disturbed by dogs became more vigilant and wary of dogs and played less than undisturbed individuals. We were very surprised to discover that people tried to stop dogs from harassing prairie dogs only 25 percent of the time and that more than half the people we polled—all dog owners—did not think prairie dogs should be protected even if dogs were a problem. Bob and I argue that proactive strategies grounded in empirical data must be developed and implemented in Boulder and elsewhere so that the interests of all parties—often called stake-holders—can be accommodated.

HUMANS *ARE* A FORCE IN NATURE

The studies reported in Part IV were relatively simple to conduct, and the results were very important for learning more about how humans influence other animals with whom we have numerous interactions. You can easily record some of the same data on your own, and they might be useful for resolving conflicts where you live.

Clearly, humans are a force in nature, and we obviously can change a wide variety of behavior patterns in many diverse species. Often, and paradoxically, these changes might make it difficult to answer reliably the research questions in which we are interested. By stepping lightly into the lives of other animals, we can enjoy their company and learn about their fascinating lives without making them pay for our interest. Our curiosity about other animals need not harm them. Coexistence of humans with other animals is essential.

The potential power of humans to do anything we want to do to animals and to nature as a whole is inextricably coupled with compelling responsibil-ities to be ethical humans beings, responsible stewards, and responsible researchers. The data we collect inform us not only about the behavior of the animals we study, but also about the similarities and differences between their behavior and ours. It is essential to collect the most reliable data possible. An important result of our being as nonintrusive as possible is that all animals, nonhuman and human, will benefit.

12   Human (Anthropogenic) Effects on Animal Behavior

HUMANS ARE HERE, there, and everywhere. We are a curious lot, and our intrusions, intentional and inadvertent, have significant impacts on a wide variety of animals and plants, as well as water, the atmosphere, and inanimate landscapes. When humans influence the behavior of animals the effects are referred to as being "anthropogenic" in origin. Often our influence on the behavior of animals and the unbalancing of nature is very subtle and long-term. Often we become at odds with the very animals with whom we choose to live when they become nuisances, dangerous to us or to our pets, or destroy our gardens and other landscapes.

Many of the animals whom we want to study, protect, and conserve experience deep emotions, and when we step into their worlds we can harm them mentally as well as physically. They are sentient beings with rich emotional lives. Just because psychological harm is not always apparent, this does not mean we do not do harm when we interfere in animals' lives. It is important to keep in mind that, when we intrude on animals we are influencing not only what they do but also how they feel.

In my home state of Colorado, many people enjoy the outdoors and many people also work to protect a wide variety of animals. Many of us live in one place and travel elsewhere to experience nature. Our understanding and appreciation of wildlife result from various types of research and "just being out there."

Some examples of behavior patterns influenced by various research methods and other forms of human intrusion include nesting and other reproductive activities (abandonment of nests. increased egg loss, disruption of pair bonds), mate choice, dominance relationships, the use of space, vulnerability to predators, patterns of vigilance, foraging, resting, and feeding and caregiving behaviors. Often animals are so stressed that they are unable to acquire the energy they need to thrive and to survive. Intrusions include such activities as using various devices and instruments to study behavior, marking and handling animals, censuring animal populations, visiting nests, urbanization (urban development and sprawl, the development of bodies of water, changes in vegetation, installing power lines, the need for more electric power) and recreational activities, including the use of snowmobiles and other off-road vehicles, environmental pollution including oil spills, photography, travel, and ecotourism. In November 2003 it was reported that only two years after a new finch-like bird, the Carrizal blue-black seedeater, was discovered in Venezuela, its habitat was destroyed so that a hydroelectric dam could be built!

Models that are generated from these studies can be misleading because of human intrusions that appear to be neutral. It is ironic that often our intrusions preclude collecting the data we need to answer specific questions. I have picked representative studies to show how wide-spread human influences can be and the diversity of species that are affected. Many of these findings apply to other situations and species. The topic of human-animal interactions is relevant to studies of applied ethology. Detailed ethological studies are needed because we need to take into account just how our research influences the behavior of other animals, otherwise we risk drawing the wrong conclusions. Also, it is increasingly important to conservation efforts to understand how humans influence and change the behavior of animals.

RESEARCH EFFECTS

Patterns of finding food can be affected by human intrusions. The foraging behavior of Little penguins (average mass of 1,100 grams) is influenced by their carrying a small device (about 60 grams) that measures the speed and depth of their dives. The small attachments result in decreased foraging efficiency. Changes in behavior such as these are called the "instrument effect." In another example of the influence of humans on penguins, researchers discovered that tourism and nest site visitation caused behavioral and hormonal changes.

Marking animals also influences their behavior. Placing a tag on the wing of ruddy ducks leads to decreased rates of courtship and more time sleeping and preening. In this case, data on mating patterns, activity rhythms, and maintenance behaviors would be misleading.

Mate choice in zebra finches is influenced by the color of the leg band used to mark individuals, and there may be all sorts of other influences that have not been documented. Females with black rings and males with red rings had higher reproductive success than birds with other colors. Blue and green rings were especially unattractive on both females and males. Leg-ring color can also influence song tutor choice in zebra finches and mate-guarding in bluethroats.

Fitting animals with radio collars can also affect their behavior. For example, the weight of radio collars influences dominance relationships in adult female meadow voles. When voles wear a collar that is greater than 10% of their live body mass, there is a significant loss of dominance. Here, erroneous data concerning dominance relationships would be generated in the absence of this knowledge. Radio collars can also influence pair bonding and breeding success in snow geese. However, when female spotted hyenas wear radio collars weighing less that 2% of their body weight, there seems to be little effect on their behavior. Similar results have been found for small rodents, for which small radio-collars do not increase the risk of predation by birds.

Methods of trapping can also lead to spurious results. Trapping methods can bias age ratios and sex ratios in birds. For example, mist nets capture a higher proportion of juveniles, whereas traps captured more adults. Furthermore, dominant males tend to monopolize traps that are baited with food, leading to erroneous data on sex ratios. These are extremely important results because age and sex ratios are important data for many different researchers interested in behavior, behavioral ecology, and population biology.

It also is known that capturing and recapturing large grey mongooses influences their use of space. It is important to ask if the use of space really is the use of space by individuals avoiding traps or avoiding human observers. If, for example, cages are being designed to take into account animals' movement and activity patterns, then data that are used to make decisions about designing enclosures need to be based on information that reliably indicates what the animals typically use and need in the wild.

Not only do research methods influence a wide variety of behavior patterns, but they can also influence susceptibility to infection. For example, ear-tagging white-footed mice led to higher infestations by larval ticks because the tags impeded grooming by these rodents. Thus, for researchers interested in grooming and maintenance behavior, the presence of ear tags could influence results.

Discerning the effects of human intrusions, even those that are meant to help animals, can be extremely complicated. A highly disputed example of the possible effects of human interference into wild populations concerns the plight of African wild dogs. Interference into the lives of wild dogs involved vaccinating them against rabies and canine distemper. While some scientists maintain that handling the dogs and inoculating them was indirectly responsible for their decline because the handling weakened the dogs' immune system making them less resistant to stress, others conclude just the opposite, namely that handling and inoculating were not the cause of their decline. Here we have an example of extremely competent scientists, all of whom care deeply about African wild dogs, not being able to discern what caused their decline. This is because the problems are so incredibly difficult. Some questions that these researchers pondered included: Should the researchers interfere and possibly cause animals to die or let nature take its course? If the rabies and distemper were introduced by domestic dogs who would not have been there in the absence of people (an anthropogenic cause), are we more obligated to try to help the wild dogs than if the rabies and distemper were natural? There are no simple answers to these questions and they are an example of the sorts of questions that are raised when humans intrude into the lives of other animals.

The above examples stem from research on mammals and birds, but there also are indications that human disturbance can influence the behavior and movement patterns of numerous insects (bedbugs, termites, yellow jackets, and ants), [and] skinks (lizards) and can also delay reproduction in snakes. Undoubtedly, future studies will show that humans influence the behavior of numerous diverse species.

Just Being There

Not only does "hands on" contact have an influence, but so might "just being there." Mere human presence influences the behavior of many different animals' behavior. In the early 1900s titmice in England learned to pry off the lids of milk bottles that were delivered to peoples' homes. Elk and numerous other animals avoid skiers. Research performed by my students and myself showed that humans have a large influence on prairie dogs such that individuals who have a lot of contact with humans are less wary of their presence than individuals who do not. The same is true for various species of deer. Similarly, magpies not habituated to human presence spend so much time avoiding humans that it takes time away from essential activities such as feeding. Researchers interested in feeding patterns must be sure that their presence does not alter species-typical behavior, the very information they want to collect.

People often enjoy watching animals from cars, boats, or airplanes. However, the noise and presence of vehicles can produce changes in movement patterns (elk), foraging (mountain sheep), and incubation. In swans, the noise and presence of cars results in increases in the mortality of eggs and hatchlings. Once again, these effects are not obvious when they occur, but data show they are real.

Adélie penguins exposed to aircraft and directly to humans showed profound changes in behavior including deviation from a direct course back to a nest and increased nest abandonment. Overall effects due to exposure to aircraft that prevented foraging penguins from returning to their nests included a decrease of 15% in the number of birds in a colony and an active nest mortality of 8%. There are also large increases in penguins' heart rates. Here, models concerning reproductive success and parental investment would be misleading, once again because of the methods used. Trumpeter swans do not show such adverse effects to aircraft. However, the noise and visible presence of stopped vehicles produced changes in incubation behavior by Trumpeter females that could result in decreased productivity due to increases in the mortality of eggs and hatchlings. Data on the reproductive behavior of these birds would be misleading.

Many people adore young animals and try to get close to nests or dens without disturbing residents. In various research projects it is important to observe parental behavior and to count eggs and young so as to learn about patterns of survival and morality. However, when the nests of some birds (for example, white-fronted chats and ducks) are visited regularly by humans, these birds often suffer higher predation than when their nests are visited infrequently. It has been suggested that some animals may become so accustomed to intrusions by humans who do not kill them that they subsequently allow other animals, including natural predators who will kill them, to get too close.

Activities such as mountain climbing are also intrusive. Climbers can influence activity patterns of birds such that they fly more and perch less and consequently waste energy. In Boulder, Colorado, and other places, climbing is restricted during nesting season. In a study of the effect of climbers on grizzly bears in Glacier National Park, Montana, where bears forage for moths, researchers discovered that climber-disturbed bears spent about 50 percent less time searching for moths and about 50 percent more time avoiding climbers. It was recommended that climbers be routed around areas where bears live to minimize disturbance and associated caloric losses.

Recreational trails built by humans are also associated with changes in behavior and mortality. In Boulder, within forest and mixed-grass ecosystems, nest predation is greater near trails, but we do not know if it is the trail itself, trail use by humans, trail use by predators, or all three that are responsible.

Aquatic habitats also find themselves being intruded on by gawking and intruding humans. Dolphins have become sort of a "cult" animal, and people often visit dolphins in order to swim with them. Numerous studies have discovered that swimming with dolphins in the wild may be harmful to entire groups, especially when swimmers try to be close to dolphins, who, unbeknownst to the swimmers, are resting, feeding, or mating. Swim programs may also be risky to humans. Even experts agree that we really need more detailed information about the effects of swimming with dolphins. Many researchers proffer that when we do not know the negative effects we should err on the side of the animals and leave them be.

Dolphins and other animals are often fed by humans. Feeding (and harassing) wild dolphins is illegal in the United States, and there are severe penalties for engaging in these activities, but this is not so for other countries. There are documented instances of wild dolphins being fed firecrackers, golf balls, plastic objects, balloons, and fish baits with hooks (so that hooked dolphins can be caught). Provisioning dolphins with fish has been associated with a change in the social behavior of free-ranging bottlenose dolphins in Monkey Mia, Australia. Dolphins who have been fed also change their foraging behavior and frequent heavily trafficked harbors and marinas. Some get struck by boats. People have also been seriously injured trying to feed wild dolphins. The National Marine Fisheries Service and other organizations are mounting highly visible campaigns to stop the feeding and harassment of wild dolphins. It also has been noted that some problems associated with feeding terrestrial mammals (changes in foraging patterns and hunting skills) are relevant to concerns about the feeding of dolphins.

Low frequency active sonar (LFAS) that is used to detect submarines by the United States Navy (and by other countries) can also be fatal for marine life including whales, turtles, and some fish. Low frequency active sonar can be carried as many as 400 miles through water and animals can suffer 140 decibels of sound pressure, about the noise produced by an earthquake. Less powerful sonar has been responsible for whale strandings in the Bahamas. Fish are known to suffer internal injuries, eye and auditory damage, and temporary stunning due to low frequency active sonar.

In his book *Sperm Whales: Social Evolution in the Ocean*, whale expert Hal Whitehead notes that sperm whale populations are vulnerable to many threats caused by human activity. These include the increasing use of harpoons to capture whales, collisions with ships, debris such as plastic that might resemble squid who are eaten by whales, entrapment in fishing gear, noise, chemical pollution including heavy metals that enter the food chain, and global warming. Whitehead suggests that because sperm whales seem to use culturally transmitted information about their environment, oceanic changes due to global warming and other human activities might mean that this information becomes outdated or irrelevant. And small changes in survival can influence sperm whale numbers. Many anthropogenic effects are unpredictable and this causes concern among researchers because humans might unknowingly be doing damage that is irreparable.

There also are observations of humans causing seal pups to stampede and be trampled, and humans sometimes strike and injure individuals with boats.

Habituation and Behavioral Flexibility Due to Human Presence

Habituation of wild animals to the presence of humans is also a major problem. Individuals of many species are known to habituate to the presence of humans rather than flee from them. They become less wary and less secretive and more visible. For example, black-tailed prairie dogs studied by my students and myself in and around Boulder are less wary and more tolerant in urban areas where they have a lot of contact with humans than in more remote habitats where there are fewer human intrusions. Urban prairie dogs show reduced flight distances to humans; they allow people to get closer to them and generally are less disturbed by human presence. Birds such as great crested grebes, ospreys, greylag geese, and great blue herons also show high levels of habituation in areas of high human activity.

Cougars (also called pumas and mountain lions) living in areas with dense human populations also exhibit a wide range of behavioral changes. In his book *The Beast in the Garden*, David Baron explores the behavior of cougars who repopulated their ancestral homeland in and around Boulder, Colorado. Historically, cougars were very elusive, secretive creatures. They avoided humans, tended to fear dogs, and were rarely seen during the daytime. Since cougars began to repopulate the open lands around Boulder in the late 1980s, however, biologists and ethologists have noted many behavioral changes. The cougars of Boulder tend to be less fearful of people, often coming into people's yards and even onto their decks. They have lost their fear of dogs and some cougars around Boulder even began preying on dogs.

Many of these changes in behavior are not surprising to biologists and animal behaviorists who stress that the behavior of animals is malleable and subject to change. For example, biologists know that animals are opportunistic and will identify new sources of food, as some Boulder cougars did when they began preying on domestic dogs. It is harder to understand why these cougars lost their age-old fear of dogs, although biologist Maurice Hornocker believes it may be that in areas where wolves have been exterminated, cougars no longer learn to fear canines because their ancient enemy the wolf has disappeared. It is also easy to understand why Boulder cougars tend to be more active during the daytime than their ancestors. The German ethologist Eberhard Curio has noted that predators tend to synchronize their predatory activity with their prey. Because the deer of Boulder, Colorado are more active during the day than deer in true wilderness areas, the Boulder cougars are also more active during daylight hours. It is also not surprising that the cougars, following the deer into the lowlands of Boulder, Colorado, began turning up in Boulder neighborhoods, at times even killing and stashing deer in people's backyards.

Lee Fitzhugh, a wildlife biologist at the University of California at Davis, has studied cougar-human interactions, including fatal attacks in California and other areas in the Rocky Mountain West. He has noted that in certain circumstances cougars can come to view humans as prey, whereas they had previously avoided them. Victims who survived attacks by cougars noted that the cougars crouched and swept their tails while eyeing them, which indicates that the attacks were predatory in nature, rather than defensive. The cougars were not fearful, territorial, or curious. They were assessing humans as potential meals. In his book, Baron opens with the story of a jogger in Idaho Springs (a rural community just west of Denver, Colorado) who had been killed and partially eaten by a cougar. It is important to stress that cougar attacks, while very rare, are not necessarily the result of the cougars being injured or sick. Habituation to people has led to changes in their behavior and healthy cougars will on occasion attack humans.

That the behavior of cougars and other animals can change at what is called the wild/urban interface is fascinating, for it shows that behavior can be flexible and influenced by social factors such as the presence of humans. Many animals, including urban foxes, bears, coyotes, cougars, and deer show changes in space use and activity rhythms that can influence such activities as hunting and mating. Spotted hyenas also show variations in space use as a result of human activity. We still know very little about how the behavior of animals changes when they are forced to compete with intruding humans.

Predators and prey also show behavioral flexibility and often their activity patterns are linked to each other. For example, mule deer around Boulder are more active during the daytime than are deer in the areas where there are fewer humans. The cougars around Boulder, whose primary source of food is mule deer, are also more active during the daytime. Both deer and cougars have become habituated to humans and to domestic dogs. Changes in vegetation can also alter the spacing behavior of herbivorous animals and these environmental modifications also can have far-reaching effects on a wide variety of animals.

Many animals also show changes in behavior or alterations in their ecological niche due to anthropogenic activities that are not associated with habituation to humans. Some of the species that are affected are unfamiliar to many people and these changes go unnoticed except by researchers. For example,

Preble's Meadow Jumping mice began using waterways constructed by humans over 100 years ago with the advent of agricultural irrigation. The use of these waterways changed the spatial distribution of these mice and, as a result, their patterns of interactions with other species. The giant floater mussel in Colorado was forced to change its ecological niche when humans began damming rivers. Damming increased sedimentation and the water became unsuited for the mussels. Nowadays, giant floaters live only in human-made reservoirs built since 1940. And, what is also very interesting, is that the only way that giant floaters are able to get to these reservoirs is by their larvae being carried in the gills of fish that are raised in hatcheries by the Colorado Division of Wildlife and then transported and stocked in these reservoirs. The fate of these mussels has been influenced by two separate anthropogenic activities.

One obvious conclusion that can be drawn from these and other examples is that many aspects of behavior are extremely flexible because of our presence in the lives of these animals. This is an important lesson for people to recognize. Just because some of the behavior patterns that are used in predation or mating appear to be hard-wired or innate, this does not mean that they cannot be modified due to environmental influences. And humans are part of the environment of many animals.

While there are many problems that are encountered both in laboratory and field research, the consequences for wild animals may be different from and greater than those experienced by captive animals, whose lives are already changed by the conditions under which they live. This is so for different types of experiments that do not involve trapping, handling, or marking individuals. Consider experimental procedures that include (1) visiting the home ranges, territories, or dens of animals, (2) manipulating food supply, (3) changing the size and composition of groups by removing or adding individuals, (4) playing back vocalizations, (5) depositing scents (odors), (6) distorting body features, (7) using dummies, and (8) manipulating the gene pool.

All of these manipulations can change the behavior of individuals, including movement patterns, how space is used, the amount of time that is devoted to various activities including hunting, antipredatory behavior, and to various types of social interactions including care-giving, social play, and dominance interactions. These changes can also influence the behavior of groups as a whole, including group hunting or foraging patterns, care-giving behavior, and dominance relationships and also influence nontarget individuals. There also are individual differences in responses to human intrusion. All these caveats need to be considered when a specific study is being evaluated. And perhaps these changes are long-term and open to evolution via natural selection.

How Can Animals Be Effectively Studied?

Clearly, when behavior and activity patterns are used as the litmus test for what is called "normal species-typical behavior," researchers need to be sure that the behavior patterns being used truly are an indication of who the individual is in terms of such variables as age, gender, and social status. If the information used to make assessments of well-being is unreliable, then it is likely that the conclusions that are reached and the animal models that are generated are also unreliable and can mislead current and future research programs. And, of course, human errors can have devastating effects on the lives of the animals being studied. Many believe that, as students of animal behavior, our research ethic should require that we learn about the normal behavior and natural variation of various activities so that we learn just what we are doing to the animals we are trying to study.

In addition to learning about how our intrusions influence the lives of animals, it is important to share this knowledge so that we do not inadvertently change them. Sharing involves disseminating information about what is called the "human dimension" to administrators of zoos, wildlife theme parks, aquariums, and areas where animals roam freely so that visitors can be informed of how they may influence the behavior of animals they want to see. Tourism companies, nature clubs and societies, and schools can do the same.

It is important to stress that what appear to be relatively small changes at the individual level can have wide-ranging effects in both the short- and long-term. On-the-spot decisions about what study techniques should be used often need to be made, and knowledge of what these changes will mean to the lives of the animals who are involved deserve serious attention. Many researchers believe that one guiding principle might be that the lives of the animals whom humans are privileged to study should be respected, and when we are unsure about how our activities will influence them we should err on the side of the animals and not engage in these practices until we know (or have a very informed notion about) the consequences of our acts. This precautionary principle will serve us and the animals well. Indeed, this approach could well mean that exotic animals that are so attractive to such institutions as zoos and wildlife parks need to be studied for a long time before they are brought into captivity. For those who want to collect data on novel species that are to be compared to other (perhaps more common) animals, the reliability of the information may be called into question unless enough data are available that describe the normal behavior and species-typical variation in these activities.

There is a continuing need to develop and improve general guidelines for research on free-living and captive animals. These guidelines must take into account all available information. Professional societies can play a large role in the generation and enforcement of guidelines, and many journals now require that contributors provide a statement acknowledging that the research conducted was performed in agreement with approved regulations. Guidelines should be forward-looking as well as regulatory. Much progress has already been made in the development of guidelines, and the challenge is to make them more binding, effective, and specific.

Humans are a force in nature, and obviously we can change a wide variety of behavior patterns in many diverse species. Often, and paradoxically, these changes might make it difficult to answer reliably the research questions in which we are interested. Coexistence with other animals is essential. By stepping lightly into the lives of other animals humans can enjoy their company and learn about their fascinating lives without making them pay for our interest and curiosity. Our curiosity about other animals need not harm them.

The power that we potentially wield to do anything we want to do to animals and to nature as a whole is inextricably coupled with compelling responsibilities to be ethical humans beings, responsible stewards, and responsible researchers. The data that we collect not only inform us about the behavior of the animals we study, but also about the similarities and differences between their behavior and ours. It is essential to collect the most reliable data possible. An important result of being as nonintrusive as possible is that all animals, nonhuman and human, will benefit.

REFERENCES

Baron, D. 2003. *The Beast in the Garden: A Modern Parable of Man and Nature.* W. W. Norton & Company, New York.

Bekoff, M. 2000. Field studies and animal models: The possibility of misleading inferences. In M. Balls, A.-M. van Zeller and M. E. Halder (eds.), *Progress in the Reduction, Refinement and Replacement of Animal Experimentation.* Elsevier, pages 1553–1559.

Bekoff, M. 2002. *Minding Animals: Awareness, Emotions, and Heart.* Oxford University Press, New York.

Bekoff, M., and Jamieson, D. 1996. Ethics and the study of carnivores: Doing science while respecting animals. In J. L. Gittleman (ed.), *Carnivore Behavior, Ecology, and Evolution*, Volume 2. Cornell University Press, Ithaca, New York. pp. 15–45.

Festa-Bianchet, M. and Apollonia, M. (editors). 2003. *Animal Behavior and Wildlife Conservation.* Island Press, Washington, D.C.

Goodall, J. and Bekoff, M. 2002. *The Ten Trusts: What We Must Do to Care For the Animals We Love.* HarperCollins, San Francisco.

Herrero, S. and Higgins, A. 1999. Human injuries inflicted by bears in British Columbia: 1960–97. *Ursos* 11, 209–218.

Herrero, S. and Higgins, A. 2003. Human injuries inflicted by bears in Alberta: 1960–98. *Ursos* 14, 44–54.

Traut, A. H. and Hosteller, M. E. 2003. Urban lakes and waterbirds: Effects of development on avian behavior. *Waterbirds* 26, 290–302.

JOHN P. FARRAR, KARIN L. COLEMAN, MARC BEKOFF, AND
ERIC STONE

13   Translocation Effects on the Behavior of Black-Tailed Prairie Dogs (*Cynomys ludovicianus*)

INTRODUCTION

Black-tailed prairie dogs (*Cynomys ludovicianus*) are native to The Great Plains region of North America. Since the spread of agriculture and ranching on their former range, prairie dogs have been subjected to intense government extermination programs (Clark 1979). They now occupy only a small percentage of their former range: 600,000 hectares in 1960, compared to 100 million hectares in 1900 (Koford 1958, Miller et al. 1994). But even their current range is decreasing in size due to continued human development. Prairie dogs are now becoming recognized as an essential part of healthy prairie ecosystems (Whickler and Deitling 1988, Miller et al. 1994, Robinette et al. 1995). Wildlife advocacy groups such as Wild Places, Prairie Dog Rescue, Citizens Concerned for Wildlife, Loveland Prairie Dog Action, and several Humane Societies advocate methods of management less invasive than lethal control.

Black-tailed prairie dogs typically respond to an intruder such as a human by interrupting foraging or social interactions, barking alarm calls, returning to burrow entrances, and concealing themselves underground. As such, disturbance to prairie dog colonies may affect colony persistence and survival if foraging and social behaviors are significantly interrupted.

In a previous study, Adams et al. (1987) tested the differences between prairie dogs occurring in rural and residential areas in response to human approach and showed that rural prairie dogs responded to human approach at greater distances than did residential prairie dogs. In the present study we examined whether prairie dogs exhibit increased sensitivity to human intrusion subsequent to trapping, handling, and adjusting to translocation to a new habitat. Specifically, we tested the hypothesis that sensitivity to a human intruder would be greater in colonies containing translocated prairie dogs than in native colonies (colonies inhabited only by prairie dogs that naturally dispersed into the colony or for whom this was their natal colony). Translocation is a popular alternative where residential and industrial development

Originally published in 1998 in Farrar, J. P., Coleman, K. L., Bekoff, M., and Stone, E. 1998. Translocation Effects on the Behavior of Black-Tailed Prairie Dogs (*Cynomys ludovicianus*). *Anthrozoös* 11, 164–167. Reprinted with permission, International Society for Anthrozoology (ISAZ).

is likely to disrupt or destroy prairie dog colonies. However, the effects of the translocation process on the behavior of these animals are unknown.

METHODS

Study Sites

Due to pending construction of a laboratory for the National Oceanic and Atmospheric Administration (NOAA) on the United States Department of Commerce station in Boulder, Colorado, USA, the Wild Places group worked with Phyllis Gunn of the Department of Commerce to translocate part of a prairie dog colony to a protected site on City of Boulder Open Space.

We studied three colonies, designated *Native*, *Mixed*, and *Translocated*. The Native colony consisted of prairie dogs remaining in the colony that were not moved because of construction. These prairie dogs constituted our control group. The colony was bounded by service roads restricted to motor vehicles. Pedestrians regularly used these areas and roads and their dogs often accompanied them, both on and off leash. Therefore *Native* prairie dogs were accustomed to close proximity of vehicles, humans, and potential predators.

The second site was on Boulder Reservoir Open Space (adjacent to north 51st Street.) Eighty-three prairie dogs were released onto the periphery of an existing colony from 12 July to 8 October 1996. These prairie dogs came from an area approximately 10 kilometers away, near the 63rd St. Water Treatment Plant grounds east of Boulder. This site experienced traffic similar to that of the *Native* site. Thus, the colony contained native and translocated prairie dogs, and it served as an intermediate group due to their longer adjustment time and mixed population. This population is referred to as the Mixed site. To the north of the colony is a model airplane airport and planes often "buzzed" the prairie dogs for sport. People have reportedly plugged some burrows with newspaper to prevent interference with the model planes. This and the occasional (between one and five per day) jogger or cyclist along 51st street were the only human interactions experienced by these prairie dogs.

Prairie dogs from the *Native* site were translocated onto a third site, designated *Translocated*. The city of Boulder wishes to keep knowledge of this location secret due to past incidents of people leaving privately captured prairie dogs on open space without authorization (Clint Miller, pers. comm.). Personnel from Wild Places released 117 prairie dogs from 9 September to 6 November 1996 onto a colony that was extirpated by plague three years earlier. The prairie dogs were released in the same relative burrow positions in which they were trapped. This group constituted our experimental group.

Data Collection and Analysis

From 19 October to 20 November 1996. we recorded responses of prairie dogs to human intruders at varying times at each site according to the methods used by Adams et al. (1987). Data collection began as soon as all animals were translocated and continued until we obtained twenty-one samples per site. In some cases, multiple samples were taken on the same day. Owing to the size of these colonies (>100 hectares), spacing of sample sites within a colony, and time lags between samples, we believe that these samples were independent of each other. However, pseudoreplication is a possibility and our results must be interpreted with this in mind.

Before approaching the colony, we selected a focal animal to observe attempting to select a different animal each time at a given site. This was accomplished by changing the side of the colony that was approached and using the nearest visible animal to the human intruder.

We recorded four behavioral measures as follows: 1. *bark distance* (BD)—distance from observer to the focal animal when it emitted the initial warning signal and retreated to its burrow entrance; 2. *concealment distance* (CD)—distance from observer to the burrow when the animal concealed itself; 3. *sequence time* (ST)—time the individual took to perform the avoidance sequence of running to the burrow, pausing at the burrow entrance, flattening down inside the lip of the burrow, tail-wagging, barking, and concealing itself underground; 4. *concealment time* (CT)—time from the moment that all individuals in the group concealed themselves until one reappeared above ground. At all sites J. P. Farrar approached the colony from a distance of two-hundred meters from the colony edge to control for variations in speed and the nature of the stimulus. All approach directions were determined using bearings derived from a random number table.

All response measures were log (n + 1) transformed to meet assumptions of normality and equal variances among sites. We analyzed the data using MANOVA and separate ANOVA tests to determine if significant differences occurred between sites. Missing values for some time measurements occurred when no prairie dogs resurfaced.

Our sampling scheme was designed such that individual animals were the experimental unit. True replication of the experimental unit would have us measure responses of prairie dogs from several colonies of each type (Translocated, Mixed, Native), however, this was not possible (see below).

RESULTS

Significant differences in response to a human intruder were detected using MANOVA (Wilks' Lambda=0.386, Exact F=6.858, df=8.90, p<0.001). Individual ANOVAs of the distance measurements showed highly significant differences between sites ({BD/CD} p<0.001/0.001, F=3.150/3.150, df=2.63/2.63). Prairie dogs at the *Translocated* site responded at greater distances for both concealment and barking distances. Sequence and concealment times did not vary significantly among colonies ({ST/CT} p=0.844/0.984, F=0.170/0.016, df=2.52/2.56). Natural predators were noted at the Translocated site but not at the other two areas. Prairie dogs responded to red-tailed hawks (*Buteo jamaicensis*) and a coyote (*Canis latrans*) by retreating underground.

Discussion

Translocated prairie dogs responded to disturbance at the greatest distance, Native prairie dogs at the shortest distance, and Mixed prairie dogs at intermediate distances. These results support the notion that translocated prairie dogs have a greater sensitivity to human disturbance. While this sensitivity to human intrusion may decrease with time, it highlights an additional factor to consider in prairie dog management.

Robinette et al. (1995, p. 873) recommended releasing groups larger than 60 individuals in areas with no potential immigration "to minimize the effects of random genetic drift and inbreeding." This number was well exceeded at the release site. Though Robinette et al.'s study was focused on population genetics and minimum viable population size, our results indicate that heightened sensitivity to disturbance may explain why mortality is high in the first year after translocation (Robinette et al. 1995). While heightened sensitivity to disturbance may reduce predation and hence mortality, greater response distances might also mean that individuals spend more time avoiding potential predators which in turn reduces the time available for finding and consuming food. Presently, there are no data that address this suggestion.

The most rigorous examination of translocation effects would require repeated samples from several treatment groups, permits from state and federal agencies, and sites with similar physical, topographical, and biological features for capture and release. We were unable to meet these stringent requirements. Nonetheless, the present study is the first examination of the impacts of translocation on prairie dogs, an important and timely issue for the future management of this declining species.

In summary, our results showed that translocated prairie dogs show heightened sensitivity to human intrusion when compared to individuals who were not moved. Wildlife managers and advocacy groups must take into account this increased sensitivity to human traffic (and probably to natural predators) when considering possible release sites. How increased sensitivity influences the future behavior, including reproduction and survival of translocated prairie dogs, requires further study.

Acknowledgments

We thank Clint Miller and Mark Gershman of City of Boulder Open Space, Phyllis Gunn of the United States Department of Commerce, Susan Miller of Wild Places, and Joe Mantione of Boulder Mountain Parks for their advice and assistance during the course of this study.

References

Adams, R. A. Lengas, B. J., and Bekoff, M. 1987. Variations in avoidance responses to humans by Black-tailed prairie dogs (*Cynomys ludovicianus*). *Journal of Mammalogy* 68: 686–689.

Clark, T. W. 1979. The hard life of the prairie dog. *National Geographic* 58: 270–281.

Koford, A. D. 1958. Prairie Dogs, White Faces, and Blue Grama. *Wildlife Monographs* 3: 78 pp.

Miller, B., Ceballos, G., and Reading, R. 1994. The prairie dog and biotic diversity. *Conservation Biology* 8: 677–681.

Robinette, K. W., Andelt, W. F., and Burnham, K. P. 1995. Effect of group size on survival of translocated prairie dogs. *Journal of Wildlife Management* 59: 867–874.

Whickler, A. D., and Deitling, J. K. 1988. Ecological consequences of prairie dog disturbances. *BioScience* 38: 778–785.

MARC BEKOFF AND CARRON A. MEANEY

14   Interactions Among Dogs, People, and the Environment in Boulder, Colorado

A Case Study

> The environment is not a luxury. When political movements have faded, when economic systems have changed, when ideologies have been superseded and forgotten, the environment will still be important.
> —Sylvan and Bennett 1994, p. 6

> That recreational activities disturb wildlife is well appreciated but poorly understood. Most popular forms of recreation in wildlands have yet to receive detailed study.
> —Knight and Cole 1995, p. 61

INTRODUCTION

Across the United States and in many other countries there is growing interest in how human and nonhuman animals (hereafter animals) can best share space that can be used by all parties for recreational purposes (see Knight and Gutzwiller 1995 for review). Although concern often focuses on the mutual well-being of humans and animals, when priorities have to be established, humans generally receive favorable treatment. Furthermore, when there are competing interests among humans, domestic dogs (*Canis familiaris*), wild animals, and "nature" in general, dogs' well-being and interests are often overridden (because they are "merely dogs" or "simply domesticated animals" (see Bekoff 1995, 1996a and Bekoff and Jamieson 1996 for discussion).

In the late 1800s, the people of Boulder, Colorado, had the foresight to set aside a large parcel of land backing into the foothills. Since then, additional land has been purchased under an Open Space program to create a greenbelt around the city, and to provide wildlife habitat and recreational opportunities. This program has been very successful and popular with the public.

In recent years, there has been a large increase in the use of Open Space trails in Boulder. As emphasized by Roberts (1995), Boulderites who enjoy the outdoors "love their parks to death" as they pursue recreational activities. This community resource, which is shared by humans and animals, consists of

Originally published in 1997 in Bekoff, M., and Meaney, C. A. 1997. Interactions Among Dogs, People, and Nature in Boulder, Colorado: A Case Study. *Anthrozoös* 10, 23–31. Reprinted with permission, International Society for Anthrozoology (ISAZ).

about 25,000 acres and approximately 150 miles of trails. In 1993 there were about 1.3 million visits, an increase of 13% compared to previous years (Miller 1994). In one study, it was reported that 21.3% of groups visiting Boulder City Open Space participated in exercising their companion dogs (Zeller et al. 1994). In Boulder, as in other communities, companion animals such as dogs are very important to some people and problematic to others. The resulting conflicts between different groups (pro- and anti-dog factions) of people have placed the Boulder City Council in the position of having to consider various management decisions. Empirical data are necessary and can help to deal with controversial issues such as these in a more objective and straightforward manner. The development of sound management policies that attempt to maximize the well-being of all parties in recreational areas, including the possibility of placing restrictions on dogs, require detailed consideration of perceived and actual problems. Whereas there is a significant literature on human attitudes towards domestic and wild animals (e.g. Kellert 1994; Serpell 1995a,b, and references therein), there are very few data that can inform management decisions at the local level. As the number of humans and companion animals increases, existing land use problems continue to grow in Boulder (Roberts 1995; Zaslowsky 1995) and in other communities.

Among the major issues regarding land use in Boulder and other locales is the concern that off-leash dogs disturb other dogs, people, wildlife, and the environment. Some data support this claim (see Lowry and McArthur 1978, Gentry 1983, Mainini et al. 1993, Miller 1994, Knight & Gutzwiller 1995, and references therein), whereas other data suggest either that dogs have a minimal demonstrable effect on animals such as deer (e.g. Progulske and Baskett 1958; Sweeney et al. 1971; Scott and Causey 1973) or that human impacts are equally or more invasive (e.g. Yalden and Yalden 1990). Clearly, the issues concerning the impact of dogs on wildlife and habitat require further and more detailed attention.

METHODS

Data were collected from September 1995 through April 1996 at six different locations in and around Boulder (four Open Space locations and on the University of Colorado, Boulder, campus and on the Pearl Street Mall). To achieve our goals of learning more about the behavior of off-leash dogs and about people's attitudes and perceptions towards dogs, we devised an original questionnaire and also collected detailed information on behavior. We felt that a combination of these two approaches should help to clarify distinctions between perceived problems and actual areas of conflict among dogs, people, and the environment.

Questionnaires

Our questionnaire (Appendix A) characterized the respondents by place of residence, patterns of use of Open Space, whether or not they owned and had a dog with them, their attitudes toward dogs and people, their experiences with dogs and people on Open Space, their views of the impact of dogs and people on habitat and wildlife, and their concerns about Open Space in the future. The questionnaire was developed and implemented with the input of professional pollsters and administered at the same four locations on Open Space at which data were collected on behavioral disturbances (Mt. Sanitas, Bobolink Trail, Chautauqua, Doudy Draw) where dogs are allowed to be off-leash, and also at two other locations (University of Colorado, Boulder Campus and Pearl Street Mall) where dogs are required to be on a leash. (Two other areas [Sawhill and Walden Ponds] received too little use to be included in the present data set.) All visitors with and without dogs were asked to fill out the questionnaire while the researcher waited for its completion. The questionnaires were analyzed by Market Research Services, Longmont, Colorado and cross-tabulations were run so that responses to each question could be correlated with one another.

Behavioral Disturbances

In this part of our study we were concerned with the following short-term and direct behavioral disturbances (for discussion, see Knight and Cole 1995, p. 61) by off-leash, companion dogs who were accompanied by a person. Data consisted of (i) characterization of the patterns of space use by individually observed dogs; (ii) characterization of patterns of chasing and flushing wildlife and disturbing vegetation and bodies of water; (iii) the nature of dog-dog encounters, and (iv) the nature of dog-people encounters.

Behavioral data were collected at six locations (see above). Observations were made "on trail" or from a stable vantage point, and efforts were made to minimize the effects of researchers' presence. For example, observers sat in the same place quietly and dogs generally paid little overt attention to them. At each location, beginning at the trailhead and extending for 500 meters (m), the trail was partitioned with flagging into five linear 100m sections. Other 100m sections further along a trail were randomly sampled to see if there was any "trailhead effect."

Seven different people collected field data and administered the questionnaires. Regular meetings were held to make sure that there was consistency among the different researchers. Focal animal sampling (Altmann 1974), in which individual dogs were followed during their travels within each of the 100-meter sections, was used. All of the dog's activities and its location were recorded on prepared score sheets or read into a voice-activated tape recorder. A continuous time-base was maintained using stop watches. For each 100-meter section, we recorded the frequencies and rates with which dogs were "off trail" and "on trail," the distances from the trail that dogs travelled, and whether or not leaving the trail was owner-induced (e.g. by throwing a Frisbee or a stick). We recorded all events of flushing and chasing, including and independent of the focal animal. We recorded observed instances when a dog did not appear to flush or to chase wildlife (recognizing that unobservable physiological changes can be caused by the presence of dogs; for discussion, see Gabrielson and Smith 1995). The mammalian species with which we were concerned included mule deer (*Odocoileus hemionus*), yellow-bellied marmots (*Marmota flaviventris*), black-tailed prairie dogs (*Cynomys ludovicianus*), rock squirrels (*Spermophilus variegatus*), jackrabbits (*Lepus* spp.), cottontails (*Sylvilagus* spp.), coyotes (*Canis latrans*), and red foxes (*Vulpes vulpes*). Avian species included black-billed magpies (*Pica pica*), robins (*Turdus migratorius*), dark-eyed juncos (*Junco hyemalis*), mallard ducks (*Anas platyrhynchos*), steller's jays (*Cyanocitta stelleri*), and mountain (*Parus gambeli*) and black-capped chickadees (*Parus atricapillus*).

Data were analyzed using proportions tests (Bruning and Kintz 1977, p. 222ff) which generate the z statistic. We used $p<0.05$ (two-tailed test; $z_{crit}>1.96$) to indicate significant differences between two percentages. The phrase "no significant difference" or similar terms mean that $z''1.96$ and $p>0.05$. Critical values of z for other levels of statistical significance are 2.58 ($p<0.010$) and 3.30 ($p<0.001$).

RESULTS

Behavioral Disturbances

Approximately 800 different dogs were observed for about a total of 150 hours. The behavior of dogs at different locations and at the same locale did not vary significantly (detailed analyses for the different locations are presented in Bekoff 1996b). Off-leash dogs generally travelled less than 2–5 m off trail for fewer than 1–2 minutes (min). For example, in one study (n=100 dogs) at Mt. Sanitas, 30 (=30%) dogs remained on the trail and 45 (=45%) dogs went off trail between 1–5m for less than 1 min. In a second study at Mt. Sanitas (n=80 dogs), 80% of dogs remained within 1–3m of the trail (15% remained on trail and 40% went less than 1m off trail) and in a third study at Mt. Sanitas (n=100 dogs), 93 (=93%) of dogs remained within 5m of the trail. The general impression of observers was that when dogs went far off trail, they were lured off by the people who were responsible for them (e.g. people threw sticks, Frisbees, or went off trail and then called their dogs). It is also notable that only 2 "earnest chases" of wildlife (1 deer and 1 unidentified squirrel) were observed in which it was unambiguously concluded that it was the dog who initiated and maintained the chase. Dogs also only rarely entered bodies of water. Similar behavioral data were collected at Chautauqua (n=272 dogs). In addition, information on dog-dog interactions showed that 20/26 (81%) were friendly (dogs greeted, sniffed, or played with one another) or neutral (dogs passed one another with no physical contact) and 6 (19%; $p<0.001$) had aggressive (threat) components. All observers noted that dogs off leash were friendlier than dogs on leash, although no detailed data were collected on this aspect of behavior. We also observed 172 dog-people interactions of which 146 (85%) were neutral and the rest (n=26, 15%; p<0.001) were friendly. When sufficient data could be collected, they indicated that there were no differences in the behavior of dogs in different segments of the trail (1st 100m, 2nd 100m, 3rd 100m).

Questionnaires

Four hundred and fifty (n=450) questionnaires were completed. More non-dog owners (53.2%) than dog owners (46.8%) were polled. Of all respondents, 96.4% were comfortable with dogs, and there were no significant differences (p>0.05) among different locations or between dog owners and non-dog owners. Most people (p<0.01) thought it would lessen the quality of their own (68.3%) and their dog's (82.2%) outdoor experience if dogs had to be leashed. In general, people were more disturbed by large dogs; breeds singled out as threatening (n=35 respondents) included: Rottweilers (35.3%), Doberman Pinschers (20%), Pit Bull Terriers (17.1%), and Chows (14.3%). Many more people reported seeing other people disturb wildlife (92.2%), vegetation (78.0%), and bodies of water (60.5%) significantly more often (p<0.001 for all comparisons) than dogs (49.7%, 31.4%, and 9.0%, respectively).

While we did not detect any seasonal differences in water use by dogs, it is possible that in the hottest months of the year (when we were not in the field; June-August) they would disturb water more than at other times of the year.

This question "What do you think is the biggest problem facing those who use parks and open space?" was analyzed separately for dog owners and non-dog owners. A small, but significantly higher percentage of non-dog owners thought that there were too many dogs (10.6%) when compared to dog owners (2.9%; p<0.01), and a significantly higher proportion of non-dog owners (28.5%) thought that there were too many piles of dog feces left on or near trails when compared to dog-owners (19.5; p<0.05). Similar percentages (p>0.05) of non-dog owners and dog owners reported that there were too many people (non-dog owners: 47.3%; dog owners: 53.4%), too many unruly dogs (15.5%; 8.0%), and too many unruly people (32.4%; 28.2%). Both groups agreed that people, and not dogs, were the major problem. Regardless of location, respondents indicated that there were far too many people when compared to the number of dogs (p<0.001) and too many unruly people when compared to the number of unruly dogs (p<0.001). Disturbance by people included talking loudly, trampling vegetation, and littering.

Non-dog owners and dog owners were also asked what they thought about a number of different issues centering on purported problems with off-leash dogs. Similar proportions (p>0.05) indicated that there should be standardized obedience tests for dogs (non-dog owners: 48.2%; dog owners: 42.7%), that dogs should not be banned from Open Space (93.3%; 98.2%), and that additional areas where dogs could run free should be established (72.3%; 64.3%). A significantly higher percentage of non-dog owners (55.0%) when compared to dog owners (37.3%) believed that there should be an annual fee for dogs using Open Space, that dogs should be on leashes at all times (30.5%; 19.0%), and that there should be stricter enforcement of voice and sight control (76.6%; 66.0%).

DISCUSSION

The present study was concerned with interactions among domestic dogs, people, and the environment in Boulder, Colorado. There were few noteworthy differences when data were analyzed by location. While some of the results may be specific to this area, there seems to be a more general message that deserves serious attention from those who live in other environs. There is no doubt that *some* dogs go off trail for various amounts of time and that *some* dogs do occasionally disturb people, wildlife, and habitat. However, compared to people, dogs did not seem to do much damage to vegetation or bodies of water, and they only rarely chased wildlife. Dog-wildlife encounters are very important to study; however, it is often very difficult to identify precisely what factors directly cause wildlife disturbances (Gentry 1983). People were more disruptive than were dogs, and when dogs did go far off trails they often were lured off by people. There was no trailhead effect and dogs' behavior differed little when they first were let free, during their travels in intermediate segments of a trail, and when they completed their walks.

The results of the questionnaire support the behavioral data. In fact, the results of the questionnaire show clearly that dog owners and non-dog owners do not differ in their perceptions of major problems—essentially, too many people and too many unruly people using Open Space in Boulder. Almost 97% of people polled felt comfortable with dogs off-leash. People also reported (and direct observations confirmed the fact) that people disrupt wildlife more frequently than dogs, and people cause more damage to vegetation and to bodies of water. Less than one-third of the respondents reported that feces were a problem. There are many reasons why feces can cause problems (e.g. hygienic, environmental, aesthetic; Beck 1979) and perhaps they are more of a problem in urban areas (Dumont 1996) than in open recreational areas. Boulder is dealing with this problem by placing plastic bags and trash cans near trailheads and along trails. Interestingly, non-threatening barking by dogs was not an issue for either group. Also, all observers noted that dogs off leash were friendlier than dogs on leash, although no detailed data were collected on this aspect of behavior (see also Thomas 1996).

The relationship between people and dogs has changed greatly in Boulder over the past 25 years. In the early 1970s many uncastrated dogs ran free without their owners. Dogs occasionally formed packs, chased deer and, on at least one occasion, attacked a child. Since then, there appears to have been an increased interest in having well-behaved dogs. In 1980, the Boulder Humane Society regularly offered one obedience class, and in 1996 there are 20 concurrent classes (Nana Wills, personal communication). Dog owners have become more responsible (having their dogs castrated and watching over them more conscientiously), and rarely is a dog seen without their owner or another person in attendance.

We conclude that little needs to be done to manage dogs directly in the areas where we conducted our studies. There are always going to be "problem" dogs and "problem" people. In Boulder and perhaps in other areas, reports of unruly dogs seem to attract a lot of attention, but of course, people do not report when dogs are well-behaved. Additional enforcement may solve some problems but there really are few problems that could not largely be solved by continuing serious efforts to educate people about dog behavior and matters of etiquette and responsibility (see also Beck 1996 and Dumont 1996), and by requiring people to learn more about dog behavior and control of their companions, for people and their companions essentially are a cooperative social unit (Sanders 1990).

The fact that dog owners and non-dog owners did not disagree on important issues (that standardized obedience tests should be required and that banning dogs is not a viable option) also needs to be addressed. Although standardized obedience testing is possible and equally attractive to non-dog owners and dog owners alike, the implementation of such a practice has not been given serious attention. While the details still need to be worked out for different locations, some possibilities would entail having people attend classes, hire a professional trainer, or train their dogs themselves and then go to their local humane society for testing. A set fee would be established to cover the cost of testing and licensing; the fee might also include a donation to the society.

Further concerns could be addressed by having various stipulations that could cover different sorts of violations. The following suggestions might be helpful for implementing obedience certification. People who were first-time offenders who did not have a license would be given a certain amount of time to complete the standardized test and pay a small fine. First-time offenders who had already received their licenses would have to pay for, and repeat, the standardized test within a certain period of time, but there would be no fine. However the obedience certification process is implemented, there seems to be little doubt that dogs and people would benefit.

It seems clear to us that the well-being and interests of dogs should not summarily be compromised when dogs and people attempt to share limited space that can be used by all parties for recreational purposes. The methods used and the results from this case study can serve as a model for other locations in which dogs and people compete for limited spatial resources.

POSTSCRIPT

A recent study of dogs on the University of Colorado (Boulder) campus (Dwyer and Bekoff, unpublished data) showed that leashed dogs initiated contact with humans 5.5 times more than did unleashed dogs, and that people initiated contact with leashed dogs 3.8 times more than with unleashed dogs. Generally, unleashed dogs ignored humans and chose other unleashed dogs with whom to interact when they were not exploring their surroundings.

ACKNOWLEDGMENTS

We thank Carrie Kull, Ed Leigh, Ron Hamilton, Kristen Gacek, Shelese Pratt, Gary Renne, David Fenyvesi, and Deborah Sapienza for help with data collection, and Myanna Lahsen, Rosalind Yanishevsky, Clint Miller, Ann Wichmann, and Andrew Smith for help with the development of the questionnaire. Rosalind Yanishevsky, Colin Allen, Alan Beck, Robert Eckstein, Ann Wolfe, and an anonymous reviewer provided helpful comments on an ancestral version of this manuscript. Rosalind Yanishevsky suggested how implementation of standardized testing might be initiated. We received financial support from an anonymous donor and the Department of EPO Biology, University of Colorado, Boulder.

REFERENCES

Altmann, J. 1974. Observational study of behaviour: Sampling methods. *Behaviour* 49:227–267.

Beck, A. 1996. Ecological aspects of urban stray dogs. In *Readings in Companion Animal Behavior*, 259–263, ed. V. L. Voith and P. L. Borchelt. Trenton, New Jersey: Veterinary Learning Systems.

Beck, A. M. 1979. The impact of the canine clean-up law. *Environment* 28:28–31.

Bekoff, M. 1995. Marking, trapping, and manipulating animals: Some methodological and ethical considerations. In *Wildlife Mammals as Research Models: In the Laboratory and Field*, 31–47, ed. K. A. L. Bayne and M. D. Kreger. Greenbelt, Maryland: Scientists Center for Animal Welfare.

Bekoff, M. 1996a. Naturalizing and individualizing animal well-being and animal minds: An ethologist's naiveté exposed? In *Wildlife Conservation, Zoos, and Animal Protection: Examining the Issues*, 63–129, ed. A. Rowan. Medford, Massachusetts: Tufts University Press.

Bekoff, M. 1996b. Preliminary report on dogs and people in Boulder. Unpublished paper.

Bekoff, M., and Jamieson, D. 1996. Ethics and the study of carnivores: Doing science while respecting animals. In *Carnivore Behavior, Ecology, and Evolution*, Vol. 2. 15–45, ed. J.L. Gittleman. Ithaca, New York: Cornell University Press.

Bruning, J.L., and Kintz, B. L. 1977. *Computational Handbook of Statistics*, Glenview, Illinois: Scott, Foresman and Company.

Dumont, G. 1996. A telephone survey on attitudes of pet owners and non-owners to dogs and cats in Belgian cities. *Anthrozoös* 9:19–24.

Gabrielson, G. W. and Smith, E. N. 1995. Physiological responses of wildlife to disturbance. In *Wildlife and Recreation: Coexistence Through Management and Research*, 95–107, ed. R. L. Knight and K.J. Gutzwiller. Washington, D.C.: Island Press.

Gentry, C. 1983. *When Dogs Run Wild: The Sociology of Feral Dogs and Wildlife*, Jefferson, North Carolina: McFarland & Company, Inc., Publishers.

Kellert, S. R. 1994. Attitudes, knowledge and behaviour toward wildlife among the industrial superpowers: The United States, Japan and Germany. In *Animals and Human Society: Changing Perspectives*, 166–187, ed. A. Manning and J. Serpell. New York: Routledge.

Knight, R. L. and Cole, D. N. 1995. Factors that influence wildlife responses to recreationists. In *Wildlife and Recreation: Coexistence Through Management and Research*, 71–79, ed. R. L. Knight and K. J. Gutzwiller. Washington, D.C.: Island Press.

Knight, R. L. and Gutzwiller, K. J. (eds.) 1995. *Wildlife and Recreation: Coexistence Through Management and Research*, Washington, D.C.: Island Press.

Lowry, D. A. and McArthur, K. L. 1978. Domestic dogs as predators on deer. *Wildlife Society Bulletin* 6:38–39.

Mainini, B., Neuhaus, P. and Ingold, P. 1993. Behaviour of marmots *Marmota marmota* under the influence of different hiking activities. *Biological Conservation* 64:161–164.

Miller, C. K. 1994. Environmental impacts of passive recreational trails in riparian areas. *Proceedings of the 6th Annual Colorado Riparian Association Conference*, USA, 12 pages.

Progulske, D. R. and Baskett, T. S. 1958. Mobility of Missouri deer and their harassment by dogs. *Journal of Wildlife Management* 22:184–192.

Roberts, C. 1995. Boulderites love parks to death. *Boulder Daily Camera*, 6 November, 1C.

Sanders, C. R. 1990. Excusing tactics: Social responses to the public misbehavior of companion animals. *Anthrozoös* 4:82–90.

Scott, M. D. and Causey, K. 1973. Ecology of feral dogs in Alabama. *Journal of Wildlife Management* 37:253–265.

Serpell, J. (ed.) 1995a. *The Domestic Dog: its Evolution, Behaviour and Interactions with People*, New York: Cambridge University Press.

Serpell, J. 1995b. From paragon to pariah: some reflections on human attitudes to dogs. In *The Domestic Dog: its Evolution, Behaviour and Interactions with People*, 245–256, ed. J. Serpell. New York: Cambridge University Press.

Sweeney, J. R., Marchinton, R. L. and Sweeney, J. M. 1971. Responses of radio-monitored white-tailed deer chased by hunting dogs. *Journal of Wildlife Management* 35:707–716.

Sylvan, R. and Bennett, D. 1994. *The Greening of Ethics: From Anthropocentrism to Deep-Green Ecology*, Tucson: University of Arizona Press.

Thomas, E. M. 1996. Canine liberation. *New York Times* 1 May, page A19.

Yalden, P. E. and Yalden, D. W. 1990. Recreational disturbance of breeding golden plovers *Pluvialis apricarius*. *Biological Conservation* 15:243–262.

Zaslowsky, D. 1995. The battle of Boulder. *Wilderness* Summer: 25–33.

Zeller, M., Zinn, H. C. and Manfredo, M. J. 1994. *Boulder Open Space Visitation Study*. Unpublished manuscript.

APPENDIX A: QUESTIONNAIRE

Perceptions of the Impact of Dogs on Open Space

We are interested in learning more about how dogs and people use open space so that dogs and people can maximize the pleasure that can be had by being outdoors in the limited available space. We hope that you will take the time to answer these questions.

Date: Location: Time: Sex: Age: Children?

(1)   Do you live in Boulder? City ___
      County ___ For how long? ___ No ___

(2)   How often do you use open space? (a) daily, (b) 5 times per week, (c) 2–4 times per week, (d) 2–4 times per month, (e) less than 1 time per month, (f) 2–4 times per year or less, (g) never

(3)   How long have you used this portion of open space? _____

(4)   Why do you come to open space? (a) to exercise myself, (b) to exercise my dog, (c) to see wildlife, (d) to be alone, (e) to enjoy nature, (f) other

      Please rank your top three (3) choices by writing down the appropriate letter:
      ___   ___   ___

(5)   In what type of activity do you usually engage? (you can choose more than 1) (a) walk/hike, (b) jog/run, (c) bicycle, (d) equestrian, (e) exercise dog

(6)   Are you a dog owner? Yes: ___ No: ___

(7)   Are you comfortable with dogs? Yes: ___ No: ___

(8)   Do you have a dog with you now?
      Yes: ___ No: ___
      On leash: ___ Off Leash: ___
      Under excellent voice control: ___
      Under control most of the time: ___
      Not well-controlled: ___

(9)   Do you think dogs should be (a) on leash always, (b) off leash always if dog not a threat to people, (c) off leash in certain areas and at certain times, (d) other?

(10) Would it lessen the quality of your open space experience if your dog had to be on a leash? Yes: ___ No: ___
      How: _____

(11)   Would it lessen the quality of your dog's experience if your dog had to be on a leash? Yes: ___ No: ___
How: _____

(12)   Have you ever been attacked by a dog on open space? (a) two or more times, (b) once, (c) never. What were extent of injuries?
_____

(13)   Have you ever felt uneasy when passing someone else's dog? (a) two or more times, (b) once, (c) never.

(14)   In what ways did you feel uneasy? (a) disturbs me, (b) disturbs children, (c) disturbs my dog, (d) disturbs wildlife, (e) too many dogs, (f) dog out of control

(15)   Do certain types of dogs bother you more than others? Yes: ___ No: ___

If YES, why: Please provide more details next to your choices
(a) breed _____
(b) size _____
(c) color _____
(d) behavior _____
(e) sex _____
(f) the behavior of the person with the dog?
_____

(16)   Have you ever felt uneasy in the presence of other people on open space? (a) two or more times, (b) once, (c) never.

(17)   Have you seen other people bothered by dogs? (a) two or more times, (b) once, (c) never.

(18)   Have you seen wildlife disturbed by dogs? Yes: ___ No: ___
If YES, (a) often, (b) occasionally, (c) never.

(19)   Have you seen wildlife disturbed by people? Yes: ___ No: ___
If YES, (a) often, (b) occasionally, (c) never.

(20)   Have you seen vegetation disturbed by dogs in a harmful way?
Yes: ___ No: ___
If YES, (a) often, (b) occasionally, (c) never

(21)   Have you seen vegetation disturbed by people in a harmful way?
Yes: ___ No: ___
If YES, (a) often, (b) occasionally, (c) never

(22) Have you seen streams or other bodies of water disturbed by dogs in a harmful way? Yes: ___ No: ___
If YES, (a) often, (b) occasionally, (c) never

(23) Have you seen streams or other bodies of water disturbed by humans in a harmful way?
Yes: ___ No: ___
If YES, (a) often, (b) occasionally, (c) never

(24) What do you think is the biggest problem facing those who use open space?
Too many dogs: ___
Too many unruly dogs: ___
Too many people: ___
Too many unruly people: ___
Too much dog poop: ___
Other: _____
Comments: _____

_____
_____
_____

(25) If findings suggest that dogs are problematic, do you agree with:

(a) requiring standardized obedience testing for dogs off leash:
Yes: ___ No: ___
(b) requiring annual fee and tags for dogs using open space: Yes: ___ No: ___
(c) requiring all dogs to be on a leash at all times: Yes: ___ No: ___
(d) requiring stricter enforcement for voice and sight control:
Yes: ___ No: ___
(e) banning all dogs: Yes: ___ No: ___
(f) providing areas for dogs on leash and other areas for dogs off leash?
Yes: ___ No: ___
(g) other ___
General Comments

_____
_____
_____
_____
_____
_____

MARC BEKOFF AND ROBERT W. ICKES

15 Behavioral Interactions and Conflict Among Domestic Dogs, Black-Tailed Prairie Dogs, and People in Boulder, Colorado

INTRODUCTION

World-wide there is growing interest in how human and non-human animals (hereafter animals) can best share what is becoming a limited resource, namely space that can be used by all parties for a variety of activities (see Knight and Gutzwiller 1995 for review). In Boulder, Colorado (USA) and other locales, among the numerous issues regarding land use is the concern that free-running domestic dogs (*Canis familiaris*) cause disturbance to wildlife and habitat. Yet, there are few detailed studies on relationships between dogs and wildlife (Miller 1994, Knight and Gutzwiller 1995, Bekoff and Meaney 1997, and references therein). In Boulder, dogs and prairie dogs share areas that are used for recreational purposes by people and their companion dogs. Conflict abounds because some people argue that dogs should be allowed to run free regardless of their impact on prairie dogs, whereas others maintain that prairie dogs should be protected and that dogs should be restrained or be taken elsewhere if they are to run free. There are no formal studies of which we are aware that focus on the nature of interactions between dogs and black-tailed prairie dogs (*Cynomys ludovicianus*), specifically avoidance shown by prairie dogs in response to intrusions and harassment by dogs. Two previous studies showed that prairie dogs in rural and undisturbed areas were more sensitive to human and other disturbances than were prairie dogs in urban areas (Adams, Lengas, and Bekoff 1987, Farrar et al. 1998).

Issues concerning the impact of dogs on habitat and wildlife, including prairie dogs, require more detailed attention. Dogs and prairie dogs interact frequently in various contexts, and there is a lot of interest in the management of prairie dog colonies in and around Boulder and also nationally because of the potential harm that dogs might bring to prairie dogs. Indeed, there is a lot of popular interest in prairie dogs (e.g. Dold 1998, Long 1998; Reading, Miller and Kellert 1999), and there is a serious move to have black-tailed prairie dogs listed as "threatened" under the Endangered Species Act because only about 1% of their original number occupy about 1% of their historic

Originally published in 1999 in Bekoff, M., and Ickes, R. W. 1999. Behavioral Interactions and Conflict Among Domestic Dogs, Black-Tailed Prairie Dogs, and People in Boulder, Colorado. *Anthrozoös* 12, 105–110. Reprinted with permission, International Society for Anthrozoology (ISAZ).

range. Prairie dogs are also vital for the survival of numerous (perhaps as many as 200) species associated with prairie dog towns, including endangered black-footed ferrets (*Mustela nigripes*; Miller, Reading, and Forrest 1996), and some believe they are a keystone species (Davitt et al. 1996; but see Stapp 1998). If listed, prairie dogs would be protected from being harmed by poisons, recreational hunters, bulldozer scoops, or unrelenting human sprawl.

In this study we focused on interactions between free-running domestic dogs, black-tailed prairie dogs, and people at Dry Creek, an area designated by the city of Boulder as a Habitat Conservation Area in which attempts are made to maintain natural faunal and floral biodiversity and natural shifts in animal use and vegetation dominance. Observations were also made at a control area where there was little human and no dog use. Our general hypothesis was that prairie dogs who are less disturbed by humans will be more wary than prairie dogs who are greatly intruded on by humans. This hypothesis stemmed from earlier work in which it was shown that prairie dogs in rural and undisturbed areas were more sensitive to human and other disturbances than were prairie dogs in urban areas (Adams et al. 1987, Farrar et al. 1998). We also predicted that prairie dogs who are heavily disturbed, when compared to prairie dogs who are less disturbed, would show greater disruption of normal activity patterns than less disturbed prairie dogs. Thus, disturbed prairie dogs might be more stressed than undisturbed individuals, and they might rest, forage, or socially interact less than undisturbed animals.

Methods

Data were collected by direct observation of dogs, prairie dogs, and people during September, October, and November 1998, at Dry Creek, a recreational area in East Boulder. The prairie dog colony extends over approximately 14 acres. Trail corridors fragment prairie dog habitat. Observations were conducted by 12 researchers for approximately 250 hours, and about 150 different dogs were observed: Observations were conducted throughout daylight hours as the use of Dry Creek varies throughout the day. Data were either recorded by hand or read into an audio cassette and later transcribed. Time was measured on hand-held stopwatches and distances were determined using measuring tapes or estimated using natural landmarks between which distances were known. Different areas at Dry Creek were sampled randomly to minimize the likelihood of our seeing the same people, dogs, and prairie dogs from day-to-day. The responses of prairie dogs to humans at Dry Creek and at a control area (the Marshall Area) about 1 km southeast of Dry Creek where there was little human and no dog use, were also studied to determine if prairie dogs at Dry Creek behaved similarly to other populations of disturbed animals (Adams et al 1987, Farrar et al. 1998).

We used focal animal sampling (Altmann 1974) on all but one occasion, when one-zero sampling was used (see below). Observers selected a focal dog(s) and followed him or her from the time they arrived at Dry Creek and as they roamed about. At the same time, a focal prairie dog(s) was selected in the vicinity of the dog and its behavior was recorded before, during, and after an encounter with the dog(s). We attempted to select the prairie dog(s) nearest to the dog(s) as the focal animal(s). The focal dog was observed to see if he or she ignored or approached prairie dogs or prairie dog burrows, and the response of focal prairie dogs to this sort of disturbance was also noted. We also recorded whether the dog walked near or toward a burrow, stalked a prairie dog, ran toward a burrow before or after a prairie dog retreated, chased a prairie dog, or tried to extract a concealed animal. The behavior of people (with and without companion dogs) was also observed to see if they tried to stop dogs from harassing prairie dogs.

Frequency data were pooled for all observation periods and analyzed using proportions tests (Bruning and Kintz 1977, p. 222ff) which generate the z statistic. We used $p<0.05$ (two-tailed test; $z_{crit}>1.96$) to indicate significant differences between two proportions.

Prairie Dog–Human Interactions

Behavioral Responses to Disturbance In this part of our study we used measures that have been used in the past concerning the responses of prairie dogs to the approach of humans (Adams et al. 1987, Farrar et al. 1998). We were only concerned with physical intrusions, not the influence of olfactory or auditory infringements. The following behavioral measures were recorded:

(a) *Bark distance*—distance between focal person and focal prairie dog when the prairie dog emits the initial warning signal and retreats to its burrow entrance;

(b) *Concealment distance*—distance between focal person and the burrow when the focal prairie dog conceals itself in the burrow;

(c) *Sequence time*—time the individual takes to perform the avoidance sequence of running to the burrow, pausing at the burrow entrance, flattening down inside the lip of the burrow, tail-wagging, barking, and concealing itself underground;

(d) *Concealment time*—time from the moment that all individuals in the group conceal themselves until one reappears above ground.

Observations for concealment time at the control area were terminated at 600 sec because no prairie dogs reappeared above ground after disturbance within this time period.

We also recorded the time allotted to various behaviors by prairie dogs at Dry Creek during periods when they were relatively free of intrusions by dogs and when they were intruded on more heavily. Behavior patterns observed included being alert or vigilant (scanning for dogs while standing on hindlegs or lying down; no other terrestrial predators were present during observations and on only about five occasions were birds of prey observed) and playing (details on these and other behavior patterns performed by black-tailed prairie dogs are presented in Hoogland 1995).

In addition to information concerning dog-prairie dog interactions, we observed some general patterns of dog behavior, including how frequently they left the main trail and how far they went off trail.

Prairie Dog–Human Interactions

The response of prairie dogs to humans at Dry Creek and at the control area was studied to determine if prairie dogs at Dry Creek behaved similarly to other populations of disturbed animals.

Human Attitudes

We also administered a questionnaire that was slightly modified (to include questions about prairie dog-dog interactions) from the one used in a previous study of dog-people interactions in Boulder (see Bekoff and Meaney 1997, Appendix A; available from MB).

Results

Number, Size, and Movement Patterns of Dogs

It was difficult to estimate the total number of different dogs observed during the course of study because numerous dogs frequented Dry Creek and because different observers did not have detailed information on visitation patterns, especially visits by unnamed dogs or those who looked alike. For example, there were numerous golden retrievers and medium-large dogs who could not be reliably identified over time. However, it was reasonable to conclude that at least 150 different individuals were observed. We estimated that about 70% of dogs visiting Dry Creek were "large" (> about 25 kg). About 68% of all dogs traveled more than 5 m off the main trails. On eleven occasions dogs were lured off trail by humans throwing frisbees.

Dogs and Prairie Dogs

About 60% of all visiting dogs barked at prairie dogs, ran towards burrows, chased prairie dogs, or chased and attempted to extract concealed individuals. Some dogs were repeated nuisances, while others never disturbed prairie dogs. A detailed analysis of the behavior of 56 dogs for whom we could collect reliable information from the beginning to the end of an interaction showed that eight (14.3%) barked at prairie dogs from a distance, 18 (32.1%) ran toward a burrow(s), 18 (32.1%) chased prairie dogs, and 12 (21.4%) chased and attempted to extract a concealed prairie dog from its burrow. No prairie dogs were known to be caught or killed by any dog during the course of this study.

All observers independently agreed that large dogs disturbed prairie dogs more than smaller dogs. Prairie dogs barked at and fled from large dogs sooner (when dogs were about 11 m away) than small dogs (dogs were about 8.5 m away). How the size of intruding dogs influences the behavior of prairie dogs needs further analysis.

Prairie dogs disturbed by dogs were alert more often and played less often than undisturbed individuals. They commonly flicked their tails while scanning for intruders. Using one-zero sampling, we found that in 24 observation sessions, alertness was observed in 63% of the sessions and play was observed in 38% of the sessions during high intrusion by dogs (> 60% of dogs disturbed prairie dogs). When intrusion was low (<15% of dogs disturbed prairie dogs), alertness was observed in 33% of the observation sessions and play was observed in 50% of them. The proportion of periods during which alertness and play were observed were significantly different when compared between periods of high and low intrusion (proportions test, $p<0.05$).

Prairie Dogs and People

Prairie dogs at Dry Creek were less wary of humans than prairie dogs at the control area where there was little human and no dog traffic. It was difficult to gather data on complete sequences (from barking to concealment) of prairie dog responses to human intrusion, but for the 16 sequences for which we did, we found that prairie dogs showed statistically significant differences in behavior between Dry Creek and the control site (MANOVA, Wilks' Lambda=0.189, Exact $F_{(5.10)}$=8.56, p=0.002). Prairie dogs at Dry Creek barked at a significantly shorter distance than animals at the control site [means=74±17m(sd)] and 12±12m, respectively; $F_{(1.14)}$=41.9, $p<0.0001$), concealed themselves at a significantly shorter distance (16±9m, 60±20m, respectively; $F_{(1.14)}$=21.47, p=0.0004), and showed significantly shorter concealment times (334±237 sec, 600±0 sec, respectively; $F_{(1.14)}$=15.15, p=0.0016). There was no difference in total sequence time for prairie dogs at Dry Creek and at the control site (83±60 sec, 117±76 sec, respectively; $F_{(1.14)}$=0.814, p=0.382).

A separate analysis of these four measures from a larger data set (n=60) in which we could not record entire sequences showed the same results.

People tried to stop dogs from harassing prairie dogs only 25% of the time. Usually (about 90% of the time) people called their dogs but did not go after them. Once off trail most dogs chased prairie dogs.

Human Attitudes Towards Prairie Dogs, Dogs, and People

Our surveys (n=43 of which 41 people were dog owners) showed that people at Dry Creek believed that there were too many unruly people (29.4%) rather than too many unruly dogs (8.8%). The only two non-dog owners surveyed agreed. More than half (51.2%) reported they had seen prairie dogs disturbed by dogs, but only occasionally rather than regularly (88.9% of the people reporting seeing disturbance). Seventeen percent reported they had seen people occasionally disturb prairie dogs. Sixteen percent reported that their dog did occasionally disturb prairie dogs, and 50% of these people reported that they tried to stop their own dog from disturbing prairie dogs, whereas 26.8% said they tried to stop others' dogs from disturbing prairie dogs. Twenty-one percent said they tried to stop people from disturbing prairie dogs. The biggest problems that people identified at Dry Creek included too many people (11.8%), too many unruly dogs (8.8%), too many unruly people (29.4%), and too much dog poop (20.6%). No respondents reported that there were too many dogs. All respondents reported that dogs should not be banned from Dry Creek and 58.3% (all dog owners) said that prairie dogs should not be protected even if dogs were a problem. All respondents said that it would lessen their own and their dog's experience of the outdoors if their dog had to be leashed (see also Bekoff and Meaney 1997).

DISCUSSION

Dogs and Prairie Dogs

There is a lot of interest in prairie dogs and how they are influenced by the presence of, and intrusions by, human and non-human animals. People around Boulder and elsewhere are divided on central issues concerning the impact on wildlife of humans and their companion animals. Our main objective was to develop a basic scientific understanding of the nature of dog-prairie dog interactions, an issue that has high visibility in Boulder because some people want dogs to run free even if they disturb prairie dogs, whereas others want prairie dogs to be protected and dogs to be restrained or taken elsewhere for recreation. It would be unfortunate for all involved if these issues became contentious and could not be discussed openly using available data. Trying to manage dog or prairie dog populations before relevant data are collected would be premature and likely not solve the issues at hand.

Dogs at Dry Creek went off trail more often and further than dogs at other locations in Boulder (for comparative data see Bekoff and Meaney 1997), probably because of the presence of prairie dogs at Dry Creek and not at other locations.

Disturbed prairie dogs were less wary and more habituated to the presence of humans than undisturbed animals, a finding that is consistent with what has been reported for other locations (Adams et al. 1987, Farrar et al. 1998). Prairie dogs disturbed by dogs were more vigilant and played less than undisturbed individuals. This may indicate a higher level of stress among disturbed individuals. While prairie dogs will try to challenge small predators such as snakes (Halpin, 1983), they do not directly confront dogs. Similar to prairie dogs hunted by humans (Vosburgh and Irby 1998), prairie dogs spent more time alert, nervously scanning for intruders.

Despite the fact that prairie dogs are disturbed by dogs, neither we nor anyone else seems to know if dogs have any negative effects on the health, mortality, or reproductive success of these rodents. Little also is known about the effects of non-lethal intrusions by humans on the health, mortality, or reproductive success of prairie dogs. If dogs (or humans) have negative effects, this and other similar colonies may be in danger. Prairie dogs also have keen senses of smell but we do not know what effects dog odors and waste products have on them. However, prairie dogs are sensitive to the odors of such natural predators as black-footed ferrets (Andelt and Beck 1998). It also is not clear if plague can be introduced from one colony to another by dogs traveling from one prairie dog colony to another. Currently, it is not known if City of Boulder officials will pursue these important lines of research.

Dogs clearly influence the behavior of prairie dogs at Dry Creek. Prairie dogs are favored prey of many wild predators, but none were known to be killed by dogs. While it is known that human traffic can lead to a decrease in the presence of some predatory birds (Berry, Bock, and Haire 1998, and references therein), it is not known if dog traffic deters natural predators.

Prairie Dogs and People

People tried to stop dogs from harassing prairie dogs only 25% of the time. Our survey showed that fifty-eight percent of people surveyed at Dry Creek (all dog owners) did not believe that prairie dogs should be protected even if dogs are a problem. The only two non-dog owners polled agreed. Certainly, dog owners and people could play more active roles in preventing dogs from harassing prairie dogs. Increased human responsibility would probably go a long way towards reducing existing conflict among people wanting to protect prairie dogs and those who do not.

In the present study and our previous research, we found that people, dog owners and non-dog owners alike, agreed that the biggest problem at recreational sites in Boulder was too many unruly people (those who do not control their dogs or lure their dogs off trail, and those who leave the trails themselves), not too many unruly dogs.

Developing Proactive Strategies

There is still much to learn about the complex interactions among humans and non-humans so that all can benefit from the good fortune of having nearby recreational and wildlife areas. This information is essential for the development of proactive strategies. Can all participants be accommodated? Can a restricted area be both recreational and preservational? Should wild animals be given more consideration and protection than domesticated animals? Can animals and land be protected from interminable destruction and development? Even experts disagree about facts and possible solutions. There are no quick answers to these extremely difficult questions.

The data collected in the present study should be important for educating the public that there are indeed areas of conflict that demand careful and informed resolution, which will in turn facilitate dialogue between parties. Our data have been circulated among Boulder city officials and people using Dry Creek for recreation. Currently (June 1999), there is a plan to fence off the prairie dogs at Dry Creek to protect them from dogs. While this plan was developed before our data were available, this seems a reasonable temporary management plan until more information is available concerning the effects of dogs on the health and reproductive behavior of prairie dogs.

In the future, our data should be useful for maximizing the well-being of prairie dogs (and other wildlife), dogs, and humans in Boulder and elsewhere by identifying specific areas of potential conflict [such as the friction between people who want to protect prairie dogs (and other wildlife) and those who want dogs to run free regardless of their impact on prairie dogs]. Our data should also be useful for developing proactive strategies of management that are grounded by empirical data.

ACKNOWLEDGEMENTS

We thank Mimi Lam, Taryn Flowers, Delia Bellina, Katie Chell, Lindsay Dosch, Eliza Eubank, Jennifer Garcia, Susie Graham, Nathan Inouye, Jordan McClelland, Brian Schopfer, Jessica Taylor, John Reed, and Kyle Ashton for help with this study. Kyle Ashton, Stan Godlovitch, Carron Meaney, Bill Merkle, John Reed, Penny Bernstein, and an anonymous reviewer provided comments on a previous draft of this paper.

REFERENCES

Adams, R. A. Lengas, B. J. and Bekoff, M. 1987. Variations in avoidance responses to humans by Black-tailed prairie dogs (Cynomys ludovicianus). *Journal of Mammalogy* 68: 686–689.

Altmann, J. 1974. Observational study of behaviour: Sampling methods. *Behaviour* 49: 227–267.

Andelt, W. F. and Beck, T. D. I. 1998. Effect of black-footed ferret odors on behavior and reproduction of prairie dogs. *Southwestern Naturalist* 43: 344–351.

Bekoff, M. and Meaney, C. A. 1997. Interactions among dogs, people, and the environment in Boulder, Colorado: A case study. *Anthrozos* 10: 23–31.

Berry, M. E., Bock, C. E. and Haire, S. L. 1998. Abundance of diurnal raptors on open space grasslands in an urbanized landscape. *Condor* 100: 601–608.

Bruning, J. L. and Kintz, B. L. 1977. *Computational Handbook of Statistics*. Glenview, Illinois: Scott, Foresman and Company.

Davitt, K., Grandi, R., Neasel, C. and Skeele, T. ed. 1996. *Conserving Prairie Dog Ecosystems on the Northern Plains*. Predator Project, Bozeman, Montana.

Dold, C. 1998. Making room for prairie dogs. *Smithsonian Magazine* 28: 60–68.

Farrar, J. P., Coleman, K. L. Bekoff, M. and Stone, E. 1998. Translocation effects on the behavior of black-tailed prairie dogs (*Cynomys ludovicianus*). *Anthrozos* 11: 164–167.

Halpin, Z. T. 1983. Naturally occurring encounters between black-tailed prairie dogs (*Cynomys ludovicianus*) and snakes. *American Midland Naturalist* 109: 50–54.

Hoogland, J. L. 1995. *The Black-Tailed Prairie Dog: Social Life of a Burrowing Mammal*. Chicago, Illinois: University of Chicago Press.

Knight, R. L. and Gutzwiller, K. J. ed. 1995. *Wildlife and Recreation: Coexistence Through Management and Research*. Washington, D.C.: Island Press.

Long, M. E. 1998. The vanishing prairie dog. *National Geographic* 193: 116–131.

Miller, B. J., Reading, R. P. and Forrest, S. 1996. *Prairie Night: Black-footed Ferret and Recovery of an Endangered Species*. Washington, D.C.: Smithsonian Institution Press.

Miller, C. K. 1994. Environmental impacts of passive recreational trails in riparian areas. *Proceedings of the 6th Annual Colorado Riparian Association Conference*, 12 pages.

Reading, R. P., Miller, B. J. and Kellert, S. R. 1999. Values and attitudes towards prairie dogs. *Anthrozos* 12: 43–52.

Stapp, P. 1998. A reevaluation of the role of prairie dogs in Great Plains grasslands. *Conservation Biology* 12: 1253–1259.

Vosburgh, T. C. and Irby, L. R. 1998. Effects of recreational shooting on prairie dog colonies. *Journal of Wildlife Management* 62: 363–372.

V.

ETHICS, COMPASSION, CONSERVATION, AND ACTIVISM: REDECORATING NATURE

DISCUSSIONS ABOUT ETHICS and animals make many people squirm. Surely, they exclaim, there are more important and less difficult things to talk about. More important, no; less difficult, certainly. While ignorance may be bliss, ignoring questions about our ethical responsibilities to animals compromises not only their lives and our integrity, but also the quality of scientific research. And questions about ethics and animals will not go away, even if we try to ignore them. More and more students and practicing scientists recognize that asking questions about ethics *is* in the best interests of good science, and increasing numbers of nonresearchers are also keenly interested in animal well-being. Science and scientists are under growing scrutiny by a concerned public that questions how funds are used to support various scientific products and that wants scientists to be less arrogant and more accountable to those who support them. Everyone is much affected by the results generated by the enterprise of science, and discussions of ethics can no longer be pushed aside just because they are slippery and philosophical.

The first essay in Part V, "The Importance of Ethics in Conservation Biology," stresses this theme, which echoes throughout this volume. I also ask some general and difficult questions, such as What *should* we do in our interactions with other animals? to frame the essays that follow. I lay out some principles that I believe should be used to guide the ways in which we interact with animals. These include: do no intentional harm; respect all life; treat all individuals with compassion; and step lightly into the lives of other beings, bodies of water, and landscapes. We humans use animals in innumerable ways for our own anthropocentric ends, and the negative effects—often unintentional—that our intrusions have on the behavior of animals is wide-ranging.

Such intrusions also can have negative effects on our own well-being and psyches, a point that is made by ecopsychologists such as David Abram and Laura Sewall. Their and my point is that when nature loses, we all lose.

WHERE I AM COMING FROM AND HEADING TOWARD

I have always been very interested in the ethics of animal use (I left a Ph.D. program because I did not want to dissect animals or do live animal experimentation). My work with Dale Jamieson has helped me appreciate the importance of interdisciplinary collaboration and the subtlety of many of the arguments put forth by those interested in animal protection and environmental ethics. Our paper "Ethics and the Study of Carnivores," the last essay in Part V, argues that humans are an integral and intimate part of nature; no one is exempt from the deleterious effects of our self-centered intrusions. When we destroy nature, we destroy ourselves. Science is neither value free nor perfect, and it is human imperfection that drives us to continue to learn about the world in which we live. Time is not on our side, and we must be proactive and restrain our tendency to cause wanton destruction here, there, and everywhere with little concern for our animal kin. Although these are not the best of times for animals, Dale's and my essay is a hopeful piece that has motivated many people to do something to make the world a better and more compassionate place.

RESISTING SPECIESISM: THE WORDS *LOWER* AND *HIGHER* HAVE TO GO

Conservation efforts often center on human interests, as if the animals involved aren't as important or as valuable as people. The psychologist Richard Ryder coined and defined the term *speciesism* as "discrimination against or exploitation of certain animal species by human beings, based on an assumption of man's superiority." Speciesists make decisions about how humans are permitted to use animals based on the animals' group membership rather than on an individual's unique characteristics. Speciesism often leads to applying terms such as *higher* and *lower* to different species, a practice that usually has negative consequences for supposedly lower animals. Speciesism usually is cashed out as anthropocentrism or humanism—humans are above and separate from other animals. Furthermore, speciesist language and dogma frequently results in the creation of us (human) versus them (other animals), a dualism that does not reflect what we know about the cognitive or emotional lives of other animals. This dualism also ignores a plethora of data that support Darwin's arguments for evolutionary continuity, a topic discussed in a number of essays in this volume. In a nutshell, speciesism is bad biology.

ETHICS AND THE STUDY OF CARNIVORES: WHY STUDY ANIMALS?

In "Ethics and the Study of Carnivores," Dale Jamieson and I argue that the human relationship to nature is a deeply ambiguous one and that humans are both a part of nature and distinct from it. While we concentrate on the ethical questions that arise in the study of carnivores, it is clear that these questions also apply when we become curious about other animals and intrude into their lives. People weigh in on questions of ethics in a wide variety of ways, and informed discussion and debate are needed to flesh out the details. Dale and I argue that there is an ongoing need to develop, improve, and implement strict guidelines for research that involves the use of animals, and that professional societies have to do a better job in the ethical arena. We also argue that science must reflect and effect social change, and that all scientists must be directly engaged with society at large and strive to integrate science into the human experience.

THE VOICE OF SCIENCE

A topic related to ethics that I do not consider in any of these essays concerns the voice of science—how much of science is still written in the third person rather than in the first person. In a recent discussion with the noted and controversial researcher Rupert Sheldrake, it became clear that the use of the third person—"the researcher did this"—or "the subjects were observed by the researcher"—makes it easy for researchers to distance themselves from the animals they study and can remove them from the process of science. Third-person language also reinforces the erroneous notion that science is value free. We are part of the process, and ethics are part of the process. We do indeed speak for voiceless animals, and the way in which we speak for them might open up our hearts to who they are. In this way, we might also open up science, especially the study of animal behavior and research about the nature of human-animal interactions.

THE IMPORTANCE OF COMPASSIONATE AND PROACTIVE ACTIVISM: SILENCE AND INDIFFERENCE ARE COSTLY

I believe that it is essential to leave the ivory tower to make one's views more public. I have done this in a number of different venues, despite attempts to humiliate me or discredit my work. Ethical questions very often require activism. I believe academics should speak their hearts and minds when they are so moved. Some years ago, I organized a number of peaceful protests (including a candlelight vigil) and became active in a campaign to stop the reintroduction of Canadian lynx to southwestern Colorado because four of the first five translocated cats needlessly died of starvation, a horrifying, painful death. I became the center of a smear campaign, and the head of the project tried to convince the University of Colorado to censure me. (I had previously written an essay titled "Jinxed Lynx" that was critical of this project.) Fortunately, no one was distracted by the false claims or attempts to silence the protests, and the university unequivocally supported my right to speak out. Public outcry (due to peaceful activism) about the reintroduction project resulted in a change in the way in which lynx were reintroduced, and the number of starvation deaths decreased radically.

Activism certainly takes time away from other activities that consume us daily. But speaking one's voice—taking an active role to stick up for one's values and beliefs—is essential for creating dialogue and for making informed decisions. There are many forms of activism—*activism* is not synonymous with *radical*. Nor does activism necessitate violence or the destruction of property. Boycotts and silent candlelight vigils are forms of activism.

Activism also takes patience. Protest gently but forcefully. Changes that come about as the result of heavy-handedness usually are short-lived and make little difference. Often it takes many efforts to build the momentum needed to produce the deep changes in attitude and heart that truly make a difference. It is important to listen to all views and master opponents' arguments. Only by knowing your opponents' tactics and arguments can you mount a serious offense. I often ask students to write essays arguing for a position to which they are opposed. Many gripe at first, but just about all of them come to realize that to make change, they need to talk to their opponents and listen carefully to their arguments. Preaching to the converted is not usually a great use of time. You get applause but rarely recruit new voices for the cause at hand.

Creative, proactive, compassionate solutions drenched in deep humility, caring, respect, and love need to be developed to deal with the broad range of problems with which we are currently confronted. Activism often underlies their formulation and implementation.

THE POWER OF ONE: EVERY INDIVIDUAL COUNTS

In my work with Jane Goodall, we stress that every individual counts and every individual makes a difference. Jane often uses the phrase "the power of one" to make this point. As Margaret Mead noted: "Never doubt that a small group of thoughtful, committed citizens can change the world. Indeed, it's the only thing that ever has." Martin Luther King, Jr. once said: "A time comes when silence is betrayal." He was right. Silence and indifference can be costly—deadly—for our animal friends and for Earth. Even if you have only one minute or ten seconds a day, you can make a difference. Talk to friends and families while taking a break, while taking a walk, while just hanging out. The small fraction that we each offer can contribute to larger solutions. Even a tiny ripple—a little agitation—can spread wide and rapidly. Even if you have time to help only one individual, you can make a difference. It is thought that North Atlantic right whales might survive if only one or a few females are spared each year—one whale matters.

And be resourceful. In this hi-tech world, there are innumerable sources available almost instantaneously. As Jane Goodall and I were writing *The Ten Trusts*, she told me about an introduced plant that was overtaking Buffalo, New York, but she could not remember its name. I called a bed-and-breakfast establishment in Buffalo, figuring that someone in the tourism business might know about some of the local ecological problems, and they did! I learned that it was the purple loosestrife and that many people are indeed concerned about this nasty invasive plant that is taking over native plants in many regions.

REDECORATING NATURE: SCIENCE, NATURE, HEART, AND,...YES, LOVE

My general take on matters of science, nature, heart, and love is as follows. Today's children will live and work in a world in which (as I noted earlier) science increasingly will not be seen as a self-justifying activity but as another human institution whose claims on the public treasury must be defended. It is more important than ever for students to understand that to question science is not to be antiscience or anti-intellectual. Questioning science will make for better, more responsible science and help insure that in the future we will not repeat the mistakes of the past, that we will move toward a world in which humans and other animals share peaceably the finite resources of the planet.

My vision is to create a worldwide community in which humans perceive themselves as part of nature, not apart from it, in which humans who are overwhelmed and whose spirits and souls have been robbed and squelched by living in and amongst steel, concrete, asphalt, noise, and a multitude of invasions of their private space reconnect with raw nature—with the wind in their faces, the scent of wild flowers, and the sounds, sights, odors, and touch of other animals and inanimate environs. A world in which sensing is feeling. Nature is our unconditional friend, and reconnecting with nature can help overcome alienation and loneliness. The power of love must not be underestimated as we forge ahead to reconnect with nature.

EXPANDING HEADS AND HEARTS

The numerous issues I have considered are clearly huge. Discussions of compassion, ethics, and conservation, along with musings about the nature of science and scientism, social responsibility, reductionism, holism, who we are in the grand scheme of things, and the slippery notion of love cannot be easily simplified or cleanly packaged. I want to continue on this lifelong journey. In my concluding essay following this section I freely wander here, there, and everywhere—trespassing into disciplines other than my own. I feel comfortable being among the first penguins to jump into challenging waters, hanging it all out there, as they say—because it expands my head and my heart and forces me to confront difficult, complicated, frustrating, and very important issues. Much of my thinking has been motivated by the views of His Holiness the Dalai Lama about the importance of compassion and love.

16 The Importance of Ethics in Conservation Biology

Let's Be Ethicists not Ostriches

AM I PREACHING TO THE CHOIR?

There can be no question that ethics is an essential component in animal conservation biology. For that matter, ethics is very important in *all* conservation projects, including those that deal with botanical, aquatic, atmospheric, and inanimate environs. As I write this short piece I find myself asking isn't this so obvious that you're merely preaching to the choir? Well, yes and no. Some people seem (perhaps unintentionally) to ignore ethical issues and hope they will disappear if they play "ostrich." The origin of this essay stems from a recent issue of this journal (July/August 2001) that dealt with carnivore conservation. I wrote the editor to mention my surprise that there was no essay devoted to ethical issues among the excellent contributions on this very important topic.

Here, I am concerned solely with projects that center on animals, beings who also are stakeholders in conservation efforts. The multi-dimensional, multi-level, and interdisciplinary problems with which most conservation projects are faced are very difficult, serious, and contentious, and often demand immediate attention and quick solutions. In our haste and in the frenzy of trying to put out fires before they spread (rarely before they start), and some would correctly claim that the fires spread metastatically as do many cancers, we often overlook the basic ethical principles by which most of us operate daily. These ideals include principles such as:

- do no intentional harm.
- respect all life.
- treat all individuals with compassion, and
- step lightly into the lives of other beings, bodies of water, air, and landscapes.

Surely, these principles are politically correct, but they are also ethically and ecologically correct. They demand deep reflection and should be the foundation from which all conservation projects begin. They also raise very difficult issues that easily cause people to get angry and insult one another, and mandate that we ultimately develop guidelines for adjudicating competing and conflicting agendas, even if all parties really do have the best interests of animals in mind. There clearly is no universal agreement on just what are the "best interests."

Reprinted from Bekoff, M. 2002. The Importance of Ethics in Conservation Biology: Let's Be Ethicists Not Ostriches. *Endangered Species Update* 19 (2), 23–26, with permission from the editor.

Very few people cause intentional harm in their efforts to restore or recreate ecosystems and to maintain or to increase biodiversity. The other three ideals are easily overridden either because they get lost in the shuffle or because they are too difficult to adhere to with any degree of consistency. Indeed, in some cases while it clearly is *not* one's intention to cause harm to other animal beings, the very design of some studies, or perhaps the very reality of some conservation efforts, means that inevitably some animals will die or suffer. So, for example, is it permissible to begin a reintroduction project when it is estimated and accepted that 50% of the translocated animals will die? This was the acceptable standard for attempts to reintroduce Canadian lynx into southwestern Colorado (Kloor 1999; Scott et al. 1999; Bekoff 2001). Is it permissible to subject naive prey to introduced novel predators? Is it acceptable to do a project in which a non-prey species (e.g., coyotes in Yellowstone) will be killed by the reintroduction of a competitor (e.g., gray wolves)?

What happens in *both* locations when individuals are moved from one place to another? To my knowledge, there have been no follow-up studies in areas from which individuals have been removed to determine the effects on the remaining animals—the integrity of their social system—and on the integrity of the ecological community that remains. Are we violating one ecosystem to restore or recreate another? Is there any net gain?

While we recognize the fragility of the complex webs in most ecosystems, in many instances we do not try to understand just how delicate they are. The assumption is that we are doing no harm in the areas from which animals are removed but we really do not know this. I fully realize that these are difficult questions with many implications about what we value. But, the questions will not disappear if we ignore them. Surely, we can do better in providing solid answers.

WHAT OUGHT WE DO?

So, what are we to do? While people may disagree about which ethical principles should guide conservation efforts, it seems that no one would disagree that ethics *must* be factored into all conservation projects. This might mean that a project would go more slowly than some prefer, or that it might be delayed, or not done at all—at least not until more ethical methods are developed. This might be frustrating, but perhaps having patience, especially when the "problem" at hand does not demand an immediate solution. will make for better and more effective solutions in the long term. By showing wisdom and restraint, we learn more about nature's complexities. We also need to ask if a quick-fix is the best way to proceed, especially when we lack a solid comprehension of details that could make or break a project. Prematurely implementing a multidimensional, interdisciplinary project can simply be disastrous.

In a recent series of essays (Bekoff 2000a, 2000b, 2001), I outlined some of the questions with which conservation (and other) biologists must be concerned. These included, for example, do animals have rights and if so, what responsibilities does this entail? How *should* humans treat other animals? What *ought* we do? Can we do whatever we please to other animals? Should we interfere in animals' lives when we have spoiled their habitats or when they are sick provide food when there is not enough food to go around, or translocate them? Should our interests trump theirs? Should we be concerned with individuals, populations, species, or ecosystems? Should we let animals be and not intentionally interfere in their lives except on very rare occasions?

As big-brained, omnipresent, powerful, and supposedly omniscient mammals, we are mandated to give these questions the consideration that they demand. This requires us to develop a detailed understanding and appreciation of the behavioral and social ecology of the animals with whom we are concerned (e.g., Miller et al. 1996; Clemmons and Bucholz 1997; Caro 1998; Sutherland 1998: Berger 1999: Gosling and Sutherland 2000: Berger et al. 2001). Our understanding should also include their cognitive capacities (Berger 1998: Berger et al. 2001), emotional lives, and also their ecosystems. These efforts will lead to more relevant, appropriate approaches and solutions. To do less is to shirk our responsibilities to ourselves, other animals, and to Earth as a whole. We all love being out there in the field. Thus, doing arduous, tedious field work should be an activity to which we look forward.

There are no right or wrong answers to many questions about how humans should treat animals. However, there are better and worse answers. Perhaps in some cases what we think is the right action is not, when the big picture is carefully analyzed. A major goal of mine is to stimulate discussion about pertinent issues among all parties so that competing agendas are given due consideration. Those who hold opposing views need to cooperate and engage in open discussion with well-reasoned dissent (Ehrlich 1997). Positions should be criticized, not the people who hold them. Personal attacks are infantile and preclude compromise. The basic question remains. *what constitutes acceptable treatment of animals?*

The editors of the volume in which my 2001 essay appeared recognized the importance of ethics. They wanted an essay that would highlight just how complex and multidimensional these issues are. However, they faced the dilemma of personal bias—whoever they selected to write an essay would likely be biased. However, one person's opinion does not render another's invalid. In fact, only two of the volume's four editors shared my views. What is important is a universal agreement that ethics is an essential element of conservation biology, as it is in any other sphere of science.

Others have realized the importance of ethical discourse. An essay that I co-wrote with the Philosopher, Dale Jamieson (Bekoff and Jamieson 1996), was favorably reviewed in the journal *Ecology.* It was referred to as "a well-written and impelling plea for scientists to evaluate their experimental design and be sensitive, with respect to techniques and disturbances, to the species they are studying ... [T]his paper should be 'must reading' for all biologists, conservationists, and people interested in environmental issues" (Geidt 1997).

I mention this not to blow my own horn but rather to call attention to the fact that no matter what the problem at hand, ethical concerns must be an essential part of all proposed solutions. Ethics is as important as experimental techniques and statistical analyses. All scientists are responsible for maintaining the highest of ethical standards. When humans intervene into the lives of other animals we must do so by stepping lightly with humility, grace, respect, and compassion. We must accept that ethics might dictate the demise of certain projects. Thomas Berry cautions that we must have a "benign presence" when we go out into nature (Berry 1999). I agree.

Animals depend on our goodwill and mercy. Each person chooses to be intrusive, abusive, or compassionate, and each is responsible for her or his choices. Science, including conservation biology, is not value-free. Ultimately, we are all human beings with personal views of the world that drive our actions. Complicating the situation is the fact that values and sentiments change with time and are sensitive to demographic, political, and socioeconomic variation, along with personal whims. And some issues are so emotionally volatile that expecting rational discourse is less likely than winning the power ball lottery.

ETHICAL ENRICHMENT: WOULD WE DO IT AGAIN?

It is in the best traditions of science to ask questions about ethics: it is not anti-science nor should it be threatening to question our methods of studying animals. Ethics can enrich our knowledge of other animals and the worlds they live in and help us gain respect for them. Ethics also can broaden our range of interaction with other animals without compromising their lives. Ethical discussion can help us find alternatives to methods that do not serve us or other animals well. If we perceive ethical deliberations as unnecessary hurdles, then we lose rich opportunities to learn more about animals and ourselves. The application of ethical enrichment is a two-way street. Great discoveries come when our ethical relationship with animals is respectful and not exploitive. While animals are unable to consent to or refuse our intrusions into their lives, it is useful to ask what they might say if they could do so. We should also ask ourselves if we would do what we did again, given what we learned.

Animal rights advocates often place priority on individuals, whereas animal welfare advocates take a utilitarian position. Welfare advocates favor decisions where the presumed costs to animals are less than the benefits to humans. In conservation biology, often the interests of individuals are traded off against perceived benefits that accrue to higher levels of organization, such as populations, species, and ecosystems (Estes 1998). Biocentrists and anthropocentrists often clash because the issues are highly driven by social and personal views. These issues also are fueled by how one views man's place in nature and by what is considered to be natural (Bekoff 2001, 2002).

Having Fun, Saving the World, and Educating Students

In the end, all approaches and all levels of organization need to be considered in our deliberations about human interference in nature. It is our social responsibility to do the best we can and use all "ways of knowing" (Berkes 1999; Bradshaw and Bekoff 2001). I hope that we will all convey this message to our students, a point emphasized by the eminent ecologist, Paul Ehrlich (Ehrlich 1997). In his wonderful and bold book, *A World of Wounds*, Ehrlich wrote: "Many of the students who have crossed my path in the last decade or so have wanted to do much, much more. They were drawn to ecology because they were brought up in a 'world of wounds,' and want to help heal it. But the current structure of ecology tends to dissuade them ... Now we need to incorporate the idea that it is every scientist's obligation to communicate pertinent portions of her or his results to decision-makers and the general public." And our work should be fun. Having fun, being sentimental, and doing solid science are not mutually exclusive activities (Bekoff 2002). Once again, to quote Ehrlich (1997): "In my view, no area of science can be successful (or much fun!) without a mutually supportive interaction between theory and empiricism ... So let's stop arguing about theory versus empiricism and worrying about the end of our science. Instead, let's cooperate more, change some of our priorities, and have fun while we're trying to save the world."

Minding Animals

"The earth is, to a certain extent, our mother. She is so kind, because whatever we do, she tolerates it. But now, the time has come when our power to destroy is so extreme that Mother Earth is compelled to tell us to be careful. The population explosion and many other indicators make that clear, don't they? Nature has its own natural limitations" (His Holiness the Dalai Lama 1999).

Achieving win-win situations for humans and animals involved in conservation efforts will be very difficult but we should never stop trying. If we fail to do so I fear that everyone—including our children and theirs—will lose, and much of the spark and spirit that sustain our attempts to make this a better world will be extinguished. Fortunately, many students are now interested in ethical issues, and there is a progressive trend toward caring more, not less, about the fate of individual animals in conservation biology. How we sense and feel the presence of individual animals directly influences how we interact with them (Abram 1996; Sewall 1999).

There is much to gain and little to lose if we move forward with grace, humility, respect, compassion and love. Surely, we will be more fulfilled if we know deep in our hearts that we did the best we could and took into account the well-being of the magnificent animals with whom we share the Earth— the awesome beings who selflessly make our lives richer, more challenging, and more enjoyable than they would be in the animals' absence. By "minding animals" (Bekoff 2002) we mind ourselves. The power we potentially wield to do anything we want to do to animals and to nature as a whole is inextricably tied with responsibilities to be ethical human beings. We can be no less.

ACKNOWLEDGEMENTS

I thank Jennifer Jacobus MacKay, Colin Allen, Wendy Keefover-Ring, Mark Derr, and Gay Bradshaw for their comments on an earlier draft of this essay. The development of some of the ideas in this brief essay were helped along by discussion with students in my Behavioral Ecology and Conservation Biology class and in numerous discussions with Gay Bradshaw, Laura Sewall, and Joel Berger.

LITERATURE CITED

Abram, D. 1996. The Spell of the Sensuous; Perception and Language in a More-Than-Human World. Pantheon Press, New York.

Bekoff, M. 2000a. Redecorating nature: Reflections on science; humility, community, reconciliation, spirit, compassion, and love. Human Ecology Review 7: 59–67.

Bekoff, M. 2000b. Deep science, feeling, and heart. BioScience 50: 635.

Bekoff, M. 2001. Human-carnivore interactions: Adopting proactive strategies for complex problems. Pp 34–89 in J. L. Gittleman, S. M. Funk, D. W. Macdonald, and R. K. Wayne, eds. Carnivore Conservation, Cambridge University Press. London and New York.

Bekoff, M. 2002. Minding animals: Awareness, emotion, and heart. Oxford University Press, New York.

Bekoff, M. and D. Jamieson. 1996. Ethics and the study of carnivores. Pp 16–45 in J. L. Gittleman, ed. Carnivore Behavior, Ecology, and Evolution. Cornell University Press, Ithaca, New York.

Berger, J. 1998. Future prey: Some consequences of the loss and restoration of large carnivores. Pp 80–100 in T. Caro, ed. Behavioral Ecology and Conservation. Biology. Oxford University Press, New York.

Berger, J. 1999. Anthropogenic extinction of top carnivores and interspecific animal behaviour: Implications of the rapid decoupling of a web involving wolves, bears, moose, and ravens. Proceedings of the Royal Society of London B 266: 2261–2267.

Berger, J., J. E. Swenson, and I. L. Persson. 2001. Recolonizing carnivores and naive prey: Conservation lessons from Pleistocene extinctions. Science 291: 1036–1039.

Berkes, F. 1999. Sacred knowledge: Traditional ecological knowledge and resource management. Taylor and Frances, Philadelphia.

Berry, T. 1999. The Great Work: Our Way Into the Future. Bell Tower, New York.

Bradshaw, G. A. and M. Bekoff. 2001. Ecology and social responsibility: The re-embodiment of science. Trends in Ecology and Evolution 16: 460–165.

Caro, T., ed. 1998. Behavioral ecology and conservation biology. Oxford University Press, New York.

Clemmons, J. R. and R. Buchholz, eds. 1997. Behavioral approaches to conservation in the wild. Cambridge University Press, New York.

Ehrlich, P. 1997. A world of wounds: Ecologists and the human dilemma. Ecology Institute. Oldendorf/Luhe, Germany.

Estes, J. A. 1998. Concerns about rehabilitation of oiled wildlife. Conservation Biology 12: 1156–1157.

Geidt, G. A. 1997. Review of John Gittleman, (ed.), Carnivore Behavior, Ecology, and Evolution. Cornell University Press, Ithaca, New York, Ecology 78: 1607.

Gosling, L. M. and W. J. Sutherland, eds. 2000. Behavior and conservation. Cambridge University Press, New York.

His Holiness the Dalai Lama. 1999. The path to tranquility: Daily wisdom. Viking Arkana, New York.

Kloor, K. 1999. Lynx and biologists try to recover after disastrous start; Science 285: 320–321.

Miller, B. et al. 1996. Prairie night: Black-footed ferrets and the recovery of endangered species. Smithsonian Institution Press, Washington, D.C.

Scott, J. M., D. Murray, and B. Griffith. 1999. Lynx reintroduction, Science 286: 49.

Sewall, L. 1999. Sight and Sensibility: The Ecopsychology of Perception. Jeremy P. Tarcher/Putnan, New York.

Sutherland, W. J. 1998. The importance of behavioral studies in conservation biology. Animal Behaviour 56: 801–809.

Marc Bekoff and Dale Jamieson

17 Ethics and the Study of Carnivores
Doing Science While Respecting Animals

THE HUMAN RELATIONSHIP to nature is a deeply ambiguous one. Human animals are both a part of nature and distinct from it. They are part of nature in the sense that, like other forms of life, they were brought into existence by natural processes, and, like other forms of life, they are dependent on their environment for survival and success. Yet humans are also reflective animals with sophisticated cultural systems. Because of their immense power and their ability to wield it intentionally, humans have duties and responsibilities that other animals do not (Bekoff and Jamieson 1991).

One striking feature of humans is that they are curious animals, and this curiosity has produced a wealth of knowledge about humans, nonhuman animals (hereafter "animals"), other forms of life, and the abiotic environment. Along with the acquisition of knowledge *about* nature come numerous intrusions *into* nature, even from activities such as photographing wildlife that seem to be harmless (Duffus and Wipond 1992). As Cuthill (1991:1008) has observed, "We have to tamper with nature to understand it." Though it sometimes appears that an examination of some part of nature is not harmful, often what seemed initially to be a minor intrusion turns out to have serious consequences for what has been affected (Caine 1992). Sometimes human intrusions even make it difficult to gain the knowledge that we seek, or to attain well-meaning goals (as may be the case with wild pandas: Bertram 1993; Schaller 1993).

In this chapter we focus primarily on ethical questions that arise in studies of behavior and behavioral ecology in wild carnivores under field conditions (see also Cuthill 1991; Kirkwood 1992). There are many important questions that we will not address, including those involved in the physiological analyses of carnivore behavior under field conditions (e.g., hibernation). Furthermore, we say little about domestic dogs and cats, even though they are carnivores and are used in many research projects, including some in behavioral ecology (for references, see Beck 1973; Daniels and Bekoff 1989a, b, c; Bradshaw 1992; Thorne 1992; Orlans 1993, chap. 13; Clutton-Brock, this volume). A 1988 report from the U.S. Department of Agriculture states that 140,471 dogs and 42,271 cats were used in various sorts of experimentation

Reprinted from Bekoff, M., and Jamieson, D. 1996. Ethics and the Study of Science While Respecting Animals. In J. L. Gittleman (ed.), *Carnivore Behavior, Ecology, and Evolution, Volume 2.* Copyright © 1996 Cornell University Press, Ithaca, NY. pp. 15–45. Used by permission of the publisher, Cornell University Press.

in that year alone (cited in Singer 1990:37), and Kew (1991:160) reports data indicating that about 10,000 dogs and 5,000 cats are killed annually in scientific research in the United Kingdom. Domestic dogs and cats are also used for various nonscientific purposes that involve breeding for human-desired traits, many of which are injurious to the animals themselves (Daniels and Bekoff 1990).

A great many problems, both methodological and ethical, are unique to field studies of particular carnivores or other species. Many of the issues we are concerned with, however, are not restricted to the study of wild carnivores, and our essay should also inform discussions that center on other taxa, perhaps even insects (Wigglesworth 1980; Eisemann et al. 1984; Fiorito 1986; Lockwood 1987), and on various human activities that involve using captive animals in zoos and wildlife parks (Jamieson 1985a, 1995; Peterson 1989; Chiszar et al. 1990; Kiley-Worthington 1990; Bostock 1993) and in research laboratories.

DIVERGENT VIEWS ON THE ROLE OF ETHICS

Although a consideration of ethical questions that centers on how humans use animals in science could be viewed as anti-science, it is rather in the best traditions of science. For it involves applying to science itself the scientific spirit of skepticism, rationality, and a demand for evidence. Indeed, consideration of the ethical issues meriting serious attention in field studies of carnivore behavior may make for better science; to this end, Roger Ewbank (1993), editor-in-chief of the journal *Animal Welfare*, has recently called for papers that specifically address these problems.

There is a strong trend for more, rather than less, concern for the ethical issues that arise from animal use in a wide variety of contexts (Huntingford 1984; Rowan 1984, 1988; Dickinson 1988; Rolston 1988; Hettinger 1989; Goodall 1990; Rachels 1990; Bekoff and Jamieson 1990, 1991; Cuthill 1991; Elwood 1991; Bekoff et al. 1992; Hargrove 1992; Bekoff and Gruen 1993; Benton 1993; Broom and Johnson 1993; Cavalieri and Singer 1993; Farnsworth and Rosovsky 1993; Guillermo 1993; Orlans 1993; Peterson and Goodall 1993; Preece and Chamberlain 1993; Quinn 1993; Singer 1993a; Zimmerman et al. 1993; Wilkie 1993; Bekoff 1994a; for historical accounts, see Carson 1972 and Ryder 1989). And the trend is seen among people with diverse backgrounds and interests (Plous 1991; Galvin and Herzog 1992; McAdam 1992). Those interested in animal welfare comprise a group that is as heterogeneous as many professional societies (Bekoff et al. 1992). Scientists such as Richard Dawkins (1993) have called for legal rights for chimpanzees, gorillas, and orangutans; even Desmond Morris (1990) has become a spokesperson for animal welfare, and presents what he calls a "Bill of Rights for animals" (pp. 168–169). Top-level administrators in the United States such as President Clinton's science advisor, John Gibbons, have indicated the need for ethical reflection on the use of animals in research. Nowadays many professional societies have guidelines, which are constantly updated, to which authors must adhere if they are to publish in the journals sponsored by these societies (American Society of Mammalogists 1987; Anonymous 1992; Stamp Dawkins and Gosling 1992; see also Rollin 1989; Bekoff et al. 1992; and Bekoff 1993a, for lists). Indeed, the Association for the Study of Animal Behaviour (United Kingdom) and the Animal Behavior Society (United States) jointly devoted a special issue of the journal *Animal Behaviour* to ethics in research on animal behavior.

Despite the great interest in animal welfare, there are divergent views concerning what is justifiable with respect to the treatment of animals in research and in other activities. Moreover, it is clear that people have diverse opinions about the moral acceptability of various of these activities. For example, in a recent debate about experimentally induced infanticide in birds (Bekoff 1993a; Emlen 1993), the authors disagree about what should have been done to prevent further harm to the chicks who were being killed by intruding females. Not only is this question important to consider, but so is the question concerning the value of the knowledge that accumulates from studies of this sort. Suffice it to say, people differ in terms of the benefits that they perceive to be coming from different types of research. Given that there is growing concern about animal welfare, it is important to note that Cuthill (1991) concluded that in his opinion there *were* no ethical problems with the field studies that he reviewed. Although Elwood (1991:847) concluded from his review of studies on rodents that "it is clear that many of the experiments conducted in the field of infanticide and maternal aggression could have been improved from the ethical point of view," he also notes that "in recent years there has been a decreased use of the more questionable experimental paradigms." Nevertheless, even in reviews of experimental field studies in which individuals are removed or added to groups there often is no mention of ethical considerations, for either the target animals or the nontarget animals (e.g., Sih et al.'s 1985 review of field experiments used to study competition; see also Pimm 1991, chap. 12).

Moreover, there are still those who claim that concern for issues of animal welfare is the privilege of "those who have independent sources of wealth, no family obligations, and a lamented shortage of concrete worries" (Hardy 1990:11). Some even claim that "animal usage is not a moral or ethical issue" (White 1990:43; for a reply, see Bekoff 1992). Jamieson (1985b) has called people who do not see issues concerning the regulation and use of animals as moral issues "moral privatists." These people do indeed take an ethical position, but do not acknowledge it. For the view that it is nobody else's business what one does with animals is itself an ethical position.

In this essay we will raise many questions but not always provide clear-cut answers. We hope to open the door for informed, nonpolarized debate. This approach does not, however, mean that these questions are unanswerable, or that we are neutral about how they are answered. Indeed, many of the questions we ask are being answered every day in animal care and use committees, and in the choices that we make about experimental design. Our general point of view is that we should have respect for the animals that we study, and for the diverse habitats in which they live, and that respect for individual animals cannot be separated from embracing a sound, thoroughgoing environmental ethic (Ryder 1992). Many people agree with these general sentiments, but a great deal of work remains to be done in translating them into clear, specific directions for action.

PHILOSOPHICAL BACKGROUND

This chapter is not intended to be a primer on moral philosophy, but any serious consideration of the ethics of carnivore research must begin with a discussion of the philosophical background. Public attitudes about animals are changing, in part owing to a shift in the philosophical climate. Beginning with Peter Singer's landmark *Animal Liberation* (1975, 1990), there has been an explosion of writing and activism on behalf of animals (see Magel 1989; Bekoff and Jamieson 1991; and Jamieson 1993a for bibliographies; and Finsen and Finsen 1994 for a discussion of the animal-rights movement). Concern about animals is only likely to grow in the future. Behavioral research, because it does not seem to contribute directly to human health or welfare, may be especially vulnerable to criticism, and if the research community does not effectively regulate itself in ways that are consistent with prevailing public values and attitudes, then it is likely to be increasingly regulated by government agencies. For these reasons it is important for carnivore researchers to be aware of some of the major currents of thought regarding the human and humane treatment of animals.

In recent years philosophers have devoted intense attention to questions about the moral status of animals. Though the debate has been vigorous, few moral philosophers today would defend our present treatment of animals in scientific contexts. As DeGrazia (1991:49) notes, "There is no well-developed theory explicitly addressing the moral status of animals that supports such current practices as factory farming, animal research, and hunting." Although there is a great deal of disagreement about the theoretical bases for these results, and many different views about the details of what morality requires, most contemporary moral philosophers would support significantly more restrictive policies regarding our treatment of animals than those currently in place.

Arguments for animal protection grow largely out of traditional moral theory. The basic structure of such arguments typically involves embracing some theory or principle, and then arguing that partisans of this theory or principle either have overlooked its applications to animals or have held beliefs about animals that we now know to be false.

Singer, for example, is a utilitarian in the tradition of Bentham and Mill. He believes that right actions are those that maximize utility summed over all those who are affected by the actions. Much of what we do to animals only appears to be justified, from a utilitarian point of view, because we ignore the consequences of these actions on the animals themselves. Once we take the interests of animals seriously it becomes clear that the misery that we cause them in factory farming and in some areas of research outweighs any benefits that we may gain from exploiting them. Tom Regan (1983) argues from the perspective of rights theory. One traditional view in moral philosophy is that humans have rights, and therefore it is wrong to kill or torture them even if the overall consequences of doing so would be good. Regan then goes on to show that many of the reasons that have been given for supposing that humans have rights also imply that many animals have rights. If we are to be consistent rights theorists, we must therefore recognize the rights of many animals. Thus, Regan believes that just as it is wrong to kill or torture a human even if the benefits of doing so would be very great, so it is wrong to treat animals in these ways even if doing so benefits humans. Animal-protectionist conclusions have also been reached from a neo-Aristotelian basis (Rollin 1981), from commonsense morality (Sapontzis 1987), and from concerns about character (Midgley 1983). What this suggests is that some of the most profound conclusions regarding our treatment of animals are relatively insensitive to initial theoretical assumptions. That most major theories appear to converge from different directions on the conclusion that we ought to alter our behavior with respect to animals makes the case for animal protection even more compelling in many people's minds.

The widespread criticism within the philosophical community of our practices with respect to animals may come as a surprise to many nonphilosophers. Efforts have been made to portray philosophers such as Singer and Regan as fruitcakes or radicals, and to promote the idea that critics of animal-liberationist philosophy such as Cohen (1986), Frey (1980, 1983), and Carruthers (1989, 1992) represent the true philosophical consensus. Although we cannot discuss their work in detail here, the writings of Cohen, Frey, and Carruthers have been subjected to criticism that many find devastating (see for example McGinn 1980; Singer 1990; E. Johnson 1991; Bekoff and Jamieson 1991; Jamieson and Bekoff 1992; Jamieson 1993a; Pluhar 1993; Rothschild 1993). Carruthers himself (1992:194) has changed his mind about the force of his previous arguments.

Although there is widespread agreement within the philosophical community that our practices with respect to animals need to be reformed, there are differences regarding the extent of the needed reforms. Regan is an "abolitionist"; he believes that all invasive animal research is immoral. Other philosophers, such as Singer, hold that at least in principle some animal research can be defended. There are many subtleties and complications in this rigorous, well-reasoned body of literature that cannot be explored here, but any serious rethinking of the ethics of carnivore research should take these challenges seriously.

WHY STUDY ANIMALS?

Perhaps the most fundamental question regarding field research is why do it at all. Even the least-invasive research can be disruptive, and costs time and money. In recent years anthropology has been going through a disciplinary soul-searching, and it is probably time for behavioral biology to go through one as well. Many people study animals for deeply personal reasons—they like being outdoors, they like animals, they don't know what else they would do with their lives—but these sentiments hardly amount to a justification. Several other reasons for doing this sort of research are also frequently given: that animal research benefits humans, that it benefits animals, and that it benefits the environment.

Animal research that benefits humans falls into two categories. One category subsumes research that contributes to human health; the other subsumes research that provides economic benefits. Little field research on carnivores can be defended on the grounds that it contributes to human health. Animal models for human diseases and disorders are better constructed under laboratory conditions, and even then many of them are quite controversial on both scientific and moral grounds. Animal research that contributes economic benefits often concerns the control of predators. Much of this research employs morally questionable methods, and also raises questions about where science ends and industry begins. Predator management may be informed by science, but in itself it is not science; and if producing direct economic benefits were the only justification for studying animals, then very little behavioral research would be justified.

The idea that behavioral research benefits animals and the environment is an appealing one. The thought is that only by studying carnivores will we know how to preserve them, and that only by preserving carnivores can we protect the natural environment. As noble as these sentiments are, they are rife with dangers. For this attitude can lead very quickly to transforming science into wildlife management; and wildlife management itself poses important moral challenges.

Humans face an environmental crisis in part because of their attempts to control, dominate, and manage nature. These attempts have led to the destruction of important aspects of nature, and even to serious threats to human well-being. In attitude and intention, much wildlife management is more of the same. A new generation seems to think that though in the past we were incompetent managers, we now know how to do it right. Our track record, however, does not inspire confidence (Mighetto 1991; for discussion of various projects and wildlife research in general, see Gray 1993). Ludwig et al. (1993) call into question the idea that we can manage animal populations in a sustainable way. They argue that science is probably incapable of predicting sustainable levels of exploitation of an animal population, and that even if it were possible to make such predictions, human shortsightedness and greed would prevent us from acting on them.

Some people argue that human intervention has already so disrupted natural processes that we have no choice but to manage populations and habitats—that the decision *not* to manage is just a form of unreflective, irrational management. Moreover, some would say that management approaches are part of a strategy to convince humans that much more must be done to preserve habitat and to save the animals that we have. No doubt there is something to these arguments. Still, we should be suspicious of them because they are so self-serving. Whether people are pro- or anti-environment, they seem to agree that humans should manage and manipulate nature. But if we are convinced that we must manage the natural world, we should remember that the best of intentions are no substitute for minimizing harm.

The deepest problem with wildlife management may be the tendency to confuse scientific ideas with philosophical ones. When managers argue that a population should be "culled" or otherwise managed and controlled, as for example has been suggested for Alaskan wolves (e.g., Grooms 1993, chap. 12), their view is often seen as a scientific recommendation. Appeals are made to what are presented as irrefutable scientific data concerning interactions between wolves and their prey. But the models that are used are often simplistic (important variables are omitted, including the effects of weather and food availability), and estimates of the actual numbers of supposed problem predators can be inaccurate, as can be estimates of the number of individuals hunted and killed annually by sports hunters or by managers. It is also possible that only a small percentage of people living in a given area actually want to control predators such as wolves (Grooms 1993), and the arguments put forth for doing so can therefore be self-serving. Indeed, Alaskans as a whole have been identified "as one of the two demographic groups with the greatest affection for wolves" (Grooms 1993:168). Economic factors (e.g., tourism, fees for hunting licenses) frequently provide the primary motivation for controlling predator populations, and their compelling nature can result in failures to look for other ways to deal with predator/prey interactions. But most important, recommendations about population control presuppose various philosophical positions, each with its ethical dimensions and assumptions. And when these presuppositions are made explicit, it is clear that not everyone agrees with them. Scientific data, even those that are judged to be accurate, are not the only sorts of information that are relevant to establishing management practices. Issues concerned with population control bring with them commitments to various views about human authority, the value of species versus individuals, and the importance of human versus nonhuman interests (Shapiro 1989; Jamieson 1995).

The purest motivation for studying carnivores may be simply the desire to understand them. But even if this is our motivation, we should proceed cautiously and reflectively. For in quenching our thirst for knowledge we impose costs on these animals. In many cases they would be better off if we were willing to accept our ignorance, secure in the knowledge that they are leading their own lives in their own ways (for a similar point about cetaceans, see Jamieson and Regan 1985). If, however, we do make the decision to study animals, we should recognize that we are doing it primarily for ourselves and not for them, and we should proceed respectfully and harm them as little as possible.

THE CONTEXT OF RESEARCH

Field research is conducted in contexts that influence how data are collected and used, and the results that one obtains. When scientists "go into the field" they go to a particular place, often a foreign country, with a human population, with its own government, culture, way of life, and attitudes toward both foreigners and the animals the scientists are studying. In the past, many researchers marched into foreign lands (getting permission from government officials, if needed), studied the animals in whom they were interested, and departed, often with little thought about the legacy they were leaving behind. Not only must foreign researchers be sensitive to local customs concerning animal use (e.g., Brenes 1988; Croft 1991; Rabinowitz 1986, 1991; Wenzel 1991; Freeman et al. 1992; Lynge 1992; Bekoff and Gruen 1993; Schaller 1993), but they should also do what they can to help develop the scientific capability of the host country. They should appreciate that it is a privilege to be permitted to work where they want to, and they should recognize that there may be a good deal of indigenous knowledge about the animals they are interested in studying. Furthermore, foreign researchers should not assume that they are doing their host country a favor by coming there.

There are many reasons to respect local customs and abilities. First, better science will be done in the long run if different kinds of knowledge are exploited and expertise is democratized. Second, the study of animal behavior, like anthropology, is historically rooted in Western dominance, imperialism, and colonialism (Haraway 1989). Making a contribution to the society in which researchers work is part of showing respect for the human population and making small amends for the exploitation of the past. Finally, the enlistment of local researchers may help foreigners come to terms with local attitudes and customs.

But the use of local workers may also present problems, because of difficulties in communicating about what needs to be done (e.g., Rabinowitz 1991; Schaller 1993; see also Terborgh 1993) and what data should be collected, and because of problems that might develop concerning the ownership of data and how they are to be disseminated and used. Rabinowitz (1986:155), an American scientist who has worked in various countries, also makes the point that it is often difficult to work with officials from his home country, who too often interfere with his research abroad. He recalls an incident when he was studying jaguars in Belize in which an official for a U.S. agency was willing to break Belize law to allow a visitor who "puts a lot of U.S. dollars into this country" to hunt jaguars. Such incidents create conflicts between researchers, who are concerned to protect the animals they study, and the sometimes differing values of people whose decisions affect the future of the work. Conflicts in values also inevitably arise between those who are trained in the traditions of western science and those in host countries who may have very different attitudes toward knowledge, animals, and nature.

RESPONSIBILITY FOR DATA COLLECTION, ANALYSIS, AND DISSEMINATION

In recent years there has been increasing concern about scientific integrity and even fraud in science (for discussion and references, see Goodstein 1991; LaFollette 1992; Altmann 1993; Bulger et al. 1993; Dresser 1993). Pushed along by such requirements as that of the National Institutes of Health that all training grants must have an ethics component, these issues are beginning to attract the attention of practicing scientists. Indeed, a recent book in which articles on animal behavior are reprinted begins with a section concerned with integrity in science (Sherman and Alcock 1993). Furthermore, an entire issue of the journal *Ethics and Behavior* (1993:3[3]) is devoted to the general themes of whistle-blowing and misconduct in science.

Trust is an important part of virtually all scientific endeavors (Woolf 1988; Hardwig 1985, 1991; Kitcher 1993; Webb 1993). Science proceeds by amplifying, theorizing, or rejecting one's own findings and those of others. In many areas of science, including field studies, replication is difficult and in some cases even rare. Against this background the very act of citing a report can be seen as an act of trust. Using other scholars' reports of recent work, such as information contained in book reviews, also involves trust. Though there is usually no reason to believe that someone is knowingly altering his or her view of a colleague's work, it happens: the senior author recently learned of a case in which a book was given a more favorable review than it would otherwise have received, because of the ill health of the author of the book being considered. Trust is also placed in the hands of journal editors, but this, too, is sometimes misguided: there are instances, for example, of collusion among editors so as to influence when certain types of results appear (Collins and Pinch 1979:258).

Trust also comes into question when principal investigators or project leaders who play a major role in writing a research proposal do not do much of the field work that is later reported in published articles. Thus, there is often a gap between the design of an experiment and the actual procedures by which data are collected. Individuals disappear into the field and emerge with data, but the type of guidance that is given during the process of data collection is often inconsistent or even nonexistent, and is rarely open to public scrutiny. These problems can be acute in field studies because of the difficulty involved in asserting control over many of the variables that are encountered in field projects, and also because decisions often have to be made on the spot, lest data be lost; wild animals typically do not wait around while scientists make decisions.

Because field research is often a highly collaborative activity, questions of authorship arise (for general discussion, see part V of Bulger et al. 1993). Principal investigators generally are listed as authors even if they have had little to do with data collection. The fact that the principal investigator raised the money for the research and took part in data analysis is often regarded as sufficient for his or her being the lead author. In recent years in literary studies there have been interesting discussions of authorship (e.g., Foucault 1984), and the discussion is spreading into ethics. Professional research assistants, graduate students, and postdoctoral fellows are often in a very weak position to assert claims to authorship. They may have done much or all of the data collection and made important contributions to the conceptual framework, yet they may be listed as junior authors, mentioned in the acknowledgments, or excluded from recognition altogether. There are also risks for principal investigators whose names appear on every publication from their laboratory or research project, quite apart from growing suspicions about actual participation in authorship. For if such a coauthor has played little role in the collection of the data on which the report is based, then he or she cannot be sure that everything that was claimed to have been done was done; a great deal of trust is invested in all of the participants in a field project.

Though these problems are not unique to field endeavors, they can become magnified in research efforts of this type. All those involved in such projects need to be aware of the trust that is invested in all co-workers, and aware as well that each individual shares responsibility for the integrity of the project as a whole and for the integrity of the results.

OBSERVATION AND MANIPULATION

Field projects bring along a whole host of problems concerning observation and manipulation that are usually not of much concern to laboratory endeavors (Cuthill 1991), although both sorts of research can involve intrusions into the privacy of animals' lives. The problems most apparent in field research are those that center on the lack of control over the behavior of the animals being studied, over variables that influence the behavior of the animals being studied, and, as mentioned above, the potential lack of control over the individuals who do the actual research. Furthermore, because animals living under field conditions are generally more difficult to observe than those living under more confined conditions, various manipulations are often used to make them more accessible to study (see Mills, this volume). These include such activities as handling, trapping (and retrapping) using various sorts of mechanical devices (which might include luring using live animals as bait), and marking (and remarking) individuals, none of which is unique to field studies, but all of which can have important and diverse effects on wild animals who may not be accustomed to being handled by humans or even to their presence.

Just "being there" and visiting individuals, groups, nests, dens, or ranging areas can also have a significant influence on the behavior of the animals (for discussion and bibliographies, see Michener 1989; Bekoff and Jamieson 1991; Cuthill 1991; Bekoff et al. 1992; Caine 1992; Shackley 1992; Isbell and Young 1993; Mainini et al. 1993). Kennedy and Knight (1992) found that magpies who are not habituated to human presence spend so much time avoiding the humans that the avoidance effort itself takes time away from such essential activities as feeding. Burley et al. (1982) showed that mate choice in zebra finches is influenced by the color of the leg band used to mark individuals, and there may be all sorts of other human-engendered influences that have *not* been documented. Similar data for most carnivores are lacking (but see Laurenson and Caro 1994). Furthermore, the filming of animals so as to establish permanent records can also have a negative influence on the animals being filmed; reflections from camera bodies, the noise of motor-driven cameras and other sorts of video devices, and the heat and brightness of spotlights (A. Pusey, pers. comm.) can all be disruptive.

Although many problems are encountered both in laboratory and field research, the consequences for wild animals may be different from and greater than those experienced by captive animals, whose lives are already changed by the conditions under which they live. This can be so whether experiments entail handling, trapping, and marking individuals or not. Consider experimental procedures that include (1) visiting the home ranges, territories, or dens of animals, (2) manipulating food supply and other resources, (3) changing the size and composition of groups (age, sex ratio, kin relationships) by removing or adding individuals, (4) playing back vocalizations, (5) depositing scents, (6) distorting phenotypes, (7) using dummies, and (8) manipulating the gene pool. All of these manipulations can change the behavior of individuals, including their movement patterns, how they make use of space, the amount of time they devote to various activities (including hunting and anti-predatory behavior), and the various types of social interactions they engage in (including care-giving, social play, and dominance interactions). These changes can in turn influence the behavior of groups as a whole, including group hunting or foraging patterns, care-giving behavior, and dominance relationships, and can also influence nontarget individuals (Cuthill 1991; see also Hofer et al. 1993 for discussion of how snaring migratory herbivores can influence the population dynamics and demography of spotted hyenas). Though we often cannot know about various aspects of the behavior of animals before we arrive in the field, our presence does seem to influence what animals do, at least when we initially enter into their worlds with some degree of regularity. For example, the coyotes that were observed in one long-term study (Bekoff and Wells 1986) initially spent a great deal of time staring and barking at observers who remained at least 1–2 km distant, but eventually settled down and seemed to go about their daily activities with little concern; their behavior reverted to what we assume was typical of what they did before we arrived. Furthermore, changes in the behavior of individuals and groups, including those animals who are (re)introduced to a specific area, can have far-ranging effects on local and distant ecosystems. Consider, for example, the reintroduction of red wolves into areas where coyotes already live (Wayne and Gittleman 1995).

The point here is that what appear to be relatively small changes at the individual level can have drastic and wide-ranging effects in both the short and the long term. Certain activities that were designed outside of the field situation may be impossible to perform, others, though possible to implement, may have unanticipated negative effects on the animals, and still others that seemed impossible to perform may turn out to be possible and less intrusive than those manipulations that were previously planned. On-the-spot decisions often need to be made, and expectations about what these changes will mean to the lives of the animals who are involved, and how ethical considerations might inform these decisions, need to be given serious attention. We should take as our guiding principle that when we are unsure about how our activities will influence the lives of the animals being studied, we should err on the side of the animals and not engage in these practices until we know their consequences. Recently, it has been claimed that we should take this stance even regarding insects (Wigglesworth 1980; Eisemann et al. 1986). Eisemann et al. (1986:167) conclude that this attitude "helps to preserve in the experimenter an appropriately respectful attitude towards living organisms whose physiology, though different, and perhaps simpler than our own, is as yet far from completely understood."

QUESTIONS WITHOUT ANSWERS: A BAKER'S DOZEN

Field workers engage in many different activities, and we cannot address them all here. The following list of questions is meant, rather, to provoke thought and open discussion: it is certainly not exhaustive, and there is no order to the questions being posed, in terms of their relative importance, although some questions might be viewed as being more important than others. The fact that there may be little consensus about the answers to these questions at this time does not mean that there are not better and worse answers. As a general principle we should err on the side of the animals, and never forget that respect for the animals is of utmost importance. But real progress in the future will involve developing ever more precise guidelines about what is permissible.

Here we pose 13 questions, among which there is some unavoidable overlap in the areas considered. The first four questions are concerned with general issues that center on ethical responsibilities to wild and domestic animals, captive-breeding programs, concerns about individuals and groups, and the validity of data stemming from studies of captive animals and individuals who are studied and manipulated in the field. Questions 4, 5, and 6 are concerned with methods of study and the relationship between researchers and the animals they use, and questions 7, 8, and 9 consider whether or not researchers should interfere in natural predation or employ staged encounters either between predators and prey or in studies of infanticide or dominance. The tenth question deals with relationships between animal cognition and animal welfare, the eleventh asks what principles we should use as ethical guides, and questions 12 and 13 are concerned with scientists' responsibility for how their results are used and how to deal with ethical misconduct.

1. Do wild animals have different moral status than domestic animals? This is an important question, because field studies are performed on both

domestic and wild carnivores, often in the same habitat. Callicott (1980/1989:30) writes that "domestic animals are creations of man. They are living artifacts, but artifacts nonetheless, and they constitute yet another mode of the extension of the works of man into the ecosystem" (see also Katz 1993). According to Howard (1993:234–235), "Domestic species are genetically programmed to depend upon humans for their safe existence and, fortunately, they always die relatively humanely rather than suffering one of nature's brutal deaths" (for a reply to Howard, see Bekoff and Hettinger 1994). Since these animals may live longer, have a higher quality of life, and die less painfully than do wild animals, Howard concludes that animal research actually "produces an improvement of life for some individuals of these species" (p. 235; for similar views made without any empirical support, see Gallup and Suarez 1987; Lansdell 1988; Greenough 1992; Grandin 1992; and Raynor 1992; for rebuttal, see Singer 1992a). Greenough (1992:9) goes as far as to claim, "In fact, it is very rare for research animals to be subjected to significant amounts of pain. For most animals, life in the laboratory is considerably more comfortable than [that] for their counterparts in the wild." Colwell (1989:33) maintains that "our moral responsibility for the appropriate care of *individual* organisms in agriculture, zoos, or gardens does not depend on whether they are wild or domesticated in origin." He also writes, "I contend, however, that the role of domesticated *species* as coevolved members of our ancestral component community ... places them in a biologically and ethically distinct class from 'wild' species" (emphasis original).

2. Are we ever justified, and if so under what conditions, in bringing wild animals into captivity? The most frequently cited reason for bringing animals into captivity is to preserve endangered species by allowing individuals to live in a protected environment that will facilitate breeding, thus maintaining the species' gene pool. It is sometimes said that the goal of these programs is the eventual return of these animals to the wild, but there are serious philosophical questions involved here. For example, do animals have a right to liberty? Do species have interests? Can the welfare of individuals be sacrificed in the interests of species (for discussion, see Regan 1983; Jamieson 1985a, 1995; Rachels 1989; Shapiro 1989; Singer 1990, 1993a; DeBlieu 1991; Varner and Monroe 1991; Bekoff and Gruen 1993; Norton et al. 1995). It is noteworthy, in fact, that some of the most virulent critics of captive-breeding programs are themselves among the scientists who have been devoting their lives to these efforts and who sincerely want them to succeed.

To quote Schaller (1993:233–234), "The realization that the panda has so suffered and declined in numbers while we chronicled its life burdens me painfully. Enthusiasm and goodwill count for little when the enemy is a vast bureaucracy of local officials who myopically use obstruction, evasion, outdated concepts, activity without insight, and other tragic efforts to avoid central-government guidelines and create ecological mismanagement on a dismaying scale." And, with respect to what he calls the "rent-a-panda" program, Schaller writes (p. 249), "The politics and greed, coupled with the shameful indifference to the panda's welfare that has characterized much of the rental business, will not vanish." Peterson (1989) also is skeptical of captive-breeding programs, and focuses on the Species Survival Plan for Siberian tigers. He notes that at the time of his writing extant groups of captive Siberian tigers were "poorly distributed in terms of sex ratio and age structure" (p. 301), that only a few individuals could actually be allowed to breed, and that others might have to "be removed—probably killed (or, to use the preferred expression, 'euthanized')" (p. 301). Peterson also stresses that the ultimate goal of most captive-breeding programs, the return of endangered animals to the wild, will probably never be attained. Rabinowitz, too, is uncertain about many captive-breeding programs because "they provide no comprehensive management of captive populations and no follow-up programs to reintroduce the young to the wild" (1991:165). Furthermore, he points out, "the proper techniques of reintroduction are rarely used." Schaller (1993) is critical of attempts that entail "rescuing" pandas for purposes of protecting them and developing breeding stock. He notes the deplorable conditions at one research center and explains that "the panda rescue work, a legacy of the 1983 bamboo die-off, continued well into 1987, long after there was any justification for it" (p. 223). He asserts that "if most of those that were rescued after the bamboo die-off were given their liberty they would perhaps replenish the forests" (p. 224). Here there is some tension between the seemingly defensible act of rescuing animals who might otherwise have starved to death because of the lack of food, and the motivation of helping them along so that they might be used to replenish wild populations.

No one, however, should deny the paramount importance of the goals of captive-breeding programs. Despite the logistical and financial difficulties entailed in implementing a captive-breeding and reintroduction program, Rabinowitz (1991:166) concludes, "no price can be put on saving even a single species that might otherwise have been lost. However, a halfhearted or haphazard and incorrect approach is both a waste of resources and a source of potential harm to the animals involved." Given the fact that many experts are extremely skeptical of attaining the goals of captive breeding, specifically for establishing healthy and self-sustaining animal populations that can be successfully reintroduced to the wild, we need to reassess what we are doing and why we are doing it (see also Schaller, this volume).

3. What is the relationship between good science and animal welfare? This question arises in particular with respect to research on captive animals. Much of what we learn about animals living in zoos (for example) does not generalize beyond that sort of environment, because of the way in which individuals are housed, fed, and otherwise maintained. Thus, we need to be careful when designing a field study based solely on data from captive individuals, for the nature of the questions being asked will greatly influence the usefulness of the data that are collected. For example, information about scent-marking by captive felids (e.g., Asa 1993, Mellon 1993) appears to be useful for furthering our understanding of what happens in the wild, and detailed studies

of behavioral development can also inform field research on carnivores (Bekoff 1989).

Various field techniques can affect behavior and welfare, as well, and perhaps influence the validity of the data that are collected. Field researchers should study the behavioral effects of the techniques that they use in studying wild animals (e.g., trapping animals, marking individuals, fitting individuals with radio collars) to determine whether there are consequent behavioral changes that might influence the validity of the data that are collected, and this information might also inform welfare decisions. For example, Laurenson and Caro (1994) studied the effects of nontrivial handling on free-living cheetahs, including making them wear a radio collar, radio tracking them by air, and examining their lairs, and found no detectable influence on the cheetahs' behavior. But they stress that although their subjective assessments proved to be supported, researchers must not depend solely on their intuitions. Laurenson and Caro also note that little work that focuses on the influence of researchers' presence and their experimental manipulations on the behavior of the animals being studied has been done on other mammals (e.g., Ramsay and Stirling 1986; Orford et al. 1989). But in a long-term study of coyotes (Bekoff and Wells 1986), it was found, for example, that shiny cameras and spotting scopes made the animals uneasy, and camera bodies and spotting scopes were accordingly painted dull black so that they would reflect little light. Furthermore, when visiting dens we always wore the same clothes, so that we would be presenting the coyotes a roughly consistent odor and a consistent visual image. Many studies concerned with human intrusion have been done on birds (e.g., Pietz et al. 1993), and those who study carnivores can learn many lessons from this research (for references, see Bekoff and Jamieson 1991; Laurenson and Caro 1994).

Those who study behavior and behavioral ecology in the field are in a good position to make important contributions to animal welfare, but unfortunately they often play only a minor role in informing legislation on matters of animal welfare (Cuthill 1991). Field workers can help to provide guidelines concerning dietary requirements, space needs, the type of captive habitat that would be the most conducive to maintaining the natural activity budgets of the animals being held captive, information on social needs in terms of group size and age and sex composition, and information about the nature of the bonds that tend to be formed between animals and human researchers (Rollin 1981; Davis and Balfour 1992).

4. Should we subject individuals to harmful or painful or disturbing experiences so that we can learn how animals deal with these types of situations and how their behavior is influenced? Various carnivore studies involve trapping individuals either in leg-hold or live traps (Mills, this volume). Is this practice justified in efforts to learn more about how animals can be trapped and how trap-lines can be monitored in ways that make the experience of being trapped less harmful or painful? It seems highly unlikely that anyone who has ever worked with trapped animals could claim that being trapped is not

harmful or painful—both physically and psychologically—for the individuals involved, and more research is needed on developing alternatives to leg-hold traps and other devices that restrict an animal's movements. Researchers should have to provide persuasive evidence that there are no alternatives to the trapping methods used, and they should be able to demonstrate that they are using the most humane methods (trapping, visiting trapped animals) available. Finally, it is incumbent on researchers to show that the stress of being trapped does not influence the behavior patterns of the animals being studied, patterns that might be precisely those of interest in the study at hand.

5. How can we minimize the number of animals who are used? Elwood (1991) points out that in certain sorts of studies, it is imperative to pay strict attention to the experimental protocol, and that stress must be minimized in the animals being studied. If studies produce results whose validity can be legitimately questioned, because, for example, the data come from stressed animals, then attempts to repeat the studies, in one form or another, will result in yet more animals being used, perhaps to no further research benefit. In cases where animals have to be followed or located repeatedly, it is worth asking whether it might not be sufficient to mark or radio-collar a single individual if all others are individually identifiable on the basis of reliable behavioral or other markers? Not only would this entail less handling of individuals, but minimal labeling of the animals might also lead to less disruption of ongoing behavior.

In recent years there has been a movement in laboratory research to reduce the number of animals used by refining experimental techniques. Many of these refinements concern the use of different instruments or analgesics, but in some cases changes in experimental designs and statistical methods can also result in the use of fewer animals. Field and laboratory researchers should cooperate in designing projects that use the smallest numbers of animals possible.

6. What is the proper relationship between researchers and the animals they study? Because some form of bonding between the animals who are being studied and the researchers is probably inevitable (Davis and Balfour 1992; Bekoff 1994b, c), these bonds should be exploited in such a way as to benefit the animals. As L. E. Johnson (1991:122) notes, "Certainly it seems like a dirty double-cross to enter into a relationship of trust and affection with any creature that can enter into such a relationship, and then to be a party to its premeditated and premature destruction."

Bonding can also help to produce "better" science. "Better" means different things to different people, but the notion seems to involve practices that help to expedite data collection, contribute to a more complete understanding of the animals, reduce the number of animals to be studied, and provide less contrived explanations of the behavior patterns observed (Bekoff 1993b). Whatever one thinks about the ultimate scientific respectability of folk-psychological attributions to animals, there is little question that such attributions are helpful in hypothesis generation (Dennett 1987), and that these attributions will be better motivated on the part of those who have significant relationships with the animals in question than on the part of those who do not.

We can also ask if humans should name the animals whom they use, and whether doing so might have an effect on ongoing research (Montgomery 1991; Bekoff and Allen 1996). We believe that naming is a good idea, and in primate research, in particular, it has been the norm. Furthermore, we advocate using the words "he" or "she" or "who" rather than "it" or "which." Whether or not named animals behave according to the names they are given (e.g., Brutus, Samson, Dolly, Wimpy, Dumpy), and whether or not researchers are biased by names to see things that are not there, remain open questions. Naming animals certainly can influence the treatment to which individuals are subjected (Bekoff 1993b), because named animals are typically treated more like subjects than objects, individuals with personalities and unique characteristics (Bekoff and Gruen 1993). Having strong relationships with named individuals invites the use of anecdotes, and when these are used judiciously they can play an important role in describing and interpreting the behavior of nonhumans, and informing and motivating empirical research in areas such as animal cognition (Burghardt 1991; Bekoff 1995; Bekoff and Allen 1996).

7. Should humans interfere with natural predation? It should be noted first that most carnivores have only limited to moderate success in their predatory efforts, and in many cases in which these efforts occur (e.g., at night, in inaccessible habitat, opportunistically) humans could not intervene even if they so desired. Still, it is interesting to note that in a case that was reported in a popular magazine devoted to birds (Bonta 1991), the vast majority of letters from nonscientists (see *Bird Watcher's Digest* September/October 1991, November/December 1991, March/April 1992) maintained that a family that watched a rat snake eat some young birds should have intervened. Sapontzis (1984:36) maintains that although not all predation is avoidable, "where we can prevent predation without occasioning as much or more suffering than we would prevent, we are obligated by the principle that we are obligated to alleviate unavoidable animal suffering" (see also Sapontzis 1987, chap. 13). Sapontzis stresses that issues of practicality must figure into ethical deliberations, and that it is not immediately obvious how "unnecessary predation" can be avoided. In light of these views it is interesting that not a single field biologist who has studied predation by wild animals and who responded to a request for an answer to this question believed that natural predation should be interfered with. Though it appears that most scientists would reject the view of Sapontzis and the readers of *Bird Watcher's Digest*, it is interesting to speculate on why this should be so. For in general, students of behavior do not take a "hands-off" approach to nature. If they did, they would not be in the field in the first place.

Kirkwood (1992) presents a thoughtful essay on the welfare of wild animals and considers questions such as whether we should intervene on behalf of free-living wild animals, and, if so, to what extent and how it should be done. Although he acknowledges that there are many different views on the matter, he claims (p. 143) that "most would probably agree that when wild animals are harmed by man's very recent (in evolutionary terms) changes to the environment (such as oil spills, power lines, roads, and environmental contamination) there is a reasonable case, on welfare grounds, to intervene." (For relevant papers, see Ferrer and Hiraldo 1992 and McOrist and Lenghaus 1992.) Kirkwood also writes about veterinary intervention to treat injured or sick wild animals. He calls for "an international code on intervention for wildlife welfare to provide guidance on ethics, methods and standards" (p. 151). Though we cannot explore these issues in depth here, we do believe that there are circumstances in which humans may have to intervene for the welfare of wild animals, including some of those listed above (see also Schaller 1993). One also needs to give serious consideration to the idea that if any experimental manipulation—including the mere presence of researchers— leads to harm for either the target animal or (indirectly) any other individual, then we are obligated to intervene on the animals' behalf.

8. Should studies be allowed that employ staged encounters between predators and prey, or between animals among whom the formation and maintenance of social-dominance relationships could potentially bring harm to one or more individuals (Huntingford 1984)? The general form of this question is to ask whether researchers should intentionally stimulate preda- tory, agonistic, or other types of encounters that would not otherwise have happened, the result of which could be harm to the participants. This is not a simple question that submits to easy answers, and people can change their minds. To wit, in the 1970s the senior author performed such studies on the development of predatory behavior in captive coyotes, but on reflection found it impossible to justify them and decided that he would no longer do this sort of research (Bekoff and Jamieson 1991:26, note 20). My decision centered on the psychological pain and suffering to which the prey (mice and young chickens) were subjected by being placed in a small arena in which there were no possibilities for escape, as well as the physical consequences of being stalked, chased, caught, maimed, and killed. One result of my decision was that detailed information about the development of predatory behavior could not be obtained, because similar data cannot be collected under nonstaged field conditions. Staged-encounter studies are also performed in the field. For example, in a recent study, Small and Keith (1992) released radio-collared arctic and snowshoe hares to learn how arctic foxes preyed on them.

9. Should humans interfere with infanticide, or use staged encounters to study it? An exchange between Bekoff (1993a) and Emlen (1993) concerning research reported in Emlen et al. (1989) highlights some of the important issues concerning the experimental study of infanticide (see also Elwood 1991). Bekoff questioned whether the research had to be done in the way in which it was, namely allowing chicks to be maimed or killed by intruding females after the chicks' mothers had been killed by the researchers. One interesting aspect of Emlen's response is that he and his colleagues did indeed stop their experiments when they became bothered by the maiming and killing of wat- tled jacana chicks by females other than their mothers. It would have been

helpful to see this displeasure in the original paper. Another issue that developed in this debate concerned whether or not the experimental study of infanticide was justifiable in terms of the "costs" to the animals involved and the "benefits" of the knowledge obtained. Of the people polled by one of us (MB) concerning the value of this sort of study of infanticide, there was an almost 50-50 split concerning whether or not the study should have been undertaken in the first place. The basis of most of the no votes was that we do not know enough about infanticide to justify field experiments such as those that Emlen et al. performed (see for example Dagg 1982; Bartlett et al. 1993).

10. How can the knowledge that we gain from studies of wild carnivores inform us of their cognitive abilities and of our ethical obligations to them? Some have gone as far as to claim that if gaining knowledge of the cognitive skills of wild animals does nothing more than inform the debate about animal welfare, then these efforts are worthwhile (e.g., Byrne 1991; see also Bekoff and Jamieson 1990, 1991; Duncan and Petherick 1991; Bekoff 1995; Bekoff and Allen 1996). But students of behavior have had a very difficult time in conceptualizing cognitive ethology. Many seem to suppose that behavior is what is observed, and that cognitive states can only be inferred; and for that reason cognition is beyond the reach of empirical science. Although we believe that this view is incorrect, building a theoretical foundation for cognitive ethology poses difficult problems (Jamieson and Bekoff 1993). Even if such a foundation *can* be built, the relationships between cognition and moral standing are complicated. It is logically consistent to hold, on the one hand, that we *may* owe moral respect to creatures who are not cognitive and, on the other hand, that we may *not* owe such respect to creatures who *are* cognitive.

Questions about the relation between what animals are like and how they should be treated are often in the background of discussions about the complexity of behavior and the "inner" lives of animals. These questions need to move from the background to the foreground, and be openly discussed. Sometimes in animal research we seem to be confronted by a paradox: by conducting research that involves treating animals as if they were not morally important we sometimes discover that they have rich, complex cognitive and emotional lives. Indeed, what we may discover in some cases may convince us that it is wrong to treat them in the ways that made the discoveries possible.

11. What principles should we use as ethical guides? In particular, if human-caused pain in animals is less than or equal to what the animal would experience in the wild, is it then permissible to inflict the pain (Rolston 1988; Hettinger 1994)? For many animals it is difficult to know whether this condition is satisfied, for we do not know how most individual animals in nature experience pain. For this reason we must be careful that this principle not become just a rationalization for researchers doing what they really want to do on other grounds. Many other principles have been proposed that perhaps should guide us in our treatment of animals: utilitarian ones, rights-based ones, and so forth. Furthermore, scientists often operate on the basis of

implicit, unstated principles and guidelines. All such principles need to be brought into the open and explicitly discussed.

12. Are scientists responsible for how their results are used? For example, if we learn about how wolves live, are we responsible for making sure that this information is not used to harm them? This is not a purely "academic" question, since a great deal of research on carnivores is funded by agencies that want to reduce their populations or control their behavior. Information about the behavior of tigers or wolves may be useful to those who simply want to make rugs out of them. Those who study marine mammals have been struggling with these issues for at least a decade. Purely scientific information about populations, migration routes, and behavior can be used by those who are involved in the commercial exploitation of the animals who are being studied. Even where hunting bans and restrictions are put in place, they may be only temporary.

One idea worth considering is that a scientist who studies a particular animal may be morally required to be an advocate for that animal in the way that physicians are supposed to be advocates for their patients. On this view, the welfare of the animals whom a scientist studies should come first, perhaps even in preference to the goal of obtaining peer-reviewed scientific results. Some scientists, such as Jane Goodall and Dian Fossey, have exemplified this ethic, but they have had many critics from within the scientific community.

13. What responsibility does the research community bear in preventing ethical misconduct, and how should this responsibility be exercised? In recent years various communities of researchers have taken steps to deal with problems of misconduct by adopting codes of professional ethics and refusing to publish papers that violate the ethical guidelines. At the same time, researchers have too often behaved like physicians in being reluctant to take steps against their own. In cases of conflict there has been a tendency for many scientists to side with the more powerful members of the community against the less powerful (e.g., Lang 1993). Unfortunately, there is still little agreement about what the collective ethic should be with regard to many of the questions that we ask, and little sense that the research community should be obligated to encourage high ethical standards within its own community (for discussion of some of these issues, see *Ethics and Behavior* 1993:3(1), which is devoted to whistle-blowing and misconduct in science). In many circles there is even a sense of complacency about research misconduct. Yet, in the most exhaustive empirical study to date on the reported incidence of misconduct, Swazey et al. (1993) found that reports of fraud, falsification, and plagiarism occur at a surprisingly high rate. They conclude that this is a serious problem, one that needs immediate attention.

CONCLUDING REMARKS

There is a continuing need to develop and improve general guidelines for research on free-living (and captive) carnivores (and other animals). These guidelines should be aspirational as well as regulatory. As Quinn (1993:130) notes, "We're not destroying the world because we're clumsy. We're destroying the world because we are, in a very literal and deliberate way, at war with it." We should not be satisfied that things are better than they were in the bad old days, and we should work for a future in which even these enlightened times will be viewed as the bad old days. Progress has already been made in the development of guidelines, and the challenge is to make them more binding, effective, persuasive, and specific. If possible, we should also work for consistency among countries that share common attitudes toward animals; research in some countries (e.g., the United States) is less regulated than research in other countries (Gavaghan 1992). In this evolving process, interdisciplinary input from both field workers and philosophers is necessary; no single discipline can do the necessary work alone (Farnsworth and Rosovsky 1993; Shrader-Frechette and McCoy 1993). Researchers who are exposed to the pertinent issues, and who think about them and engage in open and serious debate, can then carry these lessons into their research projects and impart this knowledge to colleagues and students. Not knowing all of the subtleties of philosophical arguments—on the details of which even professional ethicists disagree—should be neither a stumbling block nor an insurmountable barrier to learning; finding oneself on the horns of the dilemma and then doing nothing is not the way to go. Few field workers understand how binoculars or radio transmitters work, but this does not prevent them from using them. The same should be true of the details of philosophical tradition and argument.

Flip, simplistic, and unargued dismissals from those who are deeply concerned with animal welfare will do nothing but divide those whose inputs are needed if we are to improve our behavior with respect to animals. Nor should we dismiss animal-welfare concerns on the basis of facile anthropocentric arguments, or because responding to them will cost time or money. We should use the fewest animals we can, the least invasive techniques available. We should share data when possible, and carefully survey available literature so that unnecessary duplication does not occur. Great concern should be shown for the frequency with which animals are visited, the types of traps that are used, the types, color, weight, and shape of tags that are used to label individuals, where tags are placed, the weight of radio transmitters, the behavior of the researchers, the consistency of the behavior and dress of the researchers, the color and noise of cameras and other equipment, and any number of similar matters.

How we refer to some of our research practices also needs reconsideration. We should use words that accurately describe our actions, not euphemisms that may be intended to mask them. When animals are killed it should be explicitly stated that they are killed; words like euthanize, cull, sacrifice, and collect often are used to deflect attention from the act of killing and to give a false sense of acceptability. We need to eliminate research projects that should not be undertaken at all. Many proposed projects are not carried out because they lack scientific merit, but surely a lack of ethical merit is every bit as important. Of course, decisions like these can put one on a slippery slope, and it is not easy to know where to draw the line. For example, Hauser (1993) considers the interesting and difficult question of whether or not vervet monkey infants cry wolf to elicit parental care. Field data are ambiguous, and Hauser suggests that "one fruitful approach to resolving these issues would be to manipulate the physical condition of mother and offspring" (p. 1243). Hauser does not tell us, however, what these manipulations would consist of. Obviously, some experiments would be more ethical than others, and sorting among them would be very difficult when balancing the knowledge that would be gained against the type of manipulations that would have to be done. But just because these sorts of decisions are difficult does not mean that there are not better and worse answers.

Although it is important for debate to be as constructive and nonpolarized as possible, we should not be afraid of honest disagreement (e.g., Bekoff, 1993a; Emlen 1993). We will come to a consensus about the ethics of specific practices only if we expose our differences to the light of day, and frankly discuss the issues that are involved.

Recently, Slater (1993:188) claimed that "the assumptions one brings to bear in designing experiments are not necessarily the same as those one should adopt in deciding how to treat animals." Slater was responding to the views of Kennedy (1992), who, Slater believes, approaches problems of animal welfare "too much as a scientist." Basically, Kennedy's views on animal welfare are informed and motivated by his fear of the ill effects of false assumptions; thus, he is unhappy with erring on the side of animals in the absence of hard data that would lead one to this conclusion (see also Crockett 1993). Slater's claim needs further fleshing out by and for those interested in animal welfare. We need to know more about the assumptions that one does or should use in deciding how to treat animals, and how they connect, or even if they *can* connect, with the assumptions that influence experimental research that is supposedly more objective. It is highly likely that those who demand hard data bearing on animal welfare will not be convinced by Slater's view, and highly likely that they will shut the door to further discourse because Slater's position is merely stated, not argued. Still, Slater's challenging statement is one that should motivate considerable discussion among those interested in animal welfare.

One obvious and important affinity between assumptions underlying scientific research and views on animal welfare is that neither is completely objective. Each of us comes to science with biases, just as each of us brings biases to our views of nonhuman animals. Slater (as have many others) notes that studying animal welfare from an objective scientific viewpoint poses difficult problems. As Fumento (1993:366) observed, scientists "don't like to see a '[blending of] the natural sciences, values, and social sciences,' because inevitably this leads to the subjugation of scientific truth." Perhaps the problems associated with studying animal welfare from an objective scientific viewpoint are insoluble, for among the reasons that an objective view cannot be attained is that it may be impossible to be objective about the use of animals by humans. If this is the case, what are we to do about it? Certainly we cannot let the animals suffer simply because of our inability to accept the fact that an objective study of animal welfare is impossible (Bekoff and Jamieson 1991). We should use common sense in our interactions with animals (Bekoff 1992, 1993c). Who could doubt that the pain and suffering of carnivores and many other animals are real, and that this realization must inform our treatment of them? Neither dismissing the notion that humans have obligations to the animals whom they use in research nor ignoring the issues attendant upon that will make the problems disappear.

Finally, we should teach our children and our students well (see, for example, Dickinson 1988). They will live and work in a world in which, increasingly, science will not be seen as a self-justifying activity, but rather as another human institution whose claims on the public treasury must be justified (Jamieson 1993b). More than ever before it is important for students to realize that to question science is not to be anti-science or anti-intellectual, and that to question how humans interact with animals is not in itself to demand that humans never use animals. Questioning science will make for better, more responsible science, and questioning the ways in which humans use animals will make for more informed decisions about animal use. By making such decisions in an informed and responsible way, we can help to ensure that in the future we will not repeat the mistakes of the past, and that we will move toward a world in which humans and other animals will be able to share peaceably the resources of a finite planet.

Acknowledgments

We thank Susan Townsend, Lori Gruen, Tom Daniels, Hal Herzog, Dan Blumstein, Gordon Burghardt, and especially Ned Hettinger for discussing many of these issues with us, and Ann Pusey, David Scheel, Hal Herzog, and Tom Daniels for taking time to respond in detail to our requests for information concerning natural predation. Michael Mooring kindly shared his experiences as a foreign researcher in Zimbabwe. Ned Hettinger, Elizabeth J. Farnsworth, Susan Townsend, Colin Allen, Gordon Burghardt, Lewis Petrinovich, and John Gittleman provided helpful comments on an ancestral version of this chapter.

References

Altmann, S. 1993. Professional ethics: The ABS code of ethics. *Anim. Behav. Soc. Newsletter* Fall:3–5.

American Society of Mammalogists. 1987. Acceptable field methods in mammalogy: Preliminary guidelines approved by the American Society of Mammalogists. *J. Mammalogy* 68 (4, Suppl.): 1–18.

Anonymous. 1992. Guidelines for the protection of bat roosts. *J. Mammal.* 73:707–710.

Asa, C. S. 1993. Relative contributions of urine and anal-sac secretions in scent marks of large fields. *Amer. Zool.* 33:167–172.

Bartlett, T. Q., Sussman, R. W., and Cheverud, J. M. 1993. Infant killing in primates: A review of observed cases with specific reference to the sexual selection hypothesis. *Amer. Anthropol.* 95:958–990.

Beck, A. M. 1973. *The Ecology of Stray Dogs: A Study of Free-Ranging Urban Animals.* Baltimore: York Press.

Bekoff, M. 1989. Behavioral development of terrestrial carnivores. In: J. L. Gittleman, ed. *Carnivore Behavior, Ecology, and Evolution*, pp. 89–124. Ithaca, N.Y.: Cornell Univ. Press.

Bekoff, M. 1992. Scientific ideology, animal consciousness, and animal protection: A principled plea for unabashed common sense. *New Dir. Psychol.* 10:79–94.

Bekoff, M. 1993a. Experimentally induced infanticide: The removal of birds and its ramifications. *Auk* 110:404–406.

Bekoff, M. 1993b. Should scientists bond with the animals whom they use? Why not? *Psycholoquy* 4(37): 1–8.

Bekoff, M. 1993c. Common sense, cognitive ethology and evolution. In: P. Cavalieri and P. Singer, eds. *The Great Ape Project: Equality beyond Humanity*, pp. 102–108. London: Fourth Estate.

Bekoff, M. 1994a. Cognitive ethology and the treatment of non-human animals: How matters of mind inform matters of welfare. *Anim. Welfare* 3:75–96.

Bekoff, M. 1994b. Scientists, animals, and their social bonds. *New Sci.* 21 May:44–45.

Bekoff, M. 1995. Cognitive ethology and the explanation of nonhuman animal behavior. In: J.-A. Meyer and H. L. Roitblat, eds. *Comparative Approaches to Cognitive Science*, pp. 119–149. Cambridge, Mass.: MIT Press.

Bekoff, M., and Allen, C. 1996. Cognitive ethology: Slayers, skeptics, and proponents. In: R. W. Mitchell, N. Thompson, and L. Miles, eds. *Anthropomorphism, Anecdotes, and Animals: The Emperor's New Clothes?* Albany, N.Y.: SUNY Press.

Bekoff, M., and Gruen, L. 1993. Animal welfare and individual characteristics: A conversation against speciesism. *Ethics and Behavior* 3:163–175.

Bekoff, M., Gruen, L., Townsend, S. E., and Rollin, B. E. 1992. Animals in science: Some areas revisited. *Anim. Behav.* 44:473–484.

Bekoff, M., and Hettinger, N. 1994. Animals, nature, and ethics. *J. Mammal.* 75:219–223.

Bekoff, M., and Jamieson, D. 1990. Cognitive ethology and applied philosophy: The significance of an evolutionary biology of mind. *Trends Ecol. Evol.* 5:156–159.

Bekoff, M., and Jamieson, D. 1991. Reflective ethology, applied philosophy, and the moral status of animals. *Persp. in Ethology* 9:1–47.

Bekoff, M., and Wells, M. C. 1986. Social ecology and behavior of coyotes. *Adv. Study Behav.* 16:251–338.

Benton, T. 1993. *Natural Relations: Ecology, Animal Rights, and Justice.* New York: Verso.

Bertram, B. 1993. Prisoners of fate. *Nature* 363:219.

Bonta, M., 1991. Snake attack. *Bird Watcher's Digest* July/August:96.

Bostock, S. St. C. 1993. *Zoos and Animal Rights.* New York: Routledge.

Bradshaw, J. W. S., ed. 1992. *The Behavior of the Domestic Cat.* Wallingford, Conn.: CAB International.

Brenes, A., ed. 1988. *The Comparative Psychology of Natural Resource Management.* Cosenza, Italy: University of Calabria.

Broom, D. M., and Johnson, K. G. 1993. *Stress and Animal Welfare.* London: Chapman and Hall.

Bulger, R. E., Heitman, E., and Reiser, S. J., eds. 1993. *The Ethical Dimensions of the Biological Sciences.* New York: Cambridge Univ. Press.

Burghardt, G. M. 1991. Cognitive ethology and critical anthropomorphism: A snake with two heads and hognose snakes that play dead. In: C. Ristau, ed. *Cognitive Ethology: The Minds of Other Animals*, pp. 53–90. Hillsdale, N.J.: Lawrence Erlbaum Associates.

Burley, N., Krantzberg, G., and Radman, P. 1982. Influence of color-banding on the conspecific preferences of zebra finches. *Anim. Behav.* 30:444–455.

Byrne, R. W. 1991. Brute intellect. *Sciences* July:42–47.

Caine, N. G. 1992. Humans as predators: Observational studies and the risk of pseudoreplication. In: H. Davis and D. Balfour, eds. *The Inevitable Bond: Examining Scientist-Animal Interactions*, pp. 357–364. New York: Cambridge Univ. Press.

Callicott, J. B. 1980/1989. Animal liberation: A triangular affair. In: J. B. Callicott, ed. *In Defense of the Land Ethic: Essays in Environmental Philosophy*, pp. 15–38. Albany, N.Y.: SUNY Press.

Carruthers, P. 1989. Brute experience. *J. Philos.* 86:258–269.

Carruthers, P. 1992. *The Animals Issue: Moral Theory in Practice.* New York: Cambridge Univ. Press.

Carson, G. 1972. *Men, Beasts, and Gods: A History of Cruelty and Kindness to Animals.* New York: Scribners.

Cavalieri, P., and Singer, P., eds. 1993. *The Great Ape Project: Equality beyond Humanity.* London: Fourth Estate.

Chiszar, D., Murphy, J. B., and Illiff, W. 1990. For zoos. *Psychol. Rec.* 40:3–13.

Cohen, C. 1986. The case for the use of animals in research. *New England J. Med.* 315:865–870.

Collins, H. M., and Pinch, T. F. 1979. The construction of the paranormal: Nothing unscientific is happening. In: R. Wallis, ed. *On the Margins of Science: The Social Construction of Rejected Knowledge*, pp. 237–272. Keele, U.K.: Keele Univ. Press.

Colwell, R. K. 1989. Natural and unnatural history: Biological diversity and genetic engineering. In: W. R. Shea and B. Sitter, eds. *Scientists and Their Responsibilities*, pp. 1–40. Canton, Mass.: Watson Pub. International.

Crockett, C. M. 1993. Rigid rules for promoting psychological well-being are premature. *Amer. J. Primat.* 30: 177–179.

Croft, D. B., ed. 1991. *Australian People and Animals in Today's Dreamtime: The Role of Comparative Psychology in the Management of Natural Resources.* New York: Praeger.

Cuthill, 1. 1991. Field experiments in animal behaviour: Methods and ethics. *Anim. Behav.* 42: 1007–1014.

Dagg, 1. 1982. Harems and other horrors: Sexual bias in behavioral biology. Waterloo, Ont.: Otter Press.

Daniels, T. J., and Bekoff, M. 1989a. Spatial and temporal resource use by feral and abandoned dogs. *Ethology* 81:300–312.

Daniels, T. J., and Bekoff, M. 1989b. Population and social biology of free-ranging dogs, *Canis familiaris. J. Mammal.* 70:754–762.

Daniels, T. J., and Bekoff, M. 1989c. Feralization: The making of wild domestic animals. *Behav. Processes* 19:79–94.

Daniels, T. J., and Bekoff, M. 1990. Domestication, exploitation, and rights. In: M. Bekoff and D. Jamieson, eds. *Interpretation and Explanation in the Study of Animal Behavior, Vol. II: Explanation, Evolution, and Adaptation*, pp. 345–377. Boulder, Colo.: Westview Press.

Davis, H., and Balfour, D., eds. 1992. *The Inevitable Bond: Examining Scientist-Animal Interactions.* New York: Cambridge Univ. Press.

Dawkins, R. 1993. Gaps in the mind. In: P. Cavalieri and P. Singer, eds. *The Great Ape Project: Equality beyond Humanity*, pp. 80–87. London: Fourth Estate.

DeBlieu, J. 1991. *Meant to Be Wild: The Struggle to Save Endangered Species through Captive Breeding.* Golden, Colo.: Fulcrum Pub.

DeGrazia, D. 1991. The moral status of animals and their use in research: A philosophical review. *Kennedy Inst. of Ethics J.* March:48–70.

Dennett, D. 1987. *The International Stance.* Cambridge, Mass.: MIT Press.

Dickinson, P. 1988. *Eva.* New York: Dell Publishing.

Dresser, R. 1993. Defining scientific misconduct: The relevance of mental state. *J. Amer. Med. Assoc.* 269:895–897.

Duffus, D. A., and Wipond, K. J. 1992. A review of the institutionalization of wildlife viewing in British Columbia, Canada. *Northwest Env. J.* 8:325–345.

Duncan, I. J. H., and Petherick, J. C. 1991. The implications of cognitive processes for animal welfare. Unpublished paper presented at symposium on "Cognition and Awareness in Animals: Do Farm Animals' Perceptions Affect Their Production or Well-Being?" Lexington, Kentucky.

Eisemann, C. H., Jorgensen, W.K., Merritt, D.J., Rice, M.J., Cribb, B. W., Webb, P. D., and Zalucki, M. P. 1984. Do insects feel pain? A biological review. *Experientia* 40:164–167.

Elwood, R. W. 1991. Ethical implications of studies on infanticide and maternal aggression in rodents. *Anim. Behav.* 42:841–849.

Emlen, S. T. 1993. Ethics and experimentation: Hard choices for the field ornithologist. *Auk* 110:406–409.

Emlen, S. T., Demong, N. J., and Emlen, D. J. 1989. Experimental induction of infanticide in female wattled jacanas. *Auk* 106:1–7.

Ewbank, R. 1993. Editorial. *Anim. Welfare* 2:2.

Farnsworth, E. J., and Rosovsky, J. 1993. The ethics of ecological field experimentation. *Conserv. Biol.* 7:463–472.

Ferrer, M., and Hiraldo, F. 1992. Man-induced sex-biased mortality in the Spanish imperial eagle. *Biol. Conserv.* 60:57–60.

Finsen, L., and Finsen, S. 1994. *The Animal Rights Movement.* New York: Twayne.

Fiorito, G. 1986. Is there "pain" in invertebrates? *Behav. Processes* 12:383–388.

Foucault, M. 1984. *The Foucault Reader* (P. Robinow, ed.). New York: Pantheon.

Freeman, M. M. R., Wein, E. E., and Keither, D. E. 1992. *Recovering Rights: Bowhead Whales and Inuvialuit Subsistence in the Western Arctic.* Edmonton, Alta.: Canadian Circumpolar Institute.

Frey, R. G. 1980. *Interests and Rights: The Case against Animals.* New York: Oxford Univ. Press.

Frey, R. G. 1983. *Rights, Killing, and Suffering.* Oxford: Blackwell.

Fumento, M. 1993. *Science under Siege: Balancing Technology and the Environment.* New York: Morrow.

Gallup, G. G., and Suarez, S. D. 1987. Antivivisection: Questions of logic, consistency, and conceptualization. *Theoret. Philos. Psychol.* 7:81–94.

Galvin, S. L., and Herzog, H. A., Jr. 1992. Ethical ideology, animal rights activism, and attitudes toward the treatment of animals. *Ethics and Behavior* 2:141–149.

Gavaghan, H. 1992. Animal experiments the American way. *New Sci.* 16 May:32–36.

Goodall, J. 1990. *Through a Window.* Boston: Houghton-Mifflin.

Goodstein, D. 1991, Scientific fraud. *Amer. Scholar* 60:505–515.

Grandin, T. 1992. Author's response to M. Bekoff's "Some thoughts about cattle restraint." *Anim. Welfare* 1:230–231.

Gray, G. G. 1993. *Wildlife and People: The Human Dimensions of Wildlife Ecology.* Urbana: Univ. Illinois Press.

Greenough, W. T. 1992. More on monkeys. *Discover* June:9.

Grooms, S. 1993. *The Return of the Wolf.* Minocqua, Wisconsin: North Word Press.

Guillermo, K. S. 1993. *Monkey Business.* Washington, D.C.: National Press Books.

Haraway, D. 1989. *Primate Visions: Gender, Race, and Nature in the World of Modern Science.* New York: Routledge.

Hardwig, J. 1985. Epistemic dependence. *J. Philos.* 82:335–349.

Hardwig, J. 1991. The role of trust in knowledge. *J. Philos.* 88:693–708.

Hardy, D. T. 1990. *America's New Extremists: What You Need to Know about the Animal Rights Movement.* Washington, D.C.: Washington Legal Foundation.

Hargrove, E., ed. 1992. *The Animal Rights/Environmental Ethics Debate.* Albany, N.Y.: SUNY Press.

Hauser, M. D. 1993. Do vervet monkey infants cry wolf? *Anim. Behav.* 45:1242–1244.

Hettinger, N. 1989. The responsible use of animals in biomedical research. *Between the Species* 5:123–131.

Hettinger, N. 1994. Valuing predation in Rolston's environmental ethics: Bambi lovers versus tree huggers. *Env. Ethics* 16:3–20.

Hofer, H., East, M. L., and Campbell, K. L. I. 1993. Snares, commuting hyaenas and migratory herbivores: Humans as predators in the Serengeti. In: N. Dunstone and M. L. Gorman, eds. *Mammals as Predators*, pp. 347–366. Oxford: Clarendon Press.

Howard, W. E. 1993. Animal research is defensible. *J. Mammal.* 74:234–235.

Huntingford, F. A. 1984. Some ethical issues raised by studies of predation and aggression. *Anim. Behav.* 32:210–215.

Isbell, L. A., and Young, T. P. 1993. Human presence reduced predation in a free-ranging vervet monkey population in Kenya. *Anim. Behav.* 45:1233–1235.

Jamieson, D. 1985a. Against zoos. In: P. Singer, ed., *In Defense of Animals*, pp. 108–117. New York: Harper and Row.

Jamieson, D. 1985b. Experimenting on animals: A reconsideration. *Between the Species* 1:4–11.

Jamieson, D. 1993a. Ethics and animals: A brief review. *J. Agric. Env. Ethics* 6 (Spec. Suppl. 1):15–20.

Jamieson, D. 1993b. What will society expect of the future research community. Unpublished paper presented at National Research Council's Commission on Physical Sciences, Mathematics, and Applications, 13–15 August.

Jamieson, D. 1995. Zoos revisited. In: B. G. Norton, M. Hutchins, E. F. Stevens, and T. L. Maple, eds. *Ethics of the Ark: Zoos, Animal Welfare, and Conservation*, pp. 52–66. Washington, D.C.: Smithsonian Institution Press.

Jamieson, D., and Bekoff, M. 1992. Carruthers on nonconscious experience. *Analysis* 52:23–28.

Jamieson, D., and Bekoff, M. 1993. On aims and methods of cognitive ethology. *Philos. Sci. Assoc.* 2:110–124.

Jamieson, D., and Regan, T. 1985. Whales are not cetacean resources. In: M. W. Fox and L. Mackley, eds. *Advances in Animal Welfare Science*, 1984, pp. 101–111. The Hague: Martinus Nijhoff.

Johnson, E. 1991. Carruthers on conscious and moral status. *Between the Species* 7:190–192.

Johnson, L. E. 1991. *A Morally Deep World: An Essay on Moral Significance and Environmental Ethics.* New York: Cambridge Univ. Press.

Katz, E. 1993. Artefacts and functions: A note on the value of nature. *Env. Values* 2:223–232.

Kennedy, J. S. 1992. *The New Anthropomorphism.* New York: Cambridge Univ. Press.

Kennedy, S. P., and Knight, R. L. 1992. Flight distances of black-billed magpies in different regimes of human density and persecution. *The Condor* 94:545–547.

Kew, B. 1991. *The Pocketbook of Animal Facts and Figures.* London: Green Print.

Kiley-Worthington, M. 1990. *Animals in Circuses and Zoos: Chiron's World?* Essex: Little Eco-Farms Pub.

Kirkwood, J. 1992. Wild animal welfare. In: R. D. Ryder and P. Singer, eds. *Animal Welfare and the Environment*, pp. 139–154. London: Duckworth.

Kitcher, P. 1993. *The Advancement of Science: Science without Legend, Objectivity without Illusions.* New York: Oxford Univ. Press.

LaFollette, M. C. 1992. *Stealing into Print: Fraud, Plagiarism, and Misconduct in Scientific Publishing.* Berkeley: Univ. California Press.

Lang, S. 1993. Questions of scientific responsibility: The Baltimore case. *Ethics and Behavior* 3:3–72.

Lansdell, H. 1988. Laboratory animals need only humane treatment: Animal "rights" may debase human rights. *Internat. J. Neurosci.* 42:169–178.

Laurenson, M. K., and Caro, T. M. 1994. Monitoring the effects of non-trivial handling in free-living cheetahs. *Anim. Behav.* 47:547–557.

Lockwood, J. A. 1987. The moral status of insects and the ethics of extinction. *Florida Entomol.* 70:70–89.

Ludwig, D., Hilborn, R., and Walters, C. 1993. Uncertainty, resource exploitation, and conservation: Lessons from history. *Science* 260:17.

Lynge, F. 1992. *Arctic Waters: Animal Rights, Endangered Peoples.* Hanover, N.H.: Univ. Press of New England.

Magel, C. 1989. *Keyguide to Information Sources in Animal Rights.* Jefferson, N.C.: McFarland.

Mainini, B., Neuhaus, P., and Ingold, P. 1993. Behaviour of marmots *Marmota marmota* under the influence of different hiking activities. *Biol. Conserv.* 64:161–164.

McAdam, D. 1992. Radicals and others. *Science* 255:1448–1449.

McGinn, C. 1980. Book review of Frey 1980. *Times Lit. Suppl.* 1 August:865.

McOrist, S., and Lenghaus, C. 1992. Mortalities of little penguins (*Eudyptula minor*) following exposure to crude oil. *Vet. Record* 22 February: 161–162.

Mellon, J. D. 1993. A comparative analysis of scent-marking, social and reproductive behavior in 20 species of small cats (*Felis*). *Amer. Zool.* 33:151–166.

Michener, G. R. 1989. Ethical issues in the use of wild animals in behavioral and ecological research. In: J. W. Driscoll, ed. *Animal Care and Use in Behavioral Research: Regulations, Issues, and Applications.* Beltsville, Md.: Information Center.

Midgley, M. 1983. *Animals and Why They Matter.* Athens, Ga.: Univ. Georgia Press.

Mighetto, L. 1991. *Wild Animals and American Environmental Ethics.* Tucson: Univ. Arizona Press.

Montgomery, S. 1991. *Walking with the Great Apes: Jane Goodall, Dian Fossey, Birute Galdikas.* Boston: Houghton-Mifflin.

Morris, D. 1990. *The Animal Contract.* New York: Warner Books.

Norton, B. G., Hutchins, M., Stevens, E. F., and Maple, T. L., eds. 1995. *Ethics of the Ark: Zoos, Animal Welfare, and Conservation.* Washington, D.C.: Smithsonian Institution Press.

Orford, H. J. L., Perrin, M. R., and Berry, H. H. 1989. Contraception, reproduction, and demography of free-ranging Etosha lions (*Panthera leo*). *J. Zool. (Lond.)* 216:717–734.

Orlans, F. B. 1993. *In the Name of Science: Issues in Responsible Animal Experimentation.* New York: Oxford Univ. Press.

Peterson, D. 1989. *The Deluge and the Ark: A Journey in Primate Worlds.* Boston: Houghton Mifflin.

Peterson, D., and Goodall, J. 1993. *Visions of Calaban: On Chimpanzees and People.* Boston: Houghton Mifflin.

Pietz, P. J., Krapu, G. L., Greenwood, R. J., and Lokemoen, J. T. 1993. Effects of harness transmitters on behavior and reproduction of wild mallards. *J. Wildl. Mgmt.* 57:696–703.

Pimm, S. L. 1991. *The Balance of Nature? Ecological Issues in the Conservation of Species and Communities.* Chicago: Univ. Chicago Press.

Plous, S. 1991. An attitude survey of animal rights activists. *Psychol. Sci.* 2:194–196.

Pluhar, E. B. 1993. Arguing away suffering: The neo-Cartesian revival. *Between the Species* 9:27–41.

Preece, R., and Chamberlain, L. 1993. *Animal Welfare and Human Values.* Waterloo, Ont.: Wilfrid Laurier Press.

Quinn, D. 1993. *Ishmael.* New York: Bantam.

Rabinowitz, A. 1986. *Jaguar: Struggle and Triumph in the Jungles of Belize.* New York: Arbor.

Rabinowitz, A. 1991. *Chasing the Dragon's Tail: The Struggle to Save Thailand's Wild Cats.* New York: Doubleday.

Rachels, J. 1989. Why animals have a right to liberty. In: T. Regan and P. Singer, eds. *Animal Rights and Human Obligations.* Second edition, pp. 122–131. Englewood Cliffs, N.J.: Prentice-Hall.

Rachels, J. 1990. *Created from Animals: The Moral Implications of Darwinism.* New York: Oxford Univ. Press.

Ramsay, M. A., and Stirling, I. 1986. Long-term effects of drugging and handling free-ranging polar bears. *J. Wildl. Mgmt.* 50:619–626.

Raynor, M. E. 1992. Necessary suffering? *N. Y. Rev. Books* 13 August:664.

Regan, T. 1983. *The Case for Animal Rights.* Berkeley: Univ. California Press.

Rollin, B. E. 1981. *Animal Rights and Human Morality.* Buffalo, N.Y.: Prometheus Books.

Rollin, B. E. 1989. *The Unheeded Cry: Animal Consciousness, Animal Pain, and Science.* New York: Oxford Univ. Press.

Rolston, H., III. 1988. *Environmental Ethics: Duties to and Values in the Natural World.* Philadelphia: Temple Univ. Press.

Rothschild, M. 1993. Thinking about animal consciousness. *J. Nat. Hist.* 27:509–512.

Rowan, A. N. 1984. *Of Mice, Models, and Men: A Critical Evaluation of Animal Research.* Albany, N.Y.: SUNY Press.

Rowan, A. N., ed. 1988. *Animals and People Sharing the World.* Hanover, N.H.: Univ. Press New England.

Ryder, R. D. 1989. *Animal Revolution: Changing Attitudes towards Speciesism.* Oxford: Basil Blackwell.

Ryder, R. D. 1992. Painism: Ethics, animal rights and environmentalism. Cardiff, Wales: Centre for Applied Ethics.

Sapontzis, S. F. 1984. Predation. *Ethics and Animals* 5:27–38.

Sapontzis, S. F. 1987. *Morals, Reason, and Animals.* Philadelphia: Temple Univ. Press.

Schaller, G. B. 1993. *The Last Panda.* Chicago: Univ. Chicago Press.

Shackley, M. 1992. Manatees and tourism in southern Florida: Opportunity or threat? *J. Env. Mgmt.* 34:257–265.

Shapiro, K. J. 1989. The death of the animal: Ontological vulnerability. *Between the Species* 5:183–194.

Sherman, P. W., and Alcock, J., eds. 1993. *Exploring Animal Behavior: Readings from American Scientist.* Sunderland, Mass.: Sinauer.

Shrader-Frechette, K. S., and McCoy, E. D. 1993. *Method in Ecology: Strategies for Conservation.* New York: Cambridge Univ. Press.

Sih, A., Crowley, P., McPeek, M., Petranka, J., and Strohmeier, K. 1985. Predation, competition, and prey communities: A review of field experiments. *Ann. Rev. Ecol. System.* 16:269–311.

Singer, P. 1975. *Animal Liberation.* New York: Avon.

Singer, P. 1990. *Animal Liberation.* Second edition. N. Y. Rev. Books.

Singer, P. 1992a. Reply. *N. Y. Rev. Books* 13 August:65.

Singer, P. 1992b. Reply. *N. Y. Rev. Books* 15 November:60–61.

Singer, P. 1993a. *Practical Ethics.* Second edition. New York: Cambridge Univ. Press.

Singer, P. 1993b. Reply. *N. Y. Rev. Books* 27 May:49–50.

Slater, P. 1993. Review of Kennedy 1992. *Anim. Welfare* 2:187–188.

Small, R. J., and Keith, L. B. 1992. An experimental study of red fox predation on arctic and snowshoe hares. *Canadian J. Zool.* 70:1614–1621.

Stamp Dawkins, M., and Gosling, L. M., eds. 1992. *Ethics in Research on Animal Behaviour: Readings from Animal Behaviour.* London: Academic Press.

Swazey, J. P., Anderson, M. S., and Louis, K. S. 1993. Ethical problems in academic research. *Amer. Sci.* 81:542–553.

Terborgh, J. 1993. Solitary enigma: A review of Schaller 1993. *N. Y. Rev. Books* 23 September:12–14.

Thorne, C., ed. 1992. *The Waltham Book of Dog and Cat Behaviour.* New York: Pergamon.

Varner, G. E., and Monroe, M. C. 1991. Ethical perspectives on captive breeding: Is it for the birds? *Endangered Species Update* 8:27–29.

Wayne, R. K., and Gittleman, J. L. 1995. The problematic red wolf. *Sci. Amer.* 273:36–39.

Webb, M. O. 1993. Why I know about as much as you: A reply to Hardwig. *J. Philos.* 90:260–270.

Wenzel, G. 1991. *Animal Rights, Human Rights, Ecology, Economy, and Ideology in the Canadian Arctic.* Toronto: Univ. Toronto Press.

White, R. J. 1990. Letter. *Hastings Center Report* November/December:43.

Wigglesworth, V. B. 1980. Do insects feel pain? *Antenna* 4:8–9.

Wilkie, T. 1993. *Perilous Knowledge: The Human Genome Project and Its Implications.* London: Faber.

Woolf, P. K. 1988. Deception in scientific research. *Jurimetrics J.* Fall.

Zimmerman, M. E., Callicott, J. B., Sessions, G., Warren, K. J., and Clark, J., eds. 1993. *Environmental Philosophy: From Animal Rights to Radical Ecology.* Englewood Cliffs, N.J.: Prentice-Hall.

Afterword

Minding Animals, Minding Earth: Old Brains in New Bottlenecks

PUTTING AN END TO USELESS "US/THEM" DUALISMS

Humans are part of nature. We do not stand above or to the side of other beings or natural processes. There is no duality, no "them" and "us." If we try to separate our reality from that of other nature and Earth, a division results that causes much discontent and discord, for it is so very unnatural. I find it settling—very relaxing—to situate myself in nature and to sense and experience the magic and wonderment of allowing myself to be there. Living with all the contradictions in which we are immersed and with which we are surrounded makes life difficult for all of us. But these challenges are enriching and will make for a better future. We need animals more than ever, because we have become alienated and estranged from other nature. Animals are a way of knowing and feeling and are sources of wisdom. We have allowed this knowledge to be pushed aside and to erode as we consume animals and Earth at unprecedented rates with unanticipated negative consequences.

Perhaps if we listen to nature, we will make peace with ourselves and with others, and, as a result, we will make more rapid progress toward a unified community in which trust, happiness, peace, and love prevail over distrust, sadness, unrest, and hate. Sowing seeds for world peace among children is a must, and animals often help us in this venture. Trust is critical, for in the absence of trust we cannot move forward with a strong sense of security and unity. I propose that we must wage peace with abandon and enthusiasm among all human beings, all animal beings, and nature as a whole, for in our tumultuous world many alienated people crave deep and reciprocal interconnections with one another and with other nature. But first we must each be happy and content as individuals and be at peace with ourselves. Animals can help us achieve this peace. Reconnecting with nature can help overcome alienation and loneliness.

Not only are the topics I've discussed here very big, broad, and deep, they're also extremely challenging, frustrating, and complicated. *Animal Passions and Beastly Virtues* is a work in progress—there is still much to learn. So, I invite you to read on and kindly—with compassion and civility—to let me know where you agree and disagree with me. On-going and informed dialogue even, and perhaps especially, among, "warring parties," is much needed. I find it useful to engage just about anyone who thinks about and cares about what we're

Some of this essay has been excerpted from Bekoff, M. 2003. "Minding Animals, Minding Earth." *Human Ecology Review* 10: 56–76, with permission of the journal; and from Bekoff, M. 2002. *Minding Animals: Awareness, Emotions, and Heart.* Copyright 2002 by Oxford University Press, Inc., New York. Used by permission of Oxford University Press, Inc.

doing to our one and only Earth community, as long as they are interested in real dialogue.

I find it extremely humbling to realize that no one is exempt from our collective actions. No one, including future generations. We all suffer when other animals and nature suffer. We all suffer when we wound Earth and all of its inhabitants. A little humility will go a long way as we strive "to make things right."

My musings and feelings about our complex and ambiguous interrelationships with other animals have been influenced by a number of wonderful teachers. Of course, my journey is not my journey alone—it is yours too—and I hope that many others will join to make our one and only Earth community a better place for all beings and for all landscapes.

Since I was a youngster, I've pondered the nature of animals' minds and our responsibilities to care for other animals. By stepping lightly into the lives of other animals, we humans can enjoy their company without making them pay for our interest. We need to honor other animals for *who* they are in their worlds, not for *what* they are in our own—often narrow—minds. Our curiosity about other animals need not harm them.

That many others also recognize that humans and nature are indistinct is reflected in the rapid growth of the field of anthrozoology and the increasing interest in the nature of human-animal interactions. It is my hope that this interdisciplinary attention to the study of human-animal interactions will put an end to useless dualisms such as "us versus them," the "laboratory (where animals often are numbered objects) versus the home" (and other venues in which we interact with companion animals, where animals are named and imbued with all sorts of cognitive and emotional capacities), and "higher (humans and perhaps other primates) versus lower" animals. These dualisms do not work and surely do not foster the development and maintenance of deep, respectful, and symmetrical interrelationships between humans and other animals.

MOVING WITH OPTIMISM TOWARD MINDFUL ENGAGEMENT OF THE COMMUNITY OF EARTH

Animals are our consummate companions. Our animal friends complete us and, especially with regard to our companion animals, we complete them. I hope my essays succeed in constructing a big-picture view of the complex relationships among animals, culture, and society. I have tried to establish the importance of broadening behavioral, ecological, and conservation behavior into a more integrative, interdisciplinary, socially responsible, compassionate, spiritual, and holistic endeavor. I have emphasized the significance of studies of animal behavior—especially ethological research concerned with animal cognition and emotions in which individuals are named and recognized for their own personalities and temperaments—for helping us to learn not only about the animals with whom we share Earth, but also about who we are, our place in nature, our humanness. I have argued that we can be best understood in relationship to others, and, to this end, I have developed the notions of minding animals and of deep ethology. We must care for Earth and appreciate, respect, protect, and love our planet, and we must also recognize that Earth and all its inhabitants are mindfully engaged—mysteriously perhaps—because of interdependent interactions among them. Minding animals and minding Earth should cause us to wise up.

No one can ignore the devastating effects of humans on Earth, and none of Earth's beings, landscapes, or habitats, including water and air, is exempt from our actions. We must take a very broad perspective on a variety of questions. For instance, questions about science would explore what science is and how it is conducted, how to foster wide-ranging holistic interdisciplinary discussion, how common sense and "science sense" can be reconciled, what would encourage scientists to become more socially responsible, and, most importantly, what the roles of compassion, kindness, generosity, respect, grace, humility, and love are in what we call *science*. There is uneasiness among some scientists that nonscientists are showing increasing concern about science (and scientism) as it is typically practiced. Many people have concerns about Western biases in science, and recently I discovered a situation in which an essay submitted by a man in Zimbabwe was rejected by a scientific journal, whereas the same paper was accepted when it was submitted from Oxford University in the United Kingdom (Spinney 2004).

I would like to accomplish a number of goals in my short life on Earth. Some of my ideas have been presented in papers and books, whereas others are constantly being revisited and revised as I ponder more deeply just what animals can teach us about nature's wisdom. I am sure that some of the very ideas about which I write now will metamorphose when I revisit this essay and when I discuss it with colleagues. It is precisely the dynamic, frustrating, and very challenging topics with which I am concerned that keep me working feverishly to gain, at least for a short time, a coherent perspective. There are many ways to travel the path of nature's wisdom and to learn about its sagacious ways, and I hope that I can convince you that one path leads directly through the hearts and minds of our animal kin, and that we can learn much about nature's wisdom if we open our hearts and minds to nature's prudent ways. Given what some people do to animals, I often wish animals were not as sentient and wise as they are. But the fact is that they are, and we must change our ways and bond with and love animals because they are such wise and feeling organisms.

It is essential that heartless science be replaced with heartful and compassionate science, and that all scientists take seriously their responsibility to be socially responsible and share their findings with nonscientists and the community at large. In my view, we need much more than traditional science—by which I mean science that is not socially responsible, science that is autonomous and authoritarian, science that fragments the universe and disembodies and alienates humans and other animals—to make headway into understanding other animals and the world at large. We need to broaden science to incorporate and be drenched in feeling, heart, spirit, soul, and love. Scientists need to exit their heads and go deep into their hearts, and science needs to open its arms to people who love the world and who have a reverence for all life. Scientists should not be inhibited about being sentimental. We need a science of unity, reconciliation, and compassion.

I have also argued that some animals practice wild justice—that they cooperate when they play, that there is wisdom in being honest and just, and that it feels good to be fair. I think that being nice is doing what comes naturally. I believe that ethological studies that ask, "What is it like to be another animal?" are important for learning not only about who animals are as individuals and members of a given species, but also about who we are. Recently I discovered that scientists are now asking the same question about people, that is, "What is it like to be another person?" recognizing that every person does not sense the world in the same way.

I fully realize that it is impossible to be perfect beings, that all of us are hypocritical on occasion. But surely we can do much better than we have in our encounters with nature and Earth if we strive for a more comprehensive, respectful, and compassionate Earth ethic and respect the views of others who care about nature and Earth from a different perspective. Looking for complete consensus on most issues will be frustrating. However, if we talk to one another, many problems that appear insoluble will likely yield to reasonable compromises. Of course, we need to be very careful not to forsake the well-being of other animals for our own—we should not trump the interests of other animals for our own selfish and shortsighted ends.

These are only a few among many areas of inquiry that need to be considered, and any answers offered will necessarily be tentative and open to future revision. Nonetheless, these challenging and often frustrating questions must be dealt with *now*, for delay will result in more devastation of Earth. As His Holiness the Dalai Lama reminds us, "Mother Earth" is telling us—actually, warning us—to be careful about how we interact with and use her. Thomas Berry stresses that our relationship with nature should be one of awe, not one of use. I agree. Nonetheless, we continue to use awe-inspiring animals in a wide variety of activities, and much of this use is harmful and abusive.

Surely we do not want to be remembered as the generation that killed nature. Now is the time for everyone to work for universal planetary peace. There is no workable alternative to world peace, and we must sow seeds without hesitation to accomplish this urgent goal. It is essential that we do better than our ancestors did. No one could argue that a world with significantly less—with *no*—cruelty and with boundless compassion, respect, grace, humility, spirituality, peace, and love would not be a better world in which to live and to raise children. We are all citizens of Earth, members of a global community in which intimate reciprocal and beneficent peaceful relationships are mandatory. We have compelling responsibilities for making Earth a better and more peaceful habitat for all beings and for stopping our self-centered intrusions wherever we choose to go. Time is not on our side. We must reflect and step lightly as we redecorate nature. Humane education is critical. We must teach the children well and, above all, be kind (see Weil 2003). Children—like all of us—need wild places in which to lose themselves.

I yearn for a seamless tapestry of oneness, a warm blanket, a heartscape of deep and reciprocal friendships in which all individuals count, a single community in which each individual is at one with all others, in which the seer and the seen are one, in which it feels good and makes individuals happy to be kind to others. I plead for developing heartfelt and holistic science that allows for fun, joy, and play. Science need not be suspicious of things it cannot fully understand. We must never avert our eyes or our other senses from the eyes and voices of all other beings, our kin, our friends, who urgently beg for and truly need our immediate, uncompromising, and unconditional aid and love. We are obliged to do much more than we have done for animals and Earth.

EMBODIED AND EMERGENT WISDOM

The famed novelist Henry Miller (1957, p. 93) claimed: "If we don't always start from nature we certainly come to her in our hour of need." His words ring true for me. But why do we go to nature for guidance? Why do we feel so good when we see, hear, smell, or touch other animals, when we look at trees and smell the fragrance of flowers, when we watch a rushing stream, a quiet lake, or a rippling ocean? A recent survey has shown that 70–90 percent of the general public who were questioned in Europe and in the United States "recognizes the right of nature to exist even if not useful to humans in any way" (van den Born et al., 2001). The wisdom of nature has a right to be protected. Whether nature has its own inherent embodied wisdom that is at the same time emergent and shared, that interacts with our expectations of what nature is all about, or whether we project and imbue nature with such qualities and it is really just a state of our own mind, I find that when I am out in nature, I am never alone and neither do I feel lonely. I converse with nature, and nature converses with me.

Theologian Thomas Berry (2000, p. 97) noted: "We need the wonder of the dawn, the wonder of the forest, the wonder of a river, the wonder of a prairie." We often cannot put into words why nature has such positive effects on us—why when we are immersed in nature we become breathless, or we feel our heart rate slow because of nature's beauty, awe, mystery, simplicity, multiplicity, and generosity. Perhaps our inability to express nature's effect simply means that the feelings evoked are so very deep (perhaps primal) that there are no words rich enough to convey what we feel. We usually feel joy when we know that nature is doing well and feel deep sorrow and pain when we perceive that nature is being destroyed, exploited, and devastated. I ache when I feel nature's wisdom being compromised and forced out of balance. My primitive brain that is immersed in new and rapidly developing cultures and technologies still retains much of my close ties to nature. Perhaps the sheer joy we feel when nature is healthy, the joy we feel when we are embedded in nature's mysterious ways, is but one measure of the love we have for it.

I feel that nature trusts us not to defile it, not to humiliate it, so we'd better not do so. Surely there must have been significant consequences for our ancestors if they fooled with Mother Nature, for they did not have today's mechanical and intellectual machinery with which to work to undo their intrusions into natural processes. Indeed, they were probably so busy just trying to stay alive that they could not have wreaked the havoc that we have wreaked on Earth without paying a large price. It would be wonderful if we could tune into our old brains and let them guide us, for our brains are very much like those of our ancestors, but our sociocultural milieus and Earth have changed significantly over the last millennia. Cycles of nature are still with us and within us, although we might not be aware of their presence because we can so easily override just about anything "natural" with technology and with our busyness. And much technology and much useless busyness alienate us from nature, a rupture that in turn leads to our wanton abuse of Earth. It is all too easy to destroy something to which we are not attached, or to abuse another being to whom we are not bonded.

When I think about nature's wisdom, I am forced to come to terms with who I am in the grand scheme of things. While I usually conclude that I am very small in a very large world, this conclusion does not diminish me or make me feel a lesser being. Indeed, it frees me and envelops me in much peace, and I rejoice in who I am in this grand scheme—nature's random processes and more predictable rhythms. When I am immersed in nature, I feel its warmth deep in my heart, and all my senses tingle with its radiant beauty and sensuality.

BEWARE SILENT SPRINGS

More than forty years ago, Rachel Carson warned us in *Silent Spring* about the devastating loss of birdsong (Bekoff and Nystrom 2004), and the concerns she raised ring true today. Bernie Krause (2002) refers to the sounds of natural habitats and living organisms as "the most beautiful music on the planet. It is also its collective voice." We must beware of losing nature's voice; we must beware of suffering maladies associated not only with silent springs, but also with silent summers, autumns, and winters. The wrong path to tapping into nature's wisdom is to disrupt the precious lives of other animals and silence their voices, or to prevent leaves from blowing in the breeze, or to impede water from sloshing about. Because I study animals, I want places on Earth where animals can be safe from harm caused by humans. In our wisdom, we must provide such refuges. For instance, in an action displaying true human wisdom, the country of Mexico recently signed an accord to protect whales in its waters. It will be the largest sanctuary in the world, about 1.1 million square miles of water. Sadly, and unwisely, refuges do not always protect animals. On Cape Cod in Massachusetts, there is a wildlife refuge on Momomoy Island where animals are supposed to be protected from human disturbance, but where numerous coyotes are routinely killed. Some refuge! In the United States, animals can be hunted on so-called national refuges. Surely, if we do not protect animals in areas where they are *supposed* to be protected, to live their lives in safety, we risk losing their voices, nature's sounds.

WHAT IS WISDOM? DOES NATURE KNOW BEST?

> No people ever knew the Earth as well as we do in terms of its mechanistic processes, but no people have ever had less intimacy with the planet. We are shriveled up in our souls.
> —Thomas Berry, in an interview, 2000

In October 2002, I attended a meeting outside Graz, Austria, convened by His Holiness the Dalai Lama. The main theme was "the path to nature's wisdom," and the gathering was part of the Dalai Lama's Kalachakra for World Peace 2002. In attendance were scientists, philosophers, religious scholars and leaders, and local farmers, and the interdisciplinary discussions over wonderful beer and wine made it a most amazing experience.

My assignment was to talk about animals as a path to nature's wisdom, so I began by asking what we mean by the phrase "nature's wisdom." Anton Moser (2000, p. 381) has introduced a new term, *ecosophy*, to refer to "the science of nature's wisdom," the core of an ecological, holistic worldview. His approach is extremely interdisciplinary, multilevel, and necessarily wide-ranging, and many people will likely find it extremely challenging, and perhaps daunting and intimidating in its breadth. Moser brings to the table a holistic, macroscopic, integrated view in which the notion of wisdom includes the importance of intuition, sustainability, diversity, flexibility, self-organization, integration ("deep science," in which science, ethics, and art are integrated with nature), unity or oneness (nature as an interconnected, interdependent, and embedded whole), aesthetics and spiritual and emotional dimensions (rather than a reliance on solely experimental data), science integrated with ethics, and the use of noninvasive manipulations that respect "a feeling for other creatures" (p. 375) when we study nature. Thus, nature is seen as "the whole," and an "Earth ethics" demands that we not intrude on the integrity of integrated natural processes. Nature is a source of happiness, joy, and beauty, and beauty is the overall indicator of the quality of the "wholeness" of nature, "the glory of the whole." The importance of sensory experience is stressed in Moser's conceptualization of nature's wisdom, as is active participation in the world in which we are immersed. Our lives should be "senseful" rather than "senseless." Nature is more than logical, physical, materialistic, mechanistic, and mathematical principles and laws.

Talking about nature's wisdom suggests that nature seems to understand itself and its rhythmic dance through space and time, although this understanding might not be obvious in a narrow-minded or short-term view; that perhaps there truly is some self-organizing principle that applies to the concept of nature, taken broadly; and that in the short time each of us is on Earth we cannot possibly understand or appreciate the underlying dynamics that have allowed nature to persist for millennia, no matter how wise we are as individuals, no matter how great is our collective wisdom. One of my colleagues mentioned to me that he is concerned that talking about nature's wisdom is an anthropocentric exercise and that we need to be very careful when we discuss what we mean by the phrase "nature's wisdom." I agree, but I believe that it is a very useful way to speak about nature. And perhaps nature knows best.

While the impossibility of ever achieving a deep comprehension of nature's wisdom might be frustrating, I find the challenge inviting, because with hard work we *can* make Earth a better place for all beings, for all life, for all environs, animate and inanimate. I feel that we can truly come to terms with the big picture, in which every event is interconnected, in which we take a holistic view of Earth as a community of subjects rather than a mere collection of objects, to borrow a phrase from Thomas Berry. Berry stresses that no living being nourishes itself; each is dependent on every other member of the community for nourishment and the assistance it needs for its own survival.

EARTH AS A WISE ELDER: THE IMPORTANCE OF WORLD HAPPINESS, PEACE, AND LOVE

> Something almost unspeakably holy—I don't know how else to say this—underlies our discovery and confirmation of the actual details that made our world and also, in realms of contingency, assured the minutiae of its construction in the manner we know, and not in any of the trillion other ways, nearly all of which would not have included the evolution of a scribe to record the beauty, the cruelty, the fascination, and the mystery.
>
> —Stephen Jay Gould, *The Structure of Evolutionary Theory*

> "You have to look at the data closely," the man said, "and think about the science, but when you get up the North Slope [of Alaska], you'll hear those caribou go thundering past, and you'll get this gut feeling that you just can't ignore."
>
> —Bill Streever, "Science and Emotion, on Ice"

Humans have altered the future of biological evolution. It's estimated that species extinctions due to humans range from about one hundred to one thousand species per one million per year; the natural rate of extinction is about one species per one million per year. Meanwhile, about one new species per one million is born each year. Do the math—this is not a good situation at all, for far fewer species are born than go extinct because of human activities. It's very hard to know precisely what is happening, but there is no doubt that we are losing nature at alarming and unprecedented rates—and most species extinctions go unrecognized.

We are in the middle of the sixth major period of biotic extinction, this one caused predominantly by human activities. In the past five extinctions, it took about ten million years to restore biodiversity—this time, there may be no coming back, because of increased rates of extinction. As many as 250,000 species went extinct in the twentieth century, and as many as ten to twenty times this number will disappear in the twenty-first century. In North America alone, about 235 animal species are threatened by pollution, human encroachment on their habitat, and aggressive harvesting practices. Michael McKinney (2001) has discovered that human population size is positively correlated with threat to the numbers of birds and mammals for continental (but not island) nations, and that mammals suffer more losses than do birds during initial human impacts. His data set is large; 149 nations were analyzed for mammals and 154 were analyzed for birds.

Perhaps if we view Earth as a wise elder, and perhaps if we listen to its messages and watch it very closely, as do many indigenous peoples, we will be able to tap into and come to a deeper understanding of Earth's grand wisdom, a combination of complex and simple processes that it shares openly and generously. I often wonder if indigenous peoples who live close to and in deep interrelationship with Earth are able to solve problems that more detached "scientists" cannot. Firket Berkes (1999) stresses the importance of giving serious attention to traditional ecological knowledge and provides many examples of how Western science cannot deal with many local problems encountered in foreign lands. He notes, for example, that scientists did not know that a population of eider ducks lived year-round in Hudson Bay, but the Inuit knew. Because it was not "scientific," Inuit knowledge was for a long time ignored in summaries of the avifauna in this area. Likewise, Inuit observations and warnings about global warming are beginning to be taken more seriously by nonnative scientists, who usually have a narrower and shorter-term view of the situation at hand. According to a story in the *Washington Post* on 28 May 2002, the average temperature in Canada's Western Arctic has increased between 1.5 and 13.5 degrees Celsius, and native Inuit "cannot read the weather the way they used to." Inuit hunters and elders who depend on the land are seeing increasing numbers of deformed fish and of caribou with diseased livers. Recently, a robin was seen where none had ever been observed; there is no word for "robin" in the Inuit language. Likewise, insects the Inuit had never seen before are appearing, and similarly there is no word for them in Inuktitut.

Berkes (1999) also warns that visiting scientists often have a "seasonally limited research period," as a result of which they cannot possibly accumulate the long-term details needed to make substantive claims about ecological problems. For example, he writes that in the Keoladeo National Park in India, local people argued for years that grazing by water buffalo should be allowed because it was consistent with conservation objectives. Park authorities disagreed. A long-term study by the Bombay Natural History Society supported the local people's claim. Grazing helped counter the tendency of the wetland to turn into grassland. A ban on grazing had negatively affected the wetland and the park, which was well known for its rich bird life. Grazing by cattle was an effective solution. In some (possibly many) cases, perhaps it should be permissible to view traditional knowledge and wisdom as equivalent to "scientific" knowledge, because traditional knowledge often results from systematic observations and inquiries over long periods, without all the propaganda, authority, autonomy, and arrogance of "science."

THE CHOICES WE MAKE

Given who we are and that we are all over Earth, we do indeed have the power to dominate all other animals and landscapes, some of which might seem to have little or no value to us. We eat other animals, we hunt them, we use them in education and research, and we let them entertain and amuse us. We spread human diseases when we visit the places animals live. Our relationship with other animals is usually very lopsided, with few if any benefits going to the animals themselves.

But we can *choose* to be intrusive, abusive, or compassionate. We do not have to do something just because someone else wants us to. We do not have to do something just because we can. We each are responsible for our choices. Some ideas we should base them on include (1) putting respect, compassion, and admiration for other animals first; (2) taking seriously the animals' points of view; (3) erring on the animals' side when uncertain whether they feel pain or are suffering; (4) recognizing that almost all the methods used to study animals, even in the field, are intrusions on their lives—that much research is fundamentally exploitative; (5) recognizing how misguided are speciesistic views concerning vague notions such as intelligence and cognitive or mental complexity for informing assessments of animals' well-being; (6) focusing on the importance of individual animals; (7) appreciating individual variation and the diversity of the lives of different individuals in the worlds within which they live; (8) appealing to what some call questionable practices that have no place in the conduct of science, such as the use of common sense and empathy; and (9) using broad-based rules of fidelity and nonintervention as guiding principles. A great challenge centers on how we will reconcile common sense with "science sense." Our animal kin depend on our goodwill, mercy, and wisdom.

There may well be some studies that we want to do but cannot because there is no ethically defensible way to conduct them, at least not now. And some places we have to just leave alone. The environmental ethicist Holmes Rolston (2002, p. 134) has this to say about Antarctica, a continent that is attracting more and more attention (similar to the way an unknown or an appealing animal in a cage in a zoo often does) and that could easily be taken over by humans: "Here is one continent on the home planet that is not, cannot, and ought not be our home." I agree. Let's preserve Antarctica's integrity as much as we can; let's honor the wisdom of this magnificent continent. (I studied Adéie penguins and South Polar skuas in Antarctica in the 1970s. During my time there, my interests in science and ethics were kindled, and these concerns have been important to me since then. I often asked myself as I walked among the penguins, "What in the world am I doing here?")

KEEPING OPEN MINDS AND OPEN HEARTS: REMAINING CURIOUS AND ALIVE AND TAKING PRECAUTIONS

Here and elsewhere I have argued that while there still is much to learn about the lives of other animals—what makes them tick—we know quite a lot now that can and should inform us as to how we should interact with them. Ecologists and environmentalists have developed what they call the "precautionary principle" (Applegate 2000), which is used for making decisions about environmental problems. This principle basically states that we should not use a lack of full scientific certainty as an excuse to delay taking action on an issue. The precautionary principle can be well applied in studies of animal cognition, animal emotions, and the evolution of social morality.

I believe that we can justify using the information we now have to stop the wanton destruction of other animals' lives, of their very being, and of the places they live. Claiming that we do not know enough or that we will never know enough, and using this uncertainty to excuse our destructive ways, makes us less than human.

THE IMPORTANCE OF COMMUNITY, HOPE, AND BOUNDLESS LOVE: NO ONE IS EXEMPT

I am a hopeful person and a dreamer, and while I feel things are getting better, I also feel we need to make better decisions about how we interact with nature than we have in the past—and I do not think time is on our side. There is much to do and not much time to accomplish it. Thus I argue that we must all recognize that no one—let me emphasize, *no one*—is exempt from accountability for the wanton destruction, intentional or unintentional, of nature's wisdom and spirit and hence of our own, no matter how rich one is and no matter how removed one may become from nature. We are a single community of Earth.

It is essential to maintain hope even when things seem grim. Rather than take a doomsday view that the world won't exist in a hundred years if we humans fail to accept our unique responsibilities, it is more disturbing to imagine a world in which humans and other life coexist in the absence of any intimacy and interconnectedness.

If we forget that humans and other animals are all part of the same interdependent world—the more-than-human world (Abram 1996)—and if we forget that humans and animals are deeply connected at many levels of interaction, when things go amiss in our interactions with animals, as they surely will, and animals are set apart from and inevitably below humans, I feel certain that we will miss the animals more than the animal survivors will miss us. The interconnectivity and spirit of the world will be lost forever, and these losses will make for much loneliness in a severely impoverished universe.

In the end, in my humble opinion, it boils down to love. We need to be motivated by love, not by fear of what it will mean if we come to love animals and Earth for who they are. We can indeed love animals more and not love people less. We must love the universe and all its inhabitants—animate and inanimate.

REDUCTIONISM VERSUS HOLISM, COMPASSION, AND HEART: MOVING TOWARD UNITY

> In reality there is a single integral community of the Earth.... In this community every being has its own role to fulfill, its own dignity, its inner spontaneity. Every being has it own voice.... We have no right to disturb the basic functioning of the biosystems of the planet. We cannot own the Earth or any part of the Earth in any absolute manner.
>
> —Thomas Berry, *The Great Work*

I want to return briefly to some topics that I considered earlier. Much of my reflection centers on the deep and reciprocal interactions I have had with numerous animals, who with their profound wisdom have selflessly been my teachers and healers.

There seems to be no doubt that reductionist science misrepresents the world, the world of people, the world of animals—the entire deeply interconnected community of Earth. This has serious consequences for the quality of knowledge we gather and for how we interact in and with nature. Reductionism promotes alienation, isolation, and disconnection. It forces a separation between the seer and the seen—a false dualism. Science often impedes our truly sensing, feeling, and understanding the scope of the amazing world within which we live. We live as if we know with great certainty how whole systems work, but our knowledge is far from infallible.

Reductionism can also easily lead us away from viewing animals' worlds as they view then and toward rampant and destructive anthropocentrism. Science can indeed make nature less majestic and less magical and appear less wise. But let us not allow it to continue to do so.

Holistic and more heart-driven science is needed, science infused with spirit, compassion, and love. Closet holists need to emerge and offer their heretical views. Holistic heartfelt science reinforces a sense of togetherness and relationship, family and community, and awe. It fosters the development of deep and reciprocal friendships among humans, animals, and other nature. It helps us resonate with nature's radiance and lessens our tendency to think, egocentrically, that we are at the center of everything. Thomas Berry (1999) stresses that we should strive for a "benign presence" in nature. Native Americans are proud to claim that "animals are all our relations." Animals and inanimate landscapes need to speak for themselves, and we must listen to their messages very carefully. Trees and rocks need love too.

We need a science that incorporates who we are as the human practitioners of the business of science. Solid science *can* be driven by the stirrings of one's heart. Saturating science with spirit and compassion will help bring science, nature, and society into a unified whole. Questioning science will help insure that we will not repeat past mistakes, that we will move toward a world in which humans and other animals share peaceably the beneficence of nature. Magnificent nature—the cacophony of its deep and rich sensuality—will be respected, cherished, and loved.

Visualizing Compassion: Minding Animals, Minding Earth

> Compassion—surely that is what the earth seeks most in us.
> —Calvin Luther Martin, *In the Spirit of the Earth*

Alan Sponberg (1997, 366–67) presents a useful model of compassion in his "hierarchy of compassion." In his hierarchy, "vertical progress is a matter of 'reaching out,' actively and consciously, to affirm an ever-widening circle of expressed interrelatedness; ... progress along this spiral path confers no increasing privilege over those who are below on the path. Quite the contrary, it entails an ever increasing sense of responsibility ... for an ever greater circle of relatedness ... expressed by the Buddhist term *karunā*—compassion or 'wisdom in action.'" Sponberg's views on compassion are compelling, for they accentuate how we humans need to come to terms with who we are in a hierarchy of compassion. Sponberg also stresses that higher does not mean "better" but, rather, more responsible.

We must move forward with grace, kindness, generosity, humility, respect, compassion, and love. By minding animals, we mind ourselves. By minding Earth, we mind ourselves and the entire integrated community of Earth.

Let us make a pact to do no intentional harm, to treat all individuals with compassion, and to step lightly into the lives of other beings, bodies of water, air, and landscapes. It will be difficult, but if we set any lower goal we can be sure that we will not be able to accomplish win-win agreements. Moral progress requires moral choices. Let us expand our relatively closed human clubhouse to incorporate all of Earth.

As I write, I am at once smiling and feeling twinges of sadness, for I have touched on so many topics and so much more work needs to be done. It is unsettling that nearly half our splendid planet has been transformed so that there are "dead zones," areas where there is little or no oxygen in coastal waters. It is unsettling that so many animals are harmed and killed by humans. Perhaps the biggest and most difficult question of all is whether enough of us will choose to make the heartfelt commitment to making this a better world, a more compassionate world in which love is plentiful and shared, before it is too late. I believe we have already embarked on this pilgrimage. My optimism leads me in no other direction.

Consummate Companions: Why We Need Animals Now More Than Ever

> One means of sanity is to retain a hold on the natural world, to remain, insofar as we can, good animals.
> —Wallace Stegner, *Wilderness Letter*

> The image of the world around us that science provides is highly deficient. It supplies a lot of factual information, and puts all our experience in magnificently coherent order, but it keeps terribly silent about everything close to our hearts, everything that really counts.
> —Max Schrödinger (quoted by Revel and Ricard, 1998, p. 214)

Let us not continue to behave in ways that disrespect and destroy nature. Let us be very careful as we trespass into the world of other animals so we don't lose our animal friends, our consummate companions—and only then discover how much they truly mean to us because of *who* they are.

I hope I have convinced you that studies of animal behavior, including their passions and beastly virtues, are essential for learning more about nature's wisdom. And I hope I have convinced you that science, nature, kinship, ethics, and heart can coexist as we travel the path to and from nature's wisdom. We need to let our old brains do what comes naturally and pull us back to deep, reciprocal, passionate, and respectful interconnections with nature.

> If all the beasts were gone, men would die from a great loneliness of spirit, for whatever happens to the beasts also happens to the man. All things are connected. Whatever befalls the Earth befalls the sons of the Earth.
> —Chief Seattle of the Suwamish tribe in a letter to President Franklin Pierce

We need to appreciate and love nature with all our heart. We need wise nature, and we need wise animals.

We are all consummate companions. We complete one another. This is why we need animals now more than ever.

References

Listed here are references to the research that is discussed in the introduction to each of the five parts of this book and in my introduction and afterword. I also include some sources not discussed directly that bear on the topics under consideration.

INTRODUCTION: WHAT DOES IT FEEL LIKE TO BE A FOX?

Allen, C., and M. Bekoff. 1997. *Species of Mind: The Philosophy and Biology of Cognitive Ethology.* MIT Press, Cambridge, Massachusetts.

Auster, P. 1999. *Timbuktu.* Henry Holt, New York.

Beck, A., and A. Katcher. 1996. *Between Pets and People: The Importance of Animal Companionship.* Purdue University Press, West Lafayette, Indiana.

Beck, A. M., and N. M. Meyers. 1996. Health enhancement and companion animal ownership. *Annual Review of Public Health* 17: 247–257.

Beck, B. B. 1982. Chimpocentrism: Bias in cognitive ethology. *Journal of Human Evolution* 11: 3–17.

Becker, M. 2002. *The Healing Power of Pets.* Hyperion, New York.

Bekoff, M. 1994. Cognitive ethology and the treatment of non-human animals: How matters of mind inform matters of welfare. *Animal Welfare* 3: 75–96.

Bekoff, M. 1995. Naturalizing and individualizing animal well-being and animal minds: An ethologist's naiveté exposed? In A. Rowan (ed.), *Wildlife Conservation, Zoos, and Animal Protection: A Strategic Analysis.* Tufts Center for Animals and Public Policy, Grafton, Massachusetts. pp. 63–129.

Bekoff, M. 1998. Cognitive ethology: The comparative study of animal minds. In W. Bechtel and G. Graham (eds.), *Blackwell Companion to Cognitive Science.* Blackwell, Oxford. pp. 371–379.

Bekoff, M. 1998. Deep ethology, animal rights, and the Great Ape/Animal Project: Resisting speciesism and expanding the community of equals. *Journal of Agricultural and Environmental Ethics* 10: 269–296.

Bekoff, M. (ed.) 1998. *Encyclopedia of Animal Rights and Animal Welfare.* Foreword by Jane Goodall. Greenwood, Westport, Connecticut.

Bekoff, M. 2000. Animal emotions: Exploring passionate natures. *BioScience* 50: 861–870.

Bekoff, M. (ed.) 2000. *The Smile of a Dolphin: Remarkable Accounts of Animal Emotions.* Random House/Discovery Books, Washington, D.C.

Bekoff, M. 2000. *Strolling with Our Kin: Speaking for and Respecting Voiceless Animals.* Lantern Books, New York.

Bekoff, M. 2002. Animal reflections. *Nature* 419: 255.

Bekoff, M. 2002. *Minding Animals: Awareness, Emotions, and Heart.* Oxford University Press, New York.

Bekoff, M. 2002. Virtuous nature. *New Scientist* 13 July, 34–37.

Bekoff, M. 2003. Consciousness and self in animals: Some Reflections. *Zygon (Journal of Religion and Science)* 38: 229–245.

Bekoff, M (ed.) 2004. *Encyclopedia of Animal Behavior.* Foreword by Jane Goodall. Greenwood, Westport, Connecticut.

Bekoff, M. 2004. The great divide: A review of Wynne, C. D. L. 2004. *Do Animals Think? American Scientist* 92: 481–482.

Bekoff, M. 2004. Wild justice, cooperation, and fair play: Minding manners, being nice, and feeling good. In R. Sussman and A. Chapman (eds.), *The Origins and Nature of Sociality.* Aldine, Chicago. pp. 53–80.

Bekoff, M., C. Allen, and G. M. Burghardt. (eds.) 2002. *The Cognitive Animal: Empirical and Theoretical Perspectives on Animal Cognition.* MIT Press, Cambridge, Massachusetts.

Bekoff, M., and D. Jamieson. (ed.) 1996. *Readings in Animal Cognition.* MIT Press, Cambridge, Massachusetts.

Bshary, R., W. Wickler, and H. Fricke. 2002. Fish cognition: A primate's eye view. *Animal Cognition* 5: 1–13.

Darwin, C. 1872/1998. *The Expression of the Emotions in Man and Animals.* Third edition. With an Introduction, Afterword, and Commentaries by Paul Ekman. Oxford University Press, New York

Francione, G. L. 2000. *Introduction to Animal Rights: Your Child or the Dog?* Temple University Press, Philadelphia.

Haraway, D. 2003. *The Companion Species Manifesto: Dogs, People, and Significant Otherness.* Prickly Paradigm Press, Chicago.

Horowitz, A. C., and M. Bekoff. 2004. Embracing and naturalizing anthropomorphism: Doing what comes naturally. Manuscript, author's files.

Kaminski, J., J. Call, and J. Fischer. 2004. Word learning in a domestic dog: Evidence for "fast mapping." *Science* 304: 1682–1683.

Randour, M. L. 2000. *Animal Grace: Entering a Spiritual Relationship with Our Fellow Creatures.* New World Library, Novato, California.

Regan, T. 1983. *The Case for Animal Rights.* University of California Press, Berkeley.

Reuters, June 25, 2004. Friendly dog prevents killing spree.

Rivera, M. 2001. *Hospice Hounds.* Lantern Books, New York.

Rollin, B. E. 1989. *The Unheeded Cry: Animal Consciousness, Animal Pain and Science.* Oxford University Press, New York. (reprinted 1998, Iowa State University Press).

Rolston, H., III. 1999. *Genesis, Genes, and God: Values and Their Origins in Natural and Human History.* Cambridge University Press, New York.

Schoen, A. M. 2001. *Kindred Spirits: How the Remarkable Bond between Humans and Animals Can Change the Way We Live.* Broadway Books, New York.

Sewall, L. 1999. *Sight and Sensibility: The Ecopsychology of Perception.* Jeremy P. Tarcher/Putnam, New York.

Singer, P. 1990. *Animal Liberation.* Second edition. NewYork Review of Books, New York.

Sneddon, L. U. 2003. The evidence for pain in fish: The use of morphine as an analgesic. *Applied Animal Behaviour Science* 83: 153–162.

Stach, S., J. Benard, and M. Giurfa. 2004. Local-feature assembling in visual pattern recognition and generalization in honeybees. *Nature* 429: 758–760.

Warden, C. J., and L. H. Warner. 1928. The sensory capacities and intelligence of dogs, with a report on the ability of the noted dog "Fellow" to respond to verbal stimuli. *Quarterly Review of Biology* 3: 1–28.

PART I: EMOTIONS, COGNITION, AND ANIMALS SELVES: "WOW! THAT'S ME!"

Allen, C. 1992. Mental content. *British Journal of the Philosophy of Science* 43: 537–553.

Allen, C. 1992. Mental content and evolutionary explanation. *Biology and Philosophy* 7: 1–12.

Allen, C., and M. Bekoff. 1994. Intentionality, social play, and definition. *Biology and Philosophy* 9: 63–74.

Allen, C., and M. Bekoff. 1995. Natural design, function, and animal behavior: Philosophical and ethological considerations. *Perspectives in Ethology* 11: 1–46.

Allen, C., and M. Bekoff. 1995. Cognitive ethology and the intentionality of animal behaviour. *Mind and Language* 10: 313–328.

Allen, C., and M. Bekoff. 1997. *Species of Mind: The Philosophy and Biology of Cognitive Ethology.* MIT Press, Cambridge, Massachusetts.

Allen, C., M. Bekoff, and G. Lauder. (eds.) 1998. *Nature's Purposes: Analyses of Function and Design in Biology.* MIT Press, Cambridge, Massachusetts.

Allen, C., and M. D. Hauser. 1991. Concept attribution in nonhuman animals: Theoretical and methodological problems in ascribing complex mental processes. *Philosophy of Science* 58: 221–240.

Bekoff, M. 1994. Cognitive ethology and the treatment of nonhuman animals: How matters of mind inform matters of welfare. *Animal Welfare* 3: 75–96.

Bekoff, M. 1995. Naturalizing and individualizing animal well-being and animal minds: An ethologist's naivet exposed? In A. Rowan (ed.), *Wildlife Conservation, Zoos, and Animal Protection: A Strategic Analysis.* Tufts Center for Animals and Public Policy, Grafton, Massachusetts. pp. 63–129.

Bekoff, M. 1998. Deep ethology, animal rights, and the Great Ape/Animal Project: Resisting speciesism and expanding the community of equals. *Journal of Agricultural and Environmental Ethics* 10: 269–296.

Bekoff, M. 2000. Animal emotions: Exploring passionate natures. *BioScience* 50: 861–870.

Bekoff, M. (ed.) 2000. *The Smile of a Dolphin: Remarkable Accounts of Animal Emotions.* Random House/Discovery Books, Washington, D.C.

Bekoff, M. 2000. *Strolling with Our Kin: Speaking for and Respecting Voiceless Animals.* Lantern Books, New York.

Bekoff, M. 2002. Animal reflections. *Nature* 419: 255.

Bekoff, M. 2002. *Minding Animals: Awareness, Emotions, and Heart.* Oxford University Press, New York.

Bekoff, M. 2002. Virtuous nature. *New Scientist* 13 July, 34–37.

Bekoff, M. 2003. Consciousness and self in animals: Some reflections. *Zygon (Journal of Religion and Science)* 38: 229–245.

Bekoff, M. 2004. Wild justice, cooperation, and fair play: Minding manners, being nice, and feeling good. In R. Sussman (ed.), *The Origins and Nature of Sociality.* Aldine, Chicago. pp. 53–80.

Bekoff, M., and C. Allen. 1992. Intentional icons: Towards an evolutionary cognitive ethology. *Ethology*, 91: 1–16.

Bekoff, M., and C. Allen. 1997. Cognitive ethology: Slayers, skeptics, and proponents. In R. W. Mitchell, N. Thompson, and L. Miles (eds.), *Anthropomorphism, Anecdote, and Animals: The Emperor's New Clothes?* SUNY Press, Albany, New York. pp. 313–334.

Bekoff, M., and C. Allen. 1998. Intentional communication and social play: How and why animals negotiate and agree to play. In M. Bekoff and J. A. Byers (eds.), *Animal Play: Evolutionary, Comparative, and Ecological Perspectives.* Cambridge University Press, Cambridge and New York. pp. 97–114.

Bekoff, M., C. Allen, and G. M. Burghardt. (eds.) 2002. *The Cognitive Animal: Empirical and Theoretical Perspectives on Animal Cognition.* MIT Press, Cambridge, Massachusetts.

Bekoff, M., C. Allen, and M. C. Grant. 1999. Feeding decisions by Steller's jays (*Cyanocitta stelleri*): The utility of a logistic regression model for analyses of complex choices. *Ethology* 105: 393–406.

Bekoff, M., C. Allen, and A. Wolfe. 1998. Feeding behavior in Steller's jays (*Cyanocitta stelleri*): Effects of food type and social context. *Bird Behavior* 12: 79–84.

Bekoff, M., and D. Jamieson. 1990. Cognitive ethology and applied philosophy: The significance of an evolutionary biology of mind. *Trends in Ecology and Evolution* 5: 156–159.

Bekoff, M., and D. Jamieson. (eds.) 1990. *Interpretation and Explanation in the Study of Animal Behavior.* Vol. 1, *Interpretation, Intentionality, and Communication.* Westview Press, Boulder, Colorado.

Bekoff, M., and D. Jamieson. (eds.) 1990. *Interpretation and Explanation in the Study of Animal Behavior.* Vol. 2, *Explanation, Evolution and Adaptation.* Westview Press, Boulder, Colorado.

Bekoff, M., and D. Jamieson. 1991. Reflective ethology, applied philosophy, and the moral status of animals. *Perspectives in Ethology* 9: 1–47.

Bekoff, M., and D. Jamieson. 1991. Sport hunting as an instinct: Another evolutionary "just-so-story"? *Environmental Ethics* 13: 375–378.

Bekoff, M., and Jamieson, D. 1996. Ethics and the study of carnivores: Doing science while respecting animals. In J. L. Gittleman (ed.), *Carnivore Behavior, Ecology, and Evolution*, Vol. 2. Cornell University Press, Ithaca, New York. pp. 15–45.

Bekoff, M., and D. Jamieson. (eds.) 1996. *Readings in Animal Cognition.* MIT Press, Cambridge, Massachusetts.

Burghardt, G. M. 1991. Cognitive ethology and critical anthropomorphism: A snake with two heads and hognose snakes that play dead. In C. A. Ristau (ed.), *Cognitive Ethology: The Minds of Other Animals—Essays in Honor of Donald R. Griffin.* Lawrence Erlbaum, Hillsdale, New Jersey. pp. 53–90.

Burghardt, G. M. 1997. Amending Tinbergen: A fifth aim for ethology. In R. W. Mitchell, N. Thompson, and L. Miles (eds.), *Anthropomorphism, Anecdote, and Animals: The Emperor's New Clothes?* SUNY Press, Albany, New York. pp. 254–276.

Burghardt, G. M., and M. Bekoff. (eds.) 1998. *The Development of Behavior: Comparative and Evolutionary Aspects.* Garland, New York.

Cheney, D. L., and R. M. Seyfarth. 1990. *How Monkeys See the World: Inside the Mind of Another Species.* University of Chicago Press, Chicago.

Cheney, D. L., and R. M. Seyfarth. 1992. Précis of *How Monkeys See the World: Inside the Mind of Another Species. Behavioral and Brain Sciences* 15: 135–182.

Darwin, C. 1872/1998. *The Expression of the Emotions in Man and Animals.* Third edition. With an Introduction, Afterword, and Commentaries by Paul Ekman. Oxford University Press, New York.

Dennett, D. C. 1983. Intentional systems in cognitive ethology: The "Panglossian paradigm" defended. *Behavioral and Brain Sciences* 6: 343–390.

deWaal, F. 2001. *The Ape and the Sushi Master.* Basic Books, New York.

Goodall, J., and M. Bekoff. 2002. *The Ten Trusts: What We Must Do to Care For the Animals We Love.* HarperCollins, San Francisco.

Gould, S. J. 2000. A lover's quarrel. In M. Bekoff (ed.). *The Smile of a Dolphin: Remarkable Accounts of Animal Emotions.* Random House/Discovery Books, Washington, D.C. pp. 13–17.

Griffin, D. R. 2001. *Animal Minds.* University of Chicago Press, Chicago.

Hauser, M. 2000. *Wild Minds.* Henry Holt, New York.

Heyes, C. 1987. Cognisance of consciousness in the study of animal knowledge. In W. Callebaut and R. Pinxten (eds.), *Evolutionary Epistemology.* D. Reidel, Dordrecht, Netherlands. pp. 105–136.

Irvine, L. 2003. George's bulldog: What Mead's canine companion could have told him about the self. *Sociological Origins* 3: 46–49.

Jamieson, D., and M. Bekoff. 1992. Carruthers on nonconscious experience. *Analysis* 52: 23–28.

Kennedy, J. S. 1992. *The New Anthropomorphism.* Cambridge University Press, New York.

Long, William J. 1906. *Brier-Patch Philosophy by "Peter Rabbit."* Harper, New York.

MacLean, P. 1970. *The Triune Brain in Evolution: Role in Paleocerebral Functions.* New York, Plenum.

Miklosi, A., J. Topal, and V. Csanyi. 2004. Comparative social cognition: What can dogs teach us? *Animal Behaviour* 67: 995–1004.

Panksepp, J. 1998. *Affective Neuroscience.* Oxford University Press, New York.

Panksepp, J. 2003. At the interface of the affective, behavioral, and cognitive neuroscience: Decoding the emotional feelings of the brain. *Brain and Cognition* 52: 4–14.

Panksepp, J. 2003. "Laughing" rats and the evolutionary antecedents of human joy? *Physiology and Behavior* 79: 533–547.

Ristau, C. 1991. Aspects of the cognitive ethology of an injury-feigning bird, the piping plovers. In C. A. Ristau (ed.), *Cognitive Ethology: The Minds of Other Animals— Essays in Honor of Donald R. Griffin.* Lawrence Erlbaum, Hillsdale, New Jersey. pp. 91–126.

Rollin, B. E. 1989. *The Unheeded Cry: Animal Consciousness, Animal Pain and Science.* Oxford University Press, New York. (reprinted 1998, Iowa State University Press).

Rollin, B. E. 1990. How the animals lost their minds: Animal mentation and scientific ideology. In M. Bekoff and, D. Jamieson,(eds.), *Interpretation and Explanation in the Study of Animal Behavior.* Vol. 1, *Interpretation, Intentionality, and Communication.* Westview Press, Boulder, Colorado. pp. 375–393.

Siviy, S. 1998. Neurobiological substrates of play behavior: Glimpses into the structure and function of mammalian playfulness. In M. Bekoff and J. A. Byers (eds.), *Animal Play: Evolutionary, Comparative, and Ecological Perspectives.* Cambridge University Press, New York. pp. 221–242.

Washburn M. F. 1908. *The Animal Mind: A Text-book of Comparative Psychology.* Macmillan, London.

Wynne, C.D.L. 2004. *Do Animals Think?* Princeton University Press, Princeton, New Jersey.

PART II: THE SOCIAL BEHAVIOR OF DOGS AND COYOTES

Bekoff, M. 1974. *A General Bibliography on the Coyote*, Canis latrans: *Taxonomy, Anatomy, Pathology, Physiology, Disease, Behavior, Ecology, and Management.* Coymar Press, Boulder, Colorado.

Bekoff, M. 1974. Social play and play-soliciting by infant canids. *American Zoologist* 14: 323–340. (Reprinted in D. Müller-Schwarze, [ed.], *Benchmark Papers in Animal Behavior*, vol. 10, 1978).

Bekoff, M. 1975. The communication of play intention: Are play signals functional? *Semiotica* 15: 231–239.

Bekoff, M. 1977. Social communication in canids: Evidence for the evolution of a stereotyped mammalian display. *Science* 197: 1097–1099.

Bekoff, M. (ed.) 1978/1990. *Coyotes: Biology, Behavior, and Management.* Academic Press, New York. (Reprinted 2001 by Blackburn Press, West Caldwell, New Jersey).

Bekoff, M. 1979. Coyote damage assessment in the West: Review of a report. *BioScience* 29: 754.

Bekoff, M. 1979. Scent marking by free-ranging domestic dogs: Olfactory and visual components. *Biology of Behaviour* 4: 123–139.

Bekoff, M. 2001. Cunning coyotes: Tireless tricksters, protean predators. In L. Dugatkin (ed.), *Model Systems in Behavioral Ecology.* Princeton University Press, Princeton, New Jersey. pp. 381–407.

Bekoff, M. 2001. Demonic dogs: The alleged truth about would-be jerks. *Anthrozoös* 14: 56–59.

Bekoff, M., and E. Gese. 2003. Coyote, *Canis latrans.* In J. Chapman and G. Feldhamer (eds.), *Wild Mammals of North America: Biology, Management, and Conservation.* John Hopkins University Press, Baltimore, Maryland. pp. 467–481.

Bekoff, M., H. L. Hill, and J. B. Mitton. 1975. Behavioral taxonomy in canids by discriminant function analysis. *Science* 190: 1223–1225.

Bekoff, M., and M. C. Wells. 1981. Behavioural budgeting by wild coyotes: The influence of food resources and social organization. *Animal Behaviour* 29: 794–801.

Bekoff, M., and M. C. Wells. 1982. Behavioral ecology of coyotes: Social organization, rearing patterns, space use, and resource defense. *Zeitschrift für Tierpsychologie* 60: 281–305.

Bekoff, M., and M. C. Wells. 1986. Social behavior and ecology of coyotes. *Advances in the Study of Behavior* 16: 251–338.

Bekoff, M., T. J. Daniels, and J. L. Gittleman. 1984. Life history patterns and the comparative social ecology of carnivores. *Annual Review of Ecology and Systematics* 15: 191–232

Bekoff, M., J. Diamond, and J. B. Mitton. 1981. Life-history patterns and sociality in canids: Body size, reproduction, and behavior. *Oecologia* 50: 386–390.

Berger, J. 1979. Social ontogeny and behavioral diversity: Consequences for bighorn sheep inhabiting desert and mountain environments. *Journal of Zoology* (London) 188: 251–266.

Berger, J. 1980. The ecology, structure, and function of social play in bighorn sheep. *Journal of Zoology* (London) 192: 531–542.

Berger, J. 1986. *Wild Horses of the Great Basin: Social Competition and Population Size.* University of Chicago Press, Chicago.

Berger, J. 1994. Science, conservation, and black rhinos. *Journal of Mammalogy* 75: 298–308.

Berger, J. 1999. Anthropogenic extinction of top carnivores and interspecific animal behaviour: Implications of the rapid decoupling of a web involving wolves, bears, moose, and ravens. *Proceedings of the Royal Society of London B* 266: 2261–2267.

Berger, J., and C. Cunningham. 1994. *Bison: Mating and Conservation in Small Populations.* Columbia University Press, New York.

Berger, J., A. Hoylman, and W. Weber. 2001. Perturbation of vast ecosystems in the absence of adequate science: Alaska's Arctic refuge. *Conservation Biology* 15: 539–541.

Berger, J., J. E. Swenson, and I.-L. Persson. 2001. Recolonizing carnivores and naive prey: Conservation lessons from Pleistocene extinctions. *Science* 291, 1036–1039.

Boone, J. A. 1954. *Kinship with All Life.* HarperCollins, San Francisco.

Byers, J. A. 1983. Social interactions of juvenile collared peccaries, *Tayassu tajacu. Journal of Zoology* 201: 83–89.

Byers, J. A. 1998. *American Pronghorn: Social Adaptations and the Ghosts of Predators Past.* University of Chicago Press, Chicago.

Byers, J. A. 2003. *Built for Speed: A Year in the Life of Pronghorn.* Harvard University Press, Cambridge, Massachusetts.

Byers, J. A., and M. Bekoff. 1981. Social spacing and cooperative behavior of the collared peccary, *Tayassu tajacu. Journal of Mammalogy* 62: 767–785.

Daniels, T. J. 1983. The social organization of free-ranging urban dogs: I. Non-estrous social behavior. *Applied Animal Ethology* 10: 341–363.

Daniels, T. J. 1983. The social organization of free-ranging urban dogs: II. Estrous groups and the mating system. *Applied Animal Ethology* 10: 365–373.

Daniels, T. J., and M. Bekoff. 1989. Feralization: The making of a wild domestic animal. *Behavioural Processes* 19: 79–94.

Daniels, T. J., and M. Bekoff. 1989. Spatial and temporal resource use by feral and abandoned dogs. *Ethology* 181: 300–312.

Daniels, T. J., and M. Bekoff. 1990. Domestication, exploitation, and rights. In M. Bekoff and D. Jamieson (eds.), *Interpretation and Explanation in the Study of Animal Behavior.* Vol. 2, *Explanation, Evolution, and Adaptation.* Westview Press, Boulder, Colorado. pp. 345–377.

Darwin, C. 1859/1958. *The Origin of Species.* Mentor Book, New York.

Darwin, C. 1868. *The Variation of Animals and Plants under Domestication.* Vols. I and II. Murray, London.

Feddersen-Peterson, D. U. 2000. Vocalizations of European wolves (*Canis lupus lupus* L.) and various dog breeds (*Canis lupus f. fam.*). *Archive Tierzucht Dummerstorf* 43: 387–397.

Hare, B., M. Brown, C. Williamson, and M. Tomasello. 2002. The domestication of social cognition in dogs. *Science* 298: 1636–1639.

Hare, B., and R. Wrangham. 2002. Integrating two evolutionary models for the study of social cognition. In M. Bekoff, C. Allen, and G. M. Burghardt (eds.), *The Cognitive Animal: Empirical and Theoretical Perspectives on Animal Cognition.* MIT Press, Cambridge, Massachusetts. pp. 363–369.

Irvine, L. 2004. *If You Tame Me: Understanding Our Connections with Animals.* Temple University Press, Philadelphia.

Leonard, J. A., R. K. Wayne, J. Wheeler, R. Valadez, S. Guillén, and C. Vilà. 2002. Ancient DNA evidence for old world origin of new world dogs. *Science* 298: 1613–1616.

Limbaugh, R. H. 1996. *John Muir's "Stickeen" and the Lessons of Nature.* University of Alaska Press, Fairbanks.

Miklosi, A., E. Kubinyi, J. Topal, M. Gacsi, Z. Viranyi, and V. Csanyi. 2003. A simple reason for a big difference: Wolves do not look back at humans, but dogs do. *Current Biology* 13: 763–766.

Muir, J. 1981. *Stickeen.* Heydey Books, Berkeley, California.

Price, E. O. 2003. *Animal Domestication and Behavior.* Oxford University Press, New York.

Savolainen, P., Y. Zhang, J. Luo, J. Lundeberg, and T. Leitner. 2002. Genetic evidence for an East Asian origin of domestic dogs. *Science* 298: 1610–1613.

Svartberg, K., and B. Forman. 2002. Personality traits in the domestic dog (*Canis familiaris*). *Applied Animal Behaviour Science* 79: 133–135.

Wells, M. C., and M. Bekoff. 1981. An observational study of scent-marking in coyotes, *Canis latrans. Animal Behaviour* 29: 332–350.

Wells, M. C., and M. Bekoff. 1982. Predation by wild coyotes: Behavioral and ecological analyses. *Journal of Mammalogy* 63: 118–127.

Wells, M. C., and P. N. Lehner. 1978. The relative importance of the distance senses in coyote predatory behavior. *Animal Behaviour* 26: 251–258.

PART III: SOCIAL PLAY, SOCIAL DEVELOPMENT, AND SOCIAL COMMUNICATION: COOPERATION, FAIRNESS, AND WILD JUSTICE

Allen, C., and M. Bekoff. 1994. Intentionality, social play, and definition. *Biology and Philosophy* 9: 63–74.

Bekoff, M. 1974. Social play and play-soliciting by infant canids. *American Zoologist* 14: 323–340. (Reprinted in D. Müller-Schwarze [ed.], *Benchmark Papers in Animal Behavior*, vol. 10, 1978).

Bekoff, M. 1975. The communication of play intention: Are play signals functional? *Semiotica* 15: 231–239.

Bekoff, M. 1976. Animal play: Problems and perspectives. In P. P. G. Bateson and P. H. Klopfer (eds.), *Perspectives in Ethology.* Vol. 2. Plenum Press, New York. pp. 165–188.

Bekoff, M. 1977. Quantitative studies of three areas of classical ethology: Social dominance, behavioral taxonomy, and behavioral variability. In B. A. Hazlett (ed.), *Quantitative Methods in the Study of Animal Behavior.* Academic Press, New York. pp. 1–46.

Bekoff, M. 1978. A field study of the development of behavior in Adélie penguins: Univariate and numerical taxonomic approaches. In G. M. Burghardt and M. Bekoff (eds.), *The Development of Behavior: Comparative and Evolutionary Aspects.* Garland, New York. pp. 177–202.

Bekoff, M. 2002. Minding Animals: Awareness, Emotions, and Heart. Oxford University Press, New York.

Bekoff, M., D. Ainley, and A. Bekoff. 1979. The ontogeny and organization of comfort behavior in Adélie penguins. *Wilson Bulletin* 91: 255–270.

Bekoff, M., and C. Allen. 1992. Intentional icons: Towards an evolutionary cognitive ethology. *Ethology* 91: 1–16.

Bekoff, M., and J. A. Byers. 1978. A critical reanalysis of the ontogeny and phylogeny of mammalian social and locomotor play: An ethological hornet's nest. In

K. Immelmann, G. Barlow, M. Main, and L. Petrinovich (eds.), *Behavioral Development: The Bielefeld Interdisciplinary Project.* Cambridge University Press, Cambridge and New York. pp. 296–337.

Bekoff, M., and J. A. Byers. (eds.) 1998. *Animal Play: Evolutionary, Comparative, and Ecological Approaches.* Cambridge University Press, New York and Cambridge. 274 pages.

Bekoff, M., M. Tyrrell, V. E. Lipetz, and R. A. Jamieson. 1981. Fighting patterns in young coyotes: Initiation, escalation, and assessment. *Aggressive Behavior* 7: 225–244.

Broom, D. 2003. *The Evolution of Morality and Religion.* Cambridge University Press, New York.

Brosnan, S. F., and F.B.M. de Waal. 2003. Monkeys reject unequal pay. *Nature* 425, 297–299.

Burghardt, G. M. 2004. *The Genesis of Animal Play.* MIT Press, Cambridge, Massachusetts.

Carter, C. S., I. I. Lederhendler, and B. Kirkpatrick. (eds.) 1997. *The Integrative Neurobiology of Affiliation.* Annals of the New York Academy of Sciences, vol. 807. New York Academy of Sciences, New York.

Damasio, A. 2003. *Looking for Spinoza: Joy, Sorrow, and the Feeling Brain.* Harcourt, New York.

de Waal, F.B.M. 1996. *Good-Natured.* Harvard University Press, Cambridge, Massachusetts.

Drea, C. M., and L. G. Frank. 2003. The social complexity of spotted hyenas. In F. de Waal and P. L. Tyack (eds.), *Animal Social Complexity: Intelligence, Culture, and Individualized Societies.* Harvard University Press, Cambridge, Massachusetts. pp. 121–148.

Drea, C. M., J. E. Hawk, and S. E. Glickman. 1996. Aggression decreases as play emerges in infant spotted hyaenas: Preparation for joining the clan. *Animal Behaviour* 51: 1323–1336.

Dugatkin, L. A., and M. Bekoff. 2003. Play and the evolution of fairness: A game theory model. *Behavioural Processes* 60:209–214.

Fagen, R. M. 1981. *Animal Play Behavior.* Oxford University Press, New York.

Frith, C. D., and U. Frith. 1999. Interacting minds: A biological basis. *Science* 286: 1692–1695.

Gallese, V. 1998. Mirror neurons, from grasping to language. *Consciousness Bulletin,* Fall, 3–4.

Gallese, V., and A. Goldman. 1998. Mirror neurons and the simulation theory of mind-reading. *Trends in Cognitive Science* 2: 493–501.

Gese E. M., R. L. Ruff, and R. L. Crabtree. 1996. Social and nutritional factors influencing the dispersal of resident coyotes. *Animal Behaviour* 52: 1025–1043.

Goodenough, U., and T. W. Deacon. 2003. From biology to consciousness to morality. *Zygon (Journal of Religion and Science)* 38: 801–819.

Haraway, D. 2003. *The Companion Species Manifesto: Dogs, People, and Significant Otherness.* Prickly Paradigm Press, Chicago.

Harris, S., and P.C.L. White. 1992. Is reduced affiliative rather than increased agonistic behaviour associated with dispersal in red foxes? *Animal Behaviour* 44: 1085–1089.

Hinde, R. A. 2002. *Why Good Is Good: The Sources of Morality.* Routledge, New York.

Holekamp, K. E., and L. Smale. 1998. Behavioral development in the spotted hyena. *BioScience* 48: 997–1005.

Katz, L D. (ed.) 2000. *Evolutionary Origins of Morality: Cross-Disciplinary Perspectives.* Imprint Academic, Bowling Green, Ohio.

Kropotkin, P. 1914. *Mutual Aid: A Factor of Evolution.* Expanding Horizons Press, Boston.

Meyer, S., and J.-M. Weber. 1996. Ontogeny of dominance in free-living red foxes. *Ethology* 102: 1008–1019.

Morrison, N. K., and S. K. Severino. 2003. The biology of morality. *Zygon (Journal of Religion and Science)* 38: 855–869.

Müller-Schwarze, D., R. Butler, P. Belanger, M. Bekoff, and A. Bekoff. 1975. Feeding territories of South Polar Skuas at Cape Crozier. *Antarctic Journal of the United States* 10: 121–122.

Panksepp, J. 1998. *Affective Neuroscience.* Oxford University Press, New York.

Panksepp, J. 2003a. "Laughing" rats and the evolutionary antecedents of human joy? *Physiology and Behavior* 79: 533–547.

Panksepp, J. 2003b. At the interface of the affective, behavioral, and cognitive neuroscience: Decoding the emotional feelings of the brain. *Brain and Cognition* 52: 4–14.

Pellis, S. 2002. Keeping in touch: Play fighting and social knowledge. In M. Bekoff, C. Allen, and G. M. Burghardt (eds.), *The Cognitive Animal.* MIT Press, Cambridge, Massachusetts, pp. 421–427.

Power, T. G. 2000. *Play and Exploration in Children and Animals.* Lawrence Erlbaum, Mahwah, New Jersey.

Preston, S. D., and F.B.M. de Waal. 2002. Empathy: Its ultimate and proximate bases. *Behavioral and Brain Sciences* 25: 1–72.

Ridley, M. 1996. *The Origins of Virtue: Human Instincts and the Evolution of Cooperation.* Viking, New York.

Rooney, N. J., J.W.S. Bradshaw, and I. H. Robinson. 2001. Do dogs respond to play signals given by humans? *Animal Behaviour* 61: 715–722.

Siviy, S. 1998. Neurobiological substrates of play behavior: Glimpses into the structure and function of mammalian playfulness. In M. Bekoff and J. A. Byers (eds.), *Animal Play: Evolutionary, Comparative, and Ecological Perspectives.* Cambridge University Press, New York. pp. 221–242.

Wilson, D. S. 2002. *Darwin's Cathedral: Evolution, Religion, and the Nature of Society.* University of Chicago Press, Chicago.

Woollard, T., and S. Harris. 1990. A behavioural comparison of dispersing and non-dispersing foxes (*Vulpes vulpes*) and an evaluation of some dispersal hypotheses. *Journal of Animal Ecology* 59: 709–722.

PART IV: HUMAN DIMENSIONS: HUMAN-ANIMAL INTERACTIONS

Adams, R. A., B. J. Lengas, and M. Bekoff. 1987. Variations in avoidance responses to humans by black-tailed prairie dogs (*Cynomys ludovicianus*). *Journal of Mammalogy* 68: 686–689.

Arluke, A., and C. R. Sanders. 1996. *Regarding Animals.* Temple University Press, Philadelphia.

Baron, D. 2003. *The Beast in the Garden: A Modern Parable of Man and Nature.* W. W. Norton, New York.

Bekoff, M. 2000. Field studies and animal models: The possibility of misleading inferences. In M. Balls, A.-M. van Zeller, and M. E. Halder (eds.), *Progress in the Reduction, Refinement, and Replacement of Animal Experimentation.* Elsevier,. Amsterdam, pp. 1553–1559.

Bekoff, M. 2002. *Minding Animals: Awareness, Emotions, and Heart.* Oxford University Press, New York.

Bekoff, M., and D. Jamieson. 1996. Ethics and the study of carnivores: Doing science while respecting animals. In J. L. Gittleman (ed.), *Carnivore Behavior, Ecology, and Evolution.* Vol. 2. Cornell University Press, Ithaca, New York. pp. 15–45.

Bradshaw, I.G.A., and M. Bekoff. 2001. Ecology and social responsibility: The re-embodiment of science. *Trends in Ecology and Evolution* 8: 460–465.

Goodall, J., and M. Bekoff. 2002. *The Ten Trusts: What We Must Do to Care For the Animals We Love.* HarperCollins, San Francisco.

Irvine, L. 2004. *If You Tame Me: Understanding Our Connections with Animals.* Temple University Press, Philadelphia.

Sanders, C. R. 1999. *Understanding Dogs: Living and Working with Canine Companions.* Temple University Press, Philadelphia.

PART V: ETHICS, COMPASSION, CONSERVATION, AND ACTIVISM: REDECORATING NATURE

Abram, D. 1996. *The Spell of the Sensuous: Perception and Language in a More-Than-Human World.* Pantheon Press, New York.

Bekoff, M. 2000. Field studies and animal models: The possibility of misleading inferences. In M. Balls, A.-M. van Zeller, and M. E. Halder (eds.), *Progress in the Reduction, Refinement, and Replacement of Animal Experimentation.* Elsevier, Amsterdam,.pp. 1553–1559.

Bekoff, M. 2000. *Strolling with Our Kin: Speaking for and Respecting Voiceless Animals.* Lantern Books, New York.

Bekoff, M. 2001. Ethics and marine mammals. In W. Perrin, B. Würsig, and H. Thewissen (eds.), *Encyclopedia of Marine Mammals.* Academic Press, San Diego. pp. 398–404.

Bekoff, M. 2002. *Minding Animals: Awareness, Emotions, and Heart.* Oxford University Press, New York.

Bekoff, M., and L. Gruen. 1993. Animal welfare and individual characteristics: A conversation against speciesism. *Ethics and Behavior* 3: 163–175.

Gittleman, J. L. (ed.) 1996. *Carnivore Behavior, Ecology, and Evolution.* Vol. 2. Cornell University Press, Ithaca, New York.

Goodall, J., and M. Bekoff. 2002. *The Ten Trusts: What We Must Do to Care For the Animals We Love.* HarperCollins, New York.

Heidt, G. A. 1997. Review of J. L. Gittleman (ed.), *Carnivore Behavior, Ecology, and Evolution,* volume 2. Cornell University Press, Ithaca, New York. *Ecology* 75: 1607.

Mead, M. The source of her quotation on activism remains a mystery; see www.mead2001.org/faq_page.htm#quote

Miller, H. 1957. *Big Sur and the Oranges of Hieronymus Bosch.* New Directions, New York.

Redmond, K. 2003. Retiring Cassandra. *Conservation Biology* 17: 1473–1474.

Ryder, R. 1998. Speciesism. In M. Bekoff (ed.), *Encyclopedia of Animal Behavior.* Greenwood, Westport, Connecticut. p. 320.

Sewall, L. 1999. *Sight and Sensibility: The Ecopsychology of Perception.* Jeremy P. Tarcher/Putnam, New York.

Sheldrake, R. 1991/1994. *The Rebirth of Nature: The Greening of Science and God.* Park Street Press, New York.

Sheldrake, R. 1999. *Dogs That Know When Their Owners Are Coming Home.* Crown, New York.

AFTERWORD: MINDING ANIMALS, MINDING EARTH

Abram, D. 1996. *The Spell of the Sensuous: Perception and Language in a More-Than-Human World.* Pantheon Press, New York.

Allen, C., and M. Bekoff. 1997. *Species of Mind: The Philosophy and Biology of Cognitive Ethology.* MIT Press, Cambridge, Massachusetts.

Applegate, J. S. 2000. The precautionary preference: An American perspective on the precautionary principle. *Human and Ecological Risk Assessment* 6: 413–443.

Bekoff, M. 1998. Deep ethology, animal rights, and the Great Ape/Animal Project: Resisting speciesism and expanding the community of equals. *Journal of Agricultural and Environmental Ethics* 10: 269–296.

Bekoff, M. (ed.) 1998. *Encyclopedia of Animal Rights and Animal Welfare.* Foreword by Jane Goodall. Greenwood, Westport, Connecticut.

Bekoff, M. 1998. Resisting speciesism and expanding the community of equals. *BioScience* 48: 638–641.

Bekoff, M. 2000. Animal emotions: Exploring passionate nature. *BioScience* 50: 861–870.

Bekoff, M. 2000. Redecorating nature: Reflections on science, holism, humility, community, reconciliation, spirit, compassion, and love. *Human Ecology Review* 7: 59–67.

Bekoff, M. (ed.) 2000. *The Smile of a Dolphin: Remarkable Accounts of Animal Behavior.* Random House/Discovery Books, Washington, D.C.

Bekoff, M. 2000. *Strolling with Our Kin.* Lantern Books, New York.

Bekoff, M. 2001. Human-carnivore interactions: Adopting proactive strategies for complex problems. In J. L. Gittleman, S. M. Funk, D. W. Macdonald, and R. K. Wayne (eds.), *Carnivore Conservation.* Cambridge University Press, London and New York, pp. 179–195.

Bekoff, M. 2002. Minding Animals: Awareness, Emotions, and Heart. Oxford University Press, New York.

Bekoff, M. 2004. Conservation behavior is here to stay. *Conservation Biology* 18: 591–593.

Bekoff, M., C. Allen, and G. M. Burghardt. (eds.) 2002. *The Cognitive Animal.* MIT Press, Cambridge, Massachusetts.

Bekoff, M., and D. Jamieson. 1996. Ethics and the study of carnivores. In J. L. Gittleman (ed.), *Carnivore Behavior, Ecology, and Evolution.* Cornell University Press, Ithaca, New York pp. 16–45.

Bekoff, M., and J. A. Byers. (eds.) 1998. *Animal Play: Evolutionary, Comparative, and Ecological Approaches.* New York, Cambridge University Press.

Bekoff, M., and J. Nystrom. 2004. The other side of silence: Rachel Carson's views of animals. *Zygon (Journal of Religion and Science)* 39: 861–883.

Berkes, F. 1999. *Sacred Ecology: Traditional Ecological Knowledge and Resource Management.* Taylor and Francis, Philadelphia, Pennsylvania.

Berry, T. 1999. *The Great Work: Our Way into the Future.* Bell Tower, New York.

Berry, T. 2000. An interview with Thomas Berry. *Wild Earth*, Summer, 93–97.

Bower, B. 2004. Unsure minds. *Science News* 165: 90–92.

Bradshaw, G. A., and M. Bekoff. 2001. Ecology and social responsibility: The re-embodiment of science. *Trends in Ecology and Evolution* 8: 460–465.

Carlson, A., and A. Berleant. (eds.) 2004. *The Aesthetics of Natural Environments.* Broadview Press, Orchard Park, New York.

Darwin, C. 1859/1958. *On the Origin of Species.* Murray, London.

Darwin, C. 1872/1998. *The Expression of the Emotions in Man and Animals.* Third edition. With an Introduction, Afterword, and Commentaries by Paul Ekman. Oxford University Press, New York.

Drea, C. M., and K. Wallen. 1999. Low-status monkeys "play dumb" when learning in mixed social groups. *Proceedings of the National Academy of Sciences* 96: 12965–12969.

Goodall, J. 1990. *Through a Window: My Thirty Years with the Chimpanzees of Gombe.* Houghton Mifflin, Boston.

Goodall, J. 1999. *Reason for Hope.* Warner Books, New York.

Goodall, J., and M. Bekoff. 2002. *The Ten Trusts: What We Must Do to Care For the Animals We Love.* HarperCollins, San Francisco.

Gould, S. J. 2002. *The Structure of Evolutionary Theory.* Harvard University Press, Cambridge, Massachusetts.

Hampton, R. R. 2001. Rhesus monkeys know when they remember. *Proceedings of the National Academy of Sciences* 98 (9): 5359–5362.

Hare, B., J. Call, and M. Tomasello. 2001. Do chimpanzees know what conspecifics know? *Animal Behaviour* 61: 139–151.

Harrington, A. 2002. A science of compassion or a compassionate science? What do we expect from a cross-cultural dialogue with Buddhism? In R J. Davidson and A. Harrington (eds.), *Visions of Compassion: Western Scientists and Tibetan Buddhists Examine Human Nature.* Oxford University Press, New York. pp. 18–30.

Hill, J. B. 2000. *The Legacy of Luna.* San Francisco, HarperCollins.

His Holiness the Dalai Lama. 1999. *The Path to Tranquility: Daily Wisdom.* Viking Arkana, New York.

His Holiness the Dalai Lama. 2002. Understanding our fundamental nature. In R J. Davidson and A. Harrington (eds.), *Visions of Compassion: Western Scientists and Tibetan Buddhists Examine Human Nature.* Oxford University Press, New York. pp. 66–80.

Hollingham, R. 2004. In the realm of your senses. *New Scientist,* 31 January, 40–43.

Huffman, M. A. 1997. Current evidence for self-medication in primates: A multidisciplinary perspective. *Yearbook of Physical Anthropology* 40: 171–200.

Huffman, M. A. 2001. Self-medicative behavior in the African great apes: An evolutionary perspective into the origins of human traditional medicine. *BioScience* 51: 651–661.

Kitcher, P. 2004. Responsible biology. *BioScience* 54: 331–336.

Krause, B. 2002. The loss of natural soundscapes. *Earth Island Journal* 17 (1). Accessed at www.earthisland.org/eijournal/new_articles.cfm?articleID=449&journalID=63.

Kumar, S. 2000. Simplicity for Christmas and always. *Resurgence,* November/December, 3.

Lorenz, K. Z. 1991. *Here I Am—Where Are You?* Harcourt Brace Jovanovich, New York.

Lorrimer, D. 1999. Introduction to D. Lorrimer (ed.), *The Spirit of Science: From Experiment to Experience.* Continuum, New York.

Martin, C. L. 1992. *In The Spirit of the Earth: Rethinking History and Time.* Johns Hopkins University Press, Baltimore, Maryland.

McComb, K., C. Moss, S. M. Durant, L. Baker, and S. Sayialel. 2001. Matriarchs as repositories of social knowledge in African elephants. *Science* 292 (5516): 491–494.

McKinney, M. L. 2001. Role of human population size in raising bird and mammal threat among nations. *Animal Conservation* 4: 45–57.

Midgley, M. 2001. *Science and Poetry.* Routledge, New York.

Miller, H. 1957. *Big Sur and the Oranges of Hieronymus Bosch.* New Directions, New York.

Moser, A. 2000. The wisdom of nature in integrating science, ethics, and the arts. *Science and Engineering Ethics* 6: 365–382.

Moss, C. 2000. A passionate devotion. In M. Bekoff (ed.), *The Smile of a Dolphin: Remarkable Accounts of Animal Emotions.* Random House/Discovery Books, Washington, D.C. pp. 134–137.

O'Hara, K. 2004. *Trust: From Socrates to Spin.* Icon Books, Cambridge, UK.

Phillips, M. T. 1994. Proper names and the social construction of biography: The negative case of laboratory animals. *Qualitative Sociology* 17: 119–142.

Poole, J. 1998. An exploration of a commonality between ourselves and elephants. *Etica and Animali* 9: 85–110.

Revel, J.-F., and M. Ricard. 1998. *The Monk and the Philosopher: A Father and Son Discuss the Meaning of Life.* Schocken Books, New York.

Rolston, H., III. 2002. Environmental ethics in Antarctica. *Environmental Ethics* 24: 115–134.

Seeley, T. D. 2003. Consensus building during nest-site selection in honey bee swarms: The expiration of dissent. *Behavioral Ecology and Sociobiology* 53: 417–424.

Sewall, L. 1999. *Sight and Sensibility: The Ecopsychology of Perception.* Jeremy P. Tarcher/Putnam, New York.

Skutch, A. 1996. *The Minds of Birds.* Texas A&M University Press, College Station.

Spinney, L. 2004. Into Africa. *New Scientist,* 7 February, 44–45.

Sponberg, A. 1997. Green Buddhism and the hierarchy of compassion. In M. E. Tucker and D. R. Williams (eds.), *Buddhism and Ecology.* Harvard University Press, Cambridge, Massachusetts. pp. 351–376.

Stegner, W. 1960. Wilderness Letter. http://www.wilderness.org/OurIssues/Wilderness/wildernessletter.cfm

Streever, B. 2002. Science and emotion, on ice: The role of science on Alaska's north slope. *BioScience* 52 (2): 179–184.

Suzuki, D., and H. Dressel. 2002. *Good News for a Change: Hope for a Troubled Planet.* Stoddart, Toronto, Canada.

Trungpa, Chögyam. 1988. *Shambhala: The Sacred Path of the Warrior.* Shambhala, Boston.

van den Born, R.J.G., R.H.J. Lenders, W. T. de Groot, and E. Huijsman. 2001. The new biophilia: An exploration of visions of nature in Western countries. *Environmental Conservation* 28: 65–75.

Weil, Z. 2003. *Above All, Be Kind: Raising a Humane Child in Challenging Times.* New Society Publishers, British Columbia, Canada.

Würsig, B. 2000. Leviathan lust and love. In M. Bekoff (ed.), *The Smile of a Dolphin: Remarkable Accounts of Animal Emotions.* Random House/Discovery Books, Washington, D.C.

Index

MARC BEKOFF is a Professor of Ecology and Evolutionary Biology at the University of Colorado, Boulder. He has published numerous books including *The Smile of a Dolphin, Minding Animals, The Ten Trusts* (with Jane Goodall), and *The Encyclopedia of Animal Behavior.* His homepage is http://literati.net/Bekoff. He and Jane Goodall co-founded Ethologists for the Ethical Treatment of Animals (www.ethologicalethics.org). In 2005 Marc was presented with The Bank One Faculty Community Service Award for the work he has done with children, senior citizens, and prisoners.